SURVIVING WILD

BOOK SIX OF THE ALASKA OFF GRID SURVIVAL SERIES

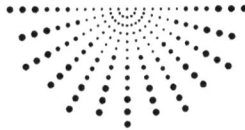

MILES MARTIN

ALASKADREAMS
PUBLISHING

Surviving Wild
By Miles Martin

Book Six of The Alaska Off Grid Survival Series
©2021 Miles Martin
Artwork, Photos, Original Poetry ©2021 by Miles Martin - All rights reserved

Published by:
Alaska Dreams Publishing
www.alaskadp.com
1st ADP Edition August 2021
PRINT PAPERBACK ISBN: 978-1-956303-08-7
PRINT HARDCOVER ISBN: 978-1-956303-09-4
This book was previously published by Miles of Alaska

Visit www.milesofalaska.com to find a bio of Miles, additional photos, stories, how-to videos, handmade artwork, and raw materials for sale.

Out along the river looking for fossils. In the boat, a 12 ft Mammoth Tusk.

I Stand in the doorway of my Nenana 1916 cabin.

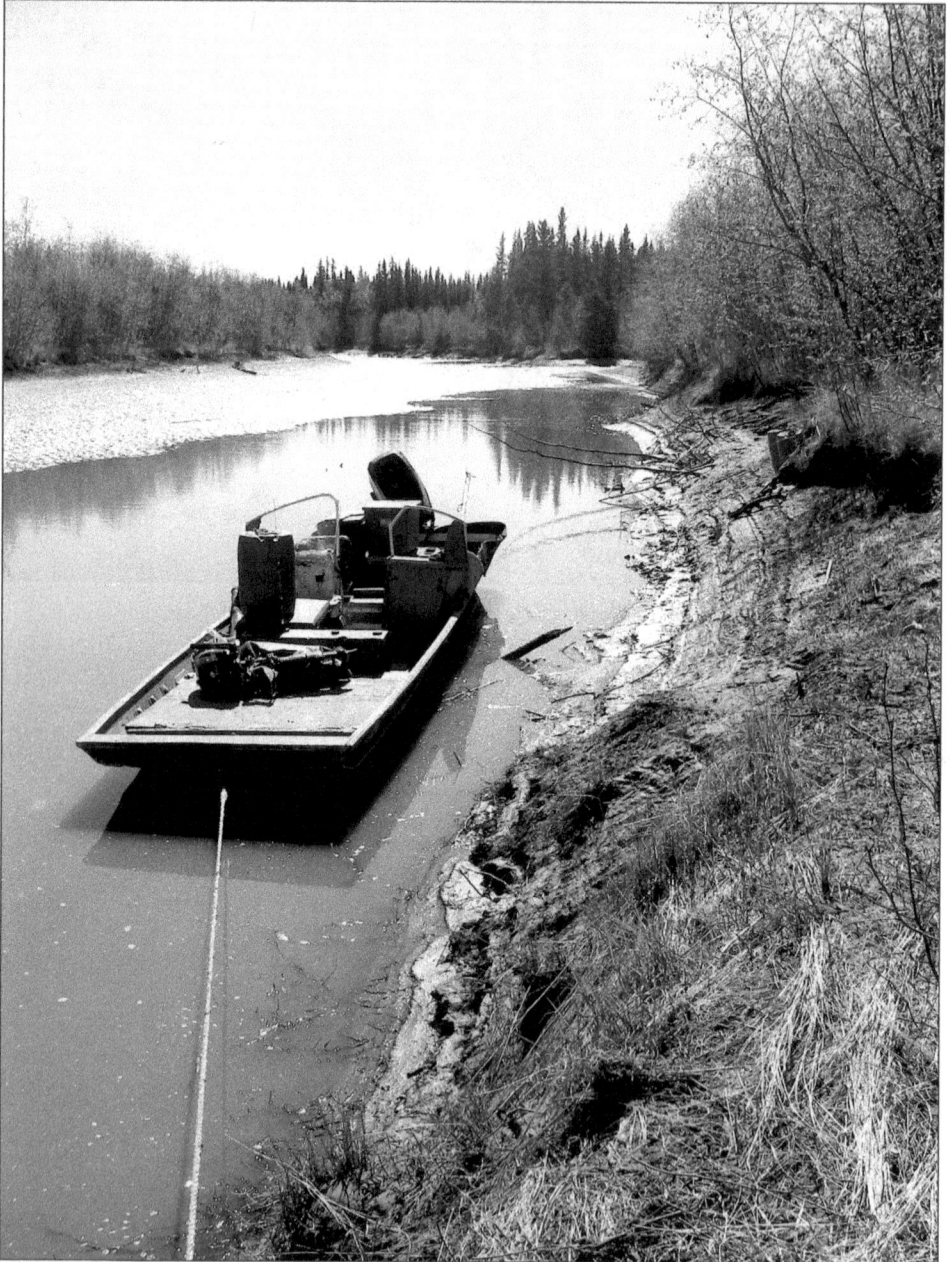

One of my favorite fishing spots.

CONTENTS

CHAPTER ONE

THE IRS, NEW COMPUTER, TUCSON SHOW TRIP

I look at the worn out sign hanging on my door as I come in the house to rest. "Work is for those who do not know how to fish!" The 1916 log cabin has a low ceiling, so even at five ft. four inches, I have to duck to get in.

It is 2010 I am almost a senior now at 58 years old. I have been working in my remote Alaska village garden all day. *No, I'm playing in the garden, not working.* My unconscious wants me to be clear what is it is we do. We are certain of the answer, but the rest of the world is not. As I sit, I ask *just what is work anyhow!* It is difficult to communicate with the rest of the world, when we do not agree on what important words and concepts mean. *So if we enjoy it, is it work? Because doesn't work mean the opposite of having fun? Isn't fun what happens on weekends when we are not working?* The idea is beyond my understanding, as I do not know this word, 'weekend.' Every day is a weekend for me. I work for myself, living a subsistence life.

The few times I get paid working for others, it is an intense seasonal work that knows no time. We work till we drop; fifteen-hour days, seven days a week, getting time and a half, double time, triple pay, for big monthly wages. Then the job is over. *I have never owned an alarm clock in my life, never woke up to one. A lot of things we never did!* I remind my unconscious! Never had a photo ID till I was forty-five, never had a bank account, credit card, or driver's license till I was fifty. Along with work, I do not know this word 'vacation.' The need to take a long break from something, by going some place else.

We jump in the boat and hunt for our meat or fish. If the weather is bad, or we do not feel like hunting or gardening, we can go look for mammoth tusks and sell them. But if we do not want to be outdoors, we stay in the shop and make art, or

7

custom knives. We can be on the computer. Fool with the web store, or add to our book. There are rocks to slice and polish, watercolors to paint. Income from writing work might not be seen for a decade. Sometimes we do repairs on a snow machine, truck, lawn mower, or four wheeler. There is firewood to cut to stay warm, flowers to arrange and sell, that we grow in our greenhouse. There are furs to catch and sell. We do not have to do any of it. We pay someone else to do stuff. 'We,' refers to me, myself and I. It's all up to us. *What part of all that is work, and what part is play?* Anyhow, who cares! *You know who cares! The IRS cares, and all those government forms!* Yes, forms that ask my income, what I do for a living, and at the end, ask if all my answers have been truthful. There is one tiny line to write down 'occupation,' when the truth would take three sheets of paper.

When I called the IRS a long time ago to get an answer, I was told to "Just make up something!" I point to the end where it states everything must be truthful. I heard a, "Good grief!" and the phone went dead.

I have nine buildings, and six wood stoves. I am adding and subtracting monetary value, conversions of trades, pleasure compared to work, materials I find, compared to gifted traded or bought. The total amount is some amazingly low number below the poverty level, a number no one cares about, anyway.

Until recently, you mean. I frown. Yes. There is this annoying issue concerning the fact we are beginning to do well and making a pile of money. *Darn.* I am not an accountant. I do income and outflow. If I have enough money to pay the bills, the rest is just details. Is income outcome going to keep working for me? *At my age, am I really going to change how I do things like keep records?* I am certain what words mean matters, especially when you live among others and try to communicate. I can go to jail for calling 'play,' 'work.'

"Did you get your taxes figured out, Miles, that one part you were wondering about? If it's work or play?" Iris reminds me of my dilemma, hollering from another room. Our own relationship often hinges on what we mean when we use words. I smile, thinking of all those mail order women and pen pals whom I corresponded with. I wrote, "And I live on a houseboat!" But no. Not even one understood what that means. They picture lots of glass, lounge chairs, bikinis, sipping wine, fanning themselves with $100 bills. Even when I sent a picture. Even when I explained. Imagination is a powerful force. *Who was out of reality, me, or them??* "Obviously, them!" I snort, "After all, it is me living the life, is that not reality? I cannot speak for how anyone else is living, I am not them." No more life on the houseboat. No more dog team transportation. No more anything worth writing in a diary about as exciting. Are those days over now?

There are certainly plenty of subsistence people like myself, living in remote villages. It is hard to know if they are like me or not. I do not visit around much. Nor do people come to visit Iris and I much. *Good fences make good neighbors.*

"Miles, let's just take the truck on the base so you can get to the VA hospital instead of walking two miles!"

I forgot. Today is the day to head for the big city. Rats. It is tax deadline time, and spring. This is the first truck trip since last fall. We do not drive in winter. Or Iris does not. I do not drive at all. Never did. I spent my life in the wilderness. Iris tells me about something called a jitney she took to work back in New Jersey. *Sounds like a public minivan of some kind?* She has had limited experience driving in Alaska on our hilly, twisty, two-lane roads.

"Miles, there is no reason to be afraid! I looked up the rules! As long as you are legal, you have nothing to worry about, the law is on your side!" I am not so sure. People in Nenana who drive to the big city simply wish each other luck. And say, "Be careful!" But I do not know what being careful means. Though it seems I had heard that part of this means to stay away from the military base! That's all I know.

"Iris, I just do not think we can get on base reliably with the truck. What if something is not in order, something goes wrong?"

"But why shouldn't everything be in order?" Iris inquired. "All we need is truck registration, our driver's license, and proof of insurance. We have all that. It's simple, it's routine."

My experience is, often these matters are not, in fact, simple and routine. We drive the fifty miles, then stop at the military base gate. In the past, I took a taxi from the gate. This cost $40, but saves an inspection.

"Sir. Mr. Martin. I see you have no updated emissions check, required by law, and you have a cracked windshield. This v–hick–all, is not legal to drive. I'm afraid I'll have to contact the local awe–thor–ee–tees."

"I understand your concern. But I am from, and have this truck registered in, Nenana. There are no such requirements, if you look at the exceptions…" He frowns. "You aren't trying to give me a hard time, are you?" Obviously he is not from around here. *It's not Alaskan unless it has a cracked windshield. Now I'm on his crap list as we wait for the local police. We will be carted off to a concentration camp screaming.* Iris knows what to do. My mind goes blank till I wake up at the VA hospital, where I go to see the *VA* Doctor, I check in.

"Mr. Martin, is that a knife you are carrying?"

"*Of course! I mean, yes it is! I mean… is there a problem?*" I do not say anything. *How does one reply to such a stupid question? Of course, it's a knife. What else would it be?* "I know you are not going to cut me up, but you will have to leave that outside." This is my hunting knife I always carry, that is just part of my clothing, like car keys and wallet.

Iris had commented earlier, "I read the rules about restrictions. Your knife is not over six inches, is it?" Rules. That's all I need, a bunch of rules. I would not even come here unless I had to. A very dangerous place.

"No, it's not over six inches. Not a problem" *Well, this is just a silly nurse.* I had my jacket on and took it off. "Oh, my God! A knife!" *Maybe it will jump out of its sheath and start flying around cutting things up.* But anyhow. My mind wanders again. *What if it had been one of the guys in uniform I came across instead? Who freaked out over an 'armed civilian' in their midst?* 'Armed civilian' meaning me, someone with a military ID card, who served my country during the Viet Nam war. In the military longer than this GI Joe who would get excited. Young enough to be my grandkid. I imagine.

"On the floor now! Hands behind your head." Headlines in the paper, "Civilian on his way to the VA doctor shot and killed with an M-16 rifle after telling guard to go blankety blank himself." Not hard to imagine. I get tired of all the crap. I am irritable, have not eaten in twelve hours in preparation for this blood test. It is easy to imagine being tired of bending over. Told to go here, jump there, wait, move, stop, go, in the wrong line, turn around, come back after lunch. Now bend over, how high, how much, yes sir, no sir, what papers sir, I'll go get them, sir. I'd be glad to come back tomorrow, sir. I understand how busy you are, Sir! "Go ahead, shoot me! Make my day!" And they would.

I just want my blood test. I'm not here to kill anyone. Just someone who cares about what America used to stand for. Freedom. Dignity. I'm not trying to make problems, make a point, stand up for anything. I have been wearing a knife since I was six years old. *A man with a knife is master of a thousand tasks.* An hour in a day hardly goes by, I do not reach for it. Open boxes, cut string, tape, pry things, open envelopes, cans, trim something, dig something. I am a custom knife maker, wearing what I make. A spiritual instrument symbolizing a way of life, the single most important and first tool Man invented.

I am not stupid, and I do not want any problems. No, I would not let that scene play out. I'd say, "Yes Sir! Sorry Sir! It will be corrected, Sir." And regret it very much, regret living in a world where I am among the sheep, being herded around—sheared at will, by whoever, for whatever reason. Increasing my blood pressure, causing me to have to come to the VA. But anyhow (smile at the irony of it all...) No. I smile and apologize for scaring the nurse, "I'll go put it in the truck, sorry, I forgot." As I take another blood pressure pill. Put my hand over my eyes to help the headache go away.

We are glad to get out of town and back home. Last time, we had walked onto the base. We had parked the truck far away and walked two miles. Iris is not as used to walking as I am, but also I did not feel so good this trip, blood sugar out of balance. *If I had stayed in the wilds, would my blood pressure be fine?* I was eating healthier wilderness food, combined with the exercise of the lifestyle. Would that have kept me off pill dependency? Does that matter? Staying in the wilderness was not an option.

"Miles, did you add up how we did in Tucson yet?" Still trying to get the taxes done.

Tucson? Nice break from Alaska. We stay with my Mom and her ninety-year-old boyfriend who still drives. He took us back and forth each day to the fossil, gem, and mineral show. We had fresh grapefruit each morning from Mom's yard. Saw hummingbirds at Mom's, flowers, and palm trees. Seventy degree weather. I was set up in a tent for $1,500 for three weeks. I got a good spot, even the best, so was excited. As last year, my spot was moved because someone who wanted the spot paid under the table to get my assigned space. That upset some of the sellers enough the manager gave me my spot back this past year. I get along with all the show people well.

We spent $500 to get everything shipped from Alaska to sell down there. Scary, as the total is half my years' income in the early days. To me, the show is about money, so the story is told in dollars. It's about making half a year's wages in three weeks. Very intense, very exciting, very wired, very Zen, very adrenaline rush. It's show time. Putting in seventeen hour work days. Part of a feast and famine lifestyle I love. Cash! *I love it!* All cash. *No records of what I made.* Making piles of thousand dollars that cover the bed as I count. We did $14,000 worth of business.

Naturally, and alas (as told to the IRS), all but about $100 went back into the business. Naturally, the boat is part of the business. The snow machine, the green-house. All my toys are business tools. Even when I go to Tucson, I tell everyone, "Darn! Got to go to Tucson. Oh well, someone has to do it, it's a business trip."

😀 :)

There are people who find, 'all this' outrageous! People who feel I am scamming the IRS, avoiding taxes. I live for my work! So 90% of my gross goes into things like rock saws, band saws, drill press, grinders, tumblers, torches, and on and on. Few know that. Few have ever watched me work. In fact, no one. Ever. The outside of my shop looks like I want it to. Crap. I'm known as a teller of tall tales. I like it that way. Implying I have a scam that works to totally avoid the concerns of the ordinary? It's a sales pitch. One truth is not even I know the details of my life. That too is how I want it. Safe.

A good friend of mine used to hang out with Mick Jagger of the Rolling Stones and tells me Mick is a businessman who knows what he is doing. He is not nuts; he does not do drugs, nor does he dispense free love to everyone he encounters. He's an actor, giving people what they ask for.

Iris came with me to Tucson, and it is the first time I had serious help. A guy shows up to sort of help. He helped last year, a guy who stays in my tent at night as security, and opens and closes the booth for us. He fills in if he's around, and we need to go some place. He only wanted a hundred bucks for the entire show, and some trade goods. So that was sweet and helpful. Tall, skinny kid, maybe Mexican, lets on he lives the life of a teen skate boarder, but he's thirty. He plays the happy-go-lucky life of a street person. Everything he owns is in his backpack, and proud of it! He has some odd habits, dresses weird, a 60s hippie judging him. *Way back when I was your age!* All I care is, he is honest, reliable, and has good energy around him. Twice he showed up with swollen eyes and bruises, saying the police beat him up, 'again.' No, he does not know why. Other than he was sleeping in a drain tunnel. Dragged out asleep, screaming, and beaten unconscious. *He must be making that up.* I mean, I could see that happening to 'one of them.' Lowlife druggie freaks. However, this kid is as harmless and happy-go-lucky as it gets. Never raises his voice or argues. Sort of a simpleton? But so what. I'd hire him over an educated idiot any day.

Iris is a good salesperson. She freed me up to tell my stories and deal with other vendors. Other vendors are at every show, among my sought after customers. We took a side trip to Mexico after the show ended. Mostly to have our teeth worked on. It had been planned, as I have done this twice before. I had extended our trip by five days to allow time to do stuff, and not be in such a rush to get back home, as often happens on trips.

So, we had both our teeth cleaned, and I had a tooth pulled. All for $140. We took the bus an hour to Nogales. Federales rode around with machine guns and wore flack coats to keep the drug lords in line. So many asked if we are afraid to go there due to the killings and such. After my life in Alaska, why would I be afraid of some thugs hopped up on drugs? In truth, I fear my own government more than Mexican drug lords, but learn that is not the correct answer to repeat.

I had my laptop computer, so during any free time, like at airports, I could work on my book. I did my taxes with my feet propped up on a table under a palm tree by a poolside, with chickee-poos in bikinis wiggling by. *It is a job, someone has to do it.* I answer Iris.

"Huh? I can't hear good!"

"You heard me!" From the other room, I smile. She can't see me. I explain about the how the snow machine and boat are a business 'write off' in a loud voice. "I do not drive. So these are my only transportation. I use the snow machine all winter to haul outgoing mail to the post office, right? I use the snow machine to haul wood to heat the shop. I trap with the snow machine and make money, I cannot trap without the snow machine. As long as I'm not having fun and do not enjoy it, it's a business expense, right?" *I'm still having a problem understanding what work is. Or more, explaining how I feel in a way others understand and accept.* The boat is used to deliver art downriver to the village stores, haul raw materials like antlers from the wilds to the shop. If I stop to catch a fish along the way, I hate doing that. It's just that we need the fish. *It's hard to keep the grin out of my voice.*

😄 :)

"Just as long as you keep track, Miles!" I keep good records. I put all my receipts in an envelope each month, a new envelope each month. I try to keep monthly totals. In my business I do not itemize, so, no requirement to turn in a quarterly report. Just a yearly 'where I am at.' Usually, the IRS owes me money. Because I survey remote lands with Seymour in summers, and he pays in–like a whole lot–like at the rate as if I were doing this all year. *We have to show a profit now and then!* "Yes, I forgot." *This might be a good year to show a profit.* "Yes, there are some numbers I can manipulate, once every 3-4 years." I converse with myself. "When I buy equipment, I can decide if I want, or need to, write the entire value off, or depreciate it over time." *Anything I stick in a retirement IRA or CD is not taxed.* If I hang on to it till I retire, there is a tax exemption or something. If I do not need the money, sometimes it is good to stick it in a retirement program. *Town life, geez!* I have an extremely good accountant as a friend.

My accountant, Bean, was Jagger's accountant for a short time. He knows what to do when people get wads of cash handed to them. "Wads?" My unconscious frowns, jabs me in the gut angrily! "Well, what I meant was. 'Wads' is a relative nonspecific term, not good evidence in a court of law. After all, it was not so long ago we lived on $2,000 a year! So when I pull in fourteen grand cash in two weeks? It seems like a ton of money, right? "Right, and do not forget the horrendous deductions, business expenses!" Of course! I agree, wads is gross, not profit! (Mr. IRS secret agent man!) "Like we have receipts to prove we spent a good five grand in one day alone buying gemstones and raw materials!" "We did?" "We have the receipts to prove it by God!"

My accountant points out, "Miles, imagine an IRS agent looking at this pile of moose antler in your yard. Imagine trying to put a value on it from his position." I see the point. I value it highly, but I, of course, am the village idiot. In truth, if I died today, the executor of my estate would pay someone to haul this garbage away. I find antlers, or buy it dirt cheap as is, dirty, rough, cracked. I leave it out in the weather to get rained on and chewed on by squirrels. Much of it rots before it sells. *I let all this happen because?* I do not wish to offer high end trophy, or number one grade anything. I sell materials almost half the price of my competitors. I can, because I have so much less overhead costs than competitors. No storage, no cleaning, sorting, grading, preserving, labeling, weighing, recording. No inventory taxes. No employees. Until someone buys it, it has zero value. When a customer tells me they want a moose antler tine, I go to the backwoods with a hacksaw and cut a tine off whatever is sticking up out of the leaves. If half the antler rots, I still make a lot of money. "But Miles, isn't that wasteful!?"

"I found it in the woods where it was meant to rot in the first place." I add. I put a lot of miles boating and find antler sheds in the woods. "But then you have that time, and huge boat costs, invested."

"Invested in what? I was out there in the boat anyhow, fishing, getting firewood, looking for herbs, berries, rocks I sell. I get to write off the boat and all its gas and costs. As much as $10,000 a year." I explain I have several truckloads of moose antlers. Who else does? Who has the room to store it? If I sell even a third of it, I make big money. Anyhow, raw materials are not my main interest. I want time to do my own art. "I do not have time to fool with raw materials a lot. Even though it is making me more money." This whole attitude is bothersome to most civilized people.

"Miles, I have struggled with my website and have thousands of dollars invested in getting high ratings in the search engines! I'm lucky to average three visits a day! I value each customer! Now you tell me you spend nothing, and have dozens a day, and chase them off because there are too many?"

"Well. I cannot speak for you. I do not know what you are doing, how, or why. I have enough issues keeping track of what I do, why, and how." I am not smarter than anyone else! I think I just use my brain differently, that is all. I hear the voice of a non–believer. "This taxes thing, Miles, how is this possible as you speak of it! I have no way to record trades, for example! How can I trade! That's absurd!"

"Listen to yourself! If you cannot imagine something, then it can never be! So what is absurd about it?" I reply to the doubter. "Absurd is in the mind of the beholder." The infidel says, "Well, the IRS does not recognize trades, and there is no place in a tax program to even record it!"

"The IRS indeed allows trades, they just do not like it. If you are too afraid of the IRS to do it, I do not know what to tell you. The IRS, as far as I am told, just wants us to keep track and pay the extortion money." I explain I do not let my computer run my life. I run the life of the computer. I am not the computers tool, it is my tool. In Quick'–books, my banks are listed as Trade' and 'Coffee can.' When I trade, I go to the trade bank. I have 'trade in' under income and 'trade out' under expense. I acquire something in trade, I give it a monetary value, and enter it in the trade bank. Hopefully, I trade up for a profit. Whatever goes out in trade, I assign a value. At the end of the year, I have the in and out for the bank. Items I got 'in' are not recorded as 'income' until the item is traded, sold or goes out in some way. It's just inventory. When the material or item I got in trade is sold, then I have an amount to report at another bank. Likewise, the amount I spent acquiring what I traded out is recorded as an expense. For my own purposes, I want to know what per cent of my business is trade, and what value it has. Likewise, I can deal with gifts, services exchanged, and what not. Joe civilized thinks only about 'money.' Middle class, you mean! "Maybe." I think on that. Ok, subsistence, poor, and the rich understand favors, trades, and the wonderful world of gifts. Middle class are serfs, working for the poor and the rich. Once you figure out how it operates, you decide where on the sliding scale you want to fit in. When Joe public says, "That's absurd!" I am relieved! Glad you do not get it! Glad you are footing the bills! As I often say, "If there were no sheep, where would fleece come from?" *We can't all be happy, that's absurd!*

😄 :)

That is not a tax fraud. In a good mood, I might see my antler pile as 200 grand in the bank. According to the IRS, it is only worth what I paid for it. Nothing. Sweet. Considering what banks are about. Most people are not listening when I speak, or it is over their head. Or I am wrong and do not know it yet. All they see is what they want to see.

"Miles, going down the street without a care in the world, all dirty, acting like he owns the world and happy. It's not fair. I have to work so hard just to make ends meet and I am still not happy! What right does Miles have!" They are going to figure out my scam and turn me in by God! "Anyhow, have you noticed the changes in Miles? Isn't he supposed to be a mountain man, subsistence guy? Now he wants to pretend he is a high roller financial wizard needing an accountant and a Swiss account? Is he off his rocker?"

I do not wish to run a business with employees. I in fact turn a good third of my customers away saying, "No thanks, I'm too busy." "No, that does not interest me." Some customers envy me, and say so, wishing they could live as they feel, do what they wish, turn business away so they can go fishing. Good for me! Others come very unglued.

"That's discrimination I'm turning you in!" Or, "Aren't you in business! You can't do that!" "You can't talk to me that way!" I say, "Next!" I explained to Iris when we met. "Customers choose where they buy things. Customers go to the mall, and might not have any money, have no intention of buying. They go in shops for entertainment. Pick up chicks, see the bright lights." Iris says this is true. I reply to that basic truth, "What is good for the goose should be good for the gander." Meaning, maybe I am open and not selling today. Maybe I pick my customers, as customers pick their suppliers. Maybe I am just jiggling the hook to see what bites and not taking every fish I snag. Maybe I'm just picking up chicks today. Watching the bright lights. Enjoying listening to the sound of my own voice giving my sales pitch, and the haggle response. But no thanks, I'm not selling today, maybe tomorrow. I do not owe an explanation, any more than the shop owner has a right to grab a customer and rudely ask why the customer came in the shop and did not buy anything. What is wrong with me saying, "Just looking!" As the customer might say?

Partly I do not see this as being rude, but conscientious. At least sometimes. I sell one of a kind items–raw materials that are animal products. As a medicine-man, shaman, spiritual guru, (to some) it is my responsibility to ensure customers get 'the right medicine' to the best of my ability. As such, I need the right to say yes or no.

An item may or may not be available to you. As with any medicine. If a patient says to a doctor, "I am in pain, doc! I need some opiate!" It would be unethical, also illegal to sell that to just anyone who asked. There is the spiritual angle I prefer not to discuss, involving respect for my environment and the animals in it. Such as a Christian may not hand out crosses to everyone who asks. "I wish to melt the silver cross down to cast a forked hoofed creature." The main reason though, is that I think some people will not be happy with the product.

"I want a wolf fang for a key fob!" No. it will break. I'm not supposed to care what happens with my product, and have no right to care, as long as customers buy it? Are you trying to tell me how to run my business? An ethical car dealer should not sell a fast sports car to someone who says they need it for off-road camping and clearly needs a jeep. *Good business in the long-term means satisfied customers, not quick income.*

I would like regulars, loyal to me, as I am loyal to them. I gather around me those who understand my product, those I feel I can trust, who as well trust me. Like-minded people. If I get 100 emails, I need a way to sort them. I cannot give half an hour personal service to 100 people a day. I have right on my website how to get to the head of the line. Because I may not serve customers in the order they arrive. One of the beauties of the Internet I discover is, you do not know where you are in line! I can arrange my emails in any order I wish and do. The bottom line being, I call this a form of freedom, being rich, living life on my terms in a way that pleases me. Is it possible to be rich and not have tons of money? Is that an oxymoron? I wonder. I get the 'moron' part. Or have I just spent way too many years alone in the wilderness and am not properly socialized, or simply a French fry short of a happy meal?? The billion-dollar question. Part of the truth is, I have less than one in a thousand dissatisfied customer responses. Oh, I may dissatisfy them before they become a customer! I tell such customers, "Aren't you glad you didn't give me any money and are not out anything? How much worse it would be to pay me, then end up with a product you do not like. I have your money, ripped you off, and you hate me! The way it all came down, you can just hate me, and have the satisfaction of not spending money with me!"

I'm living subsistence, camping along the river while looking for materials used in my art.

I remember as well, one on one, personal service means a person we may or may not get along with The advantage of dealing with a machine and eliminating the human aspect of business is, machines do not talk back or rearrange the order of those standing in line. You can yell at, insult, a machine, and it says, "Yes, Sir." "We value you!" I wonder if people have forgotten how to deal with humans? *Obviously, the problem is yours, dear customer, not mine!* Anyhow, focus on the good customers, and good people.

Fooling with my new computer. A new E-machine. My previous one was eight years old. The new one was on sale for only $300! As in–"Dang, why not get one!" Turns out Microsoft office is only a trial version, and cost $400 to buy. Norton antivirus is the same. By the time I am done, I am into the cost to the tune of $1,000. I get to my emails for the day.

I just wanted to say that I really enjoyed wandering around your site; so much that I bought your book! I'm way down in Iowa, the account is in my wife's name. I have my own one man internet business, so I was laughing my #$@# off at your comments about customers, I can totally relate. Particularly to the time wasting, so don't waste any time responding to this if you don't feel like it. Happy to give you a little business! Christopher Warnock Renaissance **Astrology & Astrological Magic**

I reply with thanks. The next email requires some thought.

Hello Miles,

The piece I was looking for was 2" wide, 2-1/2" tall and about 4" long. A hair line crack is ok, but a large one will not work too well. Discoloration is ok too - the main issue is a sound structure. Hope that helps.

Cheers, Konrad

Hello Konrad

I understand now why I have not contacted you yet on having found the ivory you want. Your dimensions do not describe mammoth ivory well. Mammoth ivory does not want to be those dimensions. Ivory has growth rings like a tree and wants to delaminate. Usually a quarter inch thick.

'Solid' in the price range quoted, is defined in only 2 dimensions, not 3. Some ivory is solid as you request, but tends to be $200 a pound and up, not in the $50 a pound range you seek. I do have a guy who says he has some legal elephant ivory he is going to bring by when he visits again. I'd rather not deal in elephant ivory. I go to the biggest show in the world in Tucson each year, if you remind me mid Jan., just before I go. I see mammoth ivory there by the ton, and can find something then for sure. The price of what you seek is a bit scary. That cost per pound can come down by half, If you can accept 1 inch as your thickness, and not two inches. **Later then, Miles**

I just found your website - cannot tell you how refreshing it is to read your philosophical views and values. It speaks volumes (all good as far as I am concerned). I feel that I can simply tell you what I want to do and say "send me five pieces of (? whatever?)" - And leave the choice up to you. And know that you would send me the best pieces for my needs.

Your being an artist too, gives me even more confidence I do wood carving - Sculpture. Some small items are half the size of your little finger. I'm currently doing a commission seven ft. tall and eight ft wide (at present weighs about 750 lbs, but I am slowly reducing it; chip-by-chip. This one is a large relief (historic logging scene). In addition, I have a small studio where I teach others.

As of late, I have begun expanding my world by doing some scrimshaw, & 18th century items pertaining to the French & Indian War. It's a small market, but its' something I really enjoy doing. This will require that I find a better source for claws, teeth, horn, and bones from animals native to the North East and Southern Canada over to the Great Lakes around 1750. Materials (locally) are hard to come by & kind of expensive. I am rarely in a hurry for anything.

Would it be possible for me to tell you what I want/need? You gather up the appropriate materials/items into a pile/box/envelope - send me an email informing me of the cost - And I could send you a money order - And you ship it (when money arrives) -keep it on a "cash" basis. I would like to keep it simple & as easy for you as possible. I don't need a bunch of emails - photos - etc. going back & forth.

Best Wishes, Richard Lamphier

I have learned to keep a file on some customers, so I can keep track of their interests and better serve them. Richard sounds like someone I can work with and help. If some of his projects involve 'scientific displays, historical items', this offers legality to some materials I have few customers I can sell to. I decide to send him a box of 'this and that,' asking him to pick it over, buy what he can use, and return the rest. In other situations, I ask someone to pay up front, giving them the option to return items they cannot use. I issue a refund or more materials. It is hard, with raw materials, to know what works, since each is unique. It is usually not cost effective to show each item for sale with a picture. Not when I have 12,000 lynx claws, all different, for example.

Iris has been learning to clean, sort, and grade these claws. Spring is a time I get the 'carcass cooker' out. This is a 55-gallon drum cut in half the long way, set in a stand with an oil furnace burner under it for heat. 55 gallons can be brought to a boil with half a gallon of fuel. I have a timer so the furnace goes off and on in a sequence that keeps the liquid at a slow boil for days. Right now it is the bags of lynx claws we need to clean up. This requires cooking lynx feet to get the claws lose.

"Geez Miles, how did you end up with so many!!I explain how fur dealers cut the claws off lynx hides. "Because the sharp claws tear up the thin skinned fur in the tanning process." The fur is desired for coats. The claws have little value, so often get tossed out in the garbage, same as the bones and guts. In this case, the fur dealer had bags of lynx feet stacked in bags in his garbage pile. He had no special plans for them. They are smelly, wet, with maggots crawling out of the bags. If I did not buy them, he was tossing them out.

I forget what I paid, but think 12,000 claws cost me $300. "One of my biggest money makers!" Some of the biggest are worth up to $25 each. The biggest 100 are as big as lion claws. I show Iris the four grades of claws, so she can help me sort. Cooking claws works, but the biggest issue is the hull comes off the bone. We have to be sure not to lose the bone! In most cases, we dry the claws, then glue the bone into the hull to ensure they will not separate. A hundred claws at a time go in my rock tumbler, with some special grit I discovered, that works for cleaning and polishing the claws. Specialty knowledge not many others have that I get paid for.

"It stinks up the house though, Miles! Yuck!"

"The smell of money, honey!" That's the business we are in, so we deal with it. There is a lot of surplus green furry goop that ends up in the compost for the garden and greenhouse. This as well ends up part of our business. We have seedlings growing in the greenhouse. There is a market for starter plants. Tomatoes especially, with cucumbers being the next favorite.

I tell Iris, "If we can break even with this part of the business, and cover our own costs for growing what we eat, I'll be happy!" Each year I need batteries for the timers, sometimes new timers, and new hoses. We make a list to replace things now, while it is on our mind and early in the season. I usually need new misters, sprayers, hose fittings, and a little potting soil. "But Iris, we generally use our own soil as starter. Sterilize it in the oven. Usually this mix needs some store bought potting soil for the right texture." My records, averaged over the past few years, let me know I usually spend $300 a season on the garden. "So if we make $300 selling plants, that is fine."

"Miles, maybe in the late summer we can sell some pickles, pickled beets, and things, even at the local bazaars." Yes, we'll see how it goes. Meanwhile, the carcass cooker has some wolf carcasses to process. I have been buying them from local trappers, mostly subsistence natives, who save the fur, then toss the carcass out in the woods. Again, a waste product with little value I wish to create a market for.

"Iris, I pay $25 for the carcass. I cook it down and sell the skull. The leg bones are for knife handles. There is a new market for knuckle bones for beads, and runes for some ancient game the magic people seek out." It's a very niche market, but one of the beauties of the internet is, if 'wolf bones' are keywords on my website, then anyone in the world putting this in a search engine will find me. If there are only 100 people in the entire world interested and looking, I can get their business. *Who else would have 'wolf bones' as key search words in their website??* [1]With my low overhead, I do not need a constant flow of volume. I can afford to sit on inventory, sometimes for a decade or longer.

It's not easy. I think it is great! Being the garbage man, cleaning up, making a living on miscellaneous items tossed out. The ultimate in recycling, that makes it a way of life, and not just words about conservation, or one day a year picking up beer cans. In the village, it's a little weird.

A guy who stacks up frozen wolf carcasses in his yard! Some react with, "Is that legal?!" First thing some people want to do is call in the Gestapo, rather than being tolerant. While others think as I do, a good thing to be doing, making a living without a big carbon footprint. What I am doing fits in with my subsistence beliefs. One issue is, I am in the village now, and this life costs more than my wilderness life!

There is less profit from my art because the pipeline money of the last two decades is dwindling. The messages from civilization are so mixed. I feel off balance and confused a lot. I begin conversations and never know for sure where they are going to end up. I meet bubbly open-minded excited people who appear to be at one with nature and all I stand for. They buy my book one. I excitedly go into detail about the lifestyle I am so ready to share and discuss, only to end up in a heated defensive argument. It has not helped to have had the nickname 'Wild Miles' most of my life! Though I do not get called this much anymore. Often I get called 'Sunshine Miles,' for the way I sign my letters, and my generally happy disposition.

Wild Miles got started as an insult based on a joke I never understood about a guy and a buffalo in a bar. I heard, whisper, whisper, "Doesn't it remind you of Miles over there?" "Ha ha, laugh, laugh, point, point, giggle, yea, Wild Miles!" I turned an insult into a nickname I am proud of. A name I take on as a compliment. *I'd rather be a savage than civilized!* 'Normal' is an insult. I see nothing especially wrong with wild animals compared to people. For the most part, wild animals seem kinder, certainly to their own species. *Or at least this is what I believed in my younger years.* Wild animals are rarely 'cruel.' Wild animals seem rarely to go out of their way to make problems. For the most part, they are trying to eat, stay warm, enjoy life. To say to me,

"I am civilized, while you are a savage!" I take as a compliment. *Tarzan was a savage. In my view, so was Jesus. All He had was sandals and a robe to his name. Born in a barn, in the straw. Living from hand to mouth, a beggar. 'Normal and civilized,' was the cheering crowd watching Him get nailed. Is there a reason God would choose this sort of life for His son?* I failed to grasp till I got older and wiser, what the price would be for being known as Wild Miles. Wild and savage, to the civilized, translates, 'crazy, not dependable, dangerous, not very bright, to be avoided, lower class, among the unprotected.'

Images of drugs, and party hardy, come to the civilized mind. While I may think this is funny, and I may have a secret smile at how 'wrong' everyone is, still, we are judged by what people think. Speculation, rumors, opinions, becomes fact. In the long haul, it did not help me much in life. But! *Oh well! Would we take any of it back and be sorry? Not especially. We have no regrets about life, do we?*

Another hundred claws are cleaned, sorted, graded, glued, run through the tumbler. The stack of wolf carcasses eventually gets cooked down to bones that are dried, sorted, graded and priced. Leftover cooked guts, fur, and 'what not,' is stirred into the compost worm farm! A big box with a glass lid to cook in the sun. This is layered with grass, eggshells, coffee grounds, raked up leaves, and the stuff plants love to grow in.

"Miles, isn't it odd the ravens do not touch anything in the yard? Considering the meat scraps and garbage?" We have talked about this before. It does seem odd. Around town, the ravens have a field day with trash bags, bones, fish skins, and anything else they can find that is edible in yards, lying in the streets. Yet I have never had an issue with the ravens, though they roost in the trees all around me. I do know I am constantly talking to them, clucking in their language. My survey boss Seymour commented one time, he cannot tell by listening, the difference between the ravens and me. Is it possible ravens understand ownership, understand messing with people and animals, and understand leaving other people's stuff alone? Understand 'polite' or 'owe a favor' or 'working together for a common good?' I cannot say. It is just odd, in the business I am in, with so much food for ravens around, that they never touch my stuff. Not ever. Even when I am gone.

Iris and I share some raven stories. We saw them sliding down the neighbor's steep tin roof and laughing once. They would slide and without extending wings, tumble in the air to land in the deep fluffy snow. Shake themselves, make sounds like laughing, and fly to the rooftop to do it again. Taking turns, and sharing with the others, as some great funny thing to do. What part of all this is a fact, and what part mere speculation? There are a great many raven stories we have heard from others and seen ourselves. Raven experts deny our interpretation of what we are observing. Experts say no animal knows how to laugh because something is funny. Ravens cannot work together on a nonsense game of fun. Animals do not imitate people for entertainment, nor have a sense of humor.

I comment to Iris, "Because animals and birds do not do this in the lab. Would you?"

Miles: I enjoy looking at your web side although I'm a little confused, in particular the prices of certain items. But I really like the fact you tell it like it is when you explain time factors and what time is worth. I did order a moose leg bone as a starter. I like the walrus scales, but I cannot seem to find prices. I am a part-time knife maker, so I will not be ordering large amounts. Because of that, I'm not sure if you even want to talk with me. But when I make knives I do not believe in using "cheap" materials, so I am always looking for sites where I can find such as sheep horn, mammoth, walrus, hippo, etc. So if you do not want to fool around with a part-timer, just let me know. Thanks **Lloyd Scallan**

Hello Lloyd:

Confused? The whole world is confusing, what can I say? (smile) Some pictures have been on the site five years. I can't have prices five years outdated. Prices vary depending on who's buying, why, where they are, and other factors. In my mind, none of this stuff has an exact set in stone price. It's an animal product. It's worth whatever people will pay for it. (Up to a point) I'd go nuts listing prices on all 1,000 items on my website and keeping up. It's all I'd get done! Every day, keeping up with prices! I get paid for my time in the shop working, not web time.

Also, various 'problems' like slow speed Internet, means hard to have a shopping cart. (For technical reasons) and I don't have enough web knowledge to fix the problems. I have some nice fossil walrus in right now. Have no time to make scales, so just raw rough, but in lengths for knives, with a few baby tusks for hidden tang style. The rough is $210 a pound or there about. Baby tusks depends on which one, might be the same price, but often a little more, as just plain awesome material- and often only a few ounces. Fossil walrus ivory scales finished as you ask for are very expensive, selling for over $100 a set, where a $150 pound might get you a dozen sets if you cut them yourself. If you want to take a chance and order, and just return it if it is not going to work. Let me know. **Miles**

PART of my confusion is that most customers understand, and communicate to me what grade they wish to come in on, or what their budget is. This customer appears to be a part-time amateur, trying to upgrade for the first time. He's concerned about the price of the material. I have some ideas to keep the cost down. Engaging me in conversation. I'm personally hunting down a specific size of a specific material to show him, so he may decide. This is not the path for 'lowest price,' having me offering so much time. He appears to be hedging.

Hello Again, many thanks for your reply. I appreciate your straight forward, no bull shit advice. I am looking for a set of unusual scales that need to be about 4 1/2 X 1 1/2 X 3/8 thick. I looked at your mammoth scales, but to be honest the prices are a little steep. My question is what would a set of walrus scales (about the above size) cost, unless you have cheaper mammoth scales. If you don't have the time to reply, that's ok. **Lloyd**

Hello Lloyd: Well, mostly anything rare, unusual and cool, is going to cost. That's why it cost. Walrus is worth more than mammoth. Often $100 ivory scales go on knives selling for $1,000 and up- So ya 'steep' is a relative term. The moose bone is a good choice, the best buy for the price in my opinion. Another option is, you could get the rough mammoth to save money. Maybe $30 for enough to make a nice set of scales worth $75. You can't get around the fact what you want 'cost.' If you do even an ok job, you will have a knife worth $300 to $500 minimum.

Cheap material will give you a $100 knife. Where the moose bone works for a functional knife, there is a value limit based on the fact the material is bone. What you invest in the material is worth 10 fold when you are finished. Best advice I can offer. If it's out of your class right now, then settle for the cheaper material, sell the knives cheaper till you get better at it, or have a customer base and a reputation living up to the material. Anyhow, let me know. **Miles**

Hi Miles- once again thanks for your reply. First, I am not asking for any sort of discount or "cheap" material. I have been making knives for a few years now, and I know what they are worth and what most various materials cost. The only reason I hesitate to even mention price is the fact that in particular, some good mammoth scales are selling for about 1/3 of your prices (depending on the quality). For example, Elephant Ivory Tusk, Jantz Supply, and Texas knife makers Supply.

I have never looked at walrus for knife scales before, thus have never looked at price for that material. Down here in the New Orleans area, one major problem when selling knives is no one wants to pay what a knife is worth in other markets. I feel, and have been told, that my work is really good.

I have gone to gun and knife shows and compared my work to other professional knife makers. I would put my work up against any of other. But I am forced to sell a knife for $100.00 when the same quality and material (both steel and handle) would sell for three times that amount most anywhere else.

People here just go to a Wal-Mart and can buy a piece of crap made of 240 steel. They use a piece of fake wood or bone, and that's good enough for them. Then wonder why they have to re-sharpen the thing half way through skinning a rabbit. Actually, down here, I'm selling more fish filet knives than hunting knives and getting a fair price. I'm not trying to drive you out of business by asking you to sell me something below your cost and labor. I'm just asking the price of things.

This knife is for my personal use. I liked the look of walrus, so I asked the price, that's all. In addition, I will put my work up against yours any day. As I write this, I had a second thought, take your walrus and mammoth, package it up real nice, then shove them up your a@#$. **Warmest regards – Lloyd**

I study transactions like this. Try to figure out what went wrong, why, and how to avoid such problems. There is a frustrating issue at this time I have not figured out how to overcome. I have dial up phone Internet connection. I can go make a pot of coffee in the time it takes to download a page off the Internet or connect to email and download emails. It takes forever to upload pictures. I do wish I could put a picture up of everything for sale with a price. I am competing with others in big cities with high-speed internet. Customers expect the same level of service with prices. Trying to explain on the website what is going on is not always understood. Opening up and encouraging a dialogue with customers might not work out. Or maybe not with everyone.

I average a sale for every four contacts made. If I average half an hour per customer then

I am spending two hours per sale. This is not going to work. I appreciate Lloyd for helping me understand what I need to do.

Hi there, I found your site when I was googling for a value of walrus tusks. My father got one in Alaska about 40 years ago, and I don't even know if it is legal to sell it or not and I have no idea of its value. It is about 2 feet long and weighs about 6 to 7 pounds. Can you offer any info? Thank you, **Kathi**

I END up acquiring material from people I meet on the Internet and encourage trades. Forty years ago is before 1970, when the city's treaty was signed for animal protection. Older material is legal. A statement from her saying when her father acquired it is all I need 'as proof.'

Laws seem in flux and unclear. I talk to my ivory dealer friend, Tusk, off and on, to keep up with the latest news. No one I know trusts Fish and Wildlife as the only source of accurate information. I have known Tusk now for a lifetime, and he is more bent over, but still looks like a prospector the way he wears his floppy hat and outdoor clothes. A bushy beard adds to the image. I repeat to Tusk what we have reviewed before. "A judge friend told me once that we have to know the law, and ignorance is no excuse. However, there is no law saying those who make the laws have to make them easily available, or even tell the truth if asked."

Tusk agrees and adds personal experiences, "Miles, just asking, can get you on the person of interest list, and a search warrant served."

It is worth commenting that much is going on behind the scenes concerning laws with animal products, ivory in particular. That's a fact. The 'Why' is speculation. Tusk and I speculate: During the 70s through the 90s, Alaska was at the peak of its gas line oil business. Many people feel civilization ripped off the Eskimo and Indians royally. To make up for that, or more, to stop an outright rebellion, Fish and Game winked and looked the other way over Native hunting regulations. Eskimos could sell their ivory. It was politically incorrect to say or do anything about it. It was good and easy times for all, except maybe the walrus. After the oil was secured, in the bag, and hard to stop, there was less need to be nice to the Natives. They now have to comply more with the white man's laws. Tusk adds to that, reminding me not to forget: "At the same time, the elephants are being hunted in Africa for ivory to support revolutions."

I'm not convinced the government cares as much for the elephants' lives. It is just my opinion, that much has to do with stopping the wrong side from having access to money to fight the side the US is backing. It's a multimillion-dollar illegal business. I mention to Tusk, "Remember the Oliver North fiasco? Our government trading guns for drugs? I heard mention elephant ivory was mixed in there someplace."

Tusk replies, "If we could prove it, and tried to, the government would have us silenced."

I do not wish to take the conversation there. "I'm working on a series of books, Tusk. This is a story of how what I believe effected my life. I am not so interested in changing anyone else's views. What I am asking of others, is to be in my shoes, and try to understand the world through my eyes."

"Smart move, Miles!" he chuckles.

Miles: I am in need of the jawbone of a wolf and/or bear. Can you help? I need it for a primitive knife handle so I would say it's a combo of spiritual and practical. Blade about 6 inches. Thanks for getting back to me. **I'll call Monday**

THIS IS an example of the customers I meet who needs parts I get from the carcass cooker. I sell this guy wolf jawbones and later leg bones. I remain optimistic! So far buckets of organized bones are accumulating much faster than they sell. However, one day it will all sell, it just takes time!

I say to Iris, "If you want wolf jawbones, toe bones, how many people in the world specialize in them? I bet there are not five people in the world! Eventually those looking will find me! I can beat anyone's price because I am the source!" I explain a more complicated idea I have had. "So much today comes for overseas, China, India. What to do about it? Think of products China cannot easily get! Local animal parts, for example. If China wants them, they get them from me. I have no competition. Business 101 by Wild Miles. Yea! Stuff we would not learn in marketing class." Am I cool? Am I the man? Give me five! There are ways to beat China at their game.

It's Marcia O'hara from the Chicago area. Hope you are doing well. My daughter and I enjoyed seeing you at the Tucson gem show and are enjoying your beautiful pieces that we purchased. I am interested in any rings and bracelets you may have, especially those with opals or other stones. Could you let me know what you have available and price? Hope the show went well for you, and that you had a good trip back to Alaska. Look forward to hearing from you. Thanks----**Marcia O.**

There are return customers, those who meet and buy from me at shows who continue the connection through the website. I am learning more about 'rocks' because of the Tucson show. I especially like opals. In the beginning, I bought cut and polished stones. Already cut cost more than I could afford. The good ones anyhow! I now buy stones in the rough, and cut, polish them myself. I am acquiring rock slicers, dicers, polishers. A local brought me a diamond wheel station seven feet long with five stations. I pay $300. I'm guessing it is from the 1940's. Replacing it new is $10,000. The water dripper does not work. A minor detail, easy to fix. I drill holes in the lid, and run a gravity feed tube in, hooked to a five-gallon bucket of water, with a drip valve in it. My buddy, Crafty, who taught me a lot about the finer points of art of selling, asks me why I want to cut my own stones!

"I got a deal for you, Miles, a deal you cannot refuse. I have many rock slices. I can offer them wholesale, cheaper than you can buy raw rocks!" Yes, for me, a special deal.

I reply, "All true Crafty! I have been getting rocks and other supplies from you for a lot of years now. However…" I explain what is going on. I am now custom casting caps for rocks, creating settings for odd shaped and sized rocks by lost wax casting. No one else I have met is doing this. The rocks I find on the market are cut to fit standard settings. They all have flat backs with the dome on the other side. It would be better for me to have a dome on both sides, so the finished pendant is reversible. Likewise, it would be better if the polished cabs had a flat spot in its circumference, so I have a place to fit a cast cap better.

"As I move up in quality, over time, it is hard to afford the higher end material as a finished product!" Maybe the same problem my customer Lloyd has, only I am doing something about it. What I am doing about it is buying nicer material in the rough, cutting it to suit my needs and coming up with a unique product that does not involve standard cookie cutter stones. Raw material is incredibly cheaper than finished products! "I can buy a raw rough Australian opal for $10, that with minimal work ends up as a $100 stone. Easily, Crafty, without a lot of knowledge or experience."

Now that I go to Tucson, I do not buy from my buddy, Crafty. I am at his sources. His deals are no longer the best deal going. In fact, it is my turn to make offers to Crafty at prices he cannot refuse. Crafty only chuckles. "I taught you well, Grasshopper!" Yes, Crafty has taught me a lot over the past twenty years. As he grins, I am reminded of how much bigger he is then I am. How he looks like Grizzly Adams, and in fact has a picture of himself next to this famous TV character in his shop. Crafty is running a million dollar a year business, supplying the entire state with Alaskan craft items for the tourist industry. Crafty knows every craft person in the state, I bet. Many he has organized, working for him indirectly. Subcontracting, filling his orders for him. Crafty is reluctant to part with his cash. So he trades. His once red beard is now white. He laughs, "Miles, your hair looks like Einstein!"

I'm also going bald. I reply, "It's intelligence that does that Crafty! My brain pushes, no room, so pushes my hair out, I can't help it!" Even my face looks like Einstein. Only on a five foot short hobbit body.

Crafters working for him, get paid in raw materials, tools to work with, and a place to stay, even a place to work in his basement. I know. I was part of his operation for many years. Crafty makes the money. Most under him work as slave labor. Since he hates to part with cash, it is hard to work for him and get ahead enough so you can leave him. Crafty doles out money for specific emergency needs, like if you are about to be evicted for not paying rent. Your buddy Crafty is right there to pay the rent for you. What a guy! Not to paint him to be 'horrible.' He has a kind side. I know if I was ever down and out, he would give me a place to stay, food, a job, today. I'd make enough to get by. Crafty has driven all the way to Manly Hot Springs to give me a ride back to town. He picks me up at the airport or drops me off and often drops what he is doing to go out to lunch, and often he buys.

When I met him, he was selling out of an old trunk on the street. Selling dumpster used stuff. I am proud to know him, as someone who worked hard, had a dream, and made something of himself. If he is a little quirky, that sometimes comes with the territory. *May any of us who are perfect, cast the first stone.* Many who work for Crafty badmouth him. He takes the brunt of the problems with the industry. In truth, it is a tough occupation, being an artist. We are independent with no union on our own, with not much recourse when things go wrong. I have been treated worse than Crafty treats me by high end galleries. Many times I have left art on consignment and the paperwork gets lost, the gallery never heard of me. No art, no money. Thousands of dollars.

I knew what I was getting into. We all do, or should, as Crafty spells it out up front. He is good at his word. In the past, I did not care so much about the money as I did about my freedom. I needed craft materials, no fuss, no muss. I needed a place to stay when I came to the city. I had cash from fur sales, from surveying. Crafty provides a service and makes life simple. Many craft people hanging around Crafty cannot do any better with their life. Quite a few who leave him, end up in the gutter, homeless. My buddy Crafty. It's amazing how many gifted artists are dysfunctional street people.

"So, Crafty, how is Wess the Mess these days?" I like to keep track of some of the Crafty regulars I know.

Wess is an extremely talented artist who can't keep his life together. Crafty gives him a place to stay and work under the conditions, 'No drugs!' Wess stays sober and drug free. He then can produce some masterpieces. Crafty can make up to thousands of dollars for these masterpieces, and Wess gets a place to stay. If Wess was paid, he'd buy drugs and stop doing his art. Wess the Mess, stuck in the 60s, tie-dye clothes, covered in peace symbols, playing the bongos. Nodding his head, "Hey Man," long pause, "What's happening?"

Crafty tells me: "Last I heard, he is staying in the basement of the co-op building, living in one of the storage bins. They let him stay there. He is sort of night security." I had seen him living there in the past, sleeping on cardboard boxes. A crate set up for his carving table, running his electric Foredom, carving the Star Ship Enterprise out of ivory. Down to the tiniest detail-moving parts, every window, as good as carving gets, on a world class level. Carved by a guy living in a cardboard box. I saw the carving for sale at new Horizon's Gallery for $15,000. Unsure how it got there, but think Wess never got a dime. Crafty would have given him at least $100, some more ivory, new cutting tips for the grinder. Wess is not an unhappy person. I tried to help him, according to my opinion of what he needs. Wess brought me down faster than I brought him up. Life is interesting. If Wess the Mess is happy, being his friend means accepting him for who and how he lives.

***

Hi Miles, I know you have many customers you have to deal with. I know I could not keep track of the volume of sales you have. So, to refresh both of our memories, Here is a copy of the order I placed. PayPal did not have a place for notes on the order and there was a choice on your website for brass, silver and some other metal capping on wolf claws. So I sent an e-mail asking for two silver capped wolf claws, similar if possible. Your last e-mail said that you believed that the order was shipped 2-20-2010 tracking number 0308 2040 000 1828 6190. As of today's mail I still have not received them and when I've tried to use the tracking number you supplied on the USPS website It states "There is no record of this item." Any help here would be appreciated.
Thanks :) Todd J Perkins

THERE IS an issue with my record keeping methods. In this case, there were two customers with the same name, on the same day, ordering the same item. *What are the odds of that?* Yet it happened. I am filing customers by name. Usually, I can sort the order by the name, date and what they order. I sent the order to the wrong Todd. I'm horrible with numbers, can't get a phone number right without at least three tries. So it does not surprise me I typed in a 26 digit code wrong. I now replace the order and send him three claws instead of two, with an apology for the mixup. The guy I sent the wrong order to never returned them. If it is my mistake, it is my loss. I see it as the cost of learning how to run a business effectively. It's still less money than taking a college course. *And better, because meanwhile, I have a job! I'm getting paid as I learn! How cool is that!* An education 'paid as you go.' No student loans to pay back. *Am I ever blessed and lucky!*

Hello, could you tell me how much it would cost me with all the charges for 20 medium wolf claws. I live in Quebec, Canada. Thanks. **Alain**

SOMETIMES THERE ARE legal issues to ponder. While I have the basic export permit for $100, wolf items require a special permit issued per shipment that needs approval and inspection at a certified point of export. That point for me is Seattle. I know of no dealers who are bothering to bring packages 1,000 miles to Seattle for inspection. In general, we send the claws anyhow. The worse we expect is to have the order confiscated if there is trouble. When I went to Fish and Game, they never heard of such a permit, never issued one, did not know where to find one, and were not interested in getting an answer as to what to do. I try to talk customers into other items instead. Twenty claws seem like a lot to try to get across the border under the radar. This order I turn down. I hate to see the loss of an easy $200. But why create problems with the government?

Sir: Attached mammoth ivory rough pic... How delicate or friable are these pieces. Will they split, spall, chip, crack, etc. with time, sunlight, or firing gun? Can I get a pair whose figure is less or shallower, kinda like polished deer antler? Also, there's no shopping link on this stuff. How do I proceed with an order? Thank You! **Dan**

I LEARN to have informational sections on the website, so I do not have to explain to each customer, what things are, how they behave, how to use the material, etc. This is a long learning process. There is poor google information at this point. For a long time I reply to each and every customer who inquires one on one. There is no good shopping cart evaluable, certainly not for the web program I use. eBay, Amazon, ETSY or other selling sites have built in shop carts. EBay will not allow the selling of animal parts. I spend ten hours a day just answering emails. To sell, to make money, I need to be in the shop creating stuff. I ask this customer if what he really wants is a deer antler look. We both know deer antler is not big enough for pistol grips, but why not try moose antler? A lot cheaper than ivory and will hold up much better. Mammoth ivory is for looks, not for durability. I sell him moose antler for $30 instead of mammoth for $100. He is grateful I took the time to explain. *Will customers being grateful in the big picture lead to good business, making money?*

My name is Olivia and I was wondering if there was any way I might be able to order a wolf tooth necklace from you. Just something simple for a cap, maybe a couple cool stones in silver? Let me know if that is ok. Thank You. By the way, I just have to let you know how much I love your site. It is so easy to get around and I feel like you really know what you are doing.

SOME CUSTOMERS UNDERSTAND what I am trying to do, how the site works, have no problem with it.

Hello, I was looking at your website last night & was wondering if you still have the musk ox horns? I'm looking for a set of them or a set of them on a skull. **Thanx Mark**....

I turn down trophy mount type animal part sales. I prefer to be in the craft business selling secondary or by-product materials. I sometimes offer a whole horn, but not a set. I explain to Iris, as she seems confused by the random sense of personal ethics I base my behavior on. "The bottom line is, I do not want to supply any animal part worth a lot of money, where it is likely the animal was killed just to supply that part, and the rest wasted." She is puzzled.

"But what about trapping, you have been a trapper most of your life!" True, but it is not a lot of money, so where we live anyhow, the animal populations are holding their own and not being wiped out. There is more or less a balance. We are not talking anything 'rare.' That is also the past. During a time and in a place, there were few options to make enough money to buy the basics. I was younger and had a different view of the world, nature, trapping, trappers. I also explain, "There is a legal difference between supplying craft items and trophy items. Craft items fall within the definition of traditional barter and trade, the subsistence life. Trophies would be getting out of the realm of supporting, living, a simple subsistence life. We kill because we must and use the surplus to make tools and crafts so we are not wasteful. This is what I wish to support."

Notice I am not pushing being a fur dealer. Possibly there would be money, but there are plenty of fur dealers in the world, lots of competition. One of my priorities is to have a niche market-small, exclusive, with little competition, that I am in control of. Not about 'power.' Control does not always mean it is about power. *I wish to control my life, no one else's.*

"Iris, it can be like an artist, I control my hand in the pen stroke, smooth, fast, without a quiver, to get beautiful lines that are music to the eye. That is not power, nor money. Control of my occupation is about keeping it safe. It is less likely a competitor is going to put the squeeze on me and ace me out. I'm not trying to fix prices, or mess with anyone else."

"If you say so, Miles!" It might be a concept hard to understand, or I am deluding myself. *Yes, one or the other, what's your vote?* I think I'll pick door number three. *I'd like to buy a vowel.* Iris can be stubborn. She is German, long, dark hair, only an inch taller than me. I do not think she agrees with me.

Hello miles, my husband and I are interested in your silver capped pair of wolf toe bone beads. Please get back

THE WOLF TOE bone beads are catching on, but it is slow building up a market. I notice these toe bones are hollow and a good diameter for beads. I cut them to exact lengths, clean them out and put a silver band around at each end for decoration and to stop them from cracking. I get $10 a set. I tell Iris, "It is now possible for me to get more money for the 'garbage' wolf carcass then the trapper gets for the fur!" I'm proud of that, to make something of nothing. Creating a market out of thin air, so to speak. Make a living without the huge impact of being a big consumer. It has taken a decade to build up a market.

Hello June It might be faster and easier for me just to send samples. Give me an address…

Thank you for your reply.
    The fang I want is one that looks nice for my amulet pendant. I will prefer a fresh fang. Can you tell me more or less the length of them? Thank you and have a nice day up there in the **Great Alaska**

I learn to have a size reference in my pictures, sometimes a ruler, sometimes a coin. Telling people in inches what the size is seems not to be as effective as a reference in the picture.

THE WEATHER IS WARMING FAST. I remind Iris,
    "Alaska has two seasons! Summer and winter!" Often there is only a two-week period between zero degrees with snow on the ground, to no snow, leaves out and summer birds. "Time for the boat!" I still feel like a child, jumping up and down. Up at sunrise babbling, running around, collecting the boat gear, ready to launch! I have changed the gear oil in the lower unit, inspected plugs and water pump, made sure I have survival tools, clothes, gear, along with a fishing pole and just everything a boat needs! I hope to get some spring geese, at least one.
    "And life jacket, Miles?" I pause. Rats. 'Sort of!' I do not wear life jackets. Tried

one once for a spell. The rewind of my outboard motor got tangled in the clumsy preserver and almost pulled me into the river. Another time, while running the length of the boat over my gear, the strings of the preserver snagged on the windshield. This stopped my momentum at a critical time when I had to get to the back of the boat, fast.

I have never in my life fallen in the river. I have never in my life flipped a boat or had one sink out from under me. Never in my many years on the river been in a situation I thought a life jacket would have helped. In many cases a life jacket can create problems, even in the river. More important to me is maneuverability. Speed, reflexes. I keep a float coat on the back of the boat chair. Just in case. Iris reminds me I should put it there then! I wolf down breakfast.

My boat is tied up on the river where I keep it all summer, where I used to keep the houseboat for years. That's still sort of my private dock area no one messes with, as I am grandfathered in now. I have seniority. All the locals know that is the tree I tie up to; I put the steps in and keep a certain amount of 'stuff' there at the landing. A bike to ride in, some fuel tanks, rope hanging in a tree and such.

"Spring geese, Miles? Is that legal?" Yes and no. Usually, and in most cases, not legal. Subsistence people are allowed to harvest spring ducks and geese, but it is frowned on. We are expected to do so discreetly. The public might frown on it. *What do they know!?* I retrieve an article to show Iris. It's saved from the News Miner, our local Fairbanks paper.

"**New York-** About 800 Canada Geese around New York City's two airports have been trapped and euthanized... Officials plan to kill 2,000 within weeks... US Airways Flight 1549 had just taken off from LaGuardia on Jan 15th and was over the Bronx when it ran into geese and lost both engines."

I comment to Iris defensively, "I notice there was no mention of offering them to the hungry! Oh, it is just fine when civilization has a need to wipe some geese out for their own purposes and waste them! When hungry people wish to harvest them to eat? Suddenly there is indignation!" This leads to the next similar subject, acquiring an out of season winter moose. "The train kills an average of 800 moose a year between Anchorage and Fairbanks. There is no effort to salvage them, make a report, or let the public know. It's ok, it's the railroad. It might cost too much to come up with a solution. But let a hungry hunter snaffle one, and they go to jail, get big fines!"

Iris is not especially interested, so I calm down. No big deal to her one way or the other; she was raised in the city and is getting me to depend on Wal-Mart. But for me, it is a sore subject. I have now had thirty years of dealing with this issue with no resolution; in fact, the situation gets worse. I'm frustrated and fed up. The entire subsistence population in Alaska does not harvest more than 2,000 geese each spring. The New York airport can kill and waste this many, and it is considered taking care of a dangerous problem. Thanked for doing so. At the taxpayers' expense. I'm disgusted! However, happiness and survival is not in this direction, we must feel forgiveness in our heart!

I'm excited to test out the boat, get out on the river, show my partner the wonders of river life!

"Come on Honey! Let's go on a picnic, I have a favorite place to show you!" We pack a lunch, head for the river and boat on our four-wheeler. The engine starts, purrs, as it should. I check all the gauges, listen to the sounds, and make sure this will be a safe trip. Speed is not necessary today, so I go at a comfortable speed that creates no wind. I do not want Iris to get chilled or have a bad experience. She loves seeing the Nenana hill turning green, the various views from the boat. We go upstream in case there is an engine problem, we can always float back. Fairbanks is seventy miles ahead of us with no villages, houses or roads along our way. This direction is not called the wilderness, though. No other boats are on the river. A few fish camps are spotted.

"Iris, I showed you pictures and told you in letters of fish camps, this is what one looks like." We could stop, but she is happy just to look from the boat; I slow down, and we see the tin shack used for smoking fish. We pass the log cabin used as shelter while here. This is one of the camps used by locals who still fish for sled dogs, or get fish for personal use, to put up for the rest of the year. Some get dried, some frozen, most get smoked in this tin shed.

"Miles, how many fish would someone put up at a camp like this?" "At least hundreds. Possibly thousands." It all gets eaten during the year. Fish shows up at community gatherings, potlucks, funerals, any kind of meeting where food is served. I do not get into all the political issues. The camp is simple, a folding chair out front, a one-room log cabin ten by twenty feet, with one window, a propane stove and a single light. This is not a vacation home. This is a break more than a vacation, and is actually serious business, This is about the ability to stay alive with food we can afford and harvest ourselves, be in charge of. Healthy food, not imported, not controlled by anyone else, or affected by the economy, the stock market. Much of this I keep to myself as we travel. It takes time to take in a completely new lifestyle. I'll let Iris sort it out. I can tell she is getting overwhelmed.

It takes an hour to get to a small creek known locally as Pogey slough. Since the map was made, it has become a clear creek with two well hidden entrances. You have to be a local to know where this is. Even from twenty feet away, approaching slowly, Iris does not see it, and has no idea why we are pulling in here. There is a nice sandy beach that looks inviting to walk on and interesting driftwood logs worth viewing up close, as works of art by God. The high water during ice break up has dropped the driftwood during the past week. I know the sand will be saturated with water and soft. I am so used to this I give it no thought.

The boat noses in enough to stay put with the bow beached three feet up on the sand. Getting out requires stepping off the front onto more firm sand. I explain to Iris who goes "Uh, huh." She must not understand, as she steps off the boat at the edge of the water into sand she thinks is solid. Before she realized it, she has lost her balance. Her foot goes deep into quicksand type river silt. I gather from her expression, she has never seen this before. Her life has been on cement. She moves, and this makes the situation worse, and only causes her foot to sink deeper.

I'm still on the boat and hold her hand, trying to give her instructions. She is in panic mode. Her boot comes off, and she gets back in the boat, but has twisted her ankle and got muddy. I'm not sure. Honestly, I can't see the problem. I'm truly puzzled. I've stepped off into, gosh, a zillion times with this problem. I've been up to my waist. I've...*but never mind*. Certainly, this is no time to review how minor this is. Iris is upset. Refuses to get off the boat. I fetch her boot, and just stare at the cool creek I wanted to show her. She wants to go home. She has had enough adventure for the day, for the week, for a lifetime. We go home. So much for sharing the great river life with my partner. She is not interested in going on the river again. Maybe never. She tells everyone she can, how I goofed up, got us stuck, and almost lost her, and let her get hurt.

This is normal. I am used to this. This is what usually happens when I try to share my life, so I have learned not to share. It's personal. Iris and I get along as far as she lets me do my thing, and whatever she does, she seems happy enough. No hard feelings. We do not argue. She is happy to stay home and take care of the home front, while I go off on my adventures. This is not what I pictured relationships are. I leave it at that.

Meanwhile, nothing is stopping me from loving and spending time on the river, not my parents, not a wife, a son, friends, not even God. I even said to God, "And you cannot make me. You made a promise to mankind that we have a choice!" God only smiled, nodded this is in fact true, and thought I was funny. God did not get mad, or leave. I reason God knows everything, so understands I have an authority issue. I'm not trying to insult God. I'm saying, "If you love me, let me figure it all out on my own, please?" So, God and I have an agreement, of sorts.

Right away, I want to head out on my own on the river to see how the homestead is, and haul a few supplies. The trip has been made a hundred gazillion times. It's 120 miles one way. Enough gas is loaded to go 250 miles. I hope to leave five gallons at the homestead for the chain saw and run a generator to charge a car battery. I acquired my ham radio license-call sign, KL1VC, and carry a portable ham radio on the boat. I have not decided if I want to put in a home-base ham tower on the Kantishna.

Reliable communication is an important necessity when remote, so I spend a lot of time researching options. Ham radio has been around many years, so seems stable as something a person can depend on. There is a beauty in this. Once you buy the ham phone, the cost is over. There is no cost to connect or use them. Other's like me, have information to share. My accountant, Bean, is an avid ham operator. "Miles, all it needs is twelve volt power, and not a lot of wattage. Good antennas are important!" He specializes in five watt usage and enters contests concerning how far they reach. "All over the world, Miles!" I discuss with others, how ham could be the last form of long distance still standing in an emergency. There are emergency channels which people all over the world monitor. Ham operators are big on helping each other. It would be hard for governments to stop this communication. Hard to exploit and make it unaffordable.

It was a big decision that took a lot of thought-how to communicate in the best way. In earlier years, many of us relied on CB radio, but these days few use this. Many switched over to a big bag, analogue type radiophone. These had much more range than CB, which required illegal signal boosters to increase distance. I was thinking of getting the new bag-phone, but I have a top-notch CB with a huge antenna. The bag-phone is expensive, and before I can decide, they became obsolete. The repeater towers that support them are shut down. The new rage is a cell phone. Towers are not in yet. The talk is cell phones are not as reliable, and will not reach nearly as far with a signal. Without the tower, they are not good for long range. They are built for city people where there are cell towers all over the place. I assume there are not enough remote people to support a business catering to us. 'Who needs them to work thirty miles?' Satellite phones are in the experimental stage, expensive, unreliable. Especially since satellites are up in space to serve the lower states. Few orbit this far north; all are low on the horizon. Alaska is, so far, out of luck.

One of the issues I have heard about for cell phone owners is the incredible bills that can accumulate. Since they are new, they are spendy. One of my neighbors on the Kantishna River, where I am headed, told me, "I asked the phone supplier why the analogue bag phone is not working anymore, why the cell towers are down. Digital cell phones do not work way upriver!" I am interested in what they had to say to my neighbor, so pay attention.

"Miles, I was told the government put a ban on analogue. Everything is going to be digital because analogue phones cannot be tracked. The government does not know where such a call is made from. The goal is to have the ability to track every single phone call, and know where it came from, with the potential to record, save, and control all calls and communications."

I have no way to know if what my neighbor is told and believes is true. This statement is simply filed away in my mind to match other information coming in, and my own firsthand experiences. This sounds preposterous, like a conspiracy theory to me. *The public would not put up with a government with this goal in mind would it?* Anyhow, this is something that would be hard to prove.

"So you are headed up the Kantishna Miles?"

"Oh. Sometime, I guess, not sure when." I have learned to be vague about my whereabouts and activity. Not that I'm paranoid or anything! I feel like we are living in ending times and some people panic as the ship begins to sink. One never knows what people's behavior will be in panic survival mode. As they lose jobs and homes, I see some turning to the government for help. Part of that is to be a snitch. Part of panic mode for some is to steal. There is much instability, with life being unpredictable. I do not want my gas stolen by those who know I am loaded and ready to go, with my boat unattended in my usual spot. I keep my boat where people cannot see it unless you know where it is. I smile, "Why? You need anything checked on if I get as far as your place?" Hardly any of the original people who lived subsistence on the river are there any more. Most of us agree, we were run off the river, harassed out of a lifestyle. Nothing I want to talk about. That is not the road to peace and happiness. *Anyhow, what can we do about it? Nothing. We tried and got no place.*

"Miles, I think the roof has been leaking, and I'd like that looked at or a picture taken. A while back, we got broken into and our generator was stolen. Now we think the stove has been taken, leaving a hole in the roof with rain coming in. If we knew what to bring to fix it, that would be a big help," I make no promise, but keep this in mind. Rumor has it my neighbor's things are being pilfered by their own family living nearby. No one else has had this kind of problem. Seymour and I are the ones who surveyed these homesteads years ago.

More gas is added to the load, thinking I might do more boating than expected. Iris cooks up soup for the trip, hands me a bag of clean clothes she just washed, and gives me a big hug and kiss.

"Be careful, Honey!" With a wink I say, "Yes, I'll be careful, you know me, careful is my middle name!"

"I thought you told me 'Legal' is you middle name!"

"Oh yes, I mean safe hyphen legal. Sometimes I leave the hyphen out!" I have the ham radio to call in to home base and let Iris know what is going on. She knows what frequency to monitor. I tell her I'll be gone at least a week, but not to panic if it gets closer to two weeks.

I'm running a new sixty horse four stroke Mercury these days on a new all-weld aluminum hull, 24 feet narrow boat with only a foot of freeboard. This is not a typical-looking boat. Built for economy, it can go 800 miles without re-fueling. I run into my buddy Josh at the boat landing. He has come down to feed the twenty-five sled dogs he keeps at the river. Josh does not own the land, but no one complains. He has a log cabin and dogs here just out of town. There is a city ordinance about how many sled dogs you can keep on your lot in downtown. Josh is Athabascan Indian and was one of the first to run the famous 1,000 mile long Iditarod dog race thorough the wilderness. He has been running it now for twenty years. Josh is small like me, but still has a nice head of hair.

Josh asks, "So how are you today, Mr. Maw-tin, the man with the golden pen? Hey what happened to your Honda engine?" Josh knows I swore by that Honda for years. Very reliable-best engine I ever had, but Josh knows I felt a tad underpowered. To do what I wanted, I had to turn the engine over 5,500 rpm. I felt this was too high and would prematurely wear out the engine. 4,000 rpm would be ¾ throttle. Ideal running rpm. I was waiting for Honda to come out with a seventy horse they advertised. After two years of waiting, it had not come out yet. Honda has a ninety horse I felt was too big, heavy, and expensive.

I tell Josh, "One day I was in at Reeds, the Mercury dealer. He showed me their sixty horse. I had the cash in my pocket to buy it, $8,000."

"Cannot hear the engine idle, Miles, looks like a nice engine." I only nod, preoccupied with getting off on my journey. I do not let Josh know where I am going, or how long I will be gone. He can tell by my load I am going a long way. "Bring back another big tusk, Miles!" Josh thinks I am going on a fossil hunt, and expects me to return with another mammoth tusk. He has watched me come in many times in the past with a whole boatload of 40,000-year-old fossils. Camel bones, bison horns, mammoth leg bones as big as I am, and tusks up to twelve feet long. All from times before the last ice age when Alaska was a tropics. *Yes, there are secrets to finding fossils, not just anyone can go out and come back with them.*

I head the short distance down the Nenana River, then left down the Tanana. The bridge I go under is the last road for 1,000 miles. The last of civilization I will see till I get back. There is a spring chill in the air that will disappear when the sun is higher. For now, I put sunglasses on, staring into a low sun with a glare on the water. Engine rpm is adjusted to 4,500. The GPS is on and acquiring satellites. I will fine-tune my trim, rpm, speed, and fuel consumption to suit what I want to accomplish. Today I can burn a tad more gas since I am not expecting to go 700 miles. When the GPS comes on, I see the river map, with a dotted line showing my previously plotted trip. Sandbars change constantly, so this is not a foolproof route I can absolutely count on, but takes out some of the energy spent figuring where to go. I know the four to five spots where the sandbars tend to shift the most. I'm traveling twenty-five miles an hour downstream. A safe cruising speed as almost six is current, so twenty miles an hour water speed. A sudden stop will not likely send me crashing through the windshield or tear off the engine. The engine's lower unit will probably not be seriously damaged if we hit a log. This is a good speed that gives me time to study the water ahead, see logs, or shallows. If I put in a ten-hour day, that is 250 miles-long way into the wilderness.

Going faster seems to cost much more for each mile an hour gained. It can cost twice as much money going thirty miles an hour compared to twenty. Is it worth it? What's my big hurry? I am not one of the weekend warriors who must get back to work by Monday. Life is good, slow down to enjoy it. Hunting gets easier going this slower speed. My eyes can leave the water to scan the shore for animal sign. This time of the year we are looking for geese. There is a two-week period when they can be expected on sandbars, as the sun tends to shine on straight stretches of the river, melting snow along the sandbars. Birds arrive early to get the best nesting grounds when lakes are still covered in ice and snow. While the geese wait for their nesting areas to open, males group on sandbars. Females arrive later and tend to land directly on the lakes. I can usually tell by the behavior, size of the bird, color, density of the group, if it is mostly males. I prefer to select a male, as the female may have eggs in her already.

I pass Percy's fish camp, one of my checkpoints, just fifteen miles from Nenana. This is where I check fuel to see how much I burned. A metal rod with a loop on the end is hung on the gunnels. There are notches on the rod in five-gallon increments. My day cruise tank is an old 1950s steel tank exactly the width of my boat and stored up front to balance my load. It holds thirty gallons. I'm guessing I am burning three and a half gallons an hour, maybe four. My dipstick should show under a notch, less than five gallons. Since there is nowhere to acquire gas in the wilds, it is important to know how much gas I am consuming. Now and then, the amount is not what I think. Some factors can be running the wrong pitch propeller for the load, a bent propeller, dragging a stick I am unaware of that slows me down a mile or two an hour. I should be getting about five miles to the gallon. This is considered by local boaters to be acceptable. My houseboat used to be gallons to the mile.

I do not pull over to check, but idle the engine and drift as I check. Everything looks fine. Next checkpoint is in Old Minto. By the time I get here, the sun is higher, and the day is warmer, no breeze, clear blue sky, seagulls drifting overhead, light green beginning to show in the birch trees along the river. Birch is the first tree to show color, then the willows, and yes, a few willows are showing color too. I decide I do not need another gas check at Old Minto. Gas consumption is not so critical this trip. Old Minto is in flat country; in another hour I am moving into the hills. In the distance, I recognize Wolverine Mountain. Tolovana River is coming up next; I usually stop, shut the engine off, drink from my thermos, get out onto dry ground, and walk around a few minutes. If I need to adjust my load, I can do that here, since I have burned off some fuel weight. As the Tolovana Roadhouse comes into view, I see friends who live here. Guessing they spent break up on the river and have not yet made the first trip to town. They are glad to see me! The first person they have seen in a couple of months. All their sled dogs are tied out here. There are still fish hanging to feed them.

"Hey how d'you end up with so many fish, wasn't the season closed?"

"Yes, season was closed, but we got the job running the test wheel for Fish and Game. If you cannot beat them, join them!" They get to keep some fish after counting them, apparently. The roadhouse looks nice. I have memories of this place when the roof was on the ground, and there was just a crawl space under it to sleep. A historical grant allowed the roadhouse to be rebuilt to look as it did in the days when mail was carried by dogs and teams stopped here for the night. My friends bring tourist out here on dog trips. Running this as a real business requires permits, insurance, advertising, and a lot of work. This is a good occupation for those willing to be dedicated to it. They are avid gardeners. Their greenhouse has plants a foot tall.

"Miles, check out the green plastic we are trying this year. Especially good for tomatoes, supposedly lets the correct light rays in and blocks the bad stuff." I'd never heard of this cutting edge technology. I will keep an eye on the garden here and see how it works. In the past, they have handed me beets, turnips, carrots, tomatoes, to eat on my trips. They are growing more than they can eat. I get them caught up on the news in Nenana. They ask if I am headed past Manley Hot Springs, and if so, can I drop mail off.

"No, turning off to go up the Kantishna and the homestead, sorry. But on my return trip, if you are still here, I can bring mail to Nenana." They think they will be gone by then. I wave goodbye and am back on the river. Rock Creek is just half an hour away, where I will stop and transfer fuel as I fish. I have a favorite hole I drop a line in, and get fish almost every cast, if the fish are around. Much depends on the level of the river and water temperature.

As I approach Rock Creek, I spot some geese in the sun at the entrance. I have a special long-range goose gun with reloaded shells for just this situation. I shoot two of the twenty geese. My engine is off and I let the river drift me into the mouth of the creek where I arrive nice and quiet so as not to disturb the fish. Several pike are caught as I transfer fuel and make a small fire on the beach to cook lunch. The fish are easier to cook over a campfire than the geese, so make part of one of the pike my lunch. The other pike are alive and I let them go. I am not as desperate for food as I once was in this lifestyle. I seem to have plenty to eat now. While the pike cooks, I clean the geese, put them in plastic bags and stow them under a covered section of the boat, down below the waterline where they will be about thirty-five degrees. No flies are out yet. I see no marsh marigolds to cook with the fish, too early yet, but there are some cattail roots to dig up. I carry garlic and pepper to add.

The entire stop is under an hour. I am refreshed, alert, ready to put in another five to six hours of river running if I choose to. The Kantishna is less than a mile away. Here I turn south and begin going upstream. The color of the river changes. The Kantishna drains the Alaska Range, so is filled with gray glacial silt. The Tanana

River drains the interior flats, so has a lot of darker vegetative soil in the water. The current is a mile an hour slower, but now I am bucking the current. I maintain twenty-five miles an hour, but to do so, increase rpm to 4,900. I try never to cruise over 5,000. Fuel consumption is now over four gallons an hour. I'm careful to remember and keep track. I can expect to burn half my fuel going the next forty miles.

There are more geese and ducks along this river. I decide the two I have are enough, so just enjoy watching. I especially enjoy the swans, since they are so huge, somewhat rare worldwide, white and so majestic looking against the dark wood and sandbars. *Eight-foot wingspreads and thirty pounds!* Chunks of ice, some as large as twenty-five feet in size, remain here and there on the sandbars, left by high water at ice breakup. Sticks and rocks frozen in the ice make some look like aliens, or abstract art. Light shines through one piece like a lens, casting rainbows. Now and then, I spot black ice floating in the river I need to avoid. Some pieces are larger than my boat. I have touched bottom twice, but nothing serious. Luckily, there is just soft silt in this stretch of the river. There are not many bad places with pebbles or rocks.

Hitting submerged logs or underwater sweepers is the biggest collision issue to avoid. A spare propeller is important, but propellers for this engine are $300. Any trip I take can suddenly cost an extra $300. *Boating is not cheap!* "Yeah, b-o-a-t stands for, break-out-another-thousand." Operating costs averaged over twenty years are about $10 an hour, for every hour I run the boat. Because of this, I always like to be doing something when I am on the river, connected with, 'making money.'

This trip is about hauling supplies, but I also get two geese. I hope to find some rocks or wood useful in my craft trade. I may look for fossils in a secret spot. I have not decided yet. Much depends on ice conditions and water depth when I get further upriver. There is no weather report this far out, so I will not know until I see for myself. Rough break ups, where ice jams up to make fast high water, or where ice slams into the shore, followed by a quick water drop, combined with hot weather is what I am looking for. *Also, no other mammoth hunters around.* 'Likewise, no other humans in the area, no hunters, no planes flying around.'

Yes, it is legal. However. (Said with a meaningful pause.) Any time there is big money involved, there is the potential for trouble. If I went to any government agency, BLM, Fish and Game, and announced I found a pair of tusks on legal state land and sold them for twenty grand and I expect to do this on a regular basis? The government will want its finger in that pie, demand a permitting process, a fee, a special tax.

Likewise, there is no such thing as exempt from having any area becoming classified as an archeological site by the university. If the public knew how-where-when, there would be that segment of the population that wants a cut of the action, desperate for that kind of income. Exactly. Those in need of quick cash, in need of adventure, or desiring to rob someone else out in the pucker brush, would zoom in on where I go. Laws would have to be passed to protect the environment from the mass, or get rich quick types. The business is so highly hazardous it is off the charts. Impossible to get insurance, get bonded, The situation could be a nightmare. It's better to say, "Yup, you are right, it's illegal, I wouldn't try it if I were you!"

I smile at these thoughts as I cruise along, passing the hours on the river. There are many checkpoints, and places I have memories of. Here is where I got a huge moose in the rain with a new gun. There is where a cabin used to be before it fell in the river. Somewhere else I found a sunken ancient boat. There are dead spots where my ham radio does not connect to anything, other places I get clear signals and I have this marked in my GPS. The ham radio is on. I scan frequencies automatically. Now and then the scan stops at a conversation I listen in on. Sometimes pilots talking to each other, or homesteaders with ham radios. Now and then I break in to say 'hi' and make sure the radio works. There is a radio dead spot at the homestead. I have with me a Yagi directional ham antenna that can go high up in a tree and be aimed at the repeater on the Nenana hill. One time in winter, I was able to stand on a chair and get a signal. I'm operating on two meter and seventy centimeter.

Bean, my tax accountant and friend who is ham radio operator, helped me get my license. I call him, "KL1VC mobile in a boat looking for Bean in Nenana." I wait to see if he replies. Formally, I am supposed to ask for Beans call sign, but this is not a legal requirement, only that I give my call sign. "WLBDO" I hear Bean answer. I just let him know I am testing the radio on the river. Iris may hear the call on our home base, but she is not licensed to reply. Bean says he will call her on the landline and let her know I am ok.

I recognize a place I need to check for fossils along the riverbank. The area is only thirty feet long. But appears to me to be the correct age. Just a brief ice lens sticking up along the bank. An ancient logjam shows itself, with an accent peat bog as dark as coal. Oil oozes out. Nothing has ever been found here, but I keep looking. Global warming has been having a positive effect on the fossil business. A slow melt of the glaciers is also a slow melt of the permafrost. Erratic weather often means erratic river height and strange break up. The water depth here is not as low as I'd like to see. I tie up the boat and slowly walk around the area.

This river has been my favorite since the day I saw it. Lake Minchumina, at the base of Mt. Denali, is the headwaters of the 300 mile long Kantishna River. Only five people live on the entire river. No roads cross it. At the headwaters is a flats fifty miles across, of nothing but endless nameless lakes. An old timer in the village of Galena told me about this river when I was living in Galena on my houseboat back in the 1970s. No one else had ever heard of it. On his say so, I took off to find it. It took two years. In my prime I cut 200 miles of trapline trail by hand, built a dozen trapline cabins, acquired three homesteads along this river. The entire trapline and all its cabins burned in a forest fire in just a few days. Ashes to ashes, and dust to dust. No one can take the memories away, however.

A smaller cabin, good enough for short visits, was built at the main homestead I call 'the lower river.' Before dark, I am at the river pond by this cabin. There is no practical way to get to the cabin without a canoe., so one is hidden in the woods. A portage has to be made over a hundred foot long beaver dam. The water is seven feet higher on the other side of this dam. A beaver trail through tall grass works its way to the main open creek of black water. I almost always park the boat, tie it up, and make a quick trip to the cabin to ensure everything is all right. A light load is grabbed - a rifle, some fresh food, clothes, and anything easy as a first load. The main weight of the riverboat load is tied down, so it does not shift or blow out of the boat. A tarp is bungeed over this main load so I can choose to stay at the cabin and come back in the morning to unload.

Sometimes I think of keeping a locking shed here at the beaver damn so I can unload and lock up gas and other goods to get up to the cabin at my leisure, even another trip, maybe a trip where my main boat can float over the top of the beaver damn, which happens now and then during high water. Some items do not carry well in a canoe! Like sheets of plywood. In the old days I could leave some items and come back in winter to haul supplies from here to the cabin with the sled dogs or snow machine. I'm guessing I will not make such long trips alone with dogs or snow machine again. Not safe enough. I am not as strong, do not hear as well, and my balance is not good enough to be safe on the trail. If I break down, I can no longer walk home. I can no longer handle the cold. I have high blood pressure and marginal diabetes. I need to eat regularly or I get dizzy, can't think straight. Coming here by boat still works. If anything goes wrong with the engine, I have a spare and I can always float down to the next village, Manley Hot Springs. I think of some of this as I decide what to bring to the cabin on this first trip. *Gun, clothes, and food, that's it.*

From a distance, I see the cabin is still there and looking ok. No person or bear broke in. The paddle is half a mile. I am quiet and slow. If there is a bear around, I prefer to see it, catch it by surprise. More than once, I have startled a sleeping bear. I have the upper hand and can decide if I merely wish to teach the bear a lesson and convince it not to come back, this is my territory, or shoot it for food. My first trip here with the X, Sally, I shot a bear by the pond as the riverboat pulled in. Normal stuff for me was 'freak out' time for her. During the four years, Karen and I lived here with her two children, she shot a bear from twenty feet with my pistol. She was not going to let a bear steal our supplies!

No, I am not afraid of bears, not even a little. Certainly not compared to my fear of people! When people ask, I do not understand the question. Afraid, why? I can kill the bear if I choose. Can I kill a person, even a thief, or a crooked cop robbing me? I think not! That is fear! To be a victim and helpless. Yet, I meet few people who say, "Yes, I understand and agree!" No one understanding adds to fear. Isolated people are not safe and attract the wrath of the society. But no, this is not on my mind. I merely scan the grass and likely places a bear would be sleeping. This time, no sign of a bear until I get to the cabin.

Muddy bear prints mark the spot where one leaned against the door to test it, see if he could push it in or roll the cabin over. The windows have boarded, hinged shutters. A single bolt has a wing nut to set the window cover free to open at its hinge. A bungee hooks the shutter off to the side to let light in. I can now see to turn on the propane and get things in order, ready to stay in. As a second precaution, there is a three foot x four feet piece of plywood filled with nails, point side up, under each of the two windows. A bear cannot stand on these nails to get at the window. Grass and leaves cover the wood so the bears seem not to understand they can flip or toss the board aside. They simply avoid standing on it.

The corners of the cabin have tin sheathing to stop mice and squirrels from being able to climb, or chew their way in through any weak spot or tiny crack. A five-gallon bucket is removed from the chimney pipe. The bucket keeps rain out of the stove and stops birds or squirrels from going down the chimney. The largest window is seven feet long, which lets a lot of light in and gives a nice view of the creek. I smile, and am glad to be here, enjoying the view, the sense of ownership and well-being.

Wild rose vines, not yet in leaf, cover the yard and surround the cabin. Raspberry bushes grow along the shaded backside. Animal sign is all over. Beaver cut nearby trees. An otter has made a slide down the beaver house, mink have left piles of fish scales along the shore. A moose and calf have been through in the past day. The bear left a footprint on the door. A Kingfisher chirps and dips as it flies. A Yellow-Shafted Flicker hammers in the backwoods. I can recognize it by the sound. Roughed grouse strut along the path and run ahead of me. This is all just the first glance.I'm not tired, but hungry, so turn the propane bottle on, bleed air out of the line, turn the stove on, and soon have a pot of creek water boiling. The creek this time of year is clean water from melted ice. Fifty below zero winter temperatures sterilize the environment. There are little bacteria or germs until warmer weather. I do not need the bug and weed strainer hanging on the wall for the water later in the summer.

The squirrels managed to get in again! Dang! How did they find their way in? Squirrels and mice do more damage than bears over a long period. Squirrels have been between the wall and made paths through the fiberglass insulation. Nests are made of balls of this insulation, while some gets remove from the cabin and distributed through the spruce trees in the yard. My bookshelf is covered in husked spruce cone hulls. The wool bed blanket has holes chewed in it, along with spruce hulls and squirrel poop. I take it outdoors and shake it, but it stinks of squirrel, which makes it hard to sleep with . A squirrel outside chatters at me as if I am the invader in his world. Which I am, I guess! He's hollering for the whole world to hear, "Help! Help! Danger! Run, hide!" All true enough. I keep a single shot target 22 rifle by the door just for such situations. My squirrel gun. I kill the squirrel in one easy shot, then another chatters. Within seconds it, too, is dead.

A close inspection is made outside of the cabin to figure out how the squirrels are getting in. It looks like they leap five feet, grab the edge of the window shutter, and climb the edge to get under the eaves. Looking along under the eaves reveals a weak spot where squirrels pulled the vent screening out to gain access under the roof. The staple gun secures this section of screen in place. Tin is put on the edge of the door shutter. This is the 5th time I have felt sure the cabin is squirrel proofed and believe no more will get in. These little monsters have chain saws for heads.

A lone male Pintail duck lands in front of the cabin to check it out. He's not from around here and does not plan to stay. He's a little late. Pintails are the first ducks to arrive, and the majority have already paired up and found a nesting spot. The twenty-two makes him my dinner-*the slow, weak, and stupid get culled*. The two geese I got earlier are still packed in ice along the creek shore. I may save them to take home to Nenana.

New tree growth after the forest fire has grown seven feet tall along the creek and in the yard. There is a lifetime supply of standing dead burned spruce along the creek bank. A single, high water spring break up takes out more trees than I burn in a lifetime. Even the beaver drop more trees than I burn. The forest fire that took my cabins and trapline burned more trees than the entire population of Alaska burns for heat, and put out more smoke pollution than all of Fairbanks produced in its history.

From this perspective, it is hard to feel guilt and shame, listening to society's words on how heating with wood is evil, destructive, selfish. *Should I as well hate the actions of beaver, and God?* The forest fire took everything for 200 miles and was not even a record big fire. Just an ordinary fire few remember today, a one-day blip in the news. I still sigh; have tears in my eyes at the loss. Still in shock. However, no, not angry. No, there is no blame. The wind is out of my sails, though. A pin has been stuck in my balloon. I cannot pretend it is not so, make it go away with pleasant thoughts. One big thrill in life is gone. A lifetime of hard work, dreams, goals-gone. Doubt tossed upon the strength of my faith. I was so sure when young; civilization is the root of all evil, while nature is pure and innocent.

I had been smug. Believing I had an ace in the hole. I have it made. I felt sorry for the rest of the world stuck in civilization. I had a getaway place to fall back on when the lemming go off the cliff. I didn't have to go off that cliff! Ha Ha! So the safe wilderness life that was going to save me when civilization went tits up, failed me. Civilization saved my bacon. Go figure.

45

The irony of it all. Now what? However, this land is nice, and this shack is nice. It is nothing compared to what it was. I had a huge two-story home filled to the brim with all I needed to live a wilderness life. A beautiful treadle sewing machine, wringer washer, canning supplies with 300 jars, tools to fix everything. Everything needed to build cabins - saws, augers, levels, spikes, windows. There were spare wood stoves, with pipe to last a lifetime. Hundreds of pounds of rice and beans, traps, guns, reloading equipment, along with a lifetime of spare warm clothes, sleeping bags. I cannot bear to think of it all. I can never in a lifetime replace it all. The *'Rah, rah, lets just start over! We can do this, get up, come on, I love it!'* is gone. I gave this lifestyle my youth, the best years of my life. I cannot get that back again. I try to tell myself as I sit here in the quiet of the wilds, *Yes, but remember what life in some other countries is like. We are spoiled! There are countries where the average person lives in a cardboard box, and if you have a pot to pee in, you are the village chief. There are places in the world where genocide is practiced, and you and all your people are hunted down as we hunt squirrels.*

The truth of this is not setting me free. I am looking at the burned dog houses, and remembering all the sled dogs that lived in them. I was standing in this very spot long ago, watching four-year-old Joy collect the dog food cans. As if it were today. The clink of the cans. Joy, smaller than some of the dogs. One dog, Map, jumped on her and she almost fell over. My breath stopped, worried if she would get hurt by the dogs, or forever be afraid! She has scar marks on her face from when she was a baby, and a sled dog grabbed her and shook her like a rag doll. She was almost killed before I met her. Little Joy turns around and smacks Map on the nose with the food serving ladle, saying, "Stop that!" I can still see Map's expression! In shock, stopped in his tracks. She showed him who is in charge here! The rough sled dogs actually listened to her at four years old. Amazing. The happy laughter of Karen and May in the cabin working on home schooling. The moose hanging by the cache that used to be over there. Now all burned trees. It is hard to see where the cabin was. Seven-foot tall birch trees hide the pile of melted roof tin.

As I eat the duck and look at the view out the seven-foot picture window, I feel ok, happy enough. But this does not describe how I felt being here for twenty-five years. A new mitten in life is being knitted. A new woof to the weave. The fabric of my life has a similar appearance, but is made differently. This homestead is now more of a resting place, drop off spot, for activities up and down the river. I can store supplies here as a base camp. While getting out on day trips or overnight trips. There are plenty of nice spots along the river system that hold no memories to miss. The new light dome tents that have been on the market a few years are getting cheaper and showing up at garage sales for a few bucks. New technology makes travel and overnight camping a pleasant experience with gear getting cheaper, lighter, easier to set up and more comfortable. Now, an entire camp fits in an army duffle bag that used to hold only my sleeping bag! I keep the duffel bag on the boat. Sleeping bag, tent, stove, folding chair, a few smaller basics, all in one bag.

There is not a lot here at the homestead for me anymore. *Maybe after twenty-five years I need a new game? This is all too familiar. The sense of adventure is gone? Is this more than just the loss by fire?* My unconscious might be right. It seems to help if I can grasp what is going on, why I feel as I do. In understanding, I can gain control easier, have a plan of action. I am no longer a victim of a fire, helpless.

CHAPTER TWO

MUSHROOM PICKERS, SURREY JOB, SUBSISTENCE ARTICLE

I nformation is saved and organized that I hope will be useful for my books. Diaries, letters, and pieces of information that are not my own words and opinion, but related—identified and saved. Changes in hunting, fishing, trapping laws are followed. Fishing was once very important to me. My only winter transportation for many years was sled dogs, and fishing for them was a priority. Subsistence means your life depends on it. I come across an old article I saved, and read again now, before filing. I am reminded of the beginning of changes I am effected by.

Article in the Northland News Fairbanks, Alaska by Dan Jolins of the News Miner

April 5th **1985** Juneau-Gov. Bill Sheffield unveiled his proposed subsistence bill in early March, an attempt to match state law with regulations that have guided state fish and game management for the past three years.

The Alaska Supreme Court ruled in February that those regulations violated the state's 1978 subsistence law. Sheffield's proposal would do two things:

*Specify that subsistence users are customary and traditional users of fish and game by *rural* Alaskan residents. The Supreme Court in the Madison decision ruled that the state Board of Fisheries could not distinguish between rural and urban users until all other users commercial and sport fishing had been eliminated first.

* Establish in law "personal use net fishing" for Alaskans throughout the state. The Madison decision declared that Alaskans who used a net to catch fish and ate them themselves were subsistence users and had a higher interest than sport fishermen and commercial fishermen.

Blah, blah, blah—then Sheffield is quoted as saying the court decisions "Holds the potential to raise havoc" and goes on to say he hopes for a quick decision.

But the article says:

> But at administration briefings for the Senate Resources Committee this morning, legislators indicated that may not happen. Senator Majority Leader Rick Halford questioned why Alaskan hunters should give up a newly acquired right for priority in shooting game they consume in favor of trophy hunters and out-of-state hunters.

Later in the article, Fischer questioned whether the Madison decision would place the state in conflict with the Alaska National Interest Lands Conservation Act that defines subsistence users as 'use by rural people'. Senate President Don Bennett said he does not think the Legislature will act on the matter this year.

So I'm not understanding all the language, who all these people are, what their jobs are, what priority any of these people have, etc. But I have been listening to talk of this off and on for years. Talked to hunters, natives, lawyers, educated people, on the subject, as it affects me, and my lifestyle. This article in one of many indicating conflict of different sorts. I do not have to understand much to realize there is a problem. Like the state and the Feds can't agree. Many want the subsistence definition to include some low income, economic definition, because some rich folks live in rural villages who should not be included in having a need, like school teachers arriving from outside the state with regular salaries. Many people do not want a solution and prefer things remain in limbo. Decisions might be delayed on purpose.

I believe as well, that if this situation remains in limbo, undefined and vague, eventually the problem can be made to go away and become obsolete. I note in the article something about 'Fish nets' as a subsistence tool. Not fish wheels. I am ordered not to fish with a net, I must use a fish wheel. The fish wheel looks like a Ferris wheel. It is a big mechanical contraption the river current turns to scoop up fish in baskets. Much of this wheel is made of wood. But parts are made of materials purchased in civilization. They are costly to make, time-consuming, require skills, and tools to build that I do not have. If everyone is required to use a wheel, maybe there is no need to address subsistence net users anymore. One issue, I suspect, is that it is easy to see fish wheels turning from an airplane, thus easy to regulate and control. Nets are harder to observe and control.

One huge issue is the commercial fishing interest. It's big, big money. One of the biggest moneymakers in the state. Many politicians in the state made their fortune in the commercial fishing business. It's a business they understand, and still have friends, allies, financial partners in the business. They have a stake in protecting commercial fishing rights. Politicians may owe favors to financial contributors and friends. Subsistence priority over the fish is bad news to them, and not going to happen if they have a say so, even though ordered by the Feds to do so. People like myself are the ones paying. A small group with no clout that few care about politically.

It is not these facts that concern me most. Big government not looking out for the little guy is common, will never change, and must be lived with. What bothers me is the 'man on the street.' 'The common citizen.' 'Us.' 'We the people' buy into what suits the political view as portrayed in the news media. My group of people becomes the scapegoat, the bad guy. If Joe Citizen 'got it' and understood what was going on, 'we the people' could smile, nod, go along with the program. Likened to a phrase a Russian friend tells me. "God bless the Czar! And keep him far away!" A situation could exist where 'we the people' look out for each other, watch each other's back, understanding the government is not our friend. We do what we must, but in general, run our own lives.

When I lived in the village of Galena on the Yukon River, there was a solution I thought workable. We realized city rules did not work in our remote area. The game warden agreed. Word went ahead of the game warden coming our way. We have everything in order when he arrives. He sees nothing, knows nothing. He gets paid, stays out of trouble, and we live our lives as we know how, without being wasteful. We monitored ourselves. Those types who were wasteful, lost status and respect. No one got arrested, or went to jail. We cared about each other, the village as a unit. Our social standing mattered a lot. We depend on each other. No one was the enemy. Few were angry. We were tolerant of each other and our unique personality, understanding it takes all of our diverseness to survive. I assume this followed an old Native tradition that worked for thousands of years.

The enemy is not necessarily our government! I still have hope all we have to do is get back to what our government is! Get a grip on what its purpose is, follow our own laws! It is difficult to give up long-held beliefs. Among those beliefs is the citizen and the state taking care of itself with minimal higher up government getting involved. Without trust in the government and its laws, where are we, and what we have! I struggle with this trust. *If there is temporary trouble with a present administration, try to stay out of the way, let far away people rant and rave. Far away Federal government has too much else to deal with than some podunk wilderness place of 300 people. Heck, they do not have the resources to come clean the clock of every small community that gets uppity. I can get understanding and working with local government, as high as the state level. Made up of people one might define as 'my peers.'* Thus, if worse comes to worse, and I end up in court, it will be my peers I face, as stated by law, that I have the right to be judged by. *Yes! If I am in touch with these peers, if we are all in agreement, how bad can a situation get?* This is my logic. I explain in a conversation with my buddy Josh. My Native dog-mushing friend.

"When I was in the wilds, my life depended on understanding my environment.

You spent time in the wilds, Josh. Even during the Iditarod race, ten days alone on the trail. What runs our life? Is it rules and regulations? We listen to nature, pay attention to the weather. We understand snow and ice. We understand our transportation—the dogs."

Josh is not as interested in these kinds of issues, or pretends he is not. He is Athabascan Indian, and his culture is different from mine. "If you say so, Dr. Martin" Referring me to 'Dr.' is done when Josh is telling me I am being overly intellectual, an educated idiot. I explain anyway, even if it is only to help me figure my own thoughts out.

"If we need to understand our environment to survive, and our environment changes, we need to change as well. Though the same rules apply, 'understand your surroundings.' In civilization, what is my environment? What is it that controls our lives? It is not the weather, but the government, contracts, mechanical devices."

Josh sort of agrees, but not the same as I do. One reason is, he is of the chosen race. When it comes to use of wildlife, as an Indian, he is among the untouchable. Only up to a point. His son is in prison for life for murder. Obviously, he can't do whatever he wants. In terms of hunting and fishing he can, though. For sure, Josh does not follow my line of thinking, because he makes no effort whatever to understand the government, or try to get along. His method of survival is to avoid the government. However, as a winner of the Iditarod in the limelight, he is not keeping a low profile. His ways have in fact cost him very dearly. *Banned from the race for several years.* It is easy for me to see what went wrong with him. He was born and raised in the wilds, with that mindset and the rules that apply there. He moved to the white man's civilized world. Has a home, hot water, electric, a truck, a bank account, so is well plugged into the grid. Yet he did not change the rules he lives by.

"I am not going to compromise what I believe, Miles!"

Yes, that is his choice. Josh will pay a price that I'd prefer not to pay. My choice is, *If you can't beat them, join them. Or maybe keep your friends close, but your enemies closer.* Is that how it is? No. I try to be part of the community, be involved, do something to change things, instead of just complaining. I truly care. I have been on the library board for many years now. I have been on the board of the Chamber of Commerce for the past three years, the person in charge. I attend most city meetings. I have joined several committees of different kinds. I brought Art Train to Nenana. I help plan events. The mayor and I are friends. I know all the city council members and the tribal chief. I know all the business owners. I work with many of them. In this way, I keep a handle on what is acceptable behavior, and how various issues get solved in a way the community can agree to.

The situation is not perfect. I am still 'strange.' There are always whispers about what Miles has done with a latest story. As Iris says, "Everyone who does anything gets talked about. Today's gossip is tomorrow's outdated news, and it is someone else's turn to be the focus."

There are people in the community with better social skills than I have, who do a lot of good things, who tend to keep out of the gossip mill. If I knew what I know now and could rewind my life, I could be more like these people, perhaps. Yet I should not be sorry I am who I am. I'm friendly with a judge, know some lawyers. Ted Stevens and Don Young are senators who represent Alaska in Washington, know me by name when they see me. Both come right out and tell me the Federal government is crooked, and they will not support the Federal takeover of our state rights. I understand politicians say all kinds of things to the people, but I believe them. Their behavior, how they have voted, bills they propose and support, proves it. At least with what is called the old guard, the good old boys' group. The newer politicians seem to be more in bed with the Feds.

I agree with many—the good old boys have had their finger in the Alaska pipeline pie, and grabbed a few personal perks considered outside the law. I feel they care enough about Alaska not to take the whole pie and run. I'm not entirely pleased with lining their own pockets, but it is, in general, a thankless job, serving the public. I know a little of that. Even as head of the Chamber of Commerce, I am contacted because there is a problem; someone wants me to do something. People do not contact me to shake my hand and say thanks. People do not contact me to tell me they have an idea and lay out a plan by which they are going to do some work to help someone else. They do so when told to, when it looks good. No one has ever stepped forward with a donation voluntarily.

Half the business people asking for help tell me they can't afford $50 to join the Chamber, but want action. The temptation to grab a little extra is there, is almost part of the job. Oh well. So long as the state is doing well, and we get what we want, I am not overly upset if these guys grab some of the icing off the cake. What bothers me is the Federal icing on the cake, when the cost of that icing is, 'now you owe me, you're mine.'

I wish to be close to all these politically powerful groups. Not because I am a social person and love all these great people. I do so as part of survival. There are varieties of motivations that keep people in the loop. Partly a sense of duty, wanting to help, but yes, scratching each other's back and looking out for each other is part of the game. Same as in a wolf pack, or running sled dogs. I came across an old news clipping I saved and show Josh.

Fairbanks News Miner September 17th 2005. Small Alaska cities struggle without state Aid

One paragraph sums it up, that times are getting hard all over.

"According to the Alaska Municipal League, nine villages (that are named) have ceased day-to-day operations. Eighteen communities have serious management or financial problems. They do not hold elections, or adopt budgets, they owe money to fuel companies, the IRS, or insurance companies. Another thirty-nine communities have financial problems so severe they could be insolvent in two years."

Based on this, it is at least possible that small villages like Nenana could become nonexistent in the future. There is evidence the government is pleased and encourages small communities to move to bigger ones. It is easier to manage and control us. It costs less. Leave the outlying areas for the resources to be tapped, or as parks, controlled by the government. If no one lives there, few know the truth of how resources are used, there is little proof, no one to buy off.

The law reads right now, if a road goes in, or a company has any interest in the land, subsistence rights have priority. Meaning if I am out in the wilds and you disturb my blueberry patch, your company gets shut down Mr. Oil man. It's easy to understand Mr. Oil's view! Frown, pause. His multi-billion dollar operation is held up over some low life hippy freaks rights to blueberries?

"You, go buy this boy a case of blueberry jam, and tell him to get lost!" He is under contract with a deadline. Delays can cost millions! Not on his watch! Next plan of action, move all these clowns out of the wilds, they are a nuisance! "Good grief!" I'd feel that way myself. I sympathize. I tell Josh, "I do not like that, but this is how it is. We are not going to change that. If I want to survive, I am going to be in the game." Josh feels that is selling out. I can understand that view.

Josh adds, "Didn't you tell me you thought you could work with these companies, by being a watchman or something?"

He forgot what I told him, but yes, a way to work together. When I take off in the wilds on a trip, all these issues appear to go away. The ancient rules apply. I am true to the laws of the wild. That is an illusion. In civilization, I try to learn what story to tell. *The truth has many faces.* That is why Josh calls me 'the man with the golden pen.' I could convince people red is blue. I can sell snow to Eskimos.' Josh is not interested in the details. I'm not sure who is, Iris is not either. Me, myself, and I is about it. Me, myself and I wondered how many ways we could tell the same story, have it come out with entirely different outcomes, without lying. I often play with a simple story that is a couple of lines. The story of Jack and Jill, for example.

There is an obvious issue, and a series of questions coming from the fact of going uphill to fetch water. Does that make sense? Who goes uphill for water? Why does it take two people to get one bucket of water? Obviously, there is more to this story than meets the eye that most of us would not care to inquire and learn about! *Beginning with the fact Jack was a drug dealer!* "The tellers of this tale left that part out." Yea, and he's trying to sell to under-aged Jill. Her father finds out and follows them up the hill. He tosses them both down the hill. There is the official version, as told to the police, if you care to call that truth and facts.

I argue there is no such thing as an unbiased story. No such thing as the news, without a slant put on it. No such thing as the truth, the whole truth, and nothing but the truth. The order we tell the facts has meaning. Always, something is chosen as worth repeating, and something is left out. It is impossible to tell all the facts.

My point would be? I may not tell the same bear story the same way to Iris as to Josh, or to Fish and Game, a PETA group, my parents, or my child. Many people snort, "Miles, there is only one truth, and you cannot bend it. There is right, there is wrong, and we know the difference."

"Oh? Is that so, is it? Pray tell, just what is this truth we all know about?" Let me give an example, "This wolf claw was acquired from a local subsistence Athabascan Indian to support his simple lifestyle, and was humanely harvested." This is said to the woman with the flowers and peace symbol on her blouse, and 'recycle' printed on her handbag.

I hold up the same claw. "This wolf claw was acquired from a not so bright drunk Indian, who hates wolves, and wants to see these dangerous predatory animals exterminated, and beat the wolf with a club." This is said to the white biker wearing the razor blade earrings, sporting the white supremacy sticker on his leather jacket.

"Miles, you said the first time, killed humanely!"

"Correct. Humane is not the same word as respectfully. Look it up in the dictionary. Killed quickly with a club and it did not suffer, is humane." I can hold up the same claw and talk about the magic of a rare item handed to me by a shaman in a sacred manner. I could hold up the same claw and discuss a battle to the death between two savages, primitive man and wolf, in the same manner as has been going on for 50,000 years. I hold up the same claw, "Acquired during legal wolf trapping season in management 20C by a qualified trapper, with all permits and fees paid and filed." I may take the same set of facts and come up with a dozen true versions, to suit the customer, or a jury in court, or the IRS or my wife. None would be a lie.

"They all have a different meaning, Miles!'

"Of coarse! Absolutely! As it should be! I'm a writer, storyteller, reporter of the news covering the facts! Who is paying me to write the story? What will sell? What outcome is expected and desired?"

Like my accountant friend, Bean, who said, "What would you like the numbers to say?"

I replied, You're my man!" Lying? Oh, my goodness, what a nasty word! Oz is a humbug, a gifted storyteller, a man of magic, an optimist, inventor, psychologist, guru. All true, depending how you want to present it. It's all about the storyteller.

The truth told about acquiring the same claw. What is it you want this wolf claw to represent? Like any symbol, it can stand for many things. All this is on my mind and of great interest to me, since I have moved from one world into another. As a shaman, shape changer, traveler between worlds. I wear many hats. I cross borders few care to acknowledge exist.

Well-meaning people have an arm around me, like we are comrades who share a secret. The biker says, "Yea, I know what you mean, those Half Gas Can (Athabascan) savages give me a hard time. They need to be culled from the human race. The wolf claw symbolizes that perfect, don't you think?" Big smile, buddy arm around me. *Well, actually no, and what an odd notion.* Yet he and his kind look at me and say 'one of us.' Wow! A wolf, the predator in a pack, preying upon the helpless sheep.

Likewise, the flowered recycle lady smiles and says, "One of us!" Giving me a kiss. You know: "We who understand the earth and it's peaceful beauty, symbolized by this wolf claw." She'd like to French kiss the wolf. I smile and nod to them all, and am friends with no one. I avoid out rightly saying I agree with anyone. Or more, I appear to agree with everyone. While many, in all walks of life, feel I am 'someone who understands and agrees.'

The man with the golden tongue smiles and replies, "Interesting view." Maybe. "I see where you are coming from, yes indeed." Josh tells me that is bullshit, and what he means about not being able to behave as I describe, not wanting to be like me. "So Josh, what is *not* bullshit." He cannot tell me. I lighten up the conversation. He knows he can not tell me an Iditarod dog race story without it being bullshit, because I know too much.

"Bullshit = that which enters a bull's mouth as one thing and comes out the other end drastically altered." Adding, "I'm a Taurus, you know, did you know that? Hey aren't you a Taurus, a bunch of bull, too?"

I hear a Beatles song in my head. *"I am you, and you are me, and we are all together. I am the egg man! I am the walrus!"* I pause. I probably have the words off. *Because, "You are what you eat," belongs in another song, doesn't it?* "But could fit here." I answer myself. Because if we are what we eat, we are also that which comes out the other end, or at least responsible for it. I have Josh smiling and in a good mood. Especially when I point out that without bull manure, there would be no gardens, and nothing would grow. I do not remind him that some people think their manure doesn't stink. We all just do our best not to pass gas in public, and if we do, blame it on the person next to you.

Both of us have been told by the news media and fans we are among the best there is in the world at what we do. *So just what is that?* I'm not quite sure. However, I have a secret smile. For, in truth, we are all the best in the world at what we do! *Being ourselves!* Yes, anyone who tries to be us, is just acting, still only a copy, an imitation of us.

Josh had an interesting childhood. He tells me how his parents rejected him, and the village did not care. He lived with the dogs in the street. He has memories of fighting for raw fish eggs on the beach on his hands and knees with the village dogs, and climbing in doghouses to keep warm in the winter with the dogs. I try to imagine that. It is amazing he is alive. That experience would kill most people, mentally, spiritually. So what if he is a little tweaked. Josh is a difficult friend to have. He is on the small side; maybe bad nutrition when young? There is a cruel angry damaged side to him, but also a kind, wanting to help others, side to him. Much of this has been said about me.

I had once told Josh when he asked, "No, I do not recall a lot of my childhood, it's a blank."

Josh replied sadly. "Wow, that's horrible, at least I remember, and know."

Well! Just because I can't recall does not mean it was awful. Still, logic tells me, there is not much reason to block out good stuff. Now and then I get one second, two second, vivid bright flashes of the past I never tell anyone about. To remind me why we are forgetting. The truth will not set us free. Survival is having the truth be very vague and elusive. Often no deliberate attempt at hiding anything, I simply do not know, do not recall. Or it's not safe to.

When young (I'm told), my father had his blood linage altered so he could go to college. At that time, in Brooklyn, New York, you could not get to college unless you were Irish. "Poof! He's Irish!" It's just a piece of paper with words on it. His father had connections. I'm not sure what my father's bloodline really is, but evidence of part black, part native American. If there were passable *fake* proof at the time, then surely there would be contradictory proof now. So who knows? What is the truth? The rumors? The officially stamped piece of paper? It depends who is asking? My father was a pillar of the community, with three doctorate degrees, Dean of a college. Among the protected. Someone whose word is not questioned. Who am I to question it? History records us as Irish, and that's the one truth.

Josh introduces me to his friends. I wondered who was at the door. Tourists he has met before, who stop by and wish to get his autograph. "And this is Mr. Maw-Tin, whose father is Dean of a college!"

Followed inevitable by, "So what went wrong Miles?"

Meaning, why am I the black sheep of the family. How come I am a social outcast, at the other end of the spectrum from my father. As well, I might ask Josh! Word is, Josh's mother was a fairly famous, accomplished white pianist. His half-Athabascan, half-Russian father did a lot of sleeping around. I'm not offended by comments Josh makes to the tourists about me. I do not wish to be like my father, though I respect him. *He's passed away now.* I have an aversion to paperwork and proof. Much of it is an illusion and can be faked. People dress in certain ways, say things to impress others. It might be correct, the truth, or a view through rose-colored glasses.

I have the feeling Josh wishes he could be more like his mother, have that kind of respect. The respect of a privileged class among the white people. Josh would never admit that. I see he buys the nicest truck available, not what will serve the purpose. He likes his hot shower, fine manners, and foods when he goes out. Respect from the natives is all right, along with the privilege to hunt game whenever he wants. However, he does not value that a lot.

"My wife does not like to cook wild game, Miles!"

I smile and nod I understand. But understand what, Josh? Josh does not pick wild game at outdoor gatherings where it is offered. There are some among mixed races who value the ability to win dog sled races. Yet Josh comments on how he is treated at airports, in nice restaurants, fine hotels outside. In such places he is still 'just an Indian.' He is not so much angry, as sad and puzzled. Therefore, he wants to understand how I could turn that down, a place in a privileged class, that I do not even have to do anything to have a privilege handed to me, as is the right of the WASP son of the Dean of a college. I could in fact have gone to college free.

It is a fact that most kids I graduated from high school with are now teachers, doctors, lawyers, heads of corporations, and banks. I had better grades than most of them in school. All true. Indeed! Josh wants to know what went wrong? I smile. How could I tell Josh that if I had accomplished these goals, I would not likely, or could not likely, be his friend? My father, or his class, would not come to a gathering the likes of what Josh is putting on. My father would shake Josh's hand, say he is pleased to meet a famous dog race winner. Even invite Josh to one of his parties. But no, not attend an event Josh puts on.

After the guests leave, I ask Josh what is going on with the dog race ruling on his behavior during the last race he got in trouble over. "What matters, Miles, is that I told the truth!"

I pause. "Josh what is this truth you told?" I can guess, but want to hear it. Josh reviews with me what happened in the last race. From what I gather, Josh was struggling in deep snow during the race; being tired and driven, the sled dogs got in a fight. Josh rushed up with the only thing he could grab—the forked metal snow hook on its long rope. He broke up the dogfight and got back to trail breaking. Josh pulls into the next remote checkpoint with the team. There is a kennel for keeping dogs at this checkpoint. Josh puts his dogs up, feeds them, and takes off to eat and sleep. There are thirty people living in this village. The dog kennels are temporary outdoor cages. Bored reporters hang around, looking for snippets of news in the middle of a ten-day race. One of the reporters notices a dog with blood on its mouth. The concerned reporter calls a race official over. Now a vet comes over. Upon inspection, the sled dog has a broken tooth.

"Well, whose dog is this? Who is responsible?" Reporters see a possible story here.

"It's Josh's dog!"

Josh comes over. The news guy wants a story. Josh says into the camera, "Yes, the dogs got in a fight! I was mad, so I broke it up with a sled hook, wailed on the dogs good, and broke the dog's tooth!"

Being a white man from the city, I know exactly what happened next, and why.- Headlines in the news read, "Musher in the Iditarod beats and abuses dog!" The race officials are in panic, how can they save this situation? They have to hold a big pow-wow. The result is an official ban for two years from racing, since this behavior, 'Is not condoned or tolerated in a respectable race.' I could write the script word for word before it even happened. What did Josh expect?

"Josh, why didn't you say anything when you brought the dogs into the checkpoint?"

"Well, I did not want problems, figured no one would notice. No big deal. The dog was fine, just a chipped tooth, happens all the time." That, in fact, is true. Having run sled dogs for twenty-five years as my only transportation, I know, as well as the other racers, even the race officials. But not the news media or the public. Dogs fight, beat each other up, chew on each other. Much like bar brawls among working class humans. Often as not, fighting dogs have happy grins and great stories to tell each other after the fight. Like, I assume, football players celebrating after a game.

"Josh, this is how it could have been handled. You come into the checkpoint in distress, saying you are concerned about one of your dogs. Could a vet come look at the injury to make sure the dog is ok? You do not want to rest until you know this valued dog you love is ok and taken care of. If asked what happened, say the dogs got in a fight, when the fight was over one of the dogs had a broken tooth."

"But that's a lie, Miles!"

"What part of that is a lie, Josh? Do you know for a fact you broke the dog's tooth?" Josh looks at me, puzzled. It never occurred to him he might not have broken the tooth. Another dog might have.

"Miles, I did not even know the dog had a broken tooth till I was told by the reporter. I saw some blood on his mouth, but he was in good spirits! I kept an eye on him, he seemed ok to me."

"Josh, isn't it true you love your dogs?"

"Of course! How could I not? How could I run sled dogs all my life and not?"

"So why not say that? It's the truth."

Josh does not understand what the white man wants and expects. Life in the village is very different. Josh himself got treated worse than this dog. Did anyone care, say anything? He does not understand how a dog is worth more than a person.

In the old ways, there is not much time to discuss loving a dog. Dogs are work animals, they run loose; you catch them and make them work in winter. Stories might have more to do with how tough you are, not how kind. The Iditarod itself used to be billed as the toughest race on earth. Not the kindest. You run a tough race as a tough guy with tough dogs, you might get hurt, dah! Race car divers crash into a ball of fire, into the wall, into each other. Hockey payers slap each other around, it's part of the game. A dog fight breaks out, you break it up, and a dog has a chipped tooth. In the real world, dogs even get killed. Been there, done that.

The dog Josh got in trouble and banned from the race over, gets sold to another racer at the end of this race. It is in another winning team the same year. Meanwhile, Josh is banned from racing. This is not the first time. I tell Josh what I saw in Manley Hot Springs one time. A sled load of dead puppies. All shot. Maybe twenty of them.

"It's called 'spring culling time' Miles!"

"Yes Josh, Ok. But the dead puppies stayed in the sled for two weeks." The guy who culled them said to me, "I have not had time to go to the dump." The guy worked at the school, I think a janitor. The sled is in front of the school every day for the kids to walk by and see. I was laughed at for mentioning it, and called a pussy. Ended up being none of my business. This is normal. *Or was twenty years ago.*

"Josh, you and I went to visit Norman Vaughn one time. Remember?" Norman, the famous arctic explorer, our buddy. Norman had over 200 sled dogs and could not remember their names. Josh and I went out back to help him feed. We saw several frozen, starved to death dogs on chains. He had forgotten they were there. I was looking at this, thinking it takes two weeks or more for a dog to die of starvation. I'm trying to be in the dog's paws. Every day, barking to get fed, every day getting passed by, till too weak to bark for food anymore. Listening to all the other dogs eating. Dogs that help Norman finish a 1,000 mile race. Did nothing more wrong than get tied up where they'd get overlooked. Is Norman a bad guy? Did he, will he, ever get reprimanded? Did he call reporters over and say?, "Check this out guys!"

"I do not think so, Josh!"

Josh remembers. He thinks the white man is just picking on him, and there is nothing he can do about it. Josh knows what goes on. Most racers have incidents equal to what Josh was involved in. Who is in trouble? The rest know better than to tell a Josh version of the truth. I think they avoid Josh because no one wants a big investigation. That investigation would begin with Josh and those who hang with him. Josh knows the two top racers; he mentions them all the time. We both know them.

I remind Josh how the guy treats his dogs and picks the good ones out. "He takes off with a dog team to go fifty miles. Thirty or so young pups are expected to follow behind. Maybe four months to six months old." Josh knows how it is done.

This is life in the village, in the wilderness. The musher runs fifty miles and waits. Five hours of running time. Maybe ten puppies are capable and have the heart to run the fifty miles. He keeps them. The rest he forgets. He never sees them again. I know. I came across several starving, freezing puppies on a trail one time, and thought someone lost them. I put them in my dog sled basket and brought them into the village. The owner of the dogs was mad. He took them out of my sled and shot them right there in front of me.

"I do not want them, not good enough to make the team. Let them freeze!" This story is about one of the biggest top names in dog mushing. There are so many stories it is not worth reviewing. These stories do not reach the public.

Truth? Yes, tell me about truth. I love to hear other people's version of the truth of their world. Make my day. It's not just Josh dog racing. Name any activity that has not got a yucky truth we'd rather not see. Horse racing, boxing, car racing, hockey, baseball, football. Probably every occupation!

Look in the news at what even priests have been up to over the years! I overheard conversations my father had as Dean of a college and his wife, head of the history department. Things they had to overlook, or be part of. So, I sigh, that life is as it is for Josh, and it need not be. I as well am a little like Josh, but tend to forget that. What we have in common is, and I keep repeating, "Among the best there is at what we do, at the price of being tweaked."

I do not know what to say, or to whom, or when, and I'm often getting in trouble when those around me do not get in trouble for doing worse. Trying to stand up for some sort of ethics, reality, or honesty that is only in my head. My own sense of honor that a majority do not share.

"Miles, didn't you kill that one dog with a hunk of firewood?" Josh wants to hear that again. Something I want to forget.

"Yes, it was at the end of a normal day of mushing, an easy day." I tell the short version. All the dogs were happy. So was I. I was unhooking the sled dogs one at a time. This one dog lunged at me and grabbed my wrist! He would not let go and went nuts. I hollered, I hit him, he still would not let go. I was concerned he'd cut a vein in my wrist. Like he wanted to kill me. I was able to reach a stick of firewood nearby and killed him. He still did not let go, even in death. What an odd experience.

"Miles, I told you I know what happened! This was one of Cottons dogs, right? He had offered to sell it to me, but I did not want it. I could tell."

"Tell what Josh?"

"The dog is nuts. I think Cotton drugs his dogs, and this one flipped out. Anyhow, if you were not giving the drugs he was addicted to the dog freaked out!"

"Maybe." Josh has a common line, how everyone is using drugs to win the races. How Josh is the only one not using drugs and trying to win straight. This gets hard to believe, so I take all dog drug stories with a grain of salt. But yes, this might explain this dog's odd behavior. The relationship is not always cuddly and cute. Race and sled dogs are not bred for being the best pet. Josh thinks the very best racing dogs are slightly insane.

Others say, "To match Josh! Not every racer agrees, Miles!" I talk to and know other racers but am closest to Josh.

"Josh, I started out writing long ago with one main purpose, to tell the truth about a lifestyle few know the truth about." I explain how one reason is, I was raised on 'the dream' represented by Walt Disney, Old yeller, and mountain man books. TV shows about the great outdoors. These sources of information almost got me killed! As a result, I wanted to tell it like it is. Much is really good! Very positive! In any occupation there will be stuff that is necessary, or we are not so excited about, but needs dealing with.

"So Josh, I set out to tell it all, the good, the bad, and the ugly. In hopes it would be educational, and entertaining as well."

"How has that gone, Miles?"

"I'm not always certain that was a good idea. A world-famous writer/photographer came to stay with me to tell my story. He explains to me, the public is not looking for the truth." I pause to think about it. "I wonder, Josh, if everything is a story."

Josh changes the subject. He knows where this conversation is headed. He stops a dogfight, and a dog ends up with a broken tooth, and he is punished for it. He has been treated way worse than this in his life. Was anyone punished? He is in the very race the broken toothed dog was in, went through more pain than the dog! What is the matter with the world! Is running 1,000 miles thorough the Alaska dark, cold wilderness in record time supposed to be without physical stress and pain? It comes with the race!

"Animal rights groups control the purse-strings, and public sentiment. It's big money. With this in mind, we need to adjust what truth we tell, Josh." As a storyteller I get it, and do not mind, except when my own baggage and buttons are involved. I see myself in Josh.

"You never told me if you found any tusks on your last river trip, Miles. "Since the previous subject had a lot to do with keeping your mouth shut, I reply, "I'm hard of hearing, Mr. Josh. I did not get that question!"He laughs. "Just between us Miles!"

"Just between us, Josh? It was not long ago you started a rumor I had coffee cans of cash buried in my yard, thousands of dollars earned by selling prehistoric mammoth tusks!"

"But, Miles, it's true, you do!" Here we are, discussing what truth is, and spreading the truth around.

"You do not know for a fact I have coffee cans buried. You never saw me bury any, and I never said I buried any. I recall you saying you were sure I had hidden money and guessed it was in buried coffee cans and I only smiled."

"Yes, Miles, that meant it is true!" *This is a truth I wanted Josh to believe, not local thieves or the IRS.*

"Josh, there are lots of people in our community that, if they believe I have buried money, would feel inspired to come dig, or torture me to get the knowledge of where. This is not a safe rumor to spread."

"Speaking of river activity, Josh, I have been contacted by some mushroom pickers who are looking to me as a boat operator to go explore, find, and pick morel mushrooms. Do you know much about these mushrooms, Josh?" I am curious if the Natives used them for anything, or even ate them. I know they grow mostly right after a forest fire. Global warming seems to be behind a lot of big fires over the past several years. Last year, we had some fires near the village. Many people made extra money helping to fight them. Josh made $300 an hour with his boat. He has a commercial license and has run tugboats in the past. The community almost burned. I had been gone on a survey job with Seymour.

"No Miles, I cannot recall natives in the past harvesting these. I do not even know what they look like. I think there is no nutrition in them and a waste of time to eat." I was just wondering. I say bye to Josh and head home. The community RV park is across the street from me. This is where the mushroom people are beginning to congregate. I stop to meet with the guy in charge, Sam. Sam is an organizer. He has a crew of pickers coming in from Cambodia. First, he wants a helicopter to go looking around.

"That's a waste of money, Sam, at $1,000 an hour. You could accomplish a lot by boat and climbing up to look in the woods here and there to check. Even if you find anything by chopper, how will you get the pickers in and out on a regular basis? Especially if the chopper finds hot spots accessible by no other means! There should be plenty of mushrooms if they are around, within access of the river." Sam agrees. I go home and get some maps, but see right off Sam does not know how to read a map.

"Ok, Sam. I know this area, and where the fire has been. If you have a GPS, we can mark spots we find. We can bring crews in and maintain camps with food and supplies." There are a few independent professional morel pickers from the lower states beginning to show up in the Nenana RV park. It is obvious to me they are all out of their element. They are used to roadside picking. Sam is not a wilderness expert. I see a money angle in this for me. I can be his go-to guy.

One young couple realizes they need a boat! They go to Fairbanks and buy what they think is going to work. I still hang out at the boat landing where I check on my riverboat tied up in a back slough where I used to keep the houseboat. I happen to be there when this young couple is launching the newly acquired boat. They decide to test it first, before putting it in the river. They have started the engine and are now wondering why there is white smoke and the engine quit. I know at first glance, even before I get within fifty feet.

"No cooling water. You have to be in the water to start the boat engine or have the water intake in a bucket of water."

"Oh, ok. Well then, could you help us push the boat in the river?"

"Too late. You need a new engine now."

"No way, man! You just want all the mushroom money! Are you going to help us launch or not?"

"Sure, no problem" I help them get the boat off the trailer and into the river.

"We'll work on the engine downriver after we camp, first we need to get out where the mushrooms are, and make a camp!"

I nod wisely and watch them load the boat with gas, food, tent, gear, and help them push off into the current. They paddle downstream and smile a thanks. I smile back. It's highly likely no one will ever see them again alive. I wave.

There is no way they can do anything with a seized-up engine on the river. At best, they can float to Manley Hot Springs downriver in about a week. It will cost the price of a new engine to get someone to drive to Manley with a trailer, load them up, and get them back to civilization. *They shall have a great adventure, if they live several days without food and such; perhaps they will have a bear encounter!* Another outfit shows up the same day with a 1950s rotted fiberglass boat they paid twice too much for. *Reminds me of stories from the Soapy Smith gold rush days a hundred years ago!* Talk at the RV park is, these mushrooms are huge money out there free for the taking. Stories of people they met who are making $1,000 a day. Yet no one local is very interested.

Sam is with a group who cannot speak English. He seems to be their leader and takes care of them, does all the translating, showing them what to do. The RV park owners are friends of ours. Iris tells me what the RV owners say about the Cambodians. "They took all the toilet paper and rolled it up on sticks, along with the twenty spare rolls. They helped themselves to all the coffee filters at the free coffee machine in the Laundromat. All the floor mats are now sleeping pads and covers by campfires. They love America, smile, nod, and thank us."

Sam and I, and one other guy, go out with the GPS exploring the river for good mushroom spots. Sam knows a lot about what it takes for mushrooms to grow.

"No use pulling in here, to dry, no, not there either, to sunny, not enough sand. Up ahead, this is it!"

Sure enough, there in the fireweed flowers, and growing on the old burn among fallen, charcoaled trees, are carpets of morel mushrooms. I am not especially interested in any situation I see, in terms of wanting to make big money picking. It is hard to climb over and under the charred trees. My back is not so great these days. The money sounds only ok to me. It's not as good as fossil hunting. Sam is the only local buyer. He is paying five dollars a pound for wet mushrooms. $40 a pound, for dry. I see internet buyers are offering $40 a pound for green and $600 a pound for dry. None of these pickers seems savvy enough to use the internet. Sam is making a lot of money. The usual deal. Workers in many industries are slaves. The head guy counting the money and paying the salaries is the one pulling the strings, calling the shots, getting rich.

One out-of-state kid at the RV park shows up with a backpack full of dry mushrooms and gets paid $700 by Sam. The rest in the RV park go nuts. Everyone wants to head out, like right now. Sam will sell these mushrooms for $7,000. Sam pays me to get his crew out to some places we scouted out. The closest is five miles. The farthest forty miles. Everyone wants in the boat at once so they can be on the first trip.

I try to explain, "Two trips, two trips." Hold my fingers up. No one wants to be part of a second trip. It's all about 'now.' I'm not good at saying who goes now, and who goes later. I let them figure it out, pile in the boat till it holds no more. There is only two inches of freeboard. Dangerous as hell. Very dangerous. Worse, no one but me has a clue. Everyone is happy, laughing, going from one side of the boat to the other, pointing. No matter what I say, pointing to the edge of the water and the boat, and showing what is happening when they all rush to one side. If anyone can pull off a safe trip, it will be me. That's why I'm the boatman, getting paid good wages. The boat is rated for 2,000 pounds, and I am carrying at least 5,000.

"No problem," some say in broken English. "No worry." Guessing they come from a crowded country. Everything is overcrowded—cars, busses, donkey carts, all maxed out to the limit. Boats overload, sink, not newsworthy, too many people. We survive. The trip is just incredibly slow.

Two crews are dropped off. I had not paid attention, but see when unloading, these poor pickers have nothing. Most are barefoot. No sleeping bag, no tent, no bear protection, no bug spray. No Alaska skills either. I try to help. I leave each crew with one of my spare bow saws to cut wood for a fire, leave some bug repellent. One crew I leave with a .22 rifle for bears or food.

When I get back, I see Sam, "Sam! These poor pickers have nothing, how can they pick good if they cannot stay warm or sleep? I left them some of my stuff."

"Miles, that is not smart. They do not need any help. I take care of them. You come to me. I take care of you, the one who pays you, not them. If you want to make deals with them, you can do that, but if I pay you, I am in charge. Do not bypass me and offer help." Well. Whatever. I want to be paid, but I cannot help feel for those in poverty, and wish to help.

Iris tells me the latest at the RV park. The situation is tolerable anyhow. There are thirty to forty pickers camped out, all paying. Sam takes care of his crew of thirty, pays for everyone. If there is a problem, come see Sam, he makes it right. He sets up an office in a tent in the grass. There are scales to weigh mushrooms, and a propane drying area set up to finish off half dry mushrooms. Two armed guards stand at the tent.

"Miles, I need to rent your shop space, a secure building to store dry mushrooms till I can ship them." There are several hundred pounds of dry mushrooms. I rent out my shop and give Sam a key. This is looking like a military or mob type operation. Slave labor. The RV park owners think they are illegal's without green cards, smuggled into the country. We have no clue how they could enter the country. I do not care. I do not consider it my business. I do not consider these people a threat to anyone. No local wants the job of mushroom picking. Let slaves do it. Whatever. No one is starving or complaining. Actually, these people seem happy. They are in the great Alaska! Cooking by a communal fire! They joke, laugh, eat Cambodian type food. There is a flute, stringed instrument to play, with songs sung. Life is good!

They greet each day as the sun comes up with joy and reverence. Without a worry in the world, for someone will take care of them. No one will starve. There is zero sign of stress or irritability. These people appear to accept the world as it is, with no interest in changing anything. If anything, it is we, everyone else, who needs help. It is they who are kind and forgiving of us and our quest for money and change. They, who feel sorry for the rest of the world, are slaves, but from their perspective, it is a good life. There are no bills. Not a lot is expected of them. One of them can speak some English. He is a little in charge, and talks most with Sam, representing the rest of the group. I think he has traveled around the world with Sam.

"Yes Miles, we wish we got paid more all right! Sam does not let us get ahead, while he makes all the money."

From the slave's viewpoint, I hear how it is. If these people found another buyer on their own and cut Sam out, how would that play out? These Cambodians do not know how they got here. Someone else arranged everything. They do not have a clue how to get back home on their own. If they are here illegally, then Sam holds the cards, Sam paid someone off and has an agreement. Everyone can return the same way with Sam, under Sam's umbrella. This network of people is in business, big business. Everyone along this food chain knows the deal, is working together. None in the food chain is going to let one of the slaves figure out how to bypass them, get uppity, inspire other slaves to think outside the cage. As long as the slaves cooperate, do what is expected, everything will work out wonderful. This can be done the easy way, or the hard way.

If anyone wishes to go off on their own, Sam would say, "Try it, good luck, you are on your own, enjoy your freedom."

If the free man says, "But how will I get home?"

Sam replies, "That is no longer any of my concern. You chose freedom." There are many questions.

"How do I eat? Where is the store? How do I get there? Where will I sleep?" The slaves do not speak English. They would have trouble making any deal with anyone.

"Are you willing to help us, Miles?"

Help in what way? If they are illegal's, what help can I possibly be that does not make me a felon? I would not know how to pay anyone off like Sam does. There is not enough money a handful of rebellious slaves could earn to help themselves. There is no way I could help them get passports while they are in this country. *What they really need is an education. Not formal training, but street smarts. How not to steal toilet paper from the nice generous lady giving you a deal on a place to stay that you will never see again.* I already had experience trying to help a German girl get legal working papers to come to the US to work. Reams of paperwork and questions.

There might be secret ways to siphon off some mushrooms slaves pick, and pay the slaves more money for their product under the table without Sam knowing. Sam is smart enough to know about how many pounds of mushrooms to expect from his pickers. He is a businessman, and has seen a variety of plans to try to cut him out, and is most likely smarter on the subject than I am. He would not take kindly to what in his view would be trying to rob him. I'd feel different if I saw abuse, pain, tears, heart wrenching poverty. I am seeing happy people. Sam is nice enough. We chat. I understand Sam better than his slaves!

"Miles, these people would not know what to do with money and goods."

I have trouble believing that! Everyone in the world knows what to do with stuff and money! Yet that is not true. I had a girlfriend once, and if I gave her a million dollars, she'd be flat broke again in a month.

Sam is still talking, as I think about what he is saying. "It cost me a lot to make all this happen. There is a lot to arrange, a lot is expected, others wait for their cut. There is stress, responsibility, that these people do not want to take on. No one would do it unless there was great reward."

Yes, I understand. I've experienced this in my own life. "These people have even less in Cambodia. This is their chance for a vacation, to see another country. They will return home with much to talk about. They will have a few dollars in their pocket. No stress, no mess, no fuss, no taking chances, no risk. On their own, they face worse problems than getting back home with only a few dollars."

I understand, on their own, none could ever get here to this country to see it. Back home, their greatest wealth is a tin can to pee in.

I understand business. I see this situation at the Tucson gem show all the time. People from all over the planet come to sell fossils and gems at the biggest show in the world. Making good business is not as easy as some think. There is in fact risk. It is possible, even likely, to go broke. Worse than broke. In debt. Get home owing a fortune. Worse, unable to get back home at all. This was said about what would happen to me when I announced I was going.

"You are a country bumpkin Miles, those city slickers will fleece you down to your hide and sell that too!" I've seen this. Worse off than one of Sam's workers.

We are in Sam's tent. Two mafia like armed guards stand outside guarding a drug lord. Beyond the tent flap is the community campfire. One of the slaves approaches and is let in. The workers want to humbly, respectfully, know if they can get more rice and dry fish to cook over the fire. Sam is polite and agrees, waves, orders someone to get into the food supply and issue more food for a party. I am guessing without Sam, there would be a free for all, a party. All the food would be gone in a few days. Much would get wasted.

I look around. No one looks starvation skinny, dressed in rags, or dirty, or with physical injuries of any kind not attended to. I take this in. I have only heard of the horrors of slavery, how it is worse than death. I hear it from Blacks, Indians. The greatest sin on earth. This is the first time I have been exposed to slavery first hand.

These workers get four dollars a pound, and out of this they have to pay Sam for food. I assume pay for their trip here and back, and any other expenses. Indentured slaves. Like those who came over on the Mayflower. Not a lot different from working for minimum wages here in the US. Such people are free to do what? It is not possible to ever get enough money ahead to do anything but stay alive. Buy a beer, plop themselves all wore out at the end of the day in front of the TV you hopefully finally paid off. That defines their entire life. I know such people. May as well call it slaves. Sam takes care of everything. Like Big Brother does.

Sam makes sure the theft of toilet paper stops, no more taking rugs to sleep on. The RV owners tell me flat out, if it were not for Sam in charge, they would kick this entire group out of the park. Sam keeps track and pays for everyone at the RV. It is Sam who makes sure the noise is kept down so other tourists in the RV park can sleep. Sam makes arrangements and pays me for the boat trips. Sam greases the wheels and gears of life. The individuals cannot pay me.

"Just do everything through me, Miles, that's how it works, and how everything goes smoothly."

I have notes in the computer keeping track of trips and money.

Sunday, June 06, 2010
   Money paid
   Thursday $100
   Friday $100
   Saturday gas 37 gallons total used so far paid at $3.60 = $135

Sunday receive $100 for Saturdays time
Thursday receive $250 updated for past except gas
Thursday $20 for trip across river.

While I am on the computer,I go over daily emails.

"Miles, I see in the paper a couple had to be rescued yesterday." Iris likes to keep up with the news in the paper. She tells me if there is anything interesting I might want to know. No pictures, but it reads like the couple who took off without a working engine in hopes of getting rich picking mushrooms. Iris hands me the paper so I can read all about it. Yes, they got the boat stuck, swamped the boat, lost most of their gear. Bears came around and scared them. They tried to walk out and got lost.

"Iris, looks like they got as far as below Percy's camp, fifteen miles is all they got." Fifteen miles does not sound far to civilized people, till they try to walk it in the swamps. Not one in a hundred could do it without getting lost, or totally worn out. So they ran out of food, matches, supplies, and would have died. They found the river again, and flagged a boater who called 911.

Iris says, "I wonder why the boater did not just rescue them?" I wonder as well, until I realize that would be the other mushroom crew, the drunk hauling a few independent pickers out for hire. Getting the mushroom picking crew out, making money, was more important than rescuing the competition.

I smile. "As I told you Iris, they had their adventure!" I add, "It bothers me that their preventable mistake and stupidity cost taxpayers a great deal of money." There has been talk of those being rescued, being charged. Especially if the situation looks like negligence. This couple lost their boat and supplies, got no mushrooms, and almost died. All over the mushroom God. Worse off than working for Sam, the man. I can see Sam's point. Freedom is not for the faint of heart. *For if we are free to live, we are also free to die. I want the freedom to do well and prosper, get ahead! Can such a person with this outlook turn around later saying, 'Wait, it is not working out well! Help!'*

There is a new hot spot for mushrooms that requires a trip across the Nenana River. Then walking eight miles down a swamp trail to the higher ground where the spruce trees burned. This is the same trial I travel in winter by sled dog or snow machine. I know it well. Sam wants me to take his people across the river. The one guy in the crew who speaks English tells me this is too far for some to walk. There are women and elderly in the group. He wants to know if he can rent my four wheeler and take it across the river with the cart to help these poor people, plus I can make some extra rental money. I run the idea by Sam.

"No, Miles, they do not need a four wheeler, trust me on this, do not get involved, but if you want to, I have no objection." If it helps his crew get more mushrooms and more profit for him without any cost to him, he has no issue with that.

We load my four wheeler onto the bow of the boat. This is not easy. Finally, I have the crew in the boat and we head across the river in the swift current. This is ice-cold mountain glacier water. I trust the English-speaking Cambodian somewhat, and ask if everything is ok in the front. I cannot see over all the heads to the front of the boat. It seems to me we are front heavy.

"Are we taking on any water over the bow?" The Cambodian looks, and gives a happy smile, thumb up. We only have 100 more feet to go across the river. I ask again, as the boat feels sluggish and front heavy. Again, I get a 'no problem' signal and his grin. As usual, everyone is excited, looking, chatting, without a care in the world. Till I see water around my feet and feel us going down. In another three seconds, the boat will be under water. The current will grab one side and roll the boat over, emptying all its cargo into the main current. People, gear, gas, and four-wheeler. Most of these people cannot swim, so will probably drown. However, in half a second I give the engine full throttle so we go ahead much faster. As the boat sinks, I have gotten close enough to the other side for the boat to hit bottom out of the main current. The water is over the top of the gunnels. We are 'sunk,' and grounded. There is only two feet of water between the bow and the shore, so tell everyone they need to get out in a hurry and get to shore, grabbing their stuff, before it floats away.

There is no sense of panic or rush. It's my problem. This has nothing to do with them. They all step ashore without speed. No concern whatever for me, my boat, or my four-wheeler. It's as if all that matters is what they want. They are not selfish. The situation is the same if I am on a bus I paid to get on and the engine quits. No matter how upset the driver is, it's not my problem. When I am done shopping, another bus will take me back. What it cost the bus company to replace the bus is not on my mind. In fact, if I am inconvenienced, I expect to be compensated. Or I would not, but the average civilized person deserves what they paid for.

With all eight of the people and gear gone, the boat pops up enough that the gunnels are just above the waterline. Quick bailing with a gallon can, gets enough water out I feel assured I am out of danger. Neither the four-wheeler nor the boat engine went under water. The boat bilge pump is on, and slowly empties the remaining water.

I drive the wheeler off the bow and up the riverbank. No one offers to help. I have shown the Cambodians how to run the machine, so there should be no problems. Happy munchkins head off singing up the yellow brick road, with a cart full of young and old. They are being pulled by the four-wheeler in low gear. I stare up the path as they disappear. Still in shock over what just happened. I can see life through their eyes better.

"Sam, I have a survey job for three days coming up." Sam and I set it up to where I should not be needed for three days. "Is that still the plan? I'll see you next week and gather up the pickers."

"No problem, have fun surveying, and see you when you get back. We are all paid up now, right?" I just nod yes. *I have made more than the best mushroom pickers, over $700 a day.* I like Sam. He makes sure I have been paid and happy, with genuine concern. It's a business concern, but that is all right. He is loyal. He is not telling me he will hire someone else. I am his boatman and he trusts me, depends on me.

This situation reminds me of the gold rush days. The stories of who made money and how. Some of the most consistent money was made by people plying their known trade up in the Klondike. Selling to those looking to get rich digging gold. One fellow did quite well, repairing watches in Nome, Alaska. I heard the story when visiting, because the watch shop is still there! Run by the same family! I'm sure people who owned, and knew how to operate boats, did well during the gold rush.

Seymour, the survey boss and I, meet in Manley Hot Springs as planned. I have boated there. He has flown here in his own plane with all the gear. All I had heard about the job is it is in Tanana. We need my boat, and there should be three days of Topography work. I spend the night in Manley before we take off early in the morning. Seymour clues me in on more details of the job.

"The city and the tribe are in a dispute over gravel. Our job is to survey the pile and determine how many truckloads were hauled." We had a job like this in the past. Some villages have both a white man law, and an Indian set of laws. The governments overlap in the same community. Often they do not get along and have land disputes.

"There are a couple of side jobs I drummed up for two fish camps in the area. They need a survey of their fish camps to use them as collateral on loans." Banks require surveyed sellable pieces of land. Fish camp jobs are usually interesting, and more our kind of work. Topography work is just boring level work.

The boring work is done, we are at a fish camp. I'm always amazed how Seymour can figure out how long a job will take almost to the hour! I'm reminded again how Seymour looks like John Lennon. Same glasses. Same way of walking, same intellectual air, while being very intense. I'm in the presence of a man who is one of the best in the world at what he does. We chat around the campfire after we eat. This is our chance to unwind and converse about things not related to the job.

Seymour opens the cooler saying, "Beer time!"

I do not care for beer, but recognize this is an important time that I ought to be part of—is a ritual for the boss and any crew we have. I take a beer and thank him, nursing the one beer all evening.

"Miles, tell me how the art business is doing?"

This subject has come up over the years. While Seymour and his wife collect my art and put it on the wall, he believes I cannot make any serious money at it. I am deceiving myself. Without surveying money, I am dead in the water. He worries about me. Many people I know, especially the smartest, most educated, believe art is a fun hobby one does to relax. Not a money maker, bill payer. Years ago, Seymour gave me a heads up, that we might be slowing down, heading for retirement one day. He wanted me to be ready. There is no retirement from this job. Seymour did not want to leave me in the lurch. I told him back then, I was curious if I could make a living with the art, working for myself. I'm looking forward to full-time art.

We have less work these days then we once did. The kind of work has changed and is not as fun for us. We began specializing in homesteads. Meeting homesteaders and working on our own, our way, was rewarding. However, Seymour had problems sometimes getting poor homesteaders to pay. I always got paid, so did not see that end of it. Homesteading programs slowed up. Seymour got more work doing government contract work. Putting in new airports became part of our survey work.

"Miles, one reason is my wife got certified and as a woman, we got preference for minority hire. Not a lot of female surveyors!"

More money, but more stressful for the boss. He missed the old type of work. The government has requirements. One of them is the use of GPS used in our surveys. This is expensive high tech… equipment not much related to the homestead jobs we love. We now often sit and wait for instruments to collect data. Much of the work for Seymour now is officer work downloading data into the computer and 'tweaking it in the office' as he calls it. Not real survey work. Not a survey he trusts. If the numbers do not come out right, how do you fix it when the majority of the work is not in the field? The boss is wanting to get out of the business.

Seymour has a set amount of money in the bank. He feels he can live off the interest from this money. We do not argue with each other much. We respect each other, but are not in agreement as to what a secure future looks like with retirement.

I have said, "If I had 200 grand, there are a lot of things I could do with it that would earn more money than interest in the bank." I am not inspired with confidence over what the bank is investing in and gambling with. I can gamble with my own money. I see the difference between what the bank offers me in interest when borrowing my money, compared to what the bank charges me in interest when I borrow from the bank.

Seymour feels money in the bank is better than being an artist with a dream! We chuckle and discuss our views. So now is the time to bring Seymour up to speed on how my future can expect to look, as he tells me another hundred grand is in his nest egg.[1]

"Ok, I suppose Seymour. I'm happy, doing all right." I review what has just gone on. After many years, and having cast thousands of jewelry parts, I decided to pick up the instruction book on the casting machine, and look at it closer.

Seymour is dumb struck. "Miles, you have been in business how long, and only now decide to review the instructions? I'm amazed you'd admit that! Isn't that stupid? Shouldn't you have read the instructions thoroughly when you got the machine?"

I smile and wonder how best to explain something complex.

In our society, measurement of intelligence and success is measured in how fast we learn something. The one who finishes first gets the gold star. The dummy does not learn the material during the designated education time line. If the class is six months, you better know the material in six months. After that class is over. No degree. No points, no job. Seymour wonders what my point is, and what I am getting at. I explain by giving an example.

I was in the Navy. A new officer was assigned to my ship, the aircraft carrier Wasp. A twenty-one-year-old officer right out of school, with impeccable records and top grades, among the best. He had been on the ship a week when he ordered me to open valve number J2. I am not an officer. But I know every steam and water valve on the entire ship. Over 700 of them. I answer, "Sir, that valve is below the waterline and opening it will flood the ship."

"Are you disobeying a direct order?"

I thought a moment, shrugged my shoulder and saluted.

"Sir, I will go open Valve J2!" I went below decks and opened that valve. It took a few minutes for the reaction and the water to work its way through half a mile of pipe. The compartment flooded. Divers had to go down to shut the valve off. Probably a million dollars worth of damage. It wasn't my million dollars. I was nineteen years old. I was amused. I thought of the Peter Principle, from the book I had just read. Involving people being promoted to their level of incompetence, then staying there. Now that I am older, I have a different, more expanded view.

Surveying through some tough country. My boss and friend, Seymour, at the instrument.

CHAPTER THREE

MAMMOTH IVORY HUNT, FAIR TIME, FLOOD

"It takes more than book smarts to know some things Seymour. I agree it is a good place to begin! There are also other ways to learn, that do not involve books at all."

"Miles, I agree, but those ways take a long time, and so often mean reinventing the wheel! Why? When you can learn it from experts in a brief time and bypass all the mistakes! Learn from others, those who made the mistakes and teach us how to avoid them!"

I pause because yes, that is one view. Often, however, there is a learning process in making mistakes. I learned a few basics about casting from a simple book. I spent two hours reviewing the book to get started. I bought the most simple, cheap, used equipment to get going. I began creating. I made some quite laughable mistakes. (A conversation was in my previous book with a fellow artist running a shop in Fairbanks.) *Why am I reinventing the wheel, making the most basic simple mistakes!?*

To learn, my method takes much longer than taking lessons. Many feel this makes my method not workable. This is where an entire lifestyle and way of thinking comes in. Where to begin explaining? Who cares! Seymour and I are here at a campfire passing the time, entertaining ourselves. We have till bedtime to explore this. I begin, "College classes are the option promoted and advertised. This costs money I do not have and requires I move deeper into civilization. This also takes time I do not have. Others may choose my way because they do not have the money! College teaches what most people in the business know."

Seymour nods, that yes, this makes sense, to learn the trade.

"Yet, I believe, one secret to a successful business is to offer something unique, with an identifiable style that stands out, a controllable niche market. Seymour has probably never heard such a notion before, merely waits to hear the punch line he will laugh at or dispute.

I go on anyway, "I have five dollars for a used outdated book on the subject that covers the basics. I have the first $100 it takes to buy the simplest used primitive equipment to get started." I wait to let that sink in before going on. "Within a week I have produced some castings I can sell. They are not the best. They do not fetch top dollar. I get over $200 for the first batch of thirty castings."

Seymour shrugs his shoulders, acknowledging I have a point so far. "But Miles, does $200 cover much? You have electric bills, permits, fees, insurance, taxes, etc!"

Without addressing each of these issues brought up, I admit. The first batch marginally covered expenses. Possibly I lost money. Yes, Seymour figures that.

I explain further, "But it's not a financial hardship. I simply broke even the first time. A week later out comes batch number two." I learned a lot from the first batch. "Within a month, with no financial hardship whatever, I am paying my bills and eating. There are no student loans to pay off. No waiting four years till I get a degree before working a trade that I love. I'm living life my way, on my terms, by my hours."

There is no looking for work. There in fact is no taking on a real 'work,' to pay for my education and fun. This is not a job that I hate, while I get an education about a subject I love, and hope to be doing 'someday.' I am not paying for undesired required classes. Instead, I get paid for playing at what I love. Right from the get go! In the past, the story ended here. Not especially convincing. Having fun on poverty wages. Certainly not within the first year, or two years, or even three years. There is a downside to my story. I'm making ends meet using primitive knowledge and equipment. Making less money than other jewelers doing the same thing. Being happy, but being happy does not cut it for most listeners like Seymour.

"So where is the money?" It's all about following the money. *Ok, after five years let's talk about the money.*

After five years, this is about the time I'd be getting out of college with a pile of degrees, expecting to be worth big bucks because of these degrees. Is this in fact happening to those who chose the high road? Such people have five years of classes, with 100 grand in student loans owed. To be paid off with interest. In the best case, yes, there is work for these educated people, justifying the time and money invested. There is no guarantee. A lot of times, students cannot find work in their chosen field. I meet graduates that end up with a job flipping burgers. A job they could have begun five years ago with no educational debts to pay off. Seymour and I both know people in their sixties who still have student loan debt.

Seymour hired a saw man who got interested in learning to be an instrument man. Seymour taught this hard-working, smart, young worker to run an instrument well enough to help do the basics. This friend and employee decided he wants to be a surveyor like Seymour! He's young and learns fast! He is not with us because he is in school taking needed beginning classes. Five years from now, and a lifetime in debt, he will know enough to begin basic survey work. He's already been at it a year or two and is $80,000 in debt at twenty-five years old. He is not worth any more money than I am worth to Seymour. I agree 'eventually,' and 'maybe,' he 'could be,' worth more than I am in the survey occupation. If, if and if. Meanwhile, with no guarantees, he is sitting in class, while Seymour and I are living the good life in the great outdoors. The student may even change his mind about what he wants to do for a living.

Compare this to my story. Seymour hires me same as our friend. I, too, was offered the chance to learn to run the instrument. I declined because I think I would not be good at it, not being a good numbers man. I also do not want to spend my life as a surveyor, nor five of the best years of my youth sitting in a classroom. However, if I had decided to learn from Seymour as offered, Seymour told me I could be crew boss on a survey team, working for him. No college needed. If all worked out, I can see what could have been now. Potentially a partner in the survey company. The only thing that stopped me, was me. It's not what I wanted. Yes, someone in the company has to have the license, but it does not have to be the owners. Some jobs only a specifically licensed person can sign off on. Even Seymour has to go to a bigger company as partner in order to get some jobs signed off.

On the surface, I am 'stuck' as a saw man. I'm being paid the highest wages in the state for my job, but it's fixed. I can never make more than $18 to $21 an hour, as I do now. Not that this is bad. I enjoy my work. I can think of a better example than myself, but think Seymour will only listen for a limited time. I have a neighbor with a son that just got out of high school. He did not do well, so had to repeat some grades. Not college material. His father taught him how to run heavy equipment. Forklifts, road graders, bulldozers—common equipment around these parts and in his family. This nineteen-year-old got a job making $30 an hour on his first job, running heavy equipment. No formal education. This, and other examples, is what I base my opinion on. College is good for those who want it, or feel so inclined, but there are other ways to make a lot of money, be happy, have a wonderful career.

I think times are changing. There was a period in our history when many were coming to the city from farms and we needed college-educated people! The GI bill covered education costs for many men after the Korean War. Or after the World War. Times were good, the economy was growing. Education may not have cost a fortune, and there was usually a good job waiting. I'm not so sure this is true anymore.

"If, if, and if, Seymour. If a person has the money, likes a college setting, has the kind of dream that requires this education, and the mindset, then good for them, college and a formal education work. In fact, those who get good grades, listen to the teacher, their parents, do what they are told, make good candidates for formal education!" I pause because I have just seen too many families struggling to get a child into college, as if that is the only answer. My own father, for example. Dad wanted to be a gunsmith when he was a teen. He loved being out in a sailboat. His father forbid it. "We are no one without an education!" I do not agree.

Seymour yawns and puts another stick on the campfire. The evening is cooling off with fewer mosquitoes. We can scoot out of the smoke now! No gagging on smoke as I talk!

"So let's look at my art and casting occupation, Seymour. Within a month I had paid for my equipment and basic education." From then on I am in business making a profit. Within a few months I am experimenting in ways out of the box, with the box not even being visible anymore. Professionals are asking me how I did this! I had castings of three metals that looked like marble cake. It is not possible to do this. No one had ever heard of it. Likewise, no one had ever heard of lost wax casting copper. The plaster cannot handle the temperature, and I would have learned that in school, known, this is a stupid thing to try. 'Luckily' I did not know that. "Not possible? Oh. Huh." Here I am early on, doing castings no one has seen on the market before, very identifiable as done by 'Miles.' Because of my experimenting.

"I had a lot of failure! Months, even years, before there was descent money in it." I have to pause again to think how to go on. Rewind to the beginning again. "When I began casting, and began many things, I started with no specific goal. I was not goal motivated. I do what I do because I like to, as the first priority." Seymour understands this, because he chose a less stressful survey business moving into a village life, after having a more lucrative bigger business in the city.

Even though I look at a practical side of 'the bills need to be paid,' there is some minimal amount I need to make, that is a low threshold, easy to reach. When I fail, I am not depressed, discouraged, feel stupid, or panic. I do not wonder how I will pay for my education, worry how I am doing compared to anyone else. With casting, it is $100 invested. I can walk away from it at any time. I am not especially trying to do this the right way, be a perfectionist, accomplish anything. For example, after many years I have told people, it's all about watching molten metal spin into the red hot mold. There is the sound of the hiss and vibration in my hands as it quenches in the water. I close my eyes and soak it up. If the casting comes out or not, is secondary. If the entire batch is a loss, I still smile, "Wow! Don't you just love that vibration? Lets wind it up and do another batch!" It's like holding on to something alive! In truth, I have at least a 35% total product failure rate. Mouths open every time I say this with a smile.

"You admit that, Miles? I'd be totally ashamed!"

I go even further! "I have as high as a 95% rate of 'things that did not come out as I hoped.' I have a high percent I have to re-melt or cannot figure out how to use. I am not bothered in the least." Not a worry in the world. Why? "Because Seymour, there is an average of one item in thirty that knocks my socks off. There is an average of one item in 100 that pays for the other ninety-nine." I let that sink it. "In other words, one percent sells for 100 times more money than the other ninety-nine percent. If I get $500 for one cast cool item, I can afford to throw away fifty other items." I do not throw the rest away. Often I simply sell it cheaper, cheaper, and cheapest. I can undercut third world import prices. I can meet the el-cheapo tourist market at ten cents on the dollar.

My overhead might as well be zero. I get free metal from the barge line. Old propellers that weigh over 100 pounds. Pure copper water pipes made back in the 1920s are free when old buildings are torn down. I may even get paid to haul it away. I have a used kiln I paid $300 for ten years ago. Plaster is the biggest cost. Still, my average production cost per item is a dollar. I shrug my shoulders. I am having fun.

I compare my process to that of most civilized artists. They learn to do it right the first time. Product seconds are tossed out, just like anything else, 'second rate.' Do your best, show only your best. Follow the recipe, learn it well. Those who learn fast are rewarded. Those who do not tend to give up. With this method, it is easy to see mistakes and failure as bad, discouraging, and most people give up—afraid of failure! Getting to where they want to be is too hard, takes too long, and they are not good at it. Those who are good at it skyrocket forward! However.

This seems a significant 'however.'

"Such people are followers." They learned under someone else. They know how to follow directions. This method gets us quickly to some level of knowledge and income, called 'professional.' There is sort of a monetary salary connected to the craft, occupation to be achieved. They settle in a shop, get orders to fill. Shop time might be $50 to $60 an hour. With a lot of overhead. That pleases most. They 'have arrived,' at a level society smiles, nods about, and offers respect for. Ten years after going to college, working under someone else for a while, acquiring a $200,000 loan, another loan for the shop…

I happily play in the mud, content with nothing. Laughing and making mud balls. Where does that get someone? Every time I make a mistake, I learn something. I finally learn and know after five years, what the educated person learned in six months. Seymour nods that yes, this is his point. What else matters? What a waste of time. This is the punch line Seymour was waiting for.

"I noticed something, Seymour. It's not equal knowledge." I can say how it works. I can say what does not work, and why. I know why the copper casts in plaster, even though plaster cannot handle the temperature. I understand plaster in ways the other guys do not. I know what parameters I can play with, and what sorts of results to expect. When I first asked the experts, "So I am interested in casting copper, what can you tell me?"

"I haven't a clue." That is not what I reply to questions within my trade.

The attitude was that I am asking a stupid question. Stupid because 'Who cares!' Stupid because you can make a good living, a lot of money and be respected, not knowing that, and focus on what is in style, the trend now, and ride that gravy train!

"I agree." Seymour gives a look like *why are we having this conversation then? The reason is this Seymour.* "If someone like me can figure out how to do what is not being done and do the impossible, a trend might start that I am on the front wave of. I can name my price. I can make ten times the money the followers make. I could be in the top 10% of the trade. However, it's a gamble."

The result in the long haul from my perspective is… far, far out there in time. The guy who knows 'why,' pulls ahead. That valve below the waterline in my Navy story is not just a valve on a chart. It is a series of 500 valves memorized in my head. Where they all go, what purpose is served, what is connected to what. I know what rooms they are in, what they look like, what shape they are in, which one works, which one need repair. What will happen if I do anything at all to any of them is not something we learn in school. The Captain himself comes to me when he has a valve question. At the time, that was not worth any money or rank. I got out of the navy at the same rank I went in, with the same low pay. No regrets. I have no degree, no stars, no sheets of paper on the wall. However, a rear admiral in the Navy calls me 'Sir', knows me by name, and requests me when it comes to values because I'm the man when it comes to values.

There were, I assume, officers coming out of the academy that had some useful knowledge! There must have been, or otherwise why were there such schools? All the officers I respected had put a lot of time in and worked their way up the ranks. I had been offered officer rank right out of machinist school, because I had scored in the top few percent in an aptitude test and Machinist Mate School. I turned it down. Three times the pay. I knew then what I know now. On the survey job, I enjoy being the saw man. That's what I want to do. While Seymour stays up late crunching numbers mumbling and worrying. I am snoring.

Some customers buying art are discriminating and buy the name. But not all. Many like something different, interesting, that draws attention when on display. Some want a story. Exciting stories rarely come from the sheep. Beginning, "Then I went to college," may get a polite, disinterested smile. My beginning line is, "Then I went into the wilds, killed a few bears, built a houseboat, and while fixing equipment with primitive tools I discovered an art form." Suddenly the news media wants to write that up. Seymour prefers a low profile. So the conversation ends. The evening fire cracks as I put another log on. Seymour grabs another beer. I have some more food. Seymour chuckles at a memory I ask about.

"Miles, when you talked to those ravens today, I cannot tell the raven from you without looking. You really had them going!"

Yes, I am always chatting at the ravens in their language, and confess I do not know what I am saying! Over the years, I have an opinion of what certain types of sounds mean. Basics like, "follow me, here watch this, you are full of doo, doo. Your mother wears bloomers," stuff like that.

An owl hoots in the dark spruce overhead. Across the creek, a beaver splashes. My boat rocks gently in the water, as an evening breeze comes up. The moon shines on our tents outside the campfire light. It must be late because it is only dark for two hours this time of year.

"Yea, yea, Miles, so after all this business talk, I have just one question. How much money." I cannot give the reply Seymour wants to hear. Maybe someday. I'm not there yet. I saw the droves of outsiders show up at the RV park ready to sell their souls for the chance to earn $700 a day finding mushrooms. I only know I am not impressed with $700 a day. If I do not bring in $1,000 a day at shows I go to, this is not a good show. The most money I have been paid per hour? I've had two necklaces sell for over $3,000 that took a day to make. But have done better than that. I brought in a $26,000 mammoth tusk that involved three days of work. Yes, gross, not profit. Yes, out of these wages, deduct the costs. The same that can be said for the mushroom pickers getting $700 a day. Out of that comes their food, transportation, etc.

No, Seymour would not be impressed. He wants to know how much I cleared this past year. And paid in taxes. What income bracket am I in? What is my status level, based on my income. Do I own a plane? Can I fly to Norway to watch the eclipse? (As the words to a song ask, 'Where you belong!') The measurement of having arrived, as defined by society. There are a series of questions I never got to, that Seymour asked concerning permits, taxes, insurance, and such costs. My overhead is way down. That is a topic for another day, maybe.

I simply do not have the same values Seymour has. Because of how I dress, talk, live, I am, and always will be, lower class. I'm not going to change people's minds. That's fine. Or no, it would be nice actually, to be respected... but then I am respected among certain people. Just not anyone close to me! Ha!

There are some basis truths to discover. If someone else who had a degree produced the end product I have, they would not exactly be Gods among the mortals, but would be rich and famous. Galleries would more likely carry the work and pay a better percent. The public wants to know you are somebody—measured in pieces of paper in frames on your wall. Pieces of paper also make activities legal. I could be the best hunter in the world, but if I take someone out hunting without a certificate saying how qualified I am, I go to jail. I could create a masterpiece work of art. If my name is not associated with a prestigious university, or famous craft guild, it is difficult to get the public to call it good. Few will say they want it, get someone to buy it. Gem magazine would not even allow me to buy an add in their magazine. The same issue I had an article in.

People are sheep. They want to follow what others are doing, need someone else to tell them yes it is good, and yes, you want that. There are some free thinkers. There are ways to get noticed, get ahead. It just has not been as easy as I thought. Also, not just anyone could do it. There is no way Seymour could walk in my shoes. I could not walk in his shoes and have what he has. Three airplanes, and a three-story house. I will never make 200 grand profit in a year like Seymour. He will never make $26,000 in three days as I have.

"Seymour, the great perfect plan is harder than I thought, that's all. As I go along this path, I learn more how long the road is."

Seymour and I both know someone well, whose retirement plan has a glitch in it. Someone dipped into the retirement bank account, and other assets. The predicted date by which our good friend could retire is pushed ahead by a lot of years. I believed the economy would catch up to his bank account. In other words, interest paid does not even keep up with inflation. Money in the bank is going backwards. $100,000 in the bank in the 70s buys half the goods today. But interest on it left since then is not going to double your money in three decades.

My personal view is to put that money into commodities that are not likely to go down in value. In the 70s gold was under $300 an ounce. Today, well over $1,000. Closer to $2,000. Prime real estate, coins, stamp collections, antiques, memorabilia, historic records, exotic wood, and on and on… I think are pretty safe to invest in. That would do much better than one percent interest in the bank. There might be a few things that have gone down in value, but it's not rocket science to predict what is not likely to do down, stuff we need that is getting scarce, for example. Some art is timeless and will never drop in value.

"I'd rather trust the sure thing, Miles, and not gamble with my life savings. How many people do we hear of in the news that went broke trying to get rich quick and invest in a scheme of some kind or other." It's a matter of how we feel about it. There may be no sure way to predict the future, or foolproof plan to guarantee it.

The fire is low, just a bed of coals. Mosquitoes are moving in, now that the fire smoke is down. The owl has gone quiet. *I'm glad Seymour has stopped asking how my back is doing.* A bunch of years ago I got injured on the job, needed back surgery. Considered ten percent disabled. Our survey jobs are not going to be the rough ones we used to specialize in. Seymour as well, is feeling his age.

"You have time to get to your Chandler Lake property?" Part of his retirement plan was to invest in a beautiful piece of land on a lake in the Brooks range. Post card beautiful and very isolated. No one gets there without a float plane in summer.

"Yes, Miles, the wife and I took the sled dogs and hung out there over the winter to do some trapping." No. I do not envy him. He has paid dearly for his lifestyle. A price I would not pay. He dislikes the office work connected to the job very much. I'm not sure Seymour is a happy person. "Yes Miles, we had a few quiet weeks with just us and the dogs. It was a good experience."

I'm glad for him. But guess what. That two-week experience defines twenty-five years of my life. I do not say that, but think his reply would be, "Yea, but what have you got for a future? No retirement income." When Seymour retires, he will be able to support his three planes, have full medical coverage, and a hefty yearly income. He thinks I stand a good chance of ending up on the street. *We shall see. Time will tell.*

After four days of tent life and survey work, I boat Seymour back to the road system in the village. Weather has been nice. A sprinkle of rain for half an hour a day, a few clouds off and on, mixed with intense interior Alaska sun. I'm running my brand new four stroke 60 horse Mercury outboard. I need a boat and engine combination that travels economically, is fast, and hauls the load I want. A new gauge tells me rpm, engine temperature, gallons of fuel being burned per hour to the tenth of a gallon, and total gallons consumed since reset.

I use my GPS to check speed. I keep close track and adjust travel for best economy. I will end up consuming over 100 gallons of fuel traveling for three days in the wilderness. I'm very weight critical, and constantly monitoring boat trim, speed, fuel consumption. Breaking down or running out of fuel is not an option. No one but me knows where I am going next. Not even Iris knows the survey job is over. No one knows within 500 miles where I am over the next week, beyond what I chose to say about the subject. Conditions are good to go look for mammoth tusks.

I'm pleasantly surprised there is little to no traffic on the river. I assume, because of the fast rise in fuel costs. One result, is increased game on the river. In a few hours I see a bear, seven moose, lots of geese with young and eagles. I stop at two favorite fishing holes. I get one big pike, take a picture, and turn it loose. I catch several more and have a few broken fish lines from extremely big fish. I have my fun and press on. This fishing gives me a needed break in a fifteen hour river run in an open boat.

I spend a night at one of my fishing holes. My boat is set up with four holes drilled in the gunnels that accept four tent poles of my dome tent. I set the tent up on the front deck of the boat. The holes keep the tent secure and anchored... a substitute for tent pegs. This is 'relevant' because speed, efficiency, how to run camp life, has a lot to do with such a trip and its success. I am able to be in bed half an hour after stopping. I'm up at 5:00 am and traveling by 6:00 am. My travel time is checked going by various checkpoints. I'm trying to hold my fuel consumption at two gallons an hour. *Almost unheard of.* Average boats burn five gallons an hour and some burn ten gallons an hour. One guy I know burns twenty gallons an hour. Some boaters do not even believe I'm telling the truth. I smile to myself, *Many feel my entire life, my whole story is crap, made up.* It's part of being a storyteller, but hmm.

Much has to do with not necessarily wanting to be taken seriously. *If you were a gold prospector, and found a vein of gold, what would you do if you did not want others to get the gold off an area you could not stake a claim on? Bring in some fool's gold. Brag a lot about how good it is. Be inconsistent and vague with stories. Travel alone. Be eccentric. 'Oh, yeah, it's just goofy you again.' Come and go unnoticed. No one follows you, thinks of robbing you. Your doors are open. Your 'stuff' looks like, and much is, used junk you brag about. I'm paranoid? If so, I did not start out in life this way. I was taught. I am in fact concerned with my openness in my first few books coming back to bite me. People who care about me are concerned as well. I ask what 'truth' is! Is it mostly an interpretation? Shared agreements?*

I daydream. My mind wanders as I eat up the many hours behind the steering wheel. I asked a math question when my father was trying to help me. He said, "The answer depends on what math you are studying." I was annoyed. I have to pass the test. This is not helping.

"What happens when two lines are extended indefinably?" One math says they form a parabolic curve of the universe. One says they form a circle around the earth. Another says they meet at the horizon. All these answers and more are correct. Likewise, one and one is not always two. Put two people together and you might get twins. Chemical reactions can produce more than the sum of the ingredients put together. Do I really write on the test 'it depends!' I think not! My idiot father is not much help! My father with his three PhD degrees smiles and thinks I have a long road ahead of me yet. It is interesting when 'what it takes to survive in the wilds' is summed up. I'd say one basic truth is, "The ability to see many answers to the same question." Reality itself must be in flux. Real is not the same for a savage as for a civilized person. Being asked, even ordered, to stick to the facts and tell the truth is an oxymoron.

"Where are you?" Can be answered with GPS coordinates, answered spiritually, morally, legally, in my head. I am on another planet and that is the truth. I have stepped through the star gate. I am a time traveler. Shaman. Believer in things not of this world. *Am I legally insane? If so, why does it work? What then is the secret to surviving where so few have and can go?*

I'm in love with my long twenty-four foot narrow easy to push boat. It's important not to have to stop anywhere along the way for help or gas, etc., where I might get asked questions. Gas in the villages is two dollars more a gallon than in civilization. When I see what the mushroom pickers are willing to do for $700, I understand better why the truth will not set us free. People would kill to be in the situation I am in.

I get to a village early in the day and make a brief half hour stop. There is no longer a restaurant and the owner of the store is 'gone' and cannot look at my artwork, or the book I had hoped to sell to help pay for the trip. *Making a river trip to sell my art, explains why I took a trip.* It is a little scary, taking a chance to spend $500 to make this trip. I could come back empty-handed. It would be nice to at least deliver some artwork. "Oh, well!" It seems most of the small villages are dying. So I eat chips and pickles for lunch, purchased at another village store.

I see no one at fish camps, and no boats till the Yukon 800 racers zoom by. I forgot this is the weekend of the big 800 mile long river boat race. Their engine is smaller than mine, doing seventy-five miles an hour, while I feel lucky to be doing twenty miles an hour. Ha! It's pretty awesome to watch. The entire boat is out of the water, with only the propeller touching. Prop spray is twice as long as the boat, and seen before the boat.

I get to my fossil hunting spot. *One of the many legal mines and native claims I have permission to hunt on.* There is enough time to make a first look before making camp. After thirty years, this is part of the routine. First, I note someone else has been here, *but maybe a month ago.* Not great news, because anything that got exposed over the winter, and after ice breakup, might have been found already. I'm looking at a 100 foot tall, frozen bluff towering above the river, which is forty feet deep here. It cuts the cliff, and along with rain and sun, causes the cliff to calf like a glacier with pieces falling away from the face in sections the size of houses. This is the part where the sane gulp and tell me I am not taking them anywhere near this cliff. As I cruise slowly under the cliff, sections give way, dropping ahead of me, and behind me. To be hit would, of course, mean to die.

Do the math. If the cliff is two miles long, and a section fifty feet falls once a minute, what are the odds that a section will fall right where I am? Once a section fell, and I got caught by the edge and thrown flat into my boat, but it was not enough mud to sink the boat. Several times huge sections fell that made tsunami like waves. I had to turn and gun the engine to stay ahead of the wave. I figure it takes about ten seconds for the cliff to give and hit the water. I can react in about one second with several seconds to spare. Yes, nerves are somewhat on edge. Reaction time is fine tuned. *I'm told people get addicted to danger.* My sense of safety might well be an illusion. So what. If it works. *Remember the Crazy Lawson story?* Yes! He said he was camped across the bluffs at the bone yard years ago and the cliff gave way. He was camped on the other side of the river and lost his entire camp in the enormous wave sent out. *Do you believe that?* I think he lost his camp somehow and blamed it on a tidal wave.

The permanently frozen cliff is very active today, due to heat and rain. Some years produce more change in the cliff than other years. The river undercuts unevenly. The most productive areas will also be the most dangerous. There are spots that produce relics regularly, possibly daily. Most mammoth hunters feel as I do, we find less than one percent of what falls in the river and is gone forever. Today, peregrine falcons are guarding their nest. They are not happy. I hear them scream, circling overhead. I look up and the sun flits between the twisted stunted trees high overhead. The falcons dart swiftly, trying to catch the swallows that nest in holes in the cliff.

Sometimes I see evidence of more activity than just looking from a boat. Lawson has built steam contraptions from fifty-five gallon drums and hose, to steam sections of the exposed ice lens. He and others use climbing gear and go off the top. I have my own methods. Simple. I am not set up to climb, do not build equipment, do not stay long. I get the easy stuff. If there is a secret, it is to show up at the right time, regularly, for short periods of time. I try to use my brain rather than my brawn. A lot of time is spent just looking and thinking. Studying the layers, trying to be in the exact right layer. It takes experiences to recognize layers. More experience to date them. Each hunter has his own methods he swears by, and feels everyone else is not doing so well, because they will not listen.

Years ago, in one exposed spot, I found a baby mammoth jaw. Recalling this, I see the river has washed out some bones and pieces of ivory. Along the shore, more are found using a ski pole as a prod. Wood and other objects make a thud as the prod tip sticks. Ivory, or old bones, go 'tink,' as the prod tip slides off. Some pieces under a foot of water, not visible, are found by sound. I reach under water and grab up bones. It's one of my secrets. Mine owners go by the same place and find nothing. Most do not try. They have gold fever, not fossil fever. Sometimes, I give the miners a gift or payment. However, this implies I'm finding fossils on their land. They'd rather have no knowledge if asked.

What I find in this one spot might cover my gas costs. Nothing terribly exciting, just a vertebrae, some small bones good for knife handles. But I am going downstream, so cannot go slow. I know on my upstream pass I can take more time. For now, I just want to find any easy stuff before choosing where to concentrate my efforts. In my early years I would find a tiny bone, get excited, spend all day in this spot, poking in the mud, lifting logs in hopes of more. For all I know, half a mile downriver at the next Native claim is a full tusk, just lying in the mud on the beach. The tusk might fall in the river in five minutes and be lost. Now and then, well 'twice,' I found gold nuggets in the thin gravel layer where the fossils are. Gold and fossils are often together, as prospectors know. I do not have gold fever. In fact, I am even a little turned off by gold. I do not hate it, but it stands for greed, a symbol of wealth, used to back up our dollar, but a reminder nothing backs up our money but the stock market now. I do not like to be reminded. I do not turn gold down! Gold is just not my God.

I learned over the years to study the cliff and find a thin shell layer—the bottom of ancient ponds. Some mammoths might have broken through ice and drowned, or a flash flood drops a body in a hole. Old logjams are good places to look, on the upstream side, down low. A dead mammoth floating downstream is upside down, because of the heavy tusks. The hooked tusks dragging on the river bottom snag under a log jam. If I see any bones in the cliff, the tusks will usually be lower down, as they sank further because of heavier weight. By using these bits of knowledge, I am not just randomly looking all over the cliff.

The legality is more clear, if the finds come from the river, or at its edge, legally defined 'below the high water mark.' Waterways fall under state jurisdiction. For now, possibly 'today only.' The state and the Federal government do not agree on what to do about fossil hunters, or even who has jurisdiction over navigable waters. It's best not to get involved in the argument in a test case.[1] It's better to beg for forgiveness, then ask for permission. It's good to be caught between two powerful groups who hate each other and wanting to make a point to the other. In the muscle flexing, one might slip between the habeas corpus and writ of rights. *Or one might get crushed between two stone burrs.*

I'm tired, so make camp on a gravel sandbar. My camp used to be a mile up a creek in this area, out of sight. This creek has lots of mosquitoes and thick mud. In the past, I collected interesting river rocks from here, took them home, sliced them with my rock saw, polished them in a tumbler, then used them in my art. There is unique red jasper with white quartz veins, green jade like stones, and Nowitna River agate. Time and practice have shown me which rocks polish well, and are commercially desired. There is also an area with prehistoric wood, on its way to being coal. Redwood from when Alaska was a tropic. I find this useful as an art material, and known to the rest of the world as, 'bog wood.' Between the rocks and the wood, I have a variety of financial reasons to write off the boat costs.

I make camp in the open sun on the gravel and cook several days' worth of stew, which I put in two thermoses that will stay hot for two days. I eat as much as I can, gather some rocks, and go to bed. Through the night I hear the crash of the cliff falling. Almost by the hour the face of the cliff changes, exposing new materials. It is hard to guess how much falls in the river unseen. I get only the few items that fall on a beach, or get hung up or are near the surface by the cliff.

Rain falls much of the night. I'm glad. The cliff is very active with running mud and sliding ice. This makes it much more dangerous, but also more productive. I am passing one very narrow cut, trying to look up while also steering, watching where I am going. "Whump" a cliff gives way behind me. 'SSSSS' sand falls down from 100 feet above. I pay it no mind. I almost turn my head away after craning my neck, looking backwards at the small cut in the ice. Out of the corner of my eye, I spot the tip of a perfect tusk. I know immediately what it is, and begin processing in my mind how to reach it, if possible. I have in the past turned away and left tusks I could not reach. *Oh well, there goes 10 grand.*

I do not think a lot about special equipment. I'm not greedy and not trying to alter the land. I take what is offered and no more. Everyone I know who tried to build steam systems to melt ice and wash the cliff or used fancy climbing equipment and other tools, got into legal trouble. Tusk and others in the business consider the activity is not illegal. For several decades, no one actually got arrested, fined, or jailed. I only heard rumors of ivory being confiscated. No tickets given out. Mammoth hunters discuss what would happen if we demanded a receipt, asked for proof of a confiscation!

Landowners do not want anyone altering things a lot. Just grabbing up what is lying around that the owner missed is acceptable. So my operation is the ski pole, a miner's pick ax, some rope and that's about it. There is ribbon to mark items to notice on the way back, a bag to carry goods in, and clamps to put on tusks to stop them from cracking. The miners and natives whose land I am on might be upset if I did anything to deliberately speed up the ice melt or dumping their land into the river.

I spin the boat around and come up on the cut slower. Another tusk on the other side of the cut. *"Dang!"* But I will have to climb the bank 100 feet downstream, then walk across some hunks of mud fifty feet high, and come down from above. It does not look terribly difficult, except the cliff here is very active. Another huge chunk could fall at any time from above. I take a deep breath and smile. *I love the smell of the rotting 40,000 old bones and vegetation.* Ice fog is in the cut, caused by the frozen mud newly exposed to the warm day. 40,000-year-old seeds sprout after thawing. There are plants I hang on to as I climb, that scientists do not acknowledge exist. Scientists I talk to do not listen to an amateur. *What's it to me if they believe it or not?* Besides, they have proven not to be my friend, and would shut the mine down, declaring the area a national monument. The miner would kill me. Me and my big mouth. So I climb into a world that does not exist. Stuck in time. A cave man with a spear, hunting the tusked mammoth. I pause as I hear him fart around the corner. I pause as I hear the herd crunch grass, stomp, and trumpet.

This sounds so cute and quaint. Yet I have seen, and heard of many more big muscular Viking type fossil hunters, dressed in fur, stopping here. They sense the mammoth, pick up on the energy, so to speak, and cannot handle it. They scream and leave, or go mad. I offer no explanation. Beyond my belief that those who scoff do not like the mathematical odds and will not come near. While the believers feel they have a secret spiritual 'in,' that alters the odds in their favor. Just read John Glenn's story in the book, 'The Right Stuff,' the term test plane fliers used was, 'A high Jesus factor.' Yeah. Like that.

My breath is gone. I am out of shape. Climbing this mud is so hard. The tension of calving cliffs has me work fast to limit exposure to danger. Some way up the mudslide is a mud chunk the size of a skyscraper. Behind the colossal mound, fifty feet up, is another tusk! I will have to think about this one later, as it will be hard to get. Three tusks, a total of 100 grand.

I have to crawl in a mud hole. I am in a tunnel following the light, to get to the mud section with the matching tusks and see getting them will not be difficult. One pulls out easily, no longer frozen in the mud. A perfect five foot 'S' shape, easy to carry at about forty pounds. The tip reaching for the sky, a baby blue. This gets packed back to the boat below me. Once again I ascend the cliff—two eyes staring out of a mud mannequin. The cliff sloughs off so fast it changes by the minute. It is harder to get up because rain is sending down new liquid mud, making quicksand pools I have to cross that were not there an hour ago. I would not have seen up this cut if I had boated by fifteen minutes later than I did. There is little time to stop and rest. The mud sculptures are shifting, sliding, and closing the top off. Trees growing on the top, slowly lean, topple, join the mud river that smells like a compost pile.

When I get to the second tusk, I see there is a part of the skull with teeth in it next to the tusk, froze in the ice. I deal with the tusk first. The pickax has to be used to chip a foot of ice away. After half an hour of work, the tusk slides out easily enough. It matches the first tusk now in the boat, so I have a pair from the same animal. The quick-mud is getting deeper. I almost lose my boot in it. Two matching tusks are now safely in the boat. The ice fog follows me in and out of the cut as in a script out of the twilight zone. I feel like I have gone through the outer limits, each time I enter the ice tunnel.

On the trip back up the mud-scape, I look at the big tusk, and again see it will be hard to retrieve. It is under an overhang the size of a city block, with cracks indicating the mud wants to let go—soon. If it does, it will bury the tusk, me, the mammoth teeth, and maybe even my boat. Pieces of bluff are falling off as this 60,000-year-old frozen time capsule gets weaker. A nonstop hail of baseball size pieces of mud hit the ice and splash me. This was not happening even half an hour ago. These frozen clumps could kill me if they hit me on the head. They are missing me so far, randomly falling every five seconds within a few feet. I cannot hang out here figuring which piece might hit me or do much work. I expect the entire overhang to fall within minutes.

I hear descriptions of being in a war with bullets zinging all-around. The splat of bullets hitting people close by, the swish of bullets through leaves overhead effects those in combat. Some scream and run. Others know there is no way to predict, and simply go calm, and do what needs to be done.

I give up on this tusk and go back to the jaw and teeth. I chip frozen mud as much as I can, but the ice is hard. I make little headway. This could be an entire skull with all the teeth that match the two tusks, or possibly even an entire mammoth. If so, it might be worth 200 grand. The 'might be' and 'if' is the biggest factor here. The reality is, it could take a week to chip just a skull out. I may not have more than a minute or two before I and all this are buried. I need to get the two tusks back to camp and taken care of. *Maybe the ice holding these fossils will thaw more in a few hours.*

I take pictures, knowing this could be the last I see of this. I am exhausted after three round trips from the boat through the muddy slippery passageways.

The first hour is very critical when preserving a tusk. Tusks from this area have been carbon dated between 40,000 and 60,000 years old. Internal stress builds up in the tusk, and when the tight grip of the ice is released, the ivory wants to twist or warp as it thaws. The ivory must be kept out of direct sun while I use hose clamps and baling wire to bind it so it will not expand and crack. It can crack within hours! I had one perfect un-cracked tusk that sold for $26,000. Cracked it is worth $2,000. So I take care of what I have, before worrying about what I do not have yet. After binding the tusks, I tie ropes to them and sink them in the river near camp. This not only keeps them cold and out of the direct sun, it hides them from anyone who comes by, or a plane. They are already so saturated, drying takes a year and will begin when I get home.

After doing this, I am mentally rested, and up to climbing the cliff again. After giving the remaining tusk some thought, I decide I can build a ladder, *but I will have to haul the parts up and build it on the spot.* I have been alone out here, with no other boats or planes for two days. There will be no help or solutions from the outside world. When I get the ladder parts up the cliff, I see the ladder will not possibly be tall enough to be of any help. I try to chop handholds in the dryer area of the cliff. This is not going to work. I make a grapple hook and toss it up to hook the tusk to climb up a rope. The tusk is not exposed in a way to allow something to grab onto it. It is a little out of easy toss range.

The tusk and teeth may fall within easy reach on their own if the cliff does not give way first. I climb back down and slowly boat the rest of the mine claim, looking for easy stuff. There are a few bones and minor things, but I cannot get my mind off the big items out of reach. I go back to the idea of shooting at the big tusk to dislodge it. I had shot at ice around it using most of the shells from the 12-gauge shotgun, the 22 hornet, and the 357 pistol. No use, half the tusk is still frozen in the ice. I'd have to dig six feet into the ice to get it. No way will that happen. It's very dangerous to hang out half a day under an overhang, ready to let go any minute.

I climb up again to check where I had left my ladder parts, rope, carry bag, and machete because it was too hard to carry them all up and down. They have all been buried. More proof I cannot possibly hang out here to do much. I see thicker, deeper, faster moving, mud. The tunnel I crawled through to reach the area has collapsed. There is no way to get to the skull and teeth now. Maybe I can reach the tusk. I find a place to stand with some protection from falling mud where I can see the big tusk well—about six feet of it is exposed. I could shoot it in half, rather than shoot the ice to dislodge the entire tusk. Better to have 6 six feet of ivory than none.

I need to make a boat trip to the nearest village where I can buy more bullets for one of my guns—or borrow or buy a gun and ammo. If I'm lucky, the tusk could fall after more thawing, and land closer to the boat, piece of cake, no problems. The tusk might even be waiting for me at the river's edge when I get back! And the teeth? I could shoot them down too, as I can see them now from the river where I could not before, showing me that the cliff is changing fast. This section has moved twenty-five feet or more in a day.

I know the distance to the nearest village, and take off, but it is 100 miles round trip. *I will have to buy gas.* I get to the village and right off meet someone I know! My friend will lend me his moose rifle and box of old bullets! He tells me I cannot buy gas today. The two gas sources are open three days a week! *Good grief!* He lends me five gallons of gas I must replace. I travel back in pouring rain. I must get to the tusk fast and not wait until the next day. This rain will wash mud off the face of the cliff faster.

At 10:00 pm, after being on the river since 6:00 am, I climb the cliff once again. I slip and fall, but catch myself. Once, years ago, I slipped and slid to the edge of the cliff with not much to grab on to but mud. I almost went over and into the river. I think it is not possible to survive falling in the river here, because of the strong current, whirlpools, and icy cold water. Falling in is not an option.

The quick mud is terrible now, and everywhere. I had found that the best way for me to keep from sinking was to run fast over the surface. I lose both boots while running, and have to decide if I will forget my boots, and live without them. I need my boots, so lay face down in the mud; reaching out at arm's length pulling the boots out, while missiles of new mud fall all around me from above. One chunk misses my head by six inches and splashes mud in my eyes so I cannot see. Blind, I back away from the edge of the cliff, onto a safer spot.

Finally, I get to the place I can stand and shoot in relative safety. The rifle blast could start a landslide but I cannot dwell on that. After twenty-six shots, the half tusk falls within reach! Yes! But I have to go into the heaviest mud falling zones to get it. I have a piece of rope to tie to it, because the tusk is hard to carry! If it falls, it could slide down and into the river. The rope allows me to drop the tusk if I trip, or need a break, and can grab the rope to hold it in place where it lands.

This half tusk weighs about a 100 pounds and is very hard to carry in the mud. Super human strength flows through me like a drug. *Maybe $10,000 worth of ivory.* I'm not letting go, or losing it now! The cave man with his spear grunts and shoulders his find. The hairy, ill glad creature that is me walks like an ape dragging his bone. Push, pull, tug, carry. I am amazingly exhausted when I arrive at the boat. It is now midnight under the never setting sun.

I cannot leave the teeth overnight. They will be gone. As tired as I am, I bring the boat around to the teeth. If I shoot around them, they will fall—maybe land in the mud, not the river. I have to forget the thought of the whole $100,000 skull up there for sure, maybe an entire skeleton. By morning, it will all be in the river. A story about one that got away. After four shots, one tooth falls and lands in the mud! The other tooth, after more shots, pops loose! I am thrilled it lands in the boat! A nice big $400 one. But it hits the boat, bounces out, and lands in forty feet of water. My elation sinks with it. I need to focus on what I have, not what I lost. Two matched tusks, a 100 pounds of another tusk, a 100 pounds of bones, and a tooth. It is time to head home to take care of all this. I barely have enough gas to get to the village to buy more gas for the rest of the trip.

To save gas, the weight in the boat must be carefully distributed. I am headed upstream, but can barely get on step and hold there without losing that sweet spot. In the rain, I travel exactly sixteen miles an hour.

I stop at one of the fish camps along the way, now occupied by an old man who waved as I went by twice. My friend in the village told me the man's name, so I stop and introduce myself. I need to warm up, anyway—I am soaking wet from the pouring rain. My adrenaline is gone. I am shivering. The old Native lets me in his warm cabin, tells me about a boat he is excited to be building, and how the fishing is going. He has about ten King Salmon. He shows me a wind generator and solar panels he invested in. Part of his Native land settlement government money.

After a while he asks my name again. Asks if I have a book I wrote. It turns out he has a copy of my 'Going Wild,' here in the cabin! He enjoyed the book, and for sure, now knows who I am! He is nice enough to give me two gallons of gas to make sure I make it to the village. His last name is the same as the fish cop I know, Gary.

"Yes, he's my brother!" The Alaska wilderness tends to be a small world, where we know people, who know other people, who are related to those who are friends.

In the village, I return the rifle to my friend's daughter, then buy gas at six dollars a gallon. I buy five gallons for the new friend who gave me a couple gallons and replace the five I borrowed from the guy I got the rifle from. I add some more to make sure I get home. I'm into this trip for $200 more now. I do not care, considering what I found. I have never come back empty-handed. Usually what I find at least pays for the trip. Any trip could be a financial loss. There are no guarantees.

Sometimes, I arrive a day after the area has been picked clean by other hunters who may not have had the landowners' permission. *For sure, we do not want more people interested in quick, easy profits! Remember to remind excited people who ask—it took us five trips before we found any ivory at all. I have been at this for over twenty-five years.* I have to remind myself to be quiet and evasive, as my first inclination is to happily share what is going on, even happy to share a great source of income with others.

I stash my heavy find at a favorite place I can find again that no one else knows about, or can easily find. I'd be happier having my valuables away from the area I hunt, in case I get a visit.

"Yup, just hanging out fishing! Visiting my buddy just upstream."

As the engine purrs, relieved of its heavy load, I daydream. My thinking stems from something very basic, based on what our country was founded on. What is the single biggest difference between my country and any other? Maybe freedom. But that freedom is based on the belief that each of us is capable of running our own lives, and can be trusted to do so. We should all vote and have a say. We have the right to choose our occupation. There is an assumption in all this, people are inherently good and capable! There was some argument when the constitution and bill of rights were being formed, whether or not this is true! Many argued that no, only landowners should vote. And Men. And only white ones.

There has been evidence throughout history, that people cannot run their own lives, and need to be told what to do by superior beings. Secrets need to be kept. The majority need to be left in the dark. The majority just needs to work hard without knowing what they are doing, or why. It was a big deal and radical concept for the people to break from the old Feudal system. There were important people of rank, with titled positions posed to sign the constitution, that did not want to see equality! The Queen of England had granted large tracts of land, like Pennsylvania, my part of the world.

The bottom line might be, "Were we correct in assuming people are inherently good, and can run their own lives, or was that an error?" Our country today behaves as if that concept is not workable. Do I wish to join in this thought and give up my belief in the average person? To be, or not to be, is the question. I had not told the native at the fish camp I had tusks in my boat. They were under a tarp in the bilges. When he asked why I was on the river I had replied, "Look at these cool rocks!" Pointing to the bow of the boat where the rocks are proudly, prominently displayed.

All he said was, "Yes, I see." Another idiot on the river. Too polite to hurt my feelings.

I add, "Yes, I can slice and polish them. I take them to a big rock show in Tucson and make some ok money!" This native knows about the fossils not far away, but partly it is taboo among the natives to disturb any burial site. I'm not sure if the fossils might be the souls of ancestors? The term is 'Uclanny,' but do not know the translation. Also, many people consider the area too dangerous! Many try to find fossils, thinking it is easy. They do not find any on the first or second attempt and give up. I suppose it is like looking for arrowheads, cannon balls, dinosaur bones, buried treasure, any kind of artifact. It's not easy till you know how. *If you make a living at it and enjoy it, then it's easy, anything is, when you are good at it.* Some natives tell me there is no superstition against collecting these fossils. This is just an excuse to keep the white man away. I do not know the truth.

At Square Crossing, I get stuck on a sandbar. Dang! I am tired. Traveling in the pouring rain and fog, going too fast for conditions. I am on the sandbar three hours walking in the water, trying to rock the boat off the mud. I realize I am making no headway and finally get out the bumper jack I carry for emergencies, and jack the boat up, toss it off the jack, and move the boat to deep water in fifteen minutes. The rain stops. The weather gets a little clear, so the rest of the day goes better. As the fog lifts, the swans on the other side of the river wake up, making some, 'let's fly' sounds.

I spend a night at Hot Springs to rest, arriving there at 2:00 am. There is an empty guest cabin a friend keeps. He told me where the key is. It is fine for me to stay a night when I am traveling through, just leave it as it was when I arrived. I use my sleeping bag on the bed so I do not have to wash his sheets. His cabin is right off the slough, so I do not have far to carry my food and sleeping bag. Once again, "Found a lot of cool rocks, check it out!"

I am not excited about my finds until I get home, rest up and calm down. I use the old three-wheeler, since my four wheeler is rented out to the Cambodian mushroom pickers. The two matching blue tusks, the huge half tusk and other fossils are loaded into the cart, covered with tarp, and hauled home through the back roads. No one sees me. My shop is bigger than the house. Two front doors open so I can drive in with the cart. The doors are closed.

The yard has thick vegetation. I have been slowly turning this into real hedges. The plan is for the hedges to be edibles, like raspberries, currents, and dwarf fruit trees. Five crab apple trees have been planted, along with several chokecherries. The vegetation is thick enough I have privacy for the most part. I have learned from experience, hardly anyone else gets up at 5:00 am to begin having fun. Usually it is 8:00 am before there is significant activity on the road.

At five in the morning, I am out with a garden hose in the grass yard, hosing mud off the tusks, and spraying in the cracks of the larger piece, getting all the clay off. This is the first time I can inspect up close what I found and get a better idea of value. The matching blue tusks are not big, but perfect, with graceful double curves like an S. Combined weight of the two is only fifty pounds. In the raw, I think $200 a pound. My calculator is punched, my chin scratched and I think, yes, $10,000 would be reasonable 'as is.' Possibly twice this after being dried and sanded.

I rub my mix of Elmer's glue and water over the tusks, cover them with black plastic, then apply hose clamps every foot. The glue soaks into the surface, mixing with moisture in the tusk and seals the tusk so it dries slowly. Once the glue dries, moisture leaving the tusk slows. There is now an even transfer of moisture to the atmosphere, which helps stop the tusks from warping and cracking. I do the same to the big half tusk.

This one I will cut up to sell to carvers, and use on my own work. I should, potentially, make more per pound for smaller pieces. The outer bark can sell as high as $30 an ounce. Close to $500 a pound, as cut up rectangles with a flat side for knife makers. Times 100 pounds. *But no, this is the price only for the outer bark,* maybe thirty pounds… potentialy $15,000. Minus all my costs of cutting, preparing, advertising, doing shows, travel, etc., etc. So the gears in my mind spin as the calculator clicks. Potential this, maybe that, realistically some other number. This is actually a very important time in the business process. I get my mind wrapped around what I have and its value. I take into account my costs, like the 250 gallons of gas. In this way, as I am selling it off, I have an idea what I expected to get, and what I have to have. I can decide how much I want to cut up into knife scales, how much to keep for my use, what discount I can offer, and such.

"Miles, I am used to getting tusks for $100 a pound. That's $5,000."

"I agree that is normal, however, this is rare blue, and it is uncommon to have two matched tusks off the same animal. That makes $7,000 a good price. I'd normally ask $10,000, but for cash I go much less." This buyer in my shop is very interested, because he has a skull needing two tusks and these tusks will fit. His finished product of a complete mammoth head with tusks will be worth 200 grand. An investment of seven grand is nothing, considering his profit.

I'm hesitant to sell wet, and so cheap. So it is all the same to me if he does not buy them. I can dry and prepare them, and in a year get twenty grand if I chose. My buyer knows that. We do the deal on a handshake. He counts out $7,000 in piles of $100. The single bare light bulb overhead swings. We are on our hands and knees in sawdust and river silt, making piles of money on empty spaces on the floor. We are both dressed in jeans and work clothes, dirty faces. *This is a scene out of an Indiana Jones movie.*

It is fine to take much less money now, cash, no hassle, no advertising. I avoid wondering if I will get paid, or risk it getting stolen, or not drying well, and losing value. There are all the other fossils to sell. $400 for the tooth, another grand for some bones. Much is mixed into the general population of dead things. *A blend is nice.* Even I do not know what year, or the exact place any one item came from. If I do not know, how can anyone else? Nor do I know how much I made. Some is traded, some made into objects of art, sold raw, donated, or returned to me carved, I can shrug my shoulders. It would be difficult to unwind the time line, wrap and bow tie an event into a neat time/money package. I keep good records, but one piece of ivory can stretch into five years of business dealings.

Two blue mammoth tusks, wrapped in old army blankets, are loaded into a black van backed up to the big shop doors. It's a back muddy unpaved street in Nenana, Alaska, with no traffic today. I forget his name, do not know exactly where he lives, and do not want to know.

Sam, the shroom man, is interested in buying a mammoth tusk. He's a man with a lot of cash right now. I'm concerned where he got information that I have a tusk.

Guessing from Josh. I reply, "Sure, Sam, I buy, then trade them, sort of a dealer. Sometimes I find them. I have nothing right now." I am guessing Sam is not interested in the half a tusk, certainly not pieces. He may have been interested in the matching blue. Sam has no knowledge of how to properly dry them. They would not be safe for normal display in civilian hands for a year. These tusks went to the right person who is in the business and knows how to take care of them. The buyer will not come back to me later, wanting his money back because the ivory cracked. If Sam is with organized crime, he is not the sort I to want to deal with if he wants his money back later!

Sam is puzzled. "But I heard."

Well, forget what you heard! I just look puzzled. He shakes his head like, *'everyone is right, this guy is full of crap, nice enough guy, but you can't believe what he says or what you hear.'* I add a foolish, feebleminded grin to help his thoughts along. I understand why Superman has to be Clark Kent when he is not on the job.

"So how is the shroom business Sam? Pickers need supplies, anyone to pick up, need moving around? I need to check on the guys renting the wheeler from me and get paid."

Sam informs me, "I hear the wheeler is broke down. I do not know the details. You have a deal with them, not me, so it is not my concern. I suggested everything go through me. Now you are going to find out why."

I am not sure what he means. At the communal fire pit at the RV park where the Cambodians hang out, I recognize one of the guys who knows a little English and is involved in the rental. He sees me and is happy I am here.

With a big smile and outstretched hand, he speaks first. "Good see you! Va-we good. Machine, she broke. No run. Want know when you fix! We need fix, still need!"

I ask, "So where is my four wheeler?"

"Wheeler, she cross river, up trail broke! You go get, fix!"

I ask, "And where is my rent money?"

"No rent money, she broke. We no using. You fix. We rent. Hurry, fix!"

Now I have to cross the Nenana River in the boat with my bicycle to peddle out the trail, just to see what is wrong with my wheeler. Several hours later I am at my broke down four wheeler. The gear case has a hole in it. Looks to me like someone ran it over a big rock at a fast speed and bottomed out, broke the gear case. Something inside came loose, and the transmission is not transferring engine power to the wheels. The engine starts and runs, but oil squirts out the side, and no transmission. Fixing this means for sure, getting it in a shop, tearing it down, replacing vital internal parts. Hundreds of dollars minimum. Possibly, *no can fix, buy new four wheeler.* First, I have to fetch this machine from the wilds and get it to the road system.

I decide the three-wheeler can be used. Not with the cart, though. Maybe the dog sled, where I can roll the broken machine easily onto the sled and tie it in. I decide doing all this with the boat is not going to work. The best solution is to wait till winter and come across the frozen river with the snow machine and sled to haul it across the ice. I will be without it for months, and will spend hundreds of dollars. I am offered $200 for rental for the few days it was used. It is hard for the Cambodians to come up with $200. They are slave labor, getting paid nothing but room and board, with a few dollars a day left over. In my view, they owe me, they broke it. It is their fault they ran it up on a big rock at high speed!

"If it was yours, and you owned it and you ran it up on such a rock and broke it, you would have to pay the same to fix it! Treat it like it is yours!" I tell Mr. no-speak-um-good-English.

"No, no! Belong you! You fix! When done? We still need! Want to rent, you fix!" I can see well enough this crew had enough trouble coming up with $200. There is simply no way they can come up with the $2,000 they owe me for wrecking my equipment. Sam chuckles. He thinks it is funny. I say to the disappointed Cambodians, "You walk now! Me walk now!"

There is zero sense of my loss, guilt, or being sorry they broke it. Happy smiles! It is my problem. They are slaves, responsible for nothing. Sam supplies them with everything they need and gives them nothing they cannot afford. The Cambodians wonder why I am upset, what the problem is. Being upset is on me. This has nothing to do with them. They feel sorry for me.

"What good life, if you live upset?" They say to me. Yes, I see. It is better to let them walk, then have them owe $2,000 after breaking someone else's equipment. These slaves are happier dealing with mafia Sam than me. Interesting. I file this away as a life experience not learned in school.

There are camps to move, supplies to haul. Every day, trips on the river. The money rolls in as I deal with Sam, the mafia-man. There is often time to stop and fish while I wait for families to get their mushrooms packed and loaded in my boat. The guy I lent my .22 rifle to, greets me at the camp I dropped him off at. He and several others are eating a swan he shot, with feathers all over the place as evidence. I am very upset, as it is illegal for anyone but local subsistence people to hunt swans. Swans are not endangered, but not a good thing to consider as a food source! Joe public loves swans, and would go ballistic, knowing of swan feathers hanging out of illegal Cambodian mouths. As the responsible local in charge, I'd be the one going to jail.

The guys would not know or understand, so I say nothing. Not liking to see waste, I save one wing thrown off in the brush. *Perhaps I can find a use for the wing bone or feathers one day.* I can legally hunt swans and trade them to other subsistence people. In forty years I have killed only two swans. Truthfully, I am more concerned with the ethics of the situation than the legality. If something is killed, nothing should be wasted. That is a higher law than man's.

It was probably illegal for me to give these illegals a gun! I never thought of that. My first concern is bears. I suspected they would hunt hare, rabbit, and small game. *A swan! Dang!* We load the camp into the boat. This group has been drying the mushrooms on their own here in the woods. Sam pays more dry, so there is some incentive to provide a better product and earn more money.

We deliver fifty pounds of dry morels to Sam, who has two guards with machine guns in front of his tent. Under armed escort, he gets the mushrooms over to my shop in safe storage in the steel building.

Replacing the house wiring myself. Old fuse box gets breaker.

One of the joys and rewards of wilderness life is learning how to make do with what you have. Without the proper wiring tools, it is possible to modify and repair as necessary.

Since Nenana is in a flood zone, and I have been flooded out before, I work on a flood plan with Iris who is not familiar with flooding. In this way, if there is a natural disaster, or 'event,' we will have a plan to implement. Part of survival is being ready for events likely to happen that effect our survival. Having some basic skills, even drills, is helpful. I recall even mountain men of the past had survival gear stored in a bag hung in a tree away from the cabin. If there is a fire, flood, earthquake, they only have to make it out the cabin door.

Flood danger readiness ahead of time

Equipment can be stored higher. Turn old freezer on the side for storage? Use pallets to gain height. Have sandbags available. Be aware of, part of, a local community plan. Know who has a ham radio or CB if power goes out. Locate community high ground used to park cars. Is there a community freezer? Store weatherproof bag with survival gear so everyone knows where it is and can be easily grabbed if you need to run out the door. Keep a canoe in the yard if in a flood zone. Have a gas operated water pump. I mention 'division of labor.' "Iris, you focus on things indoors, food electrical appliances. I can be outdoors focusing on equipment."

THERE IS a lot of business to catch up since I have been away dealing with the shroom people. I'm involved in the library, the chamber, the Wellness group. There is the internet business to run, with emails I have delayed replying to. I review files and where I am at with my various interests.

Nenana Wellness Coalition

Minutes taken by Miles

Chaired by Tim Horn

Reports

Ah yes, here we are, what I said:

Miles briefly gave a history and update on the Chamber of Commerce because the WIN group was interested in who runs the city open market space, which some of us wish to use to sell produce from. Basically, 'yes' the Chamber runs this, but the chamber is not a strong entity at the moment, and not had a meeting in a while.

Miles is polling the Chamber board, trying to get the open market land changed over to the Lions Club. Bill and Miles are putting out fliers announcing the first free cycle. Bill made up the fliers, announcing the feed and free table. Hopefully, this will be an ongoing idea to help others in the community with items they need. Good food and clothing are a priority. This is a 'free cycle' event trying to get used goods into the hands of the needy.

We had a full agenda today and our time was totally filled with the topic of the day, a very productive meeting.

Meeting ends at 2:00 pm

This Wellness group seems to be catching on, with more community members involved, doing things for the community. I enjoy being part of this and find reward in sharing the accomplishments. I'm one of its 'founding fathers.' A Saturday open market, or farmers' market sounds like a good thing.[2] I believe in our community taking care of ourselves and not being so dependent on outside help, government grants and such. I feel a healthy community is one that can support itself. A healthy community means a healthy me. Even though I have believed in being an individual, and explored that, I realize we are social beings who depend on each other. It is not possible to stand alone and do well. Partly that is not allowed! The answer may not be to rebel, be angry, fighting for my rights! I shall explore joining my tribe. I hope to find social rewards more acceptable than I have seen in the past.

I helped get the community garden going, volunteered to rototill it, helped cover the greenhouse structure. Other volunteers did other things. Some Indian grant money got us seeds and soil. Can we live without these grants? I begin acquiring heirloom seeds and saving them for the next season.

Hi Miles: We are working on our next Made In Alaska Newsletter and will list our workshops in it. Have you been able to confirm the availability of the Communities Center for our use?

Thanks,

Bill Webb, Program Manager/Agent
Made In Alaska

THIS IS an ongoing effort to get help to artists, by authenticating their work as Alaskan. The tourists might pay more if they knew this was for sure local, made in Alaska. Bill Web is educating people on how the program works, why it matters, how to go about getting the sticker and related topics. I found a place for him to set up for his presentation. This should have been a Chamber of Commerce effort. I still do not understand why our Chamber has fallen apart. Partly the politics. Meanwhile, things need to get done!

Sarah S. McConnell [ffssm@uaf.edu]

Oh, Miles, I'm so sorry you couldn't get on the teleconference! Thank you for trying, and for sharing your comments here. I'm glad the class was helpful to you, and I'm forwarding your comments to Madeline.

Oh yes, someone from the university is working on a health fair in Nenana. There is some talk about the university experimental farm getting involved. Our community might be working with experimental far north organic varieties of seeds. My biggest interest is the possibility of us getting hold of some far north fruit trees! Siberia has come up with a variety of pear. There are rumors of far north cherries. For sure, there are some apple trees that might survive. I have crab apple trees I planted, just waiting for regular apple grafting! I need to learn how to graft! I have taken some classes but think this is more of an art than a science in the far north.

Iris is somewhat interested, as I am, in what we might grow here. She likes the concept, but it is a lot of work in her mind, compared to getting food at the store. Iris reminds me we need to be thinking of retirement now! Not work!

Iris believes in food stamps, and any program that offers help of any kind, basically for free. "Because we qualify!" *How do you argue against free stuff?* Her life situation is different from mine. She worked for others all her life. It was work—she did not get paid to have fun. I hear a similar story from many different people. My son's mother had a similar experience, having worked for a company twelve years, then was let go with no notice. Arrives at work and a sign on the door, 'closed.'

Iris is glad those years are over! They were not fun or happy years! She feels retired now. However, it will be a few years before she is really old enough to qualify for social security. Her last job sort of messed her over and forced her to quit after years of faithful service. *Why is that my problem?* While she feels retired, I'm taking care of her and still getting paid for doing stuff. I hate to use the word 'working.' Iris is an easy keeper. So even though I am taking care of her, it is not a big deal financially.

I gather Iris's situation is typical for those who have chosen to basically be a slave to the system. I feel bad for such a situation, but you chose it. I did not. As such, she feels entitled; she is owed. On one job long ago, someone ran off with the company retirement money. Everyone who invested is simply 'out.' Iris will never collect all she put in. Even what she paid into social security. She wants it back! The way to get it back is to collect off government programs, the same government who 'stole' social security she paid in.

I just have to try to be in her shoes and see it from her perspective. I am not in the same situation. I was upset from the beginning of my working career. Taking care of your own retirement was not an option when joining the workforce. All workers pay in to our government retirement program. The government will take care of you when you get old, have no fear! "Just give us your money and we will manage it for you, invest wisely, and use the profits to take care of you!" I'd rather invest my own money, and take care of myself. And have done so. Getting food stamps sure beats growing a garden, in terms of output of effort.

Iris's biggest comment about gardening and our lifestyle is, "The work never ends!" She screams in frustration.

I reply with a big smile, "Yes, isn't it great!" *Always busy, never a dull moment, being physically healthy, alive to greet a new day. When we do not look forward to taking care of ourselves, we are on the downside of life headed towards the end.* Anyhow, we have to be doing something with our time, why not something useful? This view is not the view of the majority. I know if I expect to get along, have a mate, I need to accept other views.

Iris does find some enjoyment, pride, sense of accomplishment in what we grow. In time, I see she does not eat much of the produce she puts up. It's all about me. People admire and respect us for our garden. Iris gets compliments for pickles and relishes we make. Respect is not something anyone gets for being dependent on food stamps and government programs. I think eventually she will value the rewards and find the work more acceptable, less of a pain.

It is interesting to understand, through Iris, the differences in people's views of what heaven is, what a perfect life would be like. She describes retirement, as being able to finally sit down, relax, not get up for any reason. In a perfect world, she'd sleep in till noon, get up, read the paper, not get dressed, eat something out of a bag, watch the soaps on TV, go back to bed again. Repeat the process tomorrow. Someone to feed her in bed would be even better. I'm not sure there is any activity to her, that is not a chore, work. All of what I value, to her we do because we have to. Except maybe cooking. Iris seems to truly enjoy cooking.

I'm puzzled, as that describes life in a retirement home that I'd want to avoid, and see as a sad day. Iris and I get along, and make a good couple, leaving me wondering what it is that attracts people, or is the basis for a relationship. You'd think 'things in common' would be a priority! Perhaps I am a loner, and prefer to do my thing, by myself, my way, when I want, how I want, without interference. I need no opinion offered, no help. This is not how I dreamed a partnership would be. But what we dream may not be possible in reality. That's why it's called a dream.

"Miles, like the girl next door!" Yes. I know what Iris refers to. The girl next door lives with her parents, in her thirties by now. Still a virgin, looking for the perfect man. Saying, "He has to be handsome, religious, hardworking, kind, loyal, with money." Probably more attributes.

My first thought when I heard this was, "And what are you offering such a person in return, that such a perfect person would want you?" She does not appear to be a hard worker. She is ok looking, not mean. Maybe that is enough. Will she be still looking when she is eighty years old? Iris is kind, willing to go along with what

I want on most matters. Easy to live with. She seems to honestly care for me. Do we call it love? I have said many times, I do not think many people I know, including myself, know what love is. We have strong feelings. But are tweaked, damaged goods. Will never knew 'love' as defined by most.

Unlike Iris, my hope is to play till I drop. I hope my last words will be, "Here, watch this!" Like my 100-year-old friend, Norman Vaughn.

"Iris! Did I tell you, Norman was talking to Josh and I one time, and he wants to climb Mt. Vaughn, named after him?"

"I think so Miles, but I know you like to tell stories, so tell me again." I give her the short version, since she must have heard it before.

"Anyhow, the three of us were having lunch."

Out of the blue Norman asks Josh, "You want to come with me? I'm climbing the mountain next year!"

Josh says, "Norman, you are 100 years old. Besides, last time I went with you, we got lost!"

Norman quickly replies, "Oh, that will not happen this time! It's all planned out!"

I'm listening to this, and looking at Norman, and there in no doubt whatever that he is going to climb a mountain when he is 101. No doubts, no questions. No, "If I am able and still alive." This to me describes a perfect retirement.

I've been dealing all summer with projects, meetings, issues, the garden, the Wellness meetings, my internet customers, producing product to sell. My day still begins at 5:00 am. By 5:30 I am usually in my shop creating. It's all voluntary of course. No one makes me. I am paid for some of the time, not other time, and then some other time again, then not. If there is no money today for some effort, I am not concerned, there is money for some other time later. As long as the bills are paid and we have enough. I am not going to focus on the details much.

"Miles, did Joe pay you yet?" Oh. I forgot. No, I did not bring up the subject when I saw him. "Miles, he owes you, you need to collect!"

"Yes, I suppose. But if he does not pay, that is on him. All I can do is focus on me, what I do, and the fact I did my part. My conscience is clear. My bills are paid, his are not. Who has made out best in life, him or me?"

"That is not the point, Miles! How often do you not get paid! Half the time!" Yes. It might be half the time I do not get paid. I never think about that. Except if I do not get paid, I do not go back to that person a second time with demands and threats. I give people a chance. What they do with that chance is up to them. It seems to me that chasing after people to collect money is negative energy. After I remind them a few times, I know the reason is not because they forgot. They scammed me and I never should have trusted them. That is my fault. I misread them. I accept that responsibility. Now that person has no credit, not with me, not with anyone I am asked to be a reference for when this name comes up. These are often people walking around with a five gallon can in winter begging for enough fuel oil to make it through another night. Or those with no friends or even relatives who like, or trust them.

I think of this as I watch the illegals in the campground pack up. Twenty-seven barefoot happy Cambodians, all excited by their Alaska adventure, not a care in the world. Sam still owes me for two trips and is leaving soon, so I expect to get paid.

"Oh, we are all caught up, Miles, remember?" No receipts, no records all cash, all done on a handshake. He's armed, he's leaving. What position am I in? He's trying to short-change me.

"You owe me about two grand, Sam." It's not a lot of money.

Mayor figures these visitors have moved over a million dollars worth of mushrooms in the past month. The season is over. Not one local took advantage and did any mushroom picking. It could have been our community making the million. Mayor has been our mayor now for five terms, a lot of years. He knows us. I have discussed the illegal Cambodian situation.

He nods, we are on the same page. "Yes, Miles, maybe a majority of our citizens have a lot in common with the Cambodian slaves."

"Only the illegals work. These locals put their hand out for free money." It changes my view of the tears and talk of no work available. I get caught up in the TV news and stories of poverty and the poor starving, how they need our donations. Neither Mayor nor I are going to lose sleep over this subject. Mayor has his knowing smile as he often does. Like me, going bald. He likes his black Carhartt jeans with brass rivets and red plaid shirt. Even in the office where we meet. I see furs on the wall and a twelve-gauge shotgun in the corner. I tell him about the swan and lending the gun.

"Yes, Miles, it is better to be kind. Nenana would be negatively in the news again if this got turned in. You'd be fined and in jail, maybe." No good would come of it. Those poor guys have to eat, and they'll be gone in a few days. A little money passed through our hands. I give a puzzled look. "Yeah, Sam came by and handed me five grand for letting him use our community as a base. He also paid me to rent airport property with the big open space to set up driers for the morels." I never knew this.

I add, "The RV made some good money, I think. Maybe a few meals got served here. I guess it's all good." Mayor and I agree handing over $5,000 is to help smooth over any irregular activities we may have noticed, and will now forget.

"It's called a bribe, Miles! Hush money!" I give a look of shock. We both burst out laughing. It's how the world operates. Live with it.

Sam is not paying me. No need. He thinks there is nothing I can do about it. He stands like a Mexican mafia drug lord. Two scowling guards with machine guns.

I look and just say, "Uh huh." He smiles, turns, dismisses me, things to do.

Mafia Sam still has his dry Morrell shipment locked in my shop, and will be coming by with his armed few to load up in a few hours. I go into the shop and look the boxes over. I know about what shrooms are worth by the pound so can guess what each box is worth. About $2,000, the amount I'm owed.

I smile, "Honey, fair time is coming up! The best time of the whole year!" Not to her. It is my private joy. I have been selling at the Tanana Fair for over thirty-five years. I estimate 20,000 locals know me well enough to greet me by name. This has been the feast after the famine in my life for many years. No money till fair time. I still have that 'feast or famine' mentality. *Even though there has been steady money all along this season!* Iris drives, we have a 1986 Ford crew cab. Crank up windows, no electronics, high beam is still a foot button on the floor. The truck that we will not visit the military base with, because it cannot pass their inspection. I smile. Life is good. I'll be setting up tomorrow, loading up the truck today.

Mafia Sam is loading his truck with dry shrooms, counting boxes.

"Miles, I have a box missing! Do you know anything?"

"Must be one of your crew, one of the loaders, maybe one of the pickers?" He understands by this, it could have been anyone. I'm pretty sure he notices one box missing equals the exact amount he owes me. Whoever had access to one box could have made off with many or all. He is loading, leaving. It is not worth hanging around getting to the bottom of this. We both know this. We both know he made one big pile of money this summer. He owes me. It's best to forget it and move on. He's in business, no hard feelings. Mafia Sam just nods, smiles, and is out of here. If he could prove I robbed him, he'd kill me.

I HAVE my usual spot at the Fair. The spot I have had for twenty-five years. A new tent is set up this year, new tables, new display cloth. New signage. I want to make sure I do not owe any taxes at the end of this year, or ever, so I invested a good portion of my money back into the business. Iris and I show up four days early to take our time setting up, and for me to make deals with other vendors before the fair opens.

My buddy Crafty is setting up. "Miles! It makes no sense to me to deliberately make less profits for the sole reason of not having to pay taxes!"

I chuckle. It does sound illogical, doesn't it? I decide making money is ok, as a game, a way to feel self-respect. Knowing I know how to make money, yet do not make money. I feel good about what I am worth per hour as a form of self-esteem. I do not need to lie or make things up concerning an amount of money I can and have earned. In truth, I live a frugal life and it is not more money I need. I have it, the game is over. Now what? I have no pressing bills to pay. There is nothing I need or even want, that I do not have. I'd as soon let it sit on a coffee can. However, there is this annoying thing called paying taxes on income. If it's not income, it's not taxed. If it's not profit, but goes back into the business, it is not taxable income. It's another reason to buy raw materials I do not really need, or may not use in the next twenty years.

Others say, "It is not possible to avoid taxes, Miles! Not legally anyhow!"

"Watch and behold! Nothing up my sleeve!"

"Good to see you Crafty, had a good season?"

"Miles! Have not seen you as much as the old days. You don't need supplies anymore?"

"I get supplies from the people you get them from now." Said with a grin.

"Smart man!" He laughs. I notice he dropped the subject of what we do with our money. He lives as I do and puts all his 'fortune' into Scientology. Crafty is still a source for a few things I cannot get anyplace else, mostly local things. Having a shop in town, he has locals visit him often, that I do not have connections with. We trade one of my mammoth teeth for some Alaska jade. I have a buyer in Tucson who pays top dollar for Alaska jade, which is hard to get worldwide. Watching Crafty set up, he still has the Grizzly Adams look, just white hair and bent over. Crafty is getting a bad back.

"From lifting all your money, Crafty?" We both laugh.

Money is still his God. Crafty is one who believes the internet is a short-lived fad, not worth paying attention to. He is now paying for that mistake. *Or does he realize yet that was a mistake?* Crafty could sell his jade and many other local items, and make big bucks, if he knew how to offer it on line. Lucky for me, he and others in the trade tend to be old timers who do not believe in the internet. Though this particular product and batch is headed for Tucson, more and more people look for me on line. I'm vague with Crafty about my market. Crafty cannot be trusted when it comes to business and making money. My booth is almost the size of his now.

"Miles, you seen Mr. Macho Nacho yet? He's looking for you!"

I have to go look him up. Macho wants to trade food for something he wants. Once again, my fair food is covered. Iris is not used to how I do business. No one is.

"Miles, how do you keep track of all these deals and trades!" Said with a smile at least, and hopefully a little admiration.

As a rule, I handle such questions defensively. *What's that supposed to mean?* Some would say I do not! I have an ok handle on what I value goods at, and what I need to get to make a profit. There are at least a few customers I know who are waiting for something they asked me to make. I also made a few items knowing what some customers collect, with them in mind. Before the fair opens, the lady who collects angels stops by. I have an angel I created with her in mind, and she loves it for $250.

I'm more tired than I used to be in the past. Setting up the tent, tables, and the booth has worn me out. Mr. Macho Nacho asks what I think of the fair this season. "In the past, this state fair was my biggest, most exciting social and financial event of the year. Because of this, I'd be all stoked up. I now have the Tucson fossil show, with 70,000 vendors and a million customers and the Internet. I live full time in the village."

He nods in understanding. "I think the fair has been changing, Miles. Many of us feel it." I have heard this almost every year for over thirty-five years. But it might be true. He goes on, "The booth space went from $350 to $700 in one season, with no explanation." Yes, I wonder about this as well. This fee increase hurts others a lot more than me, though. I'll be the last man standing. I expect to average $1,000 a day. Over the years, I see many craft people barely making booth space by the end of the fair!

"Some will go in debt, Macho!" He is like me, one of the survivors who always makes money. We both care about the fair, and how the others are doing. We both notice the increase in food vendors, the decrease in handcraft, increase in junk.

I tell Macho what the manager told me. "Why should I sell a space to a crafter for $350? I can get $3,000 for the same space from a food vendor!" Macho is a food vendor who has been around many years. He knows the craft people, cares about the overall fair, and has been on the fair board off and on. He looks out for what is best for the fair, what the customers want. We agree it takes a combination of a lot going on to have a good fair attendance. There are rides, the animal barn, kid events, food booths, handcrafts, commercial vendors, music, the beer tent, rodeo, and mud bogging. Even Macho says the fair can handle only so many food booths! His business gets cut when there are so many choices to the point he wants to know why he has to pay so much for the space, if the profits get spread so thin. We both understand the economy is not the same as during the pipeline days. Maybe that is the bottom line. Not the fair's fault.

"Still, Miles, the fair association is all about profits, when it could focus on a good experience, and wonderful event. Usually a good experience results in profits as well." The family pass has been done away with, parking fees have gone way up, and other things we mention.

"Macho, I see no reason to pay a big name band from the lower 48 to come here to entertain us. I think locals would be just as happy with a small town fair atmosphere, like some local music. That right there would save a pile of money! We used to have local music around a big campfire in the field in the old days, remember?"

"People, in general seemed happier back then, happier with less." I have been part of the handcraft section since the beginning. I know many people come to see them. It's an important part of their fair experience.

"All this commercialization of merchandise offered is not much different than going to the mall!"

For the first time I notice 'Craft' is not a word used anyplace in the fair ads. Likewise, the craft tent is moved to the outer limits. "Because that part of the fair needs more traffic, so the tent will bring the people over there!" I am told by management. Yet this breaks up the craft section of the fair. There is not an area anyone could refer to as the craft area now.

I tell Macho, "Management told me this is because not enough craft vendors signed up this year." Macho is aware, I know about every vendor in the area.

"What do you think, Miles?"

"I have asked around, and know at least a dozen craft vendors who wanted space a year in advance, and were told none is available. I did not come right out and call the manager a liar, but pointed out, this reply seems odd, considering what I know."

Macho, as well as other vendors feel deceived, if not outright lied to. "The manager changed tactics on me, and said one major reason for fewer craft people is that it is difficult to monitor the products. It has been found that many vendors try to get a craft booth for the lower craft price and then sell commercial products." Yet the craft people tend to monitor themselves, and know what is commercial, and report major infractions of commercial products the vendor did not make.

"Miles, maybe it is difficult once the fair starts, to kick someone out."

"That is not necessary; just point out the products are not handmade by the artist, and collect a commercial fee! Next year they go to the commercial area." I can see part of the issue management faces. It is true. I tell Macho, "More and more products offered to the public are imported because local hand crafts cost more!" We have talked in the past about the legal aspect of the term 'hand-craft' I remind Macho, "An imported commercial item only has to be altered ten percent to be legally made by you." I have in fact had vendors in the craft area set up next to me bragging they get necklaces from China for fifty cents each in bulk. They cut the cord, add a bead or two, put a cheap clasp on, and poof, it is their own—one of a kind unique hand crafted item, selling for $50. In competition with my handmade, where I make the string, each bead, and custom cast each clasp. I find, cut and polish the stone and carve, make a mold and cast the metal cap.

Macho nods, "While Alaska labor is one of the highest in the world, how can you compete?"

"It's a challenge all right!"

At first when this began, enough customers could tell the difference, and were happy to get the real thing from me! As import copies became more prevalent, I think people are less educated on how items are made, and as the economy fails, cannot afford to pay the difference. Not at a fair, anyway. I still make money, but work harder at it, and must rely on long time collectors who are now getting old. The new, younger generation, are the plastic people. Many are against animal products. To Vegetarians, the new cool is 'plastic.' I'm not even sure Macho understands. "The plastics industry is one of the most environmentally destructive, toxic, consumers of energy industries on the planet." That minor fact never hits the news, or dawns on the minds of the plastic generation.

"Maybe Miles, because the plastic industry, is a byproduct of the oil industry. Who wants to accuse this industry of doing any wrong or cutting into their profits?"

So I'm the fall guy? The scapegoat, the reason for the demise of the planet?" I know in the long haul this is going to be an issue I cannot overcome. I can see the future. I'm not amused. Ignorance is bliss, wisdom comes with a price. The future is not as bright as it once was after forty years in the business. What am I going to do? Put on a happy face and pretend trends I observe are not happening? Still, for now I am doing well, making more money every year. I will have a good fair, even if I am mixed in with the commercial people and there is no longer a designated craft area at the fair. I do not bring up a new subject I think of. Americans are not as proud as they once were. American made is not a big selling point like it once was. Wal-Mart and other big chain stores selling cheap imports may have changed our views.

I often hear from people around me, "Oh! Let's to go Wal-Mart!" as a first place to look for a product. "We can get it cheaper there!" Then complain because the clerk can't speak English. Or can't count to ten. I smile.

Macho points out, "Long ago, 'Made in Japan," was the standard product insult. Remember?" Yes, then it became Bali, India, China; now there is no focus on anyplace in particular. "Now where a product is made can be vague and not known. Keep in mind, American companies can and do subcontract outside the country. I heard talk companies like Harley Davidson, Ford, have their famous 'American made' products made overseas. I hear things like, 'there are no longer any shoe factories in the USA, not one.' I can speculate this would include other items, including the arts and crafts business. "Everyone imports so get with it Miles," no longer said with shame. "So why shop local, Miles, it all comes the same source in China anyhow!"

Macho nods, "How do we prove our product is really local? This seems to be part of an answer for us, to prove it."

I agree and have come up with ways to prove it.

It is time to sell, so conversation ends. I try to keep the flow with customers upbeat. At the end of the day, I make more than my expected $1,000. I want to get an opinion from my buddy, Crafty. I respect his ability to make money in this tough business. I tend to pick up views from a variety of spiritual doctrines. One aspect of Scientology I agree with is staying positive, with the belief our own attitude has a huge effect on the outcome of events. We tend to get what we look for. *If we are what we eat, we also are what we think.*

"Crafty, are you doing well at the fair?"

"Sure, Miles, I always do well." That is the answer I always give, the pat reply. I want the serious, between friends reply. I offer up a story we both know.

"Remember the clock man?" I do not wait for Crafty's answer. "Years ago, big wood face clocks were in style. The clock man sold a lot of his exotic wood clocks! Over time, this guy sold fewer, then even fewer. The reason he gave, is that people are stupid. The economy is down. Doom and gloom."

Crafty nods that he remembers. "Yeah, Miles, we all tried to suggest he change his product from clocks or a different kind of clock to meet the changing times, and he'd do better. Most of us were doing great, no complaints!" The clock man each year said he'd had it, was not coming back. He did come back, with more doom and gloom. Few who were doing well wanted to hear it! Eventually he never came back. This was years ago. The fair went on without him. I think about this off and on when I get discouraged.

I know the employees well at Crafty's shop. They tell me sales are way down. I can see for myself Crafty is trying to unload a lot of outdated toys, dusty rings, wore out flags. He has not invested in new inventory. He has not sold inventory he bought last year and the year before. I hoped we could honestly discuss what we think is going on, beyond everything is normal, fine, good, and on an upward trend. Crafty lives off other businesses that get discouraged and are vulnerable. He moves in for the kill, buys them out for ten cents on the dollar. It's not dishonest!

"Miles, I am up front and ask if they need cash and want to sell out cheap and get out of the business. If they say, 'No,' I do not push them. It's their choice." I do not agree and think Crafty does push people, and is overly aggressive, but it's just an opinion.

"So Miles, are you interested in selling out?" Crafty has misunderstood why I came to talk to him.

"No Crafty. People like you and me will always do well. I was just noticing changes at the fair. There is no craft area, and our booth fees doubled with no explanation. That cuts down on the competition. That's good for you and I. But if the fair association is not doing well, and half the vendors leave, that has an affect on my strategy."[3] I do not pass on any other view to Crafty. However, I am not as confident in the rightness of my views as I once was.

CHAPTER FOUR

HEAD OF CHAMBER, WELLNESS GROUP, GAME BOARD MEETING—MEET JESSIE AND HIS LEGAL PROBLEMS

Past Flash [1]

1980s. Crafty and I are on an art selling trip, on the road as salesmen. We expect to be gone two weeks. Crafty has done this many times, but it is my first. We stop at every gift shop to peddle our wares. I am learning the ropes and helping Crafty. He has a van with his shop logo on the side called, 'The Mole.' Boxes of postcards, mugs that say Alaska, antler back scratchers, bone toothpick holders, are his stock in trade. Crafty takes orders for goods he does not have in stock to be delivered for the tourist season. He is the biggest supplier in the interior of Alaska. We sleep in the van usually. There are various events Crafty knows about, that are worth attending, setting up and selling retail at. I have some of my own art that Crafty takes a percent of if I sell since it is his trip and I am tagging along as a helper. I am the grasshopper, he is the Holy One.

Crafty will make a hundred grand. I might make one grand. This is still not so bad for two weeks of fun and education in a time period when workers are happy with four dollars an hour. Or are actually paying for an education! Imagine that! I already know this is not what I aspire to be and do. Shop owners, for the most part, treat us like dirt. The wonderful world of, "Get in line and we'll get to you when we feel like it, maybe." Often we are told to come by after lunch. When we had an appointment for 10:00 in the morning. No apology. I'm not someone who stands in line well. The line forms behind me.

I tell Crafty, "The goods of the world are a pie. There is a line behind this pie and not enough to go around. Not everyone will get a piece. Those who stand in line get a fork full. No, thank you."

"Ha! Miles! There is no choice! Get in line with everyone else, or get left to starve at the back of the line!"

I do not agree. "Crafty, I discover my own pie that has no line behind it. I create that pie if I must. I cut the pie in half and slide that generous piece on my plate before anyone else discovers there is a pie. The remaining half I invite my friends over to share. By the time the world realizes there is a pie, and runs over for a forkful, three fourths is gone. I have already left with my half, looking for another new pie."

"That has its own set of problems, Miles." I agree. It may in fact not be a better way, only a different way. Citizens are not often happy watching pies get unevenly, unfairly distributed. *Surely it's illegal.* China holds no threat to me in undercutting my action. I sell wolf claws, for example. There are none in China. China wants wolf claws, there are a total of fifty major dealers in the world. Most of us know each other. The line forms behind us. It's the customer who waits till I can get to them. I make sure it's a seller's market.

Here we are in who-knows-where community. About to go to sleep in some empty parking lot, after a day of selling. The sky is octopus ink dark, midnight. The lot seems deserted. I hear voices of two young males coming near. Two teens are chatting, talking, headed somewhere. I assume a parked car in this lot. This looks normal to me. Their form flits in an out of cheap parking lot light beams. Kids well dressed, clean, sober, moving with purpose to some specific destination. I hear the sound of an order yelled out angrily by a police officer. "Hey where are you two going! What are you doing here!" Our van is closer to the kids than the cop, so I hear the one kids whisper, "What's his problem!" The other shrugs and says, "Let's just cooperate and stay out of trouble." The teens stop and wait for the policeman to come up to them. His night stick is out.

"Show me some ID!" In a nasty, demeaning voice. The one feisty kid asks what the problem is, wondering what is with the nightstick and the 'you do as I say punk' attitude. The cop does not like being questioned. Hits the kid with the nightstick, and slams him against the nearest car. The kid's buddy is shocked and says "Wow, wait, what's going on? What's the problem, Sir?" Cop screams, "You want the same thing!?" Polite kids bows his head with that, 'No, sir, I go to the back of the bus mas-ta' move the cop expects.' The kid who got hit, is upset and bloody, "What did you do that for! I have a right to know what the problem is!"

"The problem is you!" Cop begins to beat the kid to a pulp with his nightstick.

This cop does not know Crafty and I are only a few feet away watching all this. I assume the cop thinks he is alone out here and can do whatever he wants, kill a couple of punk kids for a trophy with no witnesses, is what it looks like to me. Crafty has taken all this in like me. I ask Crafty what we should do. In the past, I would not have asked. I'd have been out the door to make sure the kids did not get killed, letting the cop know there are witnesses and he better calm down! Possibly even been armed and made a citizen's arrest against the cop. Handcuffed him with his own cuffs and called in, hopefully, some honest cops. Had that cop's job. *You can't treat people like that without probable cause, for no reason!* That is how I was raised.

I hesitate as I have been learning since I have been out on my own in the world. I had been in a similar situation with my best friend, Will. He reluctantly went along with me and we 'got involved,' even though Will told me to mind my own business! In that case, it had been a woman alone on the street crying and screaming for help, saying she had just been robbed. I made Will help! It turned out we helped a prostitute rob her customer. "That," Will had calmly said, "Is why you do not get involved." Obviously, I lack social skills. I figured this time to take my cue from my streetwise buddy, Crafty.

"Mind your own business, Miles." Crafty is not concerned in the least. He has zero interest in knowing what is going on, or why. If two dead guys are in the news in the morning, Crafty will not bat an eye, nor wish we had done anything. We are alive and safe. That is all that matters. Therefore, we are entertained by watching two kids get beaten to a pulp.

"Call who, Miles? This is the police. You'll get another guy just like this, who will back up this guy. Do you want to end up like these kids? You are so naïve, Miles, how do you survive!"

"But? But Crafty, who are the police protecting? And from who?" It doesn't matter who the enemy is, as long as it is not us. Do not call the police, do not talk to the police. If you see a cop, you go to the other side of the street. So why can't I just do that. It's simple enough.[2]
Past flash ends

This is not much like my friends Dan and Vision, who run the burger stand here at the fair. I think of them as I hang out eating lunch at their fair booth.

"Miles, how is the fair going for you so far? Haven't seen you here like I used to!" I stop by each morning to visit, maybe have hot cider. I am older, getting diabetic, can't live on burgers and fries at the fair as I once could. We trade for meals, as Macho Nacho trades with me. I recall trades of $300 for ten days of meals. I just cannot eat like that anymore! Not working as physically. Dan understands. He reminds me of the days I took all his waste cooking grease to feed my sled dogs.

"Thirty to fifty gallons! Remember?" I do remember! I remember as well, he gave it free, and delivered it to my home in Nenana fifty miles away. Buddy Crafty would see a money angle. Not a problem, just different. I'd be happy to pay.

Dan says, "I'm going by there anyway, Miles!"

Still, I knew he had a lot of his own business to take care of. A lot to haul as he headed for the next fair. Yet did not forget me. There is no comment about getting nothing in return. "Dan, I brought that repaired jade piece back for Vision. That is one of my first major art pieces, with number 149 on it. I stopped recording item numbers twenty years ago, when I got to 9,999." *I used to think I'd be a well-known famous artist one day. That it would matter that I recorded each piece, keeping records, with the details and story behind each item.*

"What do I owe you, Miles?"

"Nothing. I guarantee my work for life."

"Fine, Miles, but this is over thirty years old and she dropped it! You can't cover that."

"It's me who owes you, Dan, all the things you do for me. I'm glad I have a way to do something in return!"

Most business people I know have Crafty's outlook. Dan and Vision have never told me anyone ever took advantage of them, nor do they have a bad attitude about anything at all. Life is good! They are grateful. Each day is a blessing. Glad to help where they can. They seem happy, have friends, and have money. I ask,

"So how does the fair seem to you this year, Dan?" Dan is not one to hedge or be evasive. "Normal, Miles, like most years. Attendance could be down a little from other years, but that happens. Often it is the weather." He does not comment on the taking away of the family pass, the parking lot that never seems to get fixed, or the showers that still do not work. I therefore conclude it is me who is changing, more than the fair. I should not buy into the doom and gloom so many are peddling, including the news media.

Iris points out. "You tend to want to help people, but so often you choose the wrong people to help! You get drug down faster than others are being lifted!"

I am not so good at judging character or social situations. I have noticed it is not wise to help everyone who asks for help, or even needs help. Never bet into another man's game. I want to try to choose who to give to or help. The rule can be to notice a situation where some deed is a minor thing to me, when I am in a position to easily offer time, goods, or service. Then, recognizing what is not a big deal to me, yet is a big deal to someone else. Never give anything you cannot walk away from. In this way, a gift does not have to be paid for, favor returned, or even appreciated as a condition. I gave it freely with no duct tape stuck to it.

I explain to Iris, "I spent much of my life alone in the wilds as a hermit. I did not have much practice with social skills. I was not taught these skills as a child. It's not so easy later in life to be learning what most already know as part of common sense. Common sense is common to whom? Common sense for me would be in common with nature and animals, perhaps! Anyhow, I'll figure it out. It just takes time."

"Meanwhile, Miles, you get taken to the cleaners." *Doesn't she mean, put through the wringer?*

"I still say I get ahead faster than I get behind!" I do not want to just give up on the human race and help no one, look out for number one, me. I cannot just let everyone fend for themselves. I'm just not like that. I do not wish to learn to be like that. Iris reminds me of buying the light bulbs to help the war vets. I smile. "Yea Iris, I got this phone call, pastor so and so from the church of such and such, asking if he could take a moment of my time." I'm sort of new to civilization, first time I have a phone and all that. Of course, I want to help the vets! So I order the lightbulbs guaranteed to last a lifetime, made by disabled vets. Not long after this call, I got a call asking me to help even more? Would I buy the special cleaning fluid to help the war vets? "Sure, why not?"

I ask Iris in a puzzled voice, if I somehow got put on a sucker list? "Because geez, I got ten phone calls a day to donate to the children in India, women against drunk driving, and on and on!" I got suspicious and looked into detergent I ordered from the vets, that seemed to clean no better than the products selling for one tenth the price. When I read the fine print, I see that the disabled vets get minimum wage to pack the product in peanuts for shipping. I had first assumed the disabled vets ran the entire company, made the product, the bottles, handled the labeling, and kept all the profits. "So Iris, it looked to me like some company got subsidized by the government for hiring the minimal amount of disabled employees to get tax credits so they could make more profit."

"Now you are catching on, Honey."

I'd still rather be the sucker than the suckee! I am reluctant to simply give up and assume the world is out to get us all. Give to others ten times what they give you. From the bible. This concept worked for years. Treat me nice and I multiply that back at you. Mess with me, and that too, gets returned ten fold. Christian friends reply, "Vengeance is mine, sayeth the Lord." We must turn the other cheek, let that cheek get slapped, too. Forgive, say thank you, as Jesus did while he was being nailed to the cross. I have a hard time visualizing this Jesus outlook working. I've tended to look to Clint Eastwood, and Rob Roy. Maybe Robin Hood, help the poor; stuff it to the corrupt sheriff of Nottingham. There are flaws appearing in my thinking. I now lean to the concept that no group has an exclusive on being saved, or being better than some other group. There are good and bad among all groups, be it economic, religious, or race. I may feel I have been wronged. The other swears it is me at fault and they who have been wronged. Iris reminds me of our long-time customer Dwayne. We review this on a rainy day at the fair when no customers are in sight. There are times like this, when we just keep busy until customers show up.

Dwayne is no longer a customer. He often spent a lot of money, but he was somewhat difficult all along. There were minor misunderstandings to work out in almost every deal. I'd invariably get a, "Well, that is not quite as advertised, Miles." So I'd feel obligated to make it right the next time. "Miles, I thought it would be…"

and there would be some reason he was not happy and my fault. When I made it right, I'm his best buddy again. "Yeah, Miles, there are not many people in the world you can trust. Everyone is out to screw us, but I can count on you, good buddy!" He'd call sometimes. We chatted about technical aspects of our trade, that was interesting for us both. Like me, he was experimenting. He's a knife maker like me. We want to figure out how to stabilize our own handle materials, like ivory. It is hard, and few seem to be willing to share the secrets. We share between ourselves where our experiments are going.

"Dwayne, have you tried the plastic and acetone?"

"Yes, Miles, but we still cannot get around needing to pressurize it to get it to penetrate." Yes, we are finding this out. We do not know if vacuum works, or pressure, or alternating. What sort of pressures are needed. We discuss what to buy, or sometimes how to build the right system.

"Dwayne, I am pretty sure Igor in Tucson knows, but gives no details. He gets resin to penetrate through mammoth ivory to the very center of the tusk, and not through cracks, but through the pores of the ivory!"

"Dang, Miles!" So we share this interest, and it bonds us. Like being of the same tribe. However, over time, I decide I am not making any profit from this guy. I make $20 on a $1,000 deal. Iris tells me over and over to drop the guy. He is not worth the aggravation. Oddly, Dwayne's wife says the same to him, "Drop Miles as a supplier, it is not worth this aggravation!" One deal really upsets Dwayne. I will not budge off feeling I was not out of line.

"Speaking of dropping, it is about time to find a market for a $2,000 box of morel mushrooms." Iris looks puzzled. "I got partial payment in product." I am not in the mushroom business. I go online and look around. There are some buyers listed, but they buy wholesale. Half price. I see in my search, a restaurant in Maine that offers mushrooms in meals. This would be a discounted retail sale. I contact them. "I'm in Alaska, we had a fire, lots of morels, I have sixty pounds." These mushrooms usually sell by the ounce. I get a reply of interest, but they'd like a sample since they do not know me, and this is a lot of money. I send a free sample and cover all the costs. Looks like a Mom and Pop seaside high end resort offering local clams and crabs to tourists. This is a situation I wish to support, and can express this, being a good storyteller.

They receive the sample, like the quality, and pay me $2,000 for $3,000. A simple, done deal. I want to sell some place Mafia Sam would not hear about. I actually like Sam. I am sure, if I felt inclined, I could be in business, selling to people like this restaurant owner regularly. Buy from Sam, or pass on orders for a percent as middle man. I bet I could move a million dollars' worth of mushrooms a *year if I felt like it.*

Dwayne tells me over the phone he wants a set of musk ox horns I just acquired. He wants to see a picture before he decides. He is not sure he has the money. An hour or two later, a local buyer hears about the musk ox horn set and drives fifty miles to look at them. Tusk is a local buyer I have known thirty-five years and done a lot of business with. He still has his floppy leather hat and beard. Tusk sees the horns then hands me my asking price—cash. Dwayne 'might' buy them, but might not. I did not take a, "I'm interested," as a commitment. Even a, "I want them." Tusk shows me the green. That's business. I'm loyal to friends and regular good customers. For some people I might have held the horns, set them aside. Usually it takes money down to hold something. Life is about tipping people, not haggling and wasting time or complaining. The truth is, I do not make much money dealing with Dwayne, the 'let's make a deal' man.' He is not at the head of the line. *The squeaky wheel may get the grease, but is the first wheel to get dumped when opportunity arises.*

Dwayne goes through the roof when I call to tell him the horns sold. I'm 90% sure buddy Dwayne would have somehow talked me down in price, arguing my asking price is out of line, or there is a crack in one horn, or not a perfect match. As a buyer myself, I do not have Dwayne's outlook. I want my suppliers to call me first and feel good about deals. I am 'easy.' I buy almost anything locals bring me, just to maintain good relations. I buy garbage if I have to, because I make huge profit off the really good stuff when it shows up through them. The rest is more of an investment in good relations.

In the same way mafia Sam handed Mayor money he did not have to, so there is good feeling and no complaints and a "How may I help you, Sir" attitude. "I got your back, you got my back." This happens in relationships, friendships and I say also business. Legal beagles and others cry stuff like, "Insider trading!" "Conflict of interest!" Isn't that what bringing your lady flowers and suspecting it helps get good sex is all about? Illegal? How absurd! I give my sled dogs treats and hope they pull harder. That's life. Part of the 'proof,' is folks like Dwayne, who tell me how they are broke, how business is slow. It is me saying how I have all the money and business I want, and I'm happy.

"Miles! I told you I wanted it! My word is my bond, you know that! I trusted you!" He wants me to get it back, or replace it for the same price we agreed on, a much lower price than Tusk paid. *Not going to happen, good buddy.* In his shoes, I would be disappointed, but understand. You snooze, you lose. Dwayne sort of gets over it. We do a few more deals, where I make a few dollars, but not enough to get excited about. He wants me to contact him when I get back from Tucson after I buy some Russian mammoth tusks.

Dwayne goes so far as to track down Tusk to get 'his' horns back. Tusk had sold the musk ox horn set to a local knife maker. Dwayne calls this knife maker. I'm not sure what transpired.

The knife maker contacts me. "Who is this, Dwayne? What a lunatic! Screamed at me, wants his horns back!" Dwayne tells the knife maker he should not do business with me, because the horns were not legal, and he might end up being arrested along with me.

To be legal, this set of horns needs to be separated from each other, preferably sold separately as two different transactions. This is to stop horns and antlers from being sold as trophies for high dollars. Such high dollar sales might encourage slaughter of the species. The Eskimo supplier does not know such strange technical laws of the white man. Such laws do not apply to Natives. The horns arrived attached. I had planned to separate them before offering them for sale or shipping. If Dwayne had bought them, I would have separated the horns before shipping. Tusk is a good enough friend, that when he showed up, I just turned them over to him as a raw material. He would know to separate the horns. I assumed he would cut them up to offer to knife makers, as I would. The law is not a big deal, unless someone actually tries to sell them or treats them as a trophy and has a mount made. Horns and antlers are sold at gift shops to tourists all the time—connected. The biggest legal concern would be if it is sold at low craft material prices, as intended, or a high trophy price as a display set. I sold the set at a low craft materials price. Upholding the intent of the law. I stand by that.

"Dwayne, got some choices tusks for you here!" I email some pictures of mammoth tusks I acquired from my Russian connection. Dwayne settles on a tusk he wants, telling me, "I want to cut it up for knife scales, what's your opinion on the quality?"

"Looks like a nice tusk. If it were me, I'd keep it as a display tusk. It's been restored. That adds to the cost. This tusk does not seem to me to be a good choice to cut up. I'm looking at the value per pound here. I could sell you the same thirty pounds as knife size bark scrap for $50 a pound. Why pay the $100 a pound I need for this worked display tusk?"

Dwayne does not agree. "Do you think it is solid, Miles? Sure looks nice!"

"It looks and feels solid to me. Was sold to me as a display. I am not 100% sure how the inside will look when cut up. I think this should be ok, though." Dwayne buys the tusk for $100 a pound and cuts it, then goes ballistic on me, saying the tusk has a lot of gray glue filler inside! My view is, "Bummer, too bad! Guess you screwed up, huh?" I mean, how much material have I bought and bit the bullet on as a learning process? As much as a third of what I buy!? Oh well! I dump it cheap, and make profit off the top 10% I can get ten times my investment back. That's business. I believe I know more about mammoth ivory than Dwayne. I know if I want knife material, I do not look at display tusks to cut up, because the valued knife material is mostly the outer bark of the tusk. All the inside is going to be wasted as knife material. I also do not argue with customers. A few knife makers do use the inner ivory. Buddy Dwayne did not take my advice. Why is that my fault?

Dwayne does not agree, and feels I owe him a refund. However, he cut the tusk. It is not a display anymore. It's worth half the price now per pound. I'm getting to the point, I believe. I'm not as forgiving and polite as I used to be with this guy. I did not know the tusk was full of filler, but it does not matter if sold as a display. Dwayne gets polite again, puts in another $1,000 order. I ship it off. He is going to pay me when he inspects it. I give him the option of returning it if he does not like it, since he is so hard to please.

I get word weeks down the road, Dwayne never got the shipment. I inquire, and postal tracking says it was delivered. Dwayne's story changes slightly. He tells me over the phone, "The postmaster showed up when I was gone, and left the package on the steps, or in the front door of my shop. It disappeared." That's somehow my fault. He is not paying since he did not get it. The story sounds fishy to me. He knew it was delivered to his address. I think one story was an employee picked it up. Supposedly the employee set it in the shop and no one has seen it since. I feel I am not at fault, I sent it, and it arrived. That's out of my hands. Possibly the post office is at fault for not setting the package in the hands of the recipient. I suggest he take that up with the post office. He suggests I do. I do not believe him and think he is lying. If neither of us does nothing, I am the only one out anything, not him. I think he has the ivory. I think his wife got on him about me screwing him on every deal. They think it is time to get even; that would be fair, and the right thing to do, to teach me a lesson. The $1,000 in his mind, is what I owe him for all the times I have put the screws to him. He feels as I do, "What goes around comes around. What you give me, I will return tenfold." I tell him what I think happened, that I forgive him, and am sorry he feels as he does, and not to contact me again.

This whole sequence of events might be predictable. Iris was right. I should have walked away a long time ago. This gives me insight into what 'being screwed' means, as well as 'giving back tenfold, and getting even.' This is on my mind as I struggle to run a successful business. How do I handle the variety of customers? I want to be nice, help those who could use some help, offer breaks to those who appreciate it and at the same time, make a profit. Do I treat everyone equally? Same price, same policy, never offer special deals where I lose a little money in favor of having helped someone. At the same time, never make an extra profit from people who can afford the loss? I have been experimenting with the idea we are not all equal.

The weather clears the next day at the fairgrounds. Iris and I make up for the loss of business during yesterday's rain! I sit in my chair by the booth. Blade of grass in my mouth, $5,000 necklace on, made from a rare cave bear fang. A top quality opal caps the fang. All handmade carved beads and carvings. I wear socks that do not match. Torn jeans. On my head, my leather hat with Indian beadwork, that looks like a 100-year-old hat Jim Bridger might have worn. My tee shirt has a big saber tooth cat skull on it. I'm told I look like Indiana Jones. I work on what I thought was more a 'Crocodile Dundee' look. From inside the booth, "Miles, a lot of items here are not marked! How much is this Dire wolf fang?"

I have several lines for this situation. "What do you want to pay?" "How much you got?" Or quote a price.

"I honestly have no clue, Miles, I leave it up to you to know the value." Ok. So now I know what kind of customer I have. Honest, open, trusts me. If he had said, 'How about five dollars?' I would have known he wants to play me for a sucker. I would treat him accordingly, talk him into buying a two dollar fake, for $40. If he would have said, 'I know it is rare, so guessing it might be $500?' I'd have said, "Yes, somewhat rare, could go that high under some conditions in a perfect world. This one is not huge, and has a hairline crack, see? This is the fair, with a lower overhead then a bigger show, so it would be nice to get $100." Which is within 'not rip off range,' but on the high side of normal price. Due to the answer I get, I say, "See the one similar to it over here, has a $75 tag on it. The unpriced one is about the same age and quality, but has a hairline crack. Not visible, and can be fixed, but effects the value. If you can afford $65, that would work for me."

"Dang, Miles! I have that much, but then I have no money to eat with the rest of the fair. Hate to spend my last dime here, Miles, but the fang sure is nice!"

"I'll give you a deal on it if you can part with $50." I make the sale. The customer appreciates my honesty and a fair, low price.

"It's a strange way to do business, Miles!" Iris comments, but watches how it works. Later in the day, a customer pays $100 for a similar fossil fang. Partly, I deal in animal products I did not buy, but found. There is not an established market. There are 100 levels of quality and size, since nature made it. There are few appraisers who can say truthfully, what any of this is worth. The situation is like the top opal dealer in Tucson who told me, long ago, "It's worth whatever I say it is."

I gave a puzzled, "Why is that?"

"Because I'm the man. I'm the expert everyone else comes to with questions." Yes, that is where I want to be. We do not get there by having the reputation of ripping people off. I tell Iris, "I spent much of my life away from people, not inter-acting. I arrive at my age into civilization filled with questions. Trying to run my own business that involves a lot of understanding human nature and needing knowledge how to interact." I think a little, adding, "I have known quite a few people from the wilds who would handle things Clint Eastwood style, with a gun handy, saying, 'Smile when you call me that!' If accused of being a liar or thief."

After thirty years, all of those people are dead now. There are such people who put guns in my face out on the frontier, screaming to me, "Are you calling me a liar!" What I see is misunderstanding. We should be able to work problems out with calm reasoning. Even if we agree we should not do business and ought to stay away from each other. *How many dead people would there be if we got rid of all those low life disrespectful morons, who do not have any integrity?* But worse, what an eye opener when it is me added to that list of morons! Who belongs on that list? Certainly not me! Thus, there is a flaw in giving back tenfold, that which we feel we receive.

The fair ends. It's garden harvest time.

"IRIS, the fair originated as an agriculture event, so is the time of year when the crops are finishing up." We review what grew well, how we want to put it up. Some will get frozen. We have the option to freeze, can, pickle or dry. Over the years, I have a good feel for how each batch could best be processed. Some vegetables dry well, some make great pickles, while others can or freeze without blanching. Some methods are cheaper or faster. Some methods taste better. The cucumbers in the greenhouse will be pickles for sure! We are done eating them as fast as they grow. It is time to get some quarts put up for winter! A great time of year! I love it! Putting food by for the months ahead.

"It's a lot of work, Miles. Isn't it easier to just go to Fred Meyers?" That is hard to argue with. Iris has seen, over a period of time, store food is not always what it is advertised to be. Some items are dyed to make them look ripe. Others never ripen, but simply rot first. "What would seventy-five quarts of homemade pickles cost if you had to go buy them? Even with food stamps, it would use up most of your stamps." Fresh herbs from the store are costly and require getting to the store often. We are able to have 'fresh,' daily, without having to make that fifty-mile trip to Fairbanks. We have the advantages of living remote, with low property tax, good view, and affordable home. It might be difficult to win a debate, of which is a better choice. Free food with stamps and no work, or fresh garden harvest you grew yourself. I learn the downside of home grown I never considered before. Store bought has minimum standards to meet. Old wrinkly produce is tossed out as garbage. It will always look good.

I grow vegetables that can be better than store bought, but there is no guarantee. My garden product can get outdated, and look bad, or end up with bugs, rotten spots, and in general, be lower grade then right out of the store! It could taste worse! The same with wild game, fish, or fowl! The same with home cooking. There is such a thing as a horrible home cooked meal! Not much guarantees quality!

The compromise has been that she buys food it is hard to grow, and I grow and acquire locally that which is not difficult to have. Beets, turnips, carrots, cabbage, potatoes, cauliflower, broccoli, are the usual Alaska staple vegetables we can count on. Cold weather root crops. I prefer not to grow potatoes unless I have lots of extra room.

"Iris, we can buy potatoes from local farmers cheap. I used to get 100 pounds for $10 from Dan and Vision at the fair. When the fair ends, they have potatoes left over from the French fry part of the sales. They do not want to haul the potatoes to the next fair, and could throw them out. They are glad enough I want them. This 100 pounds lasts me till the middle of next year, stored right here in the cupboard!"

"Well, they certainly would not be very fresh, Miles!" Fresh was not my priority in those days. Cost was important. At least it is real food and not powdered potatoes, or half chemicals as so much fast food is. I rarely eat out of a can. Have never had a TV dinner in my life. Every meal I eat is home cooked, homemade from scratch. Old potatoes to me, is still not a bad choice. But yes, after six months, the potatoes have long vines. I'd have trouble separating the potatoes from the leaves and vines. They would be wrinkled and half the size. However, not rotten. Maybe not as filled with nutrition. But, Oh well.

"Iris, my food bill used to be under $300 a year for most of my life here in Alaska." I agree with her that no one cares. I am not that poor anymore. All I have been is a nutcase. I have done nothing to do my part to save the waste on the planet. In the big picture, it has been negligible. Saving the planet is about grabbing as much for yourself as possible, while telling others to make sacrifices. No one I know got an award, pat on the back, or remembered, for being frugal. My view was different when young and filled with noble enthusiasm. I was confident we were living in end times. Back in the 60s when we were taught how to use bomb shelters, I was convinced we had perhaps a decade to survive. That's what I was taught. Looking around, society lived like there was no tomorrow. It made more sense back then, looking at a lot of potential years ahead to live, if I survived, to tune in and drop out in the wilds, and be the last man standing.

It would have not surprised me to come to civilization to discover it gone. A pile of rubble, with animals moving back in, and plants growing over the cement. I was resigned to it. Us getting what we deserve. Proud to be a savage, ashamed to be human. Even looking forward to Mother Earth taking the planet back. Ashes to ashes and dust to dust. Back to the beginning, a fresh start, without mankind to screw it up. A healthy planet with clean air and water. If I choose to live like the animals, perhaps I would be spared. I imagined a world in which I was the only human being. This was a happy thought. The earth recovering. Perhaps fatalistic, but look at the facts. Look at the trends and graphs. Study the history of man. Better than thoughts of the entire planet destroyed by man. I'd even sacrifice my own life if it meant the planet survived.

A decade goes by, then another and another. I still agree with the prophecies of the bible, but without a timeline. The end might take ten years, 100 or 1,000. Meanwhile, back at the ranch… life goes on. Requiring a changed battle plan. I'm at the age I am not concerned with what life holds for me. I am in my declining years, past my prime. I've already lived way longer than anyone else, or I, ever expected. The flower children of the 60s was about youth! There is an Alice Cooper song, "I'm 18, in the middle of life." We could not imagine life past thirty. Life was about 'now.' All of society catered to the baby boomers. Advertisers, music, jobs, followed us, even bowed to us. We were the new age. "The age of Aquarius," as the song goes. Even the universe aligned for us. Perhaps we are a spoiled generation. If my generation was about us, and now, it does not surprise me the generation of the 80s and 90s has issues. *What we sow, we shall reap.*

Will I spend all of my time waiting for the sky to fall? Spend it living a meager simple life, doing my part to save the planet? I gave my beliefs, my youth. What is there to show for it? Between fires and floods, I have been wiped out more times than I can count. *There will be waste, there will be destruction, get over it! I may as well enjoy that which there is to enjoy, like everyone else. Go down with the ship.* Just that, old habits die hard.

Meanwhile, food is important, one of the requirements for life! So I rejoice when I have it, when I am in control of my own food. The basic root crops! I smile. Life is good. I invested in a rototiller. There is compost to understand. A worm farm in a plastic tote to feed the garden. I get the impression Iris goes along with my idiosyncrasies with a smile, as she loves this eccentric old codger, but is not enjoying the rewards as much as I am.

"Iris, worms do not survive the Alaska winter in the wilds. I learned from a university teacher who came to talk to our community, that worms can be held easily over the winter in a tote on the floor in the corner. Feed them scraps now and then while they are mostly dormant." Yes. In spring, as it warms up, the worms wake up. They can go in the starter plants, then the greenhouse, then later into the garden. They help the soil a great deal. There is more to gardening successfully than meets the eye. I spent ten years figuring it out. But yes, almost anyone can plant a small plot, grow some basics, enough to survive. Sustaining the same garden year after year and growing the more marginal crops gets more tricky. Cucumbers, tomatoes, celery, squash, peas, are among things we grow, some easily, some a challenge. Many plants get grouped together, that grow in the same soil and conditions. There are special varieties of plants adapted to our climate, or even my garden.

Iris and I have been working with a Siberian tomato called Black Prince. I have been getting heirloom seeds, which mostly means plants that make seeds you can save and grow. This tomato is reverting to its original Siberian past. Seed companies sell seeds that you must buy again each year. We cannot save the seeds from produce. When there is a dependency on the source of these seeds, the price goes up. There is a form of control going on. I feel more comfortable having plants I can save the seeds from. Since food is a necessity of life, it is one method used to control

123

people. The Indian was controlled, partly by wiping out the buffalo and substituting a dependency on white man's weevil flour.

"Great information, Miles, but what does that have to do with now! Good grief!" The subject of 'food' encompasses a lot of ground from fertilizer types, sources of seeds, who harvests, harvest methods, storage, sale, marketing. Each of those levels has been in the news. Fertilizer is a big issue. Many people feel chemical fertilizers are not good for us, make us unhealthy. Pesticides is another big issue.

'Organic' is the word of the decade. However, I have an issue with organic. I can neither see, nor taste the difference in most products, between organic and non-organic. One might not be good for me, and the other might be better. Organic might cost twice as much. The only visual difference I can see is a sticker. I do not trust man enough to believe the sticker. It would be easy to grow cheap with chemicals and pay someone to get an organic sticker, in order to double profits. When billions of dollars are on the line, I find it easy to believe there is going to be some hanky panky going on. In the news, so and so accused of such and such. The world is shocked.

"Instead of being shocked to find out yet one more food company illegally imported watermelon fertilized with raw human crap from Mexico, and distributed to the school food program, why not grow your own?" I want to know why that is so strange, and why I am such a kook for doing so. There are many other issues, such as genetically altered foods, potentially fixed prices, and shortages. I do understand the skeptics. The sky is falling. There is a hole in the ozone, earthquakes increase, biological warfare is already upon us, pollution, cancer, Genocide in third world countries, the poor elephants, spotted owls. There are plenty of causes, problems, doom and gloom, for those who wish to choose something to stress over. There are fanatics connected to cults, ready to go to war in the name of their cause. I do get it, I really do. I'm not stressed. I hope I am not a fanatic.

The subject is part of a bigger view. If an activity that can resolve an issue is easy, fun, or the activity outweighs the disadvantage of ignoring the issue, then I consider engaging in it. Often issues are in the back of my mind, but I do nothing because activity requires more than I am willing to do. I care about spotted owls and elephants. They are not near me. They are not relevant in my life. I'm not bothering them any more than anyone else around me. I do believe we are all responsible to some degree, as we are all part of consumption, pollution, waste, overcrowding.

Perhaps I just like gardening. Playing in the dirt is healthy, good physical activity. In my view, humankind has gardened for a million years. It is in our shared genetics. The greenhouse came with the house. Judy, the old woman I got the house from, passed away in Anchorage. Her children are very glad I keep the house the same and did not tear it down. I had promised not to, but that agreement is not legally binding. I think of Judy now and then when I am in the greenhouse, or see her wooden Buddha in the garden.

"Miles, the cucumber vines are up and across the roof!" Yes, twenty-foot vines full of cucumbers. Straight eight is the old standby, but some experimental lemon did ok, and a variety from England.

"Iris, once the lemon was the only cucumber that survived. I think it can handle extra heat and dryness." I thought the early Tanana variety of cherry tomatoes would do better. I'm surprised we got hardly any. Fifty days to harvest. Some 'eighty day to harvest' did better, how odd. We had cut window blinds into strips for garden pot labels. We write the date the seed was started, when transplanted, variety, and any other information relevant to duplicating what we did different.

"Tried sand" is written on some plants, like a few cucumbers. I had read up on where plants originated and see carrots and cucumbers began in sand when in the wild. No, it did not make any difference. I love experimenting, learning, creating. There is always something to try.

We got one eggplant off two plants. *Too much of a hot weather crop.* I wondered if the twenty-four hours of sun and hot greenhouse would work, but no, because now and then the greenhouse gets cool. Many herbs do well in the greenhouse in pots. Dill, fennel, basil, sage, parsley, chives, oregano all do well. These get dried for later use. I built a big six foot dehydrator with a small wood stove in it. Recycled window screens slide in and out. It is possible to dry fifty pounds at a time. Beets, turnips, and carrots are blanched in a five gallon kettle set on a converted barbecue grill, using wood instead of charcoal.

Left over peelings and tops go in the compost bin. This is four x four x six feet tall, with a glass window for a hinged lid. The sun comes in, cooking the compost at 120 degrees. This kills any weed seeds. Leaves from the yard are added to the compost instead of paying to haul them to the dump, or burning and polluting. Sawdust and chips from cutting firewood are added, as well as grass clippings. Some garbage gets added—egg shells, coffee grounds, duck feathers, and fish guts. The compost bin has a two foot hinged locked door at the bottom that allows me to shovel compost from the bottom of the pile. The garden is twenty x thirty feet. So is the greenhouse, but two stories tall.

Our 1916 log cabin is heated mostly with wood. We have two small efficient computerized Toyo oil stoves. One in the front room, one in the back. In summer, we never need heat in the back room, so that stove comes out and goes in the greenhouse to keep night temperatures above fifty degrees. I go through $200 worth of fuel in the greenhouse. The total costs for the garden for the summer is $500. We produce about $3,000 worth of food. Some we can sell as pickles at $8 a quart and recoup some of our costs. We sell starter plants and flower baskets in late spring. The 300 foot of road frontage is covered with a hundred flower baskets, with dripper hoses to water them. The goal is to make the $500 the garden costs. So far it has not happened. It is time to move the Toyo stove from the greenhouse back to the cabin, in preparation for cooler weather soon to arrive.

"Miles, the heating hose is not working again!"

"Dang." I do not know why this project has been such a headache. I wrapped copper tubing around the outside of the trash-burning barrel. Tin went around it to help hold heat when I burn trash. I run water through the tubing, which is hooked to a hose that goes through the greenhouse, the compost, and the garden rows. A twelve volt pump run by solar panels pushes water through the system. Or it is supposed to. There is fifteen feet of head pressure. It is possible the pump cannot overcome the head pressure. Still, hot water should rise on its own, without a pump, *so what is the problem!*

Plan B. I hook a supply line to my pressured city water. Water heated by the sun is pushed through the system. At the end of the line is a hot water sprinkler. It takes about thirty minutes for water coming out of the sprinkler to be the cold supply. A battery valve timer is put in the line, so when I burn trash, the water shuts off in half an hour. In this way, I am not wasting heat when I burn trash.

I am now on the grid. I spent thirty-five years off the grid. I'm going to enjoy what the grid offers, at the same time able to easily step away. There is city water, but I still have my well. If I had to, I could go to the river for water. A generator can supply power if needed, but I have lived without electric a lot of years and been happy. I have the skills to live off the grid. I know how to run sled dogs for transportation if gas is too expensive or unavailable.

The garden is put up, and it is September. The community Wellness group I am part of has members who believe in self-sufficiency, away from government dependency. Part of taking care of ourselves is sharing and trading our resources. Iris and I have a surplus of pickles. But the beet crop was dismal. At a wellness meeting, I find out one of our members has more beets than they know what to do with, and would like some pickles. I trade for cheese, yogurt, and milk, with another local farmer. I give away potatoes, and earlier, hanging baskets of flowers. Sometimes I get a returned favor, but do not demand or expect it. A gift is just that, no expectation of a payback.

"Miles, do you need anything from town? We are headed into Fairbanks." Iris could use a gallon of milk, and I'm out of bananas. Even though we have a local grocery store, prices are twice what they are in Fairbanks. It is difficult to directly convert trades and favors into a dollar value. Did this person offer to shop for us because we gave them potatoes a year ago? Or would they have offered, anyway? Am I, in fact, getting the equivalent of the $500 in value out of the garden, which is my goal? How do you place a dollar value on helping others, having a network of connected people who look out for each other?

My financial worth is not important to me, but it is to others. 90% of our standing in the pecking order is about money. 90% of respect has to do with money, and the things we buy with it. It matters because I lost a relationship with my parents over this subject. Lost a wife over this subject. I lose credibility over this subject. When I wish to make a point at a city meeting, or influence the community, my standing in the community matters. That standing is 90% about net financial worth. Trading does not count. Those who trade drop in social status. One step above a dumpster diver.

My social standing when living alone in the wilds was quite high. I owned the world. I was at the top of the food chain. It is difficult to take such a huge step downward. It shouldn't matter, as long as I am happy. That could be the issue. I do not think I am as happy as I once was. It wasn't my choice to come out of the wilds. Or more, we always have a choice. Maybe decisions are not always clear-cut. It is nice to have Iris. It is nice to have a shop with electricity for my tools. I'm concerned and effected, that subsistence is at the bottom of the food chain. I am attending a Fish and Wildlife meeting. The subject is local moose hunting.

The meeting is fifty miles away at the next community down the road, Healy. The discussion is about moose hunting in the game management around Nenana, not Healy. Fish and Game wants local input. Local is not Healy. There appears to be no practical reason to hold the meeting in Healy instead of Nenana. I arrive already suspicious what the government is up to now!

A biologist tells us. "We are concerned there are too many moose in 20A and 20C. We need to solve this problem, because the overpopulation we have observed over the past decade may affect the health of the population. Already, we observe signs of overfeeding and stress. There is not enough food for the existing population of moose to eat." Without getting into the details, Fish and game claims to have counted all the moose in the management area by airplane. An area the size of some states.

I daydream. I was out paddling a canoe one day. From twenty feet I could not see the moose. I had to get two feet away. Able to touch it with my paddle before I saw it. I'm considered an experienced hunter. Usually when in a group I am the first to spot game, with a, "My God how did you see that!" The moose had submerged itself in the creek next to a root wad that looked just like his antlers. His head is out of the water with a five-foot antler spread and I can't see it. How is that possible? The art of disguise. He even had his head tilted to the side to better blend in with the direction of the root wad. I was not hunting, and did not need a moose. I stopped the canoe. Tilted my hat, "Have a good afternoon, Sir."

More statistics and numbers are coming from the front of the room. Few of us in the room believe the numbers. These are Healy people. The numbers are not matching what we locals see when we cover this ground living our lives. . It is time for questions and comments from the audience.

I raise my hand, "You say the moose are showing signs of stress due to overpopulation, what are these signs?"

"The cows are not having as many twins calves. We know in a healthy population there is a high percentage of twins born." This is all he has to offer as evidence.

I therefore ask, "Could the stress be caused by the forest fires in the area, and heavy smoke? Do the collars you put on the cows cause stress? Maybe bulls find cows with collars on unattractive. Would that stress them? Would flying low over them trying to count them cause stress? Global warming? Being hunted? I'm not hearing anything that convinces me this stress is lack of feed and overpopulation." In truth, I think the biologist chose overpopulation, because that fits some hidden agenda. Overpopulation, meaning there is not enough feed, would have the feed responding from the over harvest. Moose depend on willow and birch trees. Locals are not seeing a lack of these but, in fact, an increase.

"Thank you for your comment, next!"

Josh tells me his view, he is at the meeting. "Miles, Nenana is classified a native village. As such, it is a subsistence community. Nenana is the closest subsistence community to a large non-subsistence community like Fairbanks. It bothers a lot of people we can go get a moose any time we want."

Yes, I know the white man's side of this story. I hear it from hunters who want to know why these half-gas-can Indians, (Athabascan) get to hunt, when whites cannot. Many want to see the Indians clock cleaned. I believe that racial discrimination is encouraged on both sides by the government as a way to divide and conquer. Put those others in their proper place. Others who are not like us. This includes low life white people who live like Indians. Hunting guides and the rich, as well as politicians and their friends, all want to head out for a day of sport hunting without having rules to follow. Taking away the moose in Nenana would make us all equal. No moose, no preference. Has the government got a plan? Josh thinks the moose population is low, but if biologists call the population high, and lets the rich sport hunter from the city in to trophy hunt, this will gain political points, and cut the moose population so there will be no subsistence.

Josh adds, "The same as was done with the buffalo in the lower states to put the Indian under the white man's thumb." I'm not so sure the loss of buffalo was so contrived, so let the comment go. I'm guessing this is what Indians all over are telling each other. I certainly think the government is capable. I am not sure there is enough reason. It is announced at this meeting, the plan is to open moose cow season around Nenana.

Many locals are happy with the cow season! Cows are so easy to get! We have trained them over the past 100 years to not be afraid of us. Many locals have cow moose living in their yards. People have ponds, put food out, encourage moose to hang out. It is fun to see them walk up to the window of the house and look in. Cows walk the downtown streets sometimes. We know them. It's not legal to feed or interact with wild animals. Yet opening a killing season on these cows is slaughter. Cows have learned to move in close to the community in winter when wolves are about. Wolves do not come in close, because trappers will get them. The cows are safe from wolves when they come close to people. Until now, we protected them. Who will tell the cows the rules just changed?

Sure, I hunt and depend on moose for food! Part of subsistence is to not hunt in my own backyard. As a subsistence community, we all have our hunting camps spread out over several hundred miles. My area is the homestead on the Kantishna 140 miles away. Some locals are not considerate. Mad bragged last year that he was able to walk up to one of the cow moose in someone's driveway. It walked right up to him, and he shot her from ten feet.

Fish and Wildlife is advising at their Anchorage and Fairbanks office, "All hunters go hunt in Nenana, where there is a surplus of moose, and the hunting is easy."

Many locals are not subsistence, and do not eat moose. Many of these citizens are concerned with the number of cars that hit moose on the highway, cars are totaled; people killed. Such people do not think wild animals and man can coexist, so it would be fine if there were no more moose. Others have no opinion, so would simply go along with the decision and not argue with their government. Even Nenana is not in agreement on this issue.

"No Josh, I am not going to take a cow in town." I feel doing what is right, moral, just, is more important than legal. "Something is going on we do not understand, Josh. It's not about saving the moose, or the environment, or looking out for the people."

Josh adds, "This moose mismanagement reminds me of the collapse of the fishing industry starting twenty years ago."

"I know, Josh, I went to the meetings, got copies of the minutes. I still have proof of illegal government activity."

"Who are you turning this evidence in to, Miles. It would be nice to see something legal going on!"

I pause before asking, "Who would you report this to?"

After thinking about it, Josh says there is no one he trusts in the government. No agency. It's corrupt from the president on down the food chain. If you reported any wrongdoing to the wrong person, they could shut you up, made to disappear. Whistle blowers rarely come out ahead. "What about the news media, Miles?"

"I thought of that." I explain to Josh that the news media needs sensation, and an agenda. If making big government looking bad fits today's agenda, they may be interested in what I have to say. At the same time, politics owns the news media. In truth, I have nothing earth shattering, no single piece of sensational revealing document or recording that would blow some cover out of the water. What is it I am trying to accomplish? That is what I have to first ask. I am not going to try to single-handedly, right the wrongs of the world.

"It's called leverage Josh, bargaining chips." I've actually got a nice working relationship with the state level of government. I went in and talked to them, asking what issues they have with me. What would it take to make it right? I was surprised by what they said. "What we care about most is the white ivory trade. What you are doing with the teeth, claws, bones, skulls, feathers, is not so important. We can overlook all that." I in fact have legal papers for my white ivory. Legally they cannot touch me. Do I care about the law? I care about getting along with my government! I am smart enough to know that to survive, I have to be a team player. Every single package I ship is being held up and damaged. Legal items are confiscated from shops. I cannot run my business. Am I going to get justice by making my government wrong? I think not!

"How about if I voluntarily turn over all my white ivory and stay out of that business?"

"All your problems will go away."

That is what I did. It's been almost ten years now. We have both kept our word. My ability to make trouble is just in case I ever end up in court. Or more, I want Fish and Game to know what a day in court with me would be like. I mentioned some of the information I have. Embarrassing stuff. I did not see it as a threat or blackmail. It's like discussing any agreement. A scene might play out like this:

"What if we just lock you up, Miles!?" I nod, "Yes, you could try that." I push some papers over saying, "What if I decided to turn this over to my defense lawyer." Nothing said, but I believe we have an understanding. Even mutual respect. "I leave you alone, you leave me alone." In truth, I have little sympathy for the woes of the people and their government. The people allowed it and could stop it, change it, but choose not to. Considering the situation, I plan to deal with what exists, in a way I am a survivor.

Many of the game officers collect my art! Their wives wear my animal parts jewelry. It might seem strange to arrest me for creating and selling what their wives are wearing. I'm guessing, unless I get horribly out of line, I can do my thing. Life is good, I'm allowed to fit in under Indian subsistence laws. I should, I live like one. There is a strong possibility I am, in fact, part native American. I cannot prove it, records were altered. DNA might prove it, but why bother? I am obviously connected closely to the land and depend on the land. I am not asking to be above the law, or allowed to be a criminal because I have the goods on the guys with the baseball bat. I'm asking to be treated fairly, honestly, legally. *Too bad it takes threats to make that happen, but life can be like that. Not as we dream it.*

I get out some paperwork stored in the computer concerning the old issues that have not gone away. My memory is a little inaccurate. I forgot, for example, this was six years ago, while I was so sure it was over ten! I only remembered one owl claw. An undercover Agent turned in his receipts for purchase. I kept a copy. His code name was Stark. Stark posed as a friend and customer.

LAWS VIOLATED tc \l2 "Laws Violated"

16 UCS §1372 - Marine Mammal Protection Act - On or about February 1, 2003, Miles MARTIN did knowingly and unlawfully offer to sell, and did sell marine mammal products to wit: One (1) small walrus ivory box and two (2) small white walrus ivory scraps, in violation of 1372(a)(4)(B).

I'm guessing from the above note I am dealing with a Federal issue.

When I went to court, it was traffic violations being heard. *That's state then, right??* Whoever wrote the charges on the ivory did not know the entire law. *I'd like to know who is charging me. Federal laws are different from state laws.* There are exceptions to the general laws. I had proper papers for legal white ivory. The items described are finished ivory recorded by the government. I was told I can specifically have and sell, recorded and photographed as legal. There is a complication. I find the reference.

MARTIN told SA Stark that selling white ivory is illegal. MARTIN told SA Stark that MARTIN bought 80 pounds of white ivory scraps from a lady in a Fairbanks gift shop who wanted to get rid of the ivory because it was illegal. Not the greatest conversation to have recorded with an undercover agent.

I acquired the batch of ivory as described. The seller I bought from thought it might be illegal, but was not sure, and simply did not want to offer it to the public, and get involved in the controversy. I told this undercover guy posing as a customer, "Usually illegal." I did not wish to get into a legal debate reviewing all related laws and exceptions, qualifications and paperwork with a customer. Other reasons as well: I was willing to take a chance because animal parts is my specialty, not the lady I bought from, and I study the laws and know the exceptions, but more, understand the reason and intentions. She told me she got the ivory from a native, before 1972. There was no receipt, but there rarely is, even now, when dealing with village natives. She did give me old pictures. I did not tell her that before 1972 would make it legal, because the price would go up. I see proving legality could be an issue, but so would proving illegal. Much of the law has to do with intent. I'm not gong to debate the law with a customer. Even the government later told me to stop offering legal advice, I'm not a lawyer. So there is a liability issue they point out.

I never weighed the box, so the amount is unknown. To impress a customer it might be eighty pounds, when I imagine, and try to guess. The scale never used might read fifty pounds. I failed to mention 75% is pea size, not usable tiny scraps. Only a pound or two is nice size, over an ounce, golf-ball sizes. Nothing highly sought after would be the point. Truly 'scrap,' a Native carvers garbage. *No walrus was killed just to supply anyone with this ivory.* I am convinced the walrus was legally subsistence harvested, the meat was eaten, and this ivory a by-product of scraps left over from native carvers. That is what the laws are for, to protect walrus, right? *Or is this, in fact, not about protecting walrus?*

I sometimes get customers who are irritated with the government. They hate forms, rules, regulations that interfere with the ability of small people staying in business. Laws that are 'nonsense.' Laws not about protecting the game or the environment. Such customers often feel better if they think they are avoiding the government in some way, expressing their rebellion. Like buying some white ivory under the table the government does not know about for cash that goes unreported! I might say, "Yeah!" and make a sale. Or add my own government story to the fire. Why mention to such a customer this is actually a legal transaction? What a bummer.

Also, as a salesman, story teller… Well, it helps to believe what you say. *At the time you say it.* It's an art. *How to explain.* Hmmm. The desire to please, not just to sell. To 'be there,' to be in the head of the customer and understand where they are, be there with them in their time and space with their beliefs. A character in their movie. I'm with Crafty, I know what it means to be a Scientologist! I can walk and talk the talk. An hour later I am a Christian, an hour after that a seventh day Adventist. It's not just an act. I spent time with my pilot friend, Maul, and he tells me I am the best Seventh Day Adventist he knows! I take it as a compliment and enjoy the attention and pleasing my friend. Does the term 'lie' apply? I can disconnect and reconnect, now I am a great Mormon. I can argue for or against any of these spiritual beliefs and win the argument. It's an art, a gift. Is it acting? I do not call it this or feel like I am acting. I am truly there.

I assume an agent would show me a badge, tell me I am under arrest, at which time, I prove this is all just a misunderstanding, it's legal! Or, do an age test. I say it's pre 1972. Prove it's not. Go for it.

Part of the definition of a 'lie,' is knowingly misrepresenting, for the purpose of bringing about harm. A lie is not just the opposite of truth. Long ago mankind believed the earth was flat. Was it a lie to say it was? Is it a lie to say the earth is round? The earth is in fact slightly pear shaped. "Well, sorta round!" Does, 'sort of,' and 'close,' count as truth? Under what conditions? I'm not convinced I 'misrepresented.' I did not know for a certainty. The customer wanted a yes or no answer. It could go either way. It's an opinion. I, or anyone else can say whatever they want, that doesn't make it a fact. As a salesman, important to me is, we both agree, and that agreement is not likely, or knowingly, going to hurt anyone.

My buddy Josh laughs."Yes, the man with the golden pen!"

"A customer tells me there are lion claws for sale on eBay and I need to check them out!" I review this with Josh quickly, since I already told this story. This lady selling the claw on the internet visits India, and is talking to an old man who has lion or tiger claws.

He tells her, "I have a tree out back that is a lion scratching post! I go out each morning and gather the claws off the tree, and put them in this basket."

This lady put the story on eBay, explaining that her source said no lion was killed, and how environmentally sound this whole deal is. What a crock of cottage cheese! No cat sheds claws with the bone in it. There is only one way to get them. Off a dead cat. But the old man did not want to hurt the woman's feelings, so told her what she wanted to hear, out of courtesy to her feelings

I go on, "Along those lines, Josh, I listen to my customer as a man of magic." I want to figure out exactly what it is the customer wants. One common type customer comes up and whispers, "Got anything special for me?" Wink, wink, looking to the right and the left.

I get it! I smile sagely. Holding my hand up. "I have something that may interest you." *Seek and ye shall find.* I reach under the table, and, like the customer, look to the right and left and speak secretly. *"Something special. A secret between me and you. Shhhh, you are the only one who has this."*

The best example was the customer that wanted the inside claw off the right foot of a black panther five years old. With a straight face, I say, "I have just what you are looking for and deserve." I sold the customer a lynx claw that I have 12,000 of. No one can supply this item the customer wants. He is a fool to ask or look. He got what he so richly deserves. Not crap. Not a fake. Not plastic. The closest thing he will ever see to what he wants. He is happy with it. No one he knows will ever prove this is not what he says it is. He will show it off and be Mr. Cool. I did not overcharge him.

I honestly think the customer would not hate me, or be mad, if the truth came out in court. I'd get an, "I understand." Often, 'ivory' is coveted, hard to get, and many customers think it is not legal! They are told so by gift shops and customs agents at borders. This is what they read in the simple pamphlet handed out to tourists, "Avoid all ivory and be safe!" They get told. Well! They want the item, anyway! The item is in fact legal under specific conditions the customer is not interested in and may not understand, or be able to repeat if asked. They are not here for a quote of the law! So! I keep a secret, let them keep their fantasy. Secretly pass on this coveted item they think is illegal, and they will prize as the only one who has it from a secret special source they cannot reveal! A taste of the wild side! We both nod. I in fact often have the legal paperwork if there is ever an issue. Along the lines of selling pirate flags. A story of daring deeds of courage, a little on the risky side. I am, after all, Oz. You want ruby red slippers and witches? Bwalla. It is yours.

It's what some want, I supply that. So I pick up on this 'want' when an undercover agent shows up, whispering about secret forbidden items. If he would have stepped forward and said, "You are under arrest for..." and presented some charges. I would have pulled out the legal papers and proof of legality. If asked why I presented it as illegal. I'd have said, And why did you ask for something illegal? I ask myself, but say out loud, "Because that is what you wanted it to be, and I want you to be happy." Many people wish to taste of the forbidden fruit. As a man of magic, 'poof!' It is so. *Am I repeating myself?* It's scary stuff.

Here is more concerning the ivory. It is me who has to point out to my public defender.

Title 50: Wildlife and Fisheries

PART 18—MARINE MAMMALS

Subpart C—General Exceptions

§ 18.26 Collection of certain dead marine mammal parts.

(a) Any bones, teeth or ivory of any dead marine mammal may be collected from a beach or from land within ¼ of a mile of the ocean. The term "ocean" includes bays and estuaries.

(b) Marine mammal parts so collected may be retained if registered within 30 days with an agent of the National Marine Fisheries Service, or an agent of the U.S. Fish and Wildlife Service.

Such items might conceivably be bartered between subsistence people, turned into crafts, re-traded, cut up. The original receipt kept with the original major part of a tusk, since only one permit is issued for one tusk. In this case, even a very fresh looking piece of ivory might be legal.

"Wouldn't the prosecution have to prove otherwise?" There are other exceptions for ivory and bear parts, but I am not organized, and cannot easily find what I need. Google searches do not come up with the exceptions.

Monday, May 29, 2006

Hi Miles,

The equivalent in the state courts to what the attorney is talking about is what we call Strict Liability charges that are brought as a "ticket" rather than as a criminal charge. We can (and do) deal with them on a much less formal basis than we deal with criminal charges. This is allowed by the courts because the charge is considered a minor offense and carries much less serious possible penalties than if the charge is brought as a criminal case.

So yes, this note I find confirms 'all that' was considered minor, the equivalent of a traffic ticket. Easy to forget. The next letter is the same time period having to do with a resolution to my having white ivory. An acknowledgment I can have it.

Dear Mr. Martin:

This deals with some further particulars you asked about.

About the white ivory, please indicate when you could bring it to Fairbanks to USF&W. The purpose is twofold: 1. to have F&W inventory what finished ivory carvings you have and intend to sell, and 2. for you to abandon the raw ivory to F&W on one of their abandonment forms. You will be representing that the carved ivory you show them is all you have and intend to sell. They will make a record and/or photo of what it consists of. You will be instructed that the sales must be domestic sales only, not outside the United States.

The website should be cleaned up to eliminate any suggestion or hint that products may not be legal. For example "I am more interested in morality than legality"

Stephen Cooper
Assistant United States Attorney
Fairbanks, Alaska

So the government acknowledges my art work made from white walrus ivory is legal, and I can sell it. The concern is the raw material sales of white ivory. I could probably win in court if I chose to fight! However I agree to voluntarily stay out of the controversy. I have some finished pieces I can sell off. I'm happy with that at the time. I can avoid this material, as there are plenty of materials selling well. I reply to the letter.

I'll clean up my website, but want a sign off or approval or help from someone to confirm there is no issue. Preferably someone I can ask from time to time if new items listed are acceptable and if not, a law shown me or explained to me so there will be no future problems.

I ask for a sign off on my website because I am not clear exactly what the problem is, or what items are found to be offensive. As far as I was concerned, nothing on my website is illegal. The comment about being moral on my website has to do with what I think is a good way to present my business. Meaning if we have an issue, I am not going to go get a lawyer and try to sue you and go to court. Moral and ethical. That means we will work it out between us, I want to do what's right by you. I'm not looking for loopholes by which I can screw you.

Meaning I am looking for like-minded people to do business with. There is no implication, in my view, these words of ethics and morality indicate I am attempting to be a criminal. Being a criminal is immoral. Displeasing those who are in charge is about intent. My intent is to get along and be legal. *So tell me what legal is?* If I have trouble figuring it out, give me a contact so I may call, visit, ask questions, of someone who knows, and is honest and accountable. Put it in writing. If that is not going to happen, why not? Are you up to no good?

I recall showing up at the Fish and Wildlife office with a friend. As soon as I walked through the door, an officer jumps up and verbally attacks me.

"What are you doing with that owl feather in your hat, that's illegal!"

"Excuse me, Sir, but it is not illegal. I am a subsistence person. Owls are on the edible hunting list. If I can eat it, I can keep the feathers and use them as I wish, as long as I do not sell them." This is part of my spiritual belief. I have been wearing an owl feather in my hat since the beginning of time. I am on the cover of a magazine wearing this very hat and feather. No one has ever said it is illegal.

I'm grabbed like a criminal. The feather is confiscated. There is no receipt, no charges, no papers. Everyone in the room thinks it's funny. In the same way it would be funny to cut the dreadlocks off a black man. In the same way it is funny to remove a tie off a dweeb in a biker bar. Or pull the cross off a Christian, cut a hippie's hair off. I felt threatened. I was scared. I was highly offended. I was felt to be made spiritually weaker. No one at any point asked why I had come in, or if they could assist me in any way.

"I will never voluntarily come into the office ever again." I told my friend. There were a dozen laughs as I stomped out the door. I took in the setting in a few glances. There is no line of people inside, no one getting permits. There is no parking lot. No name on the building. No reception desk or secretary. All the windows are small and dirty. There is not one single plant, art piece, or thing of beauty to be seen. The room looks old and dusty. Papers are scattered all over, and full of coffee stains. Workers sit on top of desks to chat. There is zero class. I got the impression of low budget. I was reminded of scenes in spy movies of mobsters.

I compare this to the same agency, only the biologists. Big three-story building with the American flag flying, name on the building, all shiny and clean. A spacious paved parking lot filled with hustle and bustle, many people leaving and arriving. There are big clean picture windows filled with plants taken care of by secretaries who care. Art is on every wall, with displays to look at, benches to sit on while waiting. Smiling faces and happy music is playing. Bright lights, a public restroom. No dirty coffee cups lying around or papers on the floor, or people sitting on desks visiting. They are there to serve the public, and act like it. It would be easy to get a permit here, but no, it is the wrong building.

My friend says, "It seems there would be more people needing to get a permit than to visit with a biologist. The buildings should be switched around, huh?"

Another friend comments, "I had a similar experience, Miles. It is not just you. I went in to the same nondescript, hard to find building. I wanted to know if I needed a permit to keep the walrus head I inherited from a relative when they died. Officers could not, or did not, tell me. They took my name and address. A search warrant was obtained. The mount was confiscated, and I was arrested and fined." With horror stories like this being circulated, who wants to trust these people to even go ask anything? So, I want the court to assign me a specific person who is responsible for me having all the right stuff. If I do not have legal goods, it will be this guy's fault. If I have gone and asked and got in writing, but given the runaround or wrong papers, I have a face and a name and a judge's orders to point to. The judge assigns me someone named Rowland.

"Remember, this has been at my insistence, not the courts!"

"YO! MILES! HEY!" Someone I think looks familiar walks up to me at the boat landing.

"I need to look at your boat set up!" A beady eyed, curly red headed local asks me questions about what pitch propeller I use, saying, "I got a boat and engine just like yours! I want to do what you do and go fossil hunting. I hear it's a lucrative business!"

I only comment, "So they say."

"Crazy Lawson says you go to the boneyard on the Yukon! What I want to know is, how do you do that and not get caught?"

I reply, "Who says I go there?"

Snort. "Everyone knows Miles, come on. You can't keep it to yourself! Ya got to share the wealth!" Pause. I say nothing. "How much gas do you need? I heard last time you left you had 70 gallons on board. Figure 700 miles. Figure two days there, two days back, gone under a week. I figure that puts you at the boneyard. Smack in the middle of Federally protected parkland, Miles. It doesn't take a rocket scientist to figure it out."

I smile, like he got me there! *No one knows anything but what I tell them. No one knows how much gas I load, or how many days I am gone. All anyone knows is what I tell them. If this guy thinks it's easy to figure out, let him, and anyone else who wants to follow, go to this boneyard and get arrested.* I'm not in an especially good mood considering the legal questions already being asked. So here is a guy buying a boat and engine like mine so he can be like me. I notice he is not loading his boat the same way, so will not get the gas mileage I get.

I put all my gas in the front to balance the weight of the heavy engine in back. Mr. Bug Eye has not noticed. Nor does he know what pitch propeller works best. I notice an aluminum propeller while I use stainless. Important because aluminum bends and changes pitch under a load and breaks when it hits a stick. He may try to secretly follow me. *Go for it! I have a depth sounder I figured out how to get to work at 30 miles an hour. I can lead him into shallow water. But here is proof I need to be aware of my surroundings. This guy might even be capable of bushwhacking me.* Any time quick, easy money is involved, someone else will consider snaffling it. No one considers I may not even be mentioning the correct river I get fossils on.

I show up for the first meeting with this Rowland game officer I am assigned to. This is all difficult to speak of in present time as it is so horrific. I assume we will review my business. He will pile up the proper permits. Review with me what they are, and when they expire. If it cost me a $1,000, so be it. At least I can feel I am covered.

I begin, "I have a bunch of musk ox horn cut up in pieces. I understand it cannot be a trophy with two horns connected. Is this covered under the standard $100 export permit for animal products?" This is a common highly sought after material for knife makers to make handles of.

Rowland just stares at me, strumming a pencil on his desk. He finally says, "I need the name and address of who supplies this musk ox horn." This does not look like a permit we are filling out in front of him. I get the impression we are working on an arrest warrant. I catch on that I am a criminal who was caught. Now I have the status of snitch, helping to bring down all my suppliers. It's the only relation this Rowland can comprehend. There is no prevention in his vocabulary. It's all about busting people. That is his job. His training is in how to use a gun, legally subdue and interrogate. I'm the enemy. His success and promotion is based on how many arrests he makes. So what is this crap about saving people? I can see his viewpoint. He does not understand why I was assigned to him. I gather his job has nothing to do with helping people, being a public servant, or preventing crime. Preventing crime puts him out of a job. He appears to me to be not very bright. Perhaps a good yes man, who knows how to follow simple instructions to the letter.

Hello Mr. Cooper, I sent off the final $500 yesterday. I found the polar bear claw referred to. I just had not been to that spot on the site in a while and so removed it from the site. I do not have any polar bear claws in my possession. A while back, a native friend told me he could get them for me if I was interested. I wanted to see how the laws were going, since polar bear claws had just hit the galleries. I believe I can legally sell a polar bear claw signed by a native craftsman. The laws are loosening up on other bear products.

I'm of the opinion I do not have to legally remove this polar bear claw from my website. I'm doing so to be polite. Out of courtesy. I could say, "Make me!" I'd win in court. It's easier not to do that. There is legal baiting of bears. There is no closed season. It is believed by biologists there is a surplus of bears to harvest. Bears are legally hunted for food. With all this going on, are we expected to throw away teeth, claws, hides? I'm puzzled.

I'M BACK HOME TRIMMING meat off a moose I shot. While I am looking over the meat and trimming bad spots, a car stops by. I step out and close the shop door, as a tall skinny Appalachian backwoodsman looking guy comes up to me.

"You're Miles, right? Yeah, think we knew each other back in the old days!"

I do not remember him, but there are many people I forget. I'm guessing this guy calling himself Jessie is here to either sell or buy. It does not hurt if he thinks we know each other and are friends. The assumption is, we have done business before, so trust each other.

Jessie talks fast: "Trying to raise some money and have some stuff for sale." I look in the back of the truck. He points out an outboard motor for sale, some guns, a pile of antler and furs. The antler interests me. His prices are reasonable. He goes on, "I can get all kinds of stuff. My wife is Eskimo from Savoonga." This is one of the few legal places to get fossil ivory artifacts, so is an important contact to meet. Old whalebone, oosic, fossil walrus ivory, is all highly sought after. Jessie says, "All easy for me to get." He will get back to me. I hear this often, so just nod that this sounds good. Noncommittal. We shall see what he actually comes up with. I conclude we do not know each other after all. Jessie says, "Yes, I used to get goat horns from you when you had that goat farm down the road! Remember?" I only smile. I certainly never had goats, and have not sold a lot of goat horns.

It would be awkward at this point to reply, "Actually, we do not know each other."

Jessie leaves. The encounter was just one of a hundred encounters with a hundred different suppliers similar to this. There is hardly a village in the interior of Alaska where I do not know someone. Savoonga is not interior, but coastal, a contact 800 miles away. My many years of living on the river in a houseboat got me introduced to a lot of village people. I like to think I have a good reputation as honest, a good person to do business with. I'm respected by most of the natives. There are some hothead natives making trouble, but trouble for everyone, even their own people. My Internet business is gravitating to what people want, the raw materials easy for me to get, but so sought after around the world. My art sells, but not like it used to during the pipeline days. Rocks, books, wood, other items I offer get only a little interest.

Iris points out a story of interest in the local Fairbanks paper. The story involves one of the famous Rasmusons' from the big foundation that many of our Nenana grants come from. I was involved in one such grant for the library. Apparently, a member of the family, Kaplan, was held up in the Fairbanks airport coming in from somewhere else, and almost arrested for illegal transportation and possession of ivory and baleen. I glance at the article. "We were going through customs," she said. "They asked, 'What's your necklace made of?' I said, 'Ivory.' They said, 'I'm going to have to get the Fish and Wildlife agent.' "Kaplan's necklace was walrus ivory. It is legal to possess in the United States under provisions of the Marine Mammal Protection Act, but it became the ticket to a bureaucratic Twilight Zone once it left the country.

I look further along the article and read, "Oh, that's really bad," the agent said. "Anything from a whale is really bad. I'm going to probably have to confiscate your jewelry. "

Iris is puzzled why all this is an issue! "The animal is already dead, died a long time ago. What is the big deal?"

I do not answer as I read further. Kaplan—president of the Rasmuson Foundation, wife of an Alaska Native and contributor to many political causes—started making phone calls. She called Sen. Mark Begich's office, the Fish and Wildlife Service in Anchorage and officers of the National Fish and Wildlife Foundation. They advised: 'Don't hand over your jewelry. Don't sign anything. Insist on speaking to the agent's supervisor.'

During the long back-and-forth the agent said, "I don't want to get the police involved." The stand-off ended when enforcement agents at Ted Stevens Anchorage International Airport in Anchorage phoned in and spoke to the Chicago agent. A guide prepared by the USFWS specifies that 'transporting walrus ivory out of the country requires a special CITES or Convention on International Trade in Endangered Species, permit in almost all cases.' USFWS spokesman, Bruce Woods said it's required for taking a pair of personally owned walrus earrings out of the country and back. If departing through Anchorage, the ivory-transporting traveler must pay a $186 inspection fee. The fee rises to $238 for travelers taking direct flights out of state from Fairbanks or Southeast because the staff to provide such inspections is in Anchorage. The traveler must also pay for the permit, which is $75, if the earrings were made before 1972, the date when the Marine Mammal Protection Act was passed—$100 if they are "post-Act. " The certificate can only be issued by the USFWS office in Arlington, Va., and can take up to 90 days to process.

If the agent hadn't been able to exercise discretion, the jewelry would have needed the full-blown, months-long, $186 inspection CITES permit to come back to Alaska. "I always wear my ivory jewelry because it doesn't contain metal," she said. "It doesn't set off the metal detectors. It never occurred to me that this would be an issue. "

I tell Iris, "Things are changing. Kaplan has traveled all over with no problems in the past. Now, out of the blue, there is trouble over something as common and basic as a pair of earrings someone has had for years. What is going on?" We can only speculate, but of interest, since I am in the business, and need to keep up on what is going on.

One building and it's supplies.

CHAPTER FIVE

TUCSON SHOW, FOLLOW THE MONEY, LEGAL ISSUES

The next day is another article! This time about a firefighter who brought a garter snake back home to Alaska. He caught the snake in some state where he and the crew on this plane were fighting a forest fire. I am a little familiar with the routine. Long ago, I worked with the firefighters. This fireman was arrested and charged with the felony of illegally importing exotic reptiles without a permit.

"Well Miles, there is the rest of the story to read!" Iris explains the snake got loose! The fire crew caught it and were passing the snake around on the plane. Not much more is said, but I speculate a stewardess or some outsider who is a city person, found this to be unpardonable! The snake might be poisonous! Any country person knows about harmless garter snakes, and knows such a snake could not live in the wild in Alaska. There is zero chance there would be any safety or environmental issues. Someone who does not know that, got all excited and made things happen.

Iris and I come back from a trip to Fairbanks in a car we just bought. A KIA Sportage with 40,000 miles for $2,000. I pay cash to a neighbor who had been asking more money, but they are leaving, and can use cash, so we get this for half its blue book value. Good gas mileage! Now we have a truck and a car. Iris presses the answering machine button to hear our messages.

"Miles, a friend of yours, Jake, over at Alaska Air Cargo asked me to call you and warn you the Feds have you under investigation. Just a heads up." Iris and I look at each other and wonder what that is about.

I tell her, "Well honey, it is to be expected in my line of work. Whatever is going on, I'm sure it will get worked out." I'm not a criminal. Everything is legal. Some subsistence laws are untested in court. Some laws the government doesn't follow themselves. So it is hard to know for sure if there is a potential problem. I'm assuming, like with the state, if there is an issue, I'll get called in and we'll have a talk and work things out. There could be a couple of hundred dollar problems here and there to discuss. Only maybe.

I check over my shop to see if anything stands out as glaringly illegal or out of line. Many items I do not have receipts for. I have had these items thirty years. Will I have to prove that? I can if I must. Many of my suppliers of long ago are still around and could testify. What would it cost to get wilderness people in to court?

The biggest issue I see is bear claws. I have a friend on the game board who told me he was instrumental in legalizing the sale of bear claws for craft purposes. Like most laws, it has not been openly announced to the public. Most people therefore think it is still illegal. Possibly even many officers of the law. I understand the law concerning bear claw sales was opened with trepidation. There is a concern there could be an over-harvest of bears to get claws. Because I understand this concern, I sell them, but do not put big banners up and go high profile. Nor do I tell other vendors of the law change. I stay low profile. Grizzly bear claws are off-limits, *in most cases, but not all.*

Unless the bear was harvested way downriver, like near Galena, where I spent a year on the houseboat. I still have connections in Galena. Plenty of friends there can supply legal claws. Claws from bears that raided mine camps. Likewise, I have still got claws I acquired when I was there, trading my finished art for raw materials.

Anyhow, bears are state regulated, not a federal issue, unless the claw crossed state lines. Bear claws in my case would not be of federal interest. *Not their jurisdiction.* "Right!" The state, whose jurisdiction this falls under, is not upset with my activities. Not upset because the intent of the law is upheld. No one is hunting bears for parts on my account. I rarely buy bear claws twice from the same person, and always in low amounts.

"Honey, it is like getting told you can expect an audit. What do you do besides saying, 'Rats' and, 'Oh well?'" Hopefully, it will not be anything serious. I have a few border line items in my private collection I can legally have, but not sell. These items are clearly marked as not for sale. They are not in the public domain, but in my bedroom or the back shop. There is one activity I am engaged in I am sure the Feds would go through the roof over if they knew! But perfectly legal. I am dying and stabilizing fossils so they look older, or have enhanced value. Some would call that creating fakes. Within the realm of creating magic. *Is dyed turquoise fake, frowned on, illegal?*

95% of all turquoise sold on the market is dyed and stabilized. What about dyed, stabilized, stained, laminated, or veneer wood? I am sure I am more upset then customers. I consider it a crime customers so often refuse to buy #2 grade. Refuse green, red, colors in ivory. Ivory has to be blue! 99.9% of all fossil ivory I find is not sellable. After thirty years of trying, I've filled nine buildings with low-grade materials hard to sell. I see no reason I should not figure out something to do with this wasted material, rather than put it in the dump. I'm honest. "This on your right is dyed and stabilized for $75. On your left is natural, same colors, for $200." I'm experimenting with veneers, laminates, chips in resin. This all could present legality issues proving the source of all the chips. Legally, would each chip need separate proof or origin?

I have a pressure cooker and vacuum chamber. Experiments are done with a variety of methods to get dye and resin into soft materials that have little value, to create items that do have value. I might be able to make it into jewelry—if soft could be made hard. It's also possible to take barely legal material, and darken it, to make sure it is for sure dark enough to be legal fossil. Just so there are no questions. The scary part for the Feds is, some unscrupulous person might take very illegal material, and turn it into a fossil to make it legal. That would be a nightmare. This treated material might be impossible to age, carbon date, do DNA on. I am coming up with some methods of treatment so good, it is almost not possible to detect. I use chemicals from nature, but speed up the process with heat and pressure. I'm mostly artistically challenged by this. So far, too time consuming to be very practical or profitable. However, I'm working on it. As far as I have seen, no one else in the world is on the same track.

Winter arrives in a week and, as is common in the far north, sixty to seventy above one day, zero the next day. Never to get warmer for weeks. Snow arrives. It is the same snow that will be on the ground in seven months. I love all seasons in Alaska. Iris has a hard time with the cold. Getting dressed just to go out to get the newspaper is not what she enjoys. I got her a subscription to the newspaper as a Christmas gift. Winter is time for me to work in a heated shop on my art and various experiments: Jerry Lewis inventing flubber. A mad scientist's lab is one part of the shop. There are five separate shops connected by doors. The rooms are small, so easy to heat. I only heat the room I will be using that day, or for a few days. The first room is always heated; there is a Toyo oil stove and a big wood stove to heat without oil when I am around to feed it.

I show Iris again, because she still does not understand. "If you are looking for glue, that is in this front shop, the one always heated. Chemicals and things that cannot freeze are here. My foredoom carving tool is here. This is where all the fine detail of my projects is added." We enter the next room that is only four x eight. "This is the metal room where I make custom blades and do all my casting. Metal grinding and cutting equipment is here. There is the torch, the electric kiln, the electric metal melter. "If it is made of metal, look in here."

The next room is a little bigger. "This is the wood working room. Here is the bandsaw and stored pieces of wood." Iris wonders how I can move around and work. All the rooms are crowded. "The next room is the rock room." It has its own wood stove. Here, I have a main rock saw, and a separate trim saw. Rocks that need cutting are here. Cut ones are organized on a separate shelf. Another room is a huge shop area I hardly ever heat in winter. I could bring the truck or car in to work on it. There is a separate tool room as big as the wood or rock room. There is a nice, cool, dark room just for fossils to slow dry and age after they have come up out of the frozen ground. We have to move around the hanging moose quarters to get to the fossil door.

The shop is like my sanctuary. I am as a priest in my own monastery. Much in here is sacred. I do not have a troubled mind when I am in here working. Time stands still. There is just me, the material, and the tools. At one. Winter is that nice time of year we are not under a lot of pressure for anything. Tourist season is over. All that is necessary is to stay warm and sane. In summer when weather is great for being outside, it is hard to stay in the shop and work! I am gone on the river or working in the garden. Between now and the Tucson show is my most artistically productive time, about four months of intense work.

"Except to get firewood, Miles!"

True. I could gather firewood in fall as many do. Or buy wood from local cutters. I find it good exercise to be out on the snow machine once a week to go get a week's worth of firewood out in the local woods. I use the time to look for grouse or rabbits, look around, hunt, enjoy the snow for a few hours a week. In less than two hours, I can go, come back, and split a week's worth of wood for heating both the shop and house. I wonder how many hours the average person works to pay for a week's heat? I have costs too, saw and snow machine gas and maintenance. Mostly a business write off. I feel lucky to have such a life! One I am in control of. I do not have to worry about what is happening with the Arabs and the oil market. My heat source is right outside the door. If I had to, I could go back to sled dogs for hauling wood and supplies.

The story of how I live my life on the website. Many customers buy from me, wishing to support such a life, instead of supporting a big company.

Tuesday, November 29, 2011
   Hi Again!
   If you have time to send me an invoice, that would be good. I should be able to send this to you by the end of the week (:
   I've been busy finishing half a dozen rune sets in whitetail, cougar, wolf, and black bear bone. I sewed the last carved badge on the last pouch just a few minutes ago.
   Here, the weather is messed up- lots of days in the upper fifties and lower sixties. We had over a foot of snow for Halloween.

I'll get the payment to you as **soon as I can (:**

This customer is putting pouches together for a Boy Scout troop.

Tuesday, November 29, 2011 litsenberger@gmail.com;
Hey there, I spoke with you last night about your book and the knife I purchased for my father. I decided to have the book shipped to my house instead of directly to my dad, as I want to package the two together when I ship them to him. If you still had a moment to pen something into the cover that would be great, my father's name is Tom Litsenberger. I'm sure he will love it.

Hello Thilo
So today, I will go over my materials and find good stuff you can use. I have some nice musk ox and six inches is longer than usual for knife scales, but I might have some. I'll make sure you get a good deal on it. The baleen could be a problem, even if you got it safe. Baleen for sure cannot go to customers overseas, or ever get transported overseas. And might draw a lot of questions and attention at shows and stuff, so best to stay away from the baleen. Sorry to get you involved in the problems, but had that chat with a friend and was not aware of the new laws. I'll get back to you then when I see what material I have, and might find something interesting and ask if you want to try it. What might work for you is armadillo skin (!) Isn't it from where you live?

Hi Miles,
Thanks for writing back so quickly! I am very alarmed. I assumed that this Slab is old Tusk. Older than 1972 for certain. Semi fossil or whatever the term is of mineralized Tusk. It is not as pale as the pictures look and came with a 22" long, aged oosik. I believe, (know) the woman I purchased from was ignorant of what both were, and it was I who contacted her about more fossils she might have to sell. I bought both at less than $100. There was another 4" carved bone included in the purchase but I do not know what it is. Can I send a picture to you; maybe you can identify the Bone?
Do you know what a fresh cut tusk looks like inside? Is the inner part soft? Is it bloody? Have veins in it? Or hard like they all look?
All research I read explains walrus parts are legal to sell if they are older than 1972 and I see many sold at Stores online, like **Boone Trading Company.**

Hello Lou
I think the picture you show me is bear. The picture is not from my website. I do not offer bear stuff for sale. I don't in general want to mess with it. Oh yeah, I see the other emails concerning the big wolf fang necklace. I need to know if they all have to

match, and if you need two facing one way and two facing the other way as in a single necklace, but gotta run. **Miles**

TIME TO GET FIREWOOD. Josh understands why we need two of everything we depend on. "Yes Miles, two snow machines, saws, and sleds."

Those who do not have 'two,' find out why it's good to have backup, eventually. There have been several times my snow machine broke down out in the woods. We do not live where we have towing service. We are not on a road. Possibly a friend can come tow us, but often as not this will be when the friend is available in a week. It is common for a friend to notice the equipment borrowed does not run quite the same as it did before it was borrowed. Or they helped, but somehow we are sure our friend messed up our equipment! This is not the road to security and independence. I'd rather have two used machines than one brand new one so I can go fetch one, when one quits on me, or one does not start.

I have a 1990 Skidoo Tundra—one cylinder, 250 cc, easy to start, good on gas. This one is reliable and starts on the first pull, even in fifty below weather. The disadvantage is, it is hard on the body to ride, and lacks power to be safe on over- flow or breaking trail in new snow. I think I paid $800 for it seven years ago, and have not had to invest much in it since, except plugs and a new windshield. The other machine is a Skidoo Grand Touring 2000—380cc and two cylinders. This has electric start and is comfortable to ride, but needs constant work, and does not always start. Now and then, I give up, get mad, walk away from it, and take the Tundra out! Both have heated electric handle grips. The Touring, with its bigger engine, puts out more heat, so is warmer to ride. The heat from the engine comes up around the face, down around the feet. Both require oil mixed with the gas and do not get good gas mileage. The Touring gets five miles to the gallon. I get about two weeks of wood on a gallon of gas. I could haul a month's worth of wood if gas got scarce. I keep a 300-gallon gas tank in the yard—pay bulk price, off the road, no tax discount. This is enough gas to fill more than all my gas needs for the winter. *I have a year to make other plans if the gas supply dries up.*

I once used converted dog sleds for my snow machine sled. These sleds just do not hold up well. The Grand Touring is capable of traveling at fifty miles an hour all day long. It is designed for long trips, pulling camping gear and extra gas. There are fancy machines designed more for toys and having fun that do 200 miles an hour. In areas I go, these higher speeds would be unsafe. I'm happy at fifteen to twenty miles an hour on the woodland twisty trails where the firewood is. There is enough room around the community that we all seem to come up with a favorite wood cutting spot. Others leave that area alone, for the most part.

Before the big forest fire, I used to go on the river and cut dead trees piled up in logjams on sand bars. In this way, no trees are killed. Not many woodcutters do the same, because the quality of the wood is bad. Sometimes the wood is rotten or waterlogged. Worse, river silt builds up under bark and in cracks. This is very hard on the saw chain. I make up my own chain loops to save money, but it takes time. I'm often cutting with a dull saw and being made fun of. In this case, the fun is good-natured and not derogatory or mean.

Just a laughing, "Why do you bother? Do it the easy way!"

Along the river there are always animal tracks—moose, wolf, and otter. Smaller tracks of mink, grouse, rabbits, are more common. I usually carry a small shotgun, a 410, or small rifle like a twenty-two. One of my favorite guns has both a twenty-two and 410 built in. A single shot over under. I enjoy coming home with dinner while out getting wood. I bring home rabbits or grouse. Bears are not out, they hibernate in winter. It is common to see moose feeding on the willow trees along the edge of the river where the morning light hits the trees. Now and then, I see where a pack of wolves killed a moose. There will be a big gut pile with hoofs and head left behind.

After the forest fire, there are plenty of standing dead trees all over. My favorite wood cutting spot is now on airport property. The city would like to see the taller trees along the runway and on the approach cut down so the planes are safe. Only three locals are out here regularly claiming this wood area. We share a main trail to get to our woodlot. Then each person breaks off and makes a loop they keep open all winter and keeping dead trees cut. It's not polite to go exploring down someone else's loop. If you are not local, the trails go everyplace. Nothing is marked. I make a loop that lasts a winter. Each year I make a new loop somewhere within five miles of home. The loop only has to be a quarter of a mile long to offer all the dead trees I need for the year. If needed, I could come back in ten years to the same spot, and it would be ready to harvest again. We are not clear-cutting. A tree here and there is spot cut. Many trees got fire scorched and are still alive and growing, but will probably be dead in a few years. I leave behind any tree three inches or smaller in diameter. In a few years, they may grow to five inches, die, and be worth cutting. The three woods I seek are spruce, birch, and poplar.

Spruce is most commonly used, but can be hard to split and has sticky sap to deal with. Birch splits easily, has no sticky sap, and has more BTU than spruce, but tends to be wet, or rots due to the oily outer bark trapping moisture inside. Birch is classified at the low end of 'hardwood,' the hardest wood interior Alaska offers. I do not bother to split birch a year ahead of needing it. If birch is not properly dried, burning results in a cooler fire that gives off creosote, so the chimney needs cleaning more, or the creosote actually eats a hole in the chimney.

Poplar is light in weight, easiest to cut, has the fewest branches to cut off. The forest fire took the bark off, so the tree tends not to be as black and dirty with charcoal. Poplar has the least BTU of the three. I discover the new catalytic stove likes poplar. It is easy for the fire to turn the wood to charcoal, and then burn the fumes as the stove is designed to. It appears, the efficiency of burning poplar gets all the energy out of the wood, so becomes a good choice, but only for this new kind of stove. Not everyone has such a stove, so this leaves more poplar for me!

The law reads we are to go to Fairbanks and get a wood cutting permit. Yeah, right? I do not know anyone who has such a permit. Not even the mayor. Likewise, we are supposed to register and put the numbers on our snow machine, sled, and trailers. I do not know many people who would say, "Yes! I want to go to Fairbanks and give them my money, show me the way!"

I hear, "This is Nenana, our community. We are not Fairbanks, Miles! What we do, how we do it, is our business." We are not trying to be outlaws, be selfish, or hurt the environment. We mostly do not trust the big city and the rules imposed.

"It's to protect you and the resources!" But looks more like 'control.'

Nenana is not in a borough, but many, like myself, think that with the new gas discovery, with potential money, neighboring boroughs may make a move to absorb us.

"No way, Miles! This has been threatened for the past thirty years I know of, and nothing has come of it. Just scare tactics!" Maybe. In the past the area had nothing to offer a borough but costs. Boroughs take care of school costs. Nenana has a student living center we were advised from the beginning not to build. We cannot even keep up with the interest payments right now. No borough wishes to absorb this debt. The living center houses children who come to Nenana to get better schooling, or schooling not available in remote villages. We house about eighty students each year. The school gets paid for each student the center houses, but this amount does not cover all the costs.

I do not agree our small community of 300 should pay for this out of our taxes. It's a state education issue, helping villagers all over the state. The mayor feels as I do, but none of us knows the future. Many residents are concerned the money will be unfairly taken from them to pay the debt the community owes. This and other borough issues are a hot topic with strong feelings involved. 'Wood cutting' fits in the subject because if Nenana is in a borough, pollution is a borough issue. Wood burning is highly regulated, possibly soon to be completely banned in the Fairbanks borough.

There is a lack of trust among many residents. For good reason!

The current administration is frustrated trying to make ends meet with the huge bills we have. I tend to agree with our mayor, however. Eventually the state will pick up the bill for the living center, because the center is in fact a state issue. The state will not let this center get shut down due to lack of funding. It is necessary for the education of children in remote areas without a high school, or even smaller communities with no school at all! Thus, if we make an effort to pay, but show we simply cannot, the state will step in. Others do not agree and think the citizens could end up taxed to death and lose property. This again is related to a borough and sharing the burden of school costs.

The mayor tells me, "State and Federal revenue sharing has dropped since about 2000, Miles. It's now half what it was then." This money is connected to state oil revenue sharing money. Individuals get a percent we call the permanent fund. We all know about that! But also in this same structured distribution, every community is to get a cut. Nenana has been cut off! The mayor also tells me, "We no longer get state road work money for our streets that we used to get." I can understand the cuts due to a state budget problem.

My personal concern if we get forced into a borough is the feeling we would be paying another level of taxes, but getting little in return. The money would go to Fairbanks to help pay their bills. A community of 300 would be left in the dust with no say. Not even a representative on the borough board. Efforts are being made to stop the use of wood as a source of heat. There is a weather phenomenon called 'temperature inversion,' where air is trapped down low for weeks at a time in the dead of winter. This trapped air holds smoke and pollution. The EPA has determined this is unacceptable. Federal funding will get cut if Fairbanks does not solve the problem.

Visually anyone can see, and studies show, the biggest polluter by far are the three major power plants that are outdated and burning coal without the modern scrubbers. In the news, the power plants owners replied, "But we can't afford to fix the problem!" The subject was dropped. The finger gets pointed at those burning wood, it must be them causing the problem!

Anyone breathing the thick air in Fairbanks during an inversion can smell coal and car exhaust. It does not take a study to know what that smell is, and where it comes from. I know what wood smoke smells like. Even in Nenana, those of us who burn wood are considered part of a problem. The government had a wood stove exchange program. I was part of it. Iris and I got a brand new catalytic wood stove delivered from Fairbanks and installed by professionals, at a cost to the government of $6,000.

I enjoy the new stove now that I have it, but did not want it when offered. However, I see a time in the future when old stoves will be outlawed and fines issued if found. You could be forced to buy one of these new contraptions that burns the vapor, not the wood. The stove is pretty slick all right. I now have a $6,000 stove in a house not worth as much as the stove. I have no idea how many millions the government spent giving away stoves saying it will help the pollution problem. This odd behavior only contributes to Nenana wondering what is really going on.

A study was done after all the stoves were installed. There was no measurable effect on the pollution level. *I could have told them that.* "But thanks for the stove." In my opinion, which I know counts for nothing, those millions could have been spent to help build a new power plant. Or used to subsidize cab drivers or city transportation during temperature inversions. I'm certain this would be a big help. Yes, the problems and stupidity of the big city come out to touch those of us who are living remote.

The chain saw I buy has a new anti-pollution device. As if chain saws contribute anything to pollution! I doubt I burn three gallons of gas through a saw in a year. The saw will not run as well, and actually needs to be brought in for repairs because of this pollution device. Sellers show buyers what part has to be broken off with pliers before the saw is even used! "Get rid of that crap!" It's made to be easily removed, and is a small external part. The saw shop cannot legally remove it. Those who feel they are saving the planet, believe the government and love rules, regulations, and restrictions can leave the devise on. Bring the saw in for repairs in a month and need a new one in a year. Feel good you are doing your part to save the planet! In my opinion, replacing the saw prematurely contributes more to pollution than removing the anti-pollution device and having the saw last twice as long. The creation of 'stuff,' like anti-pollution devices, and new saws contributes to pollution and waste.

Few saw users live where life depends on the saw. The saw and laws are made to cover average needs. I cannot afford to take twice as long to cut wood with skip tooth safety chain. I can't have my $700 saw fail prematurely, needing repairs in as little as two weeks of use because of a smog prevention device. Likewise, it is hard these days to find a new snow machine made to last as a no nonsense, no frills work horse. The Skandic used to be such a machine, but now cost $15,000 and has more horses than it needs. My first snow machine cost me $300 new. It does not seem that long ago, in the 80s.

Out to my wood area I go, to get a sled load of firewood. I love the winter light in Alaska. Politics behind the saw, the machine, gas, pollution is not on my mind this fine morning. The sun barely gets above the horizon and stays at that level till it sets four hours later. For those few hours we have soft, cold purple light. The Nenana hill is on my left as I go out, a reference point if I get turned around exploring twisty trails. This is a snow machiner's heaven. Trails cross the river and go all the way to Nome, Alaska, almost 1,000 miles, with no other roads. Trails extend seventy miles to Fairbanks, or going the other way, to Minto, Manley, Tanana, and all points downriver. The trails can be hot and fast.

Chug, chuga, chuga. I'm moving along into the sunrise at safe economical speeds. The sled is ten feet long with three foot high sides, that makes it look like a black bathtub. Made of tough plastic, it is about indestructible and will outlast a steel or wood sled by ten times. I traded a custom knife for it. I run into a local dog musher on the trail on a race training run. I pull over and shut my engine off. This is not necessary, as dog teams are trained to pass machines with the engine running. It is just polite, saves the dogs and musher from breathing in exhaust, and putting up with the noise. In fifteen minutes I am at my wood lot. I'm burning mostly standing dry poplar wood this season. A tree along my trail is selected. I put on my otter fur work mittens. My Marten fur hat keeps my head warm.

I rarely notch the trees I cut. I can usually just face cut a tree and control where it will fall. No one is out here to hurt if the tree lands a little wrong. I try to drop the tree right next to the trail so I am walking in my snow machine trail as I section the tree. Sometimes I can only fit one tree in the sled as a weeks' worth of burning. Today I load up heavier with two trees. Ropes tied in the sled criss cross over the wood load and tie down. I have one ratchet strap to cinch across the top so there is no shifting. Some wood cutters section the trees into stove lengths right out here on the trail. I prefer to get the wood home and cut it up in the yard. This makes a pile of sawdust difficult to deal with in the lawn come spring. I shovel it up for the compost.

I tell Iris, "I think it is safer to be cutting in the yard in case there is an accident. If I stop for an hour to cut wood out there, the chances of the snow machine not wanting to start because it got cold greatly increases. There are a lot of complications if I have to walk home." She would prefer I leave the mess of bark and dust out in the woods. As I get older, I feel the cold more. I'd prefer a break, come in the house a few minutes before getting back to sectioning the trees. Sometimes I even fetch the wood one day and leave it in the sled, then section, split and stack the next day. Iris has taken on the job of stacking. She believes she does a neater job!

I call Iris out when I get home. "Honey, take a look, the sun and moon out at the same time!" We stop to admire the beauty of the sky. "More pink than purple today." I go out to cut wood every three days, getting a weeks' worth at a time. It does not take long to be months ahead on wood.Iris asks: "So why did you buy a cord of wood from that local kid?"

"I suppose I did not need it. I just wanted to help support a local kid, keep him busy, off the street. It's an investment in my community to help the youth out." I like to think we all benefit when we care about the community and help raise the young together as a group. I'm not trying to win points or be noble. I just think if we all do just a few things to help others, we ourselves benefit tenfold.

"Miles, wasn't he the kid who took your wood splitter to shop class and made it longer to accommodate longer logs for you?"

I forgot about that. I had bought a used hydraulic log splitter at our favorite second hand store, 'Used a Bit.' I've always split wood by hand with an ax, but why not let the tool do the work? This was not one of the bigger models—it only takes eighteen-inch lengths. I cut twenty-one inch lengths.

The local kid had said, "Let me fix it for you in shop class, Grandpa." I had at first been offended when the local kids referred to me as 'Grandpa.' I realized it is not said as an insult, but out of respect. Among the Natives, when you get older, the kids may refer to you as Grandpa, a respected elder, part of their extended family. Someone they will help take care of as a relative, turn to for advice. I explain to the young how it was in the good old days. So I buy wood I do not need from a kid who helped me, to teach him, that when you are kind to people, it comes back in good ways, keep it up!

I decide to cut the wood up tomorrow. It's thirty below and the wood can wait.

I explain it to Iris. "In the old days, among the Indians and other primitive people, there were no schools or old folks' homes. There were no taxes. Everyone had a role and purpose. It was assumed, that if you lived to be an elder, you must know something worth passing on to a youngster. You were qualified by the very act of having survived. The elderly helped raise the babies and teens."

"Miles, is that why you volunteer over at the student living center to work with the native kids?"

"Yes, I suppose, partly." Because I lived remotely and spent a lot of time in the villages, I understand the culture better than the school system does. There are cultural differences here at the living center that make it very hard for children of another way of life to fit in and adjust. "So partly I am teaching them something, partly helping them adjust. The school is broke, so they do not have any money to pay me anything."

Through the community wellness group, I learned of the native concerns at the living center. I volunteered to teach art after hours in the evening. The kids could voluntarily show up and learn a craft. I'd tell stories, compare old ways with today, and stuff like that. Some kids loved it, but not all the teachers did. There were complaints about their job security. Union teachers said I was taking their job away. I have no certificate. No good housekeeping seal of approval. I'd overheard some of these teachers commenting on the students,

"The poor dears." I have trouble believing this outlook is helping the children any.

Victims of poverty, ignorant of civilized ways, as if that is the worse fate a human could have. If I pick up on that just visiting, I'm sure the children are smart enough to pick up on that as well. Nenana is half Native. The same then, could be said about life in my village. Most of these teachers are from out of state, here for a school season. Many do not stay. Many live in Fairbanks and commute. They get the job because they are qualified, according to degrees. It's hard to find local qualified teachers up to government standards. I feel children will learn more from someone they know and respect, than from a stranger who disrespects them. I also believe as the Native does, if you lived long enough to be a senior, you know enough to teach something to a child.

I have taught art, taken groups out for trapping lessons in winter, and boating in late fall. There had been talk in the WIN group about locals working with the living center children. Inviting them into our homes off and on for dinner. Being mentors. Other ideas. I wanted to see on-the-job training, or apprenticeship programs in place. The community has plenty of skills represented. There are those who know how to weld, carpenters, artists, grant writers. Taking on a child as an apprentice, paying them when they learn enough, having them take a test and get qualified for a skilled job, is what I have in mind. The school superintendent at the time agrees with me and is open to ideas. I tell Iris about a conversation the superintendent and I had.

He said: "Yes Miles, programs are set up at other progressive schools for such school credit. I know two young boys who would love to have shop experience and are artistically inclined. I can talk to their parents and see if we can get them over to your shop for school credit."

I had spoken off and on about teaching a few interested kids how to use the band saw, grinders, and do the kind of work I do, maybe custom knives, or casting. Very good trades to get into, that could be taken up in the village the children are returning to. I had a specific plan in mind. It was agreed that many Native children have no plans to ever return to village life. They will end up in a city where there are malls and cool stuff. They wish to be integrated into a white society. Nothing wrong with that, even a good idea. However, there are some children who love their culture, love the wilderness life, and hope to return to the village. What can they do?

"The school has a good band and does fund raisers to compete in the lower states." This year, the band is going to Hawaii. It is costing the school, the kids, and the parents a lot of money. Shop class has been working on 'the junk yard challenge' where members of the community donate an old snow machine. The children fix up the broken machines, and get them ready for racing. There is big contest, race, prizes. I think it teaches the children a lot!

I run my idea by the superintendent, "Local artists like myself work with selected children and run a business. They would learn the trade, learn about advertising, web store building. Design brochures, business cards, marketing, taxes. Every aspect of the business." The goal, and test would be, to go to Tucson to the big show and set up to sell. The objective would be to make a profit. The bigger goal would be, instead of costing to educate this group, this group would make money for the school. I think it is possible. A whole new concept for education. Instead of raising money to send us to Tucson, we pay the school and parents. The children would have confidence, admired by teachers, parents, peers. Money talks more than gold stars and grades.

"I could get us a space in the Indian area of the show. Where buyers seek out authentic Native crafts. With a million customers passing through." I guarantee an experience these kids have never had in their life.

Iris only shakes her head. Me and my big plans and dreams. Yes. True. There is insurance, safety standards to meet. Inspections impossible to meet. I had hopes all could just be run through the school. No, it is not that simple.

I'm asked, "What if I raped one of the boys." The school would never hear the end of it. They cannot take that chance. Instead, the kids will all be handled like ticky tacky, all the same, on no budget. Some will commit suicide, A percent will never find work.

A friend tells me, "Miles, schools are government run, government controlled, government paid for. No one is going to take it out of the government hands, and make it self-sufficient."

"Let me ask this then, is the goal of the educational system to educate children or not? Educate them, to what purpose? The government will decide what you will be when you grow up?"

The superintendent agrees with my ideas, but his hands are tied. He had been to the same meeting I had.

At a WIN meeting, the head of the oil corporation doing oil gas exploration in the area was asked by the superintendent, "What classes could we be teaching to help the children get hired down the road when the gas is flowing?"

The head man said, "Teach them to be sober. Teach them to be honest. Teach them to show up on time. We can teach the rest." Absolutely what I would say if I were to hire a teen. I'd be zero interested in that piece of paper with the stars on it.

"Are you able to be loyal, can you get along with others?" I'd even hire a high school dropout, if they were easy to get along with, showed up on time. I'd pay them more than minimum wages to sweep the floor if they did so happily, without stealing anything. I would not even consider someone with college degrees who had an opinion on how to run my business better, who is hired to do preparation work. Nor am I interested in a smart person who wants to learn from me, leave and go off on their own with my ideas. A helper could compete with me, steal my ideas and run, or go to a competitor for higher pay. Ethics is everything.

The superintendent and I are in perfect agreement. This concept however puts union teachers at risk. The superintendent tells me where the majority of the funding comes from, "Federal grants. It's all about meeting Federal standards. No child left behind is the big one now." The entire school will move at the pace of the slowest child. It's all about the government tests. I have heard the concept before.

A teacher I talk to says, "We do not want to hurt the feelings of those who might get low grades. This causes them to have less confidence and lack of self-esteem."

I agree, but say, "Fine, but what does this do to the children who worked hard, earned good grades. What about their feelings, when they get the same grade or job as the one who did not care, did not show up, did no work?" What does this do to the hard workers who earned their money? I wonder. This is the basic thought behind communism. Has communism worked anyplace? Has any big government worked anyplace? History, after all, is written, and rewritten by the conqueror. Can I trust what is said about other ways of skinning the cat? Do all roads really lead to Rome? Does everyone wish to go to Rome?

Someone high up at the school tells me, "The government decides it needs more engineers in 20 years. The push in education becomes engineering skills to meet that future demand. Maybe higher math. Usually not the arts. Not even what is best for the student. It is socially efficient, economical, helps civilization have nice things cheaper."

We agree there is a point to be made, that it would not be great for children to happily learn what they like, maybe all about video games or learning to be movie critics.

"Where would society be a with a billion children qualified to be movie critics, with no engineers among them. When we need buildings, roads, bridges? Someone needs to be at the helm!"

I see the point and agree. My thought is, "God or nature comes into play here. Personalities are created, programmed, built into the system. The system being a functional society. Not everyone wants to be in charge. Not everyone wants to work hard. God creates sheep, who like to follow and do what they are told. A majority of worker bees in every hive. Only a handful of drones and just one queen. God, or nature, set it up that way. It's in the schematics, determined before we are born. We often know our place early in life. School is geared for training worker bees. Those destined for another choice will struggle to make that happen. Usually on their own time and dime." Something is gained and something is lost when dealing with the masses.

There are no tests for honest, sober or loyal. These qualities are not even rewarded. So the heck with those things. The school gets more funding only for how many students pass, with what scores. If the children earned or deserve these scores is not a big factor. Cheating is not even a factor, unless there is bad publicity over it. What sort of a society is a result of this education? This is my concern. This was my concern growing up, watching the system at work. This was a huge factor in wanting to leave.

Like my buddy, Crafty! He tells me he was pushed through school and graduated from high school unable to read or write well enough to make out a receipt! He could not spell the words ivory, baleen, tusk, or fossil. He asked me how. That was when we met, back in the 70s. In the light of this, there is not much place for my volunteerism. Or teaching anything off the agenda.

"It's not about learning, Miles, it's about the test." I recall my childhood in school, and perhaps it was the same even in the 60s.

I say: "I recall asking a question, and the teacher saying it does not matter, it is not on the test. The class laughed at me for asking a question not on the test. How stupid is that!" I repeat the good news! "Not all teachers agreed!"

Past Flash

I showed up at art class the first day. I'm in the 9th grade. The teacher asks each student, what it is we hope to accomplish this year. I explained an exact project to the teacher, involving a life-size human sculpture, making a mold, and casting it in bronze. I showed him the preliminary drawings. The teacher did not comment or reply. After a long pause, he handed me a set of keys and says, "This key fits the room next door. I want you to go there. I do not want to see you in this classroom."

I did not know if the reason is because I am a problem child. He's trying to get rid of me. He is busy, and thinks I can look out for myself and learn best on my own by 'doing.' He said, "I have nothing to teach you."

This was the best school experience I ever had and think it affected the rest of my life. A key to my own room! I can enter and leave as I wish. I sneak out of study hall to come work on my art project. I stay after school, arrive early. I got books out of the library on molds and casting. I have serious problems with the project. *Of course!* I am fourteen years old! It is all about the journey. A single teacher, single event, getting handed the keys to my dream. I finish the life size sculpture that balances on a piano wire, but am disappointed because I made a mold but do not know how to cast in bronze. No one bothered to take a picture, and I forget now what happened to the sculpture. Tossed in the trash, I assume. No one can take the memories away.

Past flash ends

I LOOKED to some older kids in the community of Nenana, already on their own. One twenty-two-year-old is extremely gifted at drawing. He pumps gas at the gas station. He wants to learn to make custom knives and is interested in working with me. I hand him some blank knife blades covered in wax, ready to etch. I told him to draw whatever he wants on the blades. I will pay him $25 each. He has six blades done in a day. I pay him $150 cash, no questions. I asked him how long it takes to make that kind of money pumping gas. Almost a week? And how fun is pumping gas compared to creating art? I wanted to know if he'd be fair with me, give me $25 worth of work per blade. It is a test. He did the best job he could. In return, I will treat him well.

I got an extra hundred dollars per blade this kid etched on. He could subcontract for me, work on his own at home, his own hours. No, probably I cannot sell six of his blades a day. However, everything begins some place. If you cannot dream it, it can never be. This kid talks it over with his girlfriend.

She says: "He*&%$ No!" He has responsibilities and bills to pay. "No fooling around having fun!" Four years later, he is still pumping gas. His girlfriend is excited he got a fifty cent raise after four years of dedicated work. I think that's disgusting! Slave labor that does not keep up with inflation. But it's his life, their decision. Others do not see life as I do. The girlfriend has learned in life that work is work, play is play, the two never meet. Cannot meet. I'm not sure what she thought when he brought a week's wages home for a few hours' work. Like he won a lottery, and of course it could never happen again? I'm up to something and the shoe is going to fall? The punch line is ahead, the hook and grab?

What do I call it when someone would rather pump gas for minimum wage all their life instead of making ten times as much at something they love? *Any idiot can pump gas, God gave you a talent few have. You are one in 10,000 people, Wake up, kid!* I call it brainwashing. His girlfriend did not want him seeing me. I am a bad influence. Regular job, regular pay, nose to the grindstone, buddy. *Well. Someone has to pump gas. I'm glad it is not me. I need to be happy there are people who raise their hand joyfully to be sheep. It saves us all from having to draw straws.*

Iris is right. Better to mind my own business. The girlfriend thinks I'm trying to scam her boyfriend. Looking at how I live, how I dress, how could I possibly know how to make money. How could I possibly care what happens to her and her boyfriend or wish to help them? No one does that unless they are up to something.

I admit to Iris, "I can explain, but so often the listener is not really listening. They have already made up their mind."

"What about your own son, Miles?"

Yes indeed. "He emailed me. He's fine. Going to college in Hawaii right now. I think my father's wife who has money, is paying the bills. I am not sure. There are a lot of secrets in the family. I've never been in the loop."

"Well Miles, as long as he is happy, huh?" "As far as I know, he has never even been on a date. Never had a job. He's 25 years old now. The good news is, he does not seem to be into drugs, is nice, good personality, liked by others. He is smart and gets good grades. Majoring right now in the art of ancient Mandarin culture."

"Is that going to help him in life in some way, Miles?"

"Well, it will, if he plans on never getting out of school, and ending up like my father, teaching that class to others." Perhaps there is a bigger plan in this I am not aware of. It's certainly not a subject I can jump in on and discuss with my son. Well, unless he contacted me every day and spent an hour explaining what this is. Or what is interesting or important about it.

He just says, "Well, it is part of required classes." I get from this, that there are classes you have to take so you can later take other classes, classes you want. I do not get it. I thought college was paying for classes. If it's my dime, then I take the classes I want or need. Is the one footing the bill dictating what classes my son takes? If so, what is the overall plan? My son cannot tell me why he is in college.

"It's what people do, dad." How do I answer that? I suppose education is always a good thing, no matter what. *"You cannot go wrong learning something!"*

Josh asks how my son is. I have to elbow Iris. "What is it he is learning, Honey?"

"The Art of Mandarin ancient culture."

Josh looks puzzled. "Learning how to peel Mandarin oranges, there's a college class for that?"

I do not have a clue. I'm as in the dark as Josh is. But think as in the dark as Mitch is when his friends ask what his father does. "Builds shelters with a knife, eats insects, stuff like that, I guess."

"People still live like that? Why? Is something wrong with your father?" All he can do is shrug his shoulders. He does not have a clue. Heck, my own mother thinks I crush bugs, leaves, sap, and mix it up to make my own paint to do the watercolors I send her. I live in an igloo, trade beads and seashells for supplies. I imagine that stops conversation.

"As long as he is happy!" is all she can say, I assume, as I do with my son.

"Your Mom does not think so any more, Miles! She knows you better now." True. She has some sense of reality of my life now. I smile at one memory after a Tucson show.

"I took a picture of Mom fanning herself with 40,000 worth of $100 bills." The amount made in two weeks doing the fossil show.

She told me, "Now I understand!"

Funny how money talks, isn't it? I cannot say I am any happier now than when I lived on $2,000 a year. I'd say I was happier then. Because I was a free man. Or maybe not happier. It is hard to measure different ways to be happy. It is nice to have Iris, nice to have a boat that runs, and a shop to work in. With all the tools I want. This is a new, different kind of happiness.

I hear a rumor my native friend Dim caught some wolves this winter. I'm surprised he has not contacted me to buy the carcasses. I do not get over to his part of the village often. He is across the tracks in Hud row. Not necessarily skid row, just the Indian part of town in government housing. I get to his place by snow machine. No one is driving a car in here. I see his large firewood pile, tools out like he is working on his snow machine.

I have to holler. "Yo! Dim, you around?" It's more polite to announce yourself in the yard rather than knock on the door. Dim answers from inside his shop. I see four wolf carcasses frozen and stacked in the snow by the shop. "Heard you got a couple of wolves!"

"Yeah, a lot around this year! Been meaning to see you. What you paying for carcasses?"

I tell him prices have not changed, "$25 a carcass." He only shrugs. It's not enough money to remember to go out of his way to haul them over to my place. "I can't afford to pay more. I have to cook the entire carcass, clean the parts I want dry, you know how it is." He has heard this from me before. How it has taken so long to find a market, all the time working on and understanding the computer. I add, "You are just going to haul them out in the woods and dump them anyhow, Dim."

"True. You want to haul them off now?" I'd rather not, because I am not going to get the cooker going till spring—many months away. I may as well get them now though, so they are under my control. I hand Dim $100, and he helps me load them in my sled. Wolves need tagging, but the tags go with the fur, not the carcass. The carcass is legally considered garbage. No one is going to kill a wolf to provide me with a carcass. The wolf is killed to supply the fur industry.

"Miles, I get $400 each for wolf furs, what do I care about $25?"

"Well, you are helping me make a living."

He laughs, "Yeah, as a garbage man!" I am not offended by that comment. I haul the wolf carcasses home and stack them next to the antler pile in the yard. I'm guessing if I had not come to get them, Dim would have hauled them off into the woods. This is what is done with most carcasses.

"Miles, got any use for fox, marten, otter, beaver, any other carcass I come up with?" I'm disappointed I do not have time, and there is not enough money in these animal skulls, claws or teeth, so trappers just toss them out. I suppose they become compost for the forest at least. I answer by nodding my head. He has asked me before, and just wonders if anything has changed.

I'm getting a lot of work done in the shop. My knife steel work is improving. One improvement people can see is the finish work. *Why should it take years to learn how to get a final high polish on a blade?! Maybe doing so in a reasonable amount of time is what takes time. Recognizing the look between each grit sizes is critical, otherwise I have to backtrack, or quit, and accept some minor scratches from a previous grit.* Some aspects of casting is seeing improvement. Mold making is getting easier. Changes are slow, by the year.

I sometimes discuss business with friends who ask and seem interested. The school superintendent's wife is looking for work. We have talked off and on about my business. She is well educated, hardworking, sober, capable of showing up on time.

"OK, Miles, how much is the business bringing in, let's start there."

I shrug my shoulders. "$1,000 days are common. Here is an example." I explain, I buy raw fossil mammoth ivory for $90 a pound. I choose my pound carefully. I polish that pound of ivory into knife handles for the knife makers market. I just spent one hour polishing one pound. I am now pricing it. A single set of knife scales weighs 3.6 ounces and is selling cheap-priced to sell fast at $95. I got five such knife handles out of the pound. If they sell for $95 each, this is $475 a pound. Subtract the $90 I paid for the pound, I now have $385 I made 'gross' in an hour shop time. Figure roughly half that cost as a high estimate being 'my costs,' including electric, heat, light, sanding belts, advertising to sell item, etc., etc. That is still $192 an hour.

She says, "This is interesting. Let's talk. Where can I fit in?"

I reply, "I could hire someone for $20 an hour to polish ivory for me, using my equipment. They make $20 an hour and I make $300 an hour. Can I move that much? Hard to know. I have 120,000 visits a year on my website. I'm in the top five in the world at what I sell in search engines worldwide. What is possible? Guessing moving ten pounds a day would not be difficult. $5,000 a day just in fossil ivory knife scales. I sell 100 other items."

Mrs. Superintendent comes over to my home and shop to look around. "A lot would have to be done to be legal, Miles. It's ok when you are the owner and only worker. No fire escape, no wheelchair access, no hazmat area, no restroom, no dust collector, crowded conditions, not properly electrically wired, not up to code, not a safe approved building, no running water."

I'm sure it does not end here. I have thought of this and am stumped. I could spend 200 grand before being legal to hire anyone. I do not know how to make these things happen, even if I said, "Let's do it!" It is beyond my ability. I do not drive. How would I get to places I need to get forms and sign papers? I do not use the phone. I am a good artist. I understand my trade. I am a good salesman. I understand business. That is a lot of abilities. I know how to build, create, solve a variety of problems. I can find a table at the dump. Use a tree limb to brace it, mount a used bearing and pulley, find an old electric motor, convert a boat engine shaft, and end up with a rock saw. For $50, and twenty hours of work.

Most people have a job, work forty hours and spend $800 on a rock saw. I saved twenty hours of work, but am not up to code. I can run used electric wire that is not color coded, put in my own air ducts for cleaning the air using a shop vacuum, some hoses and gates. It's not approved. I'm in a flood zone, can't get insurance. My property is not zoned for business. I'm used to the wild, where problems get solved without inspections, permits, approval, or getting told that standards will be and such. I was raised on free enterprise. If you can dream it and do it, go for it. Your customers will decide if they want to buy from you. Your employees will decide if they want to work in our environment.

I say, "Do you want a wheelchair ramp, color coded wires, a restroom that I pay for so I can now only afford minimum wage of $4 an hour? Or, skip all that, and you get $20 an hour?" The bottom line, "Do you want the money to go to the government, or you?"

I do not know how to work with others. I do not know how to delegate. I'm horrible with rules, regulations, and paperwork. I know how to get things done cutting through all the red tape. I am in hopes Mrs. Superintendent could 'do all that.' The stuff I do not know how to do. But right from the get go, we do not have a physical location up to code to even begin. I have nine rundown buildings I bought for $20,000. Worth nothing to anyone but me. Totally illegal to run a business out of, if I have employees. I ask, "What if I subcontract, and people work for me, away from here in their own home?"

I realize if I am turning out $5,000 worth of ivory knife scales a day, I'd need an accountant, secretary, manager. How many of these roles can be combined? This is where I am in the dark. When people call or email, they want me, not a hired flunky. I think this is why I get the business. Customers like to talk to the owner who knows something. In order for anyone to help me, everything would have to be labeled, categorized, and entered in a data base. Mrs. Superintendent agrees that would be impossible. I have nine buildings full of boxes stacked to the ceiling. In a lifetime you could not label it all. I jokingly tell her, "I have misplaced a box of $10,000 worth of fossil ivory, unable to find for the past six months. It will turn up eventually." The bottom line, I do not care enough. I'd care if I had a business making no money and I was broke. If I'm making $192 an hour, what do I care if $10,000 worth of ivory is misplaced? I do not need it.

"That can be your job, you find it. You organize it all." *Let me know in about five years, when you are done!*

"Would you make more money, Miles?" She answers the question herself. "Probably, but as a worker, I would not know where to begin. Only you know what all this stuff is. I do not know a tooth from a claw."

"Yes, I could teach you, but that might take a year."

"Well, Miles, what if we just focus on one thing, the lucrative mammoth ivory knife scale business?"

I explain that yes, I could pay someone to work at their home with just a belt sander and band saw. Cutting and polishing knife scales. But even this takes skill. It is not so easy to look at an odd shape and see how to get the most rectangles out of it with the least waste out of a round object.

"That skill could take a year to learn." I explain how I had hopes of training some young people through a school program as apprentices I could hire after they learned the trade. I had also thought of offering room and board. On-the-job training apprenticeship program. I had even advertised on my website! "Come live in Alaska, learn a trade!" Like that. I'd even pay someone's way up here. In the old days that was bondage, indentured servitude. Slavery. Promise the potential of buying your freedom someday. Sometimes referred to as having an apprentice.

I had thought of a female partner more than an employee, another artist, another adventure type person. In my dreams, someone in another country who would find my lifestyle 'rich.' Or the type who pays to go camping and be with nature. Or a young happy-go-lucky type looking for room, board, and something interesting to do. Again, in time, someone with vision could be me, replace me in a few years when I am old. Eventually own the business, the house. Think of it as a long-term investment, giving up some years in the beginning for rewards later. A way to get an education without paying, actually getting paid. A way to have the Alaska dream for someone with no other way to make that happen.

I think in some cultures it is common for a younger woman to pair up with an elder man. She takes care of him as sort of her job. He passes on while she is still young enough to find another man. Arriving in the new relation at forty years old, with a home and inheritance from the previous old man. Hmmmm

There is still concern for liability. The various legal aspects. I wondered if Mrs. Superintendent understood the various laws for hiring. I'm thinking, "Surely something could be worked out when two people want something to happen. An employee and a worker want to work together. The government can say, 'No way'?"

"Yes, that's about the size of it, Miles!"

I had looked into the local workforce available in Nenana, and thought the kid pumping gas might work out. He has artistic skills, knows something about animal parts, and could learn fast how to make knife scales from mammoth chunks. I explain what happened.

"I do not know anyone else local I might trust." I feel frustrated. I think I could run a business that keeps ten people fully employed making over $20 an hour. I have little sympathy for those telling me there is no work to be had. It's not just the mammoth scales! I have good sources for musk ox horn, and there is even more profit in that! Then there is the custom knife business. I spend an average of four hours to make a knife that sells for $400 and costs me only $30. I could train people to do the prep work, eventually make finished knives under my name. Mrs. Superintendent looks around and there is nothing for her to do. It would be illegal for her to work on my premises, and any secretarial type work would have to involve me having at least one worker. So I continue along in idle, not even in gear, because I do not, and cannot, come up with all the skills it takes to run a big smooth business properly alone. The good news is, I think this is a common story most small business faces. "Only if." *Be happy with what I have and do not get excited about aspects out of my control.*

Bean, my friend, and accountant, has said. "If you could pay just a little bit more into Social Security for two years, say another few hundred dollars a year, you could double the amount you can collect every month for the rest of your life." Something about how the government averages your income over the last four years you worked. I'm only eligible for $400 a month right now at my present reported earnings. I could get $800 a month if I pushed the next couple of years. I have an incentive now to make the most money before I retire. It would not be hard to sell off inventory of raw materials for the extra income. Not really retire as such, but do things as a hobby, for fun, and live more the subsistence lifestyle in the garden, and out fishing, hunting, gathering. *The big shows are getting hard to do!*

"MILES! Your buddy Jessie here. How you doing?" I recognize his raspy voice from this past summer. *The guy trying to sell me walrus ivory.*

"What's up Jessie?"

"Well, I have a lot of quality fossil ivory for $30 a pound." This could be worth $90 to $150 a pound. I want the details to know if this is legit.

I am suspicious and ask, "Why is the price so good, what's going on?" I already know Jessie has connections in Savoonga, an extremely remote Alaskan village, and one of the few places in the entire world where legal artifact's and fossil walrus ivory can come from. I have no good connections among Eskimos. My connections are more interior with the Athabascan Indian. A solid, up North, Eskimo connection is highly desirable to me.

Jessie explains that his wife, Loretta, is on the Savoonga village council. "There was a big storm this past fall along the entire coast." I had heard the news on the radio, so know this is true. "The village got damaged, and is trying to raise money to fix it up, get the generator fixed and the school fixed." This as well seems plausible, as I have followed the news. Remote villages all over are in trouble from lack of government funding and global warming issues. Some villages are forced to abandon their site, and move in with the bigger villages to save money. Talk is, the government is encouraging smaller villages to join bigger ones, so it is easier to financially care for them. One big generator with one stop, and large fuel drop is cheaper than two stops and two generators. Makes sense. One big school makes sense. Smaller villages are trying to figure out how to survive without government grants.

"Miles, the village has stockpiled quite a bit of fossil walrus ivory over the years for use by local carvers, and now wants to sell some off for quick cash to take care of immediate needs. Since my wife is on the council, she has inside information, and can get a good deal for someone who has cash." This as well seems like it fits what I understand of small villages. The official plan might be to offer this ivory for closer to retail, 'eventually.' But we are talking insider knowledge. Not illegal in my view.

If the village owns the ivory, wants quick cash, and is willing to do some fast deal for immediate operating cash, they have that right. The details get a little confusing from here.

"I was in Savoonga and saw the ivory, Miles. It filled a pickup truck! I did not have any cash at the time. The problem is, Loretta and I need to get back there in order to be in on the deal. We do not have the money to go. It's $1,500 each!" I know this is true as well. This is stopping buyers from going there. Before the 90s, individuals in Savoonga had stashes of ivory. Buyers would fly in and bring alcohol to trade with. The villagers often got ripped off big time. Buyers made fortunes over the years. Some of the big name buyers in the business got started this way. Buyers have been complaining in recent years, because the villagers organized after ANILCA and government land settlements.

Village corporations now control land fossils are found on. Outsiders cannot just go scavenge and pillage anymore. Corporations have money to run tribal businesses. Savoonga has a village store where locals can sell ivory for the reasonable, guaranteed subsidized government set prices of $200 a pound. I hear China is paying top dollar, cutting everyone else out. Villagers do not necessarily have good relations with Chinese buyers. The US and China may be having issues. The Federal government may control funding, suggesting business with the Chinese stop. Some materials get sold on the internet through newly emerging village websites. eBay and some other sites ban the sale of all ivory, even if it is legal. I know more of the politics in the ivory trade through my Russian friend Igor.

What Jessie is saying fits the knowledge I think I have on the subject. Many of the US big buyers of the past are hesitating to deal in any ivory at all with controversy surrounding the subject, just as EBay decided. Most of us in the trade know each other, stay in touch, and stay connected concerning changing laws and outlets. Smaller dealers are more willing to take up the slack in the market. Big money is often made out there at the edge, taking chances. I often have cash on hand to take advantage of deals. I have never liked banks, not the interest they offer on money left in their care. *Why bother with banks when I can double my money some place else?* So the story with Jessie is, he needs someone to front him the money to go to Savoonga to buy this legal fossil ivory at such a good price.

"Miles, have you got the money to front us to get to Savoonga. I promise a good return on the investment!"

"It's an issue, Jessie. I do not know you well enough to just front that kind of money. I need some collateral, just like anyone who lends money." Jessie cannot come up with anything I want to hold as collateral. I'm not fronting this kind of cash based only on a story. It would be easy to get scammed. Iris reminds me how I lose so much money helping others or getting involved in deals that do not work out.

She thinks that's where much of my profit goes, and why I seem to have so little to show for the fact I make so much money!

"Miles, like that $20,000 that guy owes you for the Bearpaw land!" I forgot about that. I'd rather focus on the good news. Jessie and I hang up with no agreement. I get to my emails.

A customer wants legal advice.

Why is it illegal to sell bear bones in the US? I see black bear skulls for sale online and not for export. In Canada, you can easily find and buy bear skulls/bones all over the place. I have to add the cost of a CITES permit to an order, but it is legal.

I'd really appreciate your help.

I reply

My selling you bear parts is not legal. There are exceptions, one being if the material is fossil. I have cave bear fangs and one cave bear lower jaw, just one side. 40,000 years old, but do not know what type of jewelry this might be good for. Usually this is a display. Fangs are in the shopping cart on my raw materials page. "Why' is partly because the government believes people will kill bears to sell the claws and endanger the bear population if made legal.

I do not bother explaining sales are state regulated, not Federally regulated. Laws vary from state to state. Mostly it is not a good idea for claws to cross state lines in a sales transaction. Using the mail can involve the Lacey Act, making any possible crime a felony. Why explain all that?

Hello Miles,

I am keeping the brass otter with the down facing tail, but am returning the bi-colored otter with the turned up tail, which I'd like to exchange for the brass turned down style. Do you have another brass whale with level sides? Thanks again, **Joe Angelico.**

I'm looking for a piece of mammoth bark ivory in a rectangular shape about 3.5" x 1.5", flat on the bottom side in beige. Can you supply this?~**Regards, Dennis**

Dealing with customers simply takes a long time. I keep saying that.

Monday, January 24, Hi Miles,

I have just sent you three PayPal payments. One was $51 for a wolf bone bead strand. One was for $140 for miscellaneous items. One was $12 for shipping (sorry about not understanding the procedure).

Blessings to you and good luck at the show,

~**Zaz**

Iris and I send thirty-five boxes of goods ahead of us to sell in Tucson. I visit with my mother and set up at the same place I am used to at the Ramada on I-10. For the first time, I have a list of items customers want and are waiting for. I am their buyer. I can see a time when I am trusted, fronted money to buy with, using their money to spend and invest. Now I am expected to use my money with the risk I may buy the wrong item and it will not be accepted!

I see, for the first time, customers with cell phones that have camera capability. Buyers are showing pictures to someone who is replying to whether they should buy it. Not long ago it was against the law to take pictures of merchandise you do not own. Not long ago it was rude to ignore the seller and engage in a cell phone conversation, ignoring or interrupting the vendor. I do not have or understand such phones, but have a digital camera that plugs into my computer. I can take a picture, put it in the computer, ask if the items are desired. The buyer can transfer funds by pay pal that I can verify and have access to, all within an hour. I can then purchase the material I have approval to buy for a customer. I see a good business in the future doing this. Possibly even to where I retire and do not come here to set up. I see moving around, taking pictures, and asking what to buy, being a middleman, making money off my experience and ability, my connections, my good prices, and relations I have with suppliers and customers. This is only an idea for now. I make a wad of cash at what I do, the way I am doing it.

RETURN HOME.

Jessie calls and says he has some stuff to show me for collateral, so he can get money to fly to Savoonga. I am dubious. He is driving to Nenana from where he lives near Wasilla, 400 miles. It seems strange to me he does not have family, business partners, friends, he can turn to on this deal. Jessie shows up. I go out to his car to see what he has to show me. He has Loretta with him, his Eskimo wife. They open the trunk. He has a trunk full of white walrus Ivory!

I tell Jessie, "No way, Jessie! I can't touch that!"

He explains the law, which I already know. "First, this is government tagged ivory, not poached. Legally harvested, meat consumed by the village. Loretta is native and can have this. The numbers are recorded. She can legally gift it to you. She can list all the numbers, and sign it over as a gift."

"Jessie, this is true. I could then legally possess it, but I cannot sell it. If you do not come through for me and deliver legal fossil ivory I can sell, then I am stuck with these tusks I can do nothing with!" I also made a deal not to get back into the fresh walrus ivory business. But I assume as collateral no one else will ever know. *He leaves it, he picks it up and I have legal fossil material that was not part of my 'no touch' agreement.* Partly the price and availability has changed on fossil material. There is a lot of profit now. Partly I have seen this material selling on a knife materials site I go to. Everything offered sells fast. For incredible amounts of money. As much as $500 for enough fossil walrus to make one knife. A mere few ounces of material. *I want that fossil material Jessie can get!* I can tell by his education level and attitude he is not Internet savvy and has no connections to sell his material retail. He has to depend on a middleman like me.

"Miles, why would I leave valuable ivory with you and not pick it back up? It's got value for Loretta and me. I can use it and sell it once she does artwork on it. We want it back!" That's true. Though I wonder why he did not just sell the ivory for the money he needs. *Why didn't Loretta do some quick artwork on it! Geez!* They are in a hurry to take advantage of this deal. This is not what I want for collateral. I am not happy. But Jessie drove 400 miles to see me and is all excited to head for Savoonga. I do not want to say no. He's now got me all excited to get my hands on some really nice top material for $30 a pound!

"Miles, I'll return with a trunk full of legal fossil ivory and trade it back for my white ivory!"

Loretta sits at a table in the shop recording tusk numbers while Jessie and I talk. I buy tickets for Jessie and Loretta to fly to Savoonga for $2,100. I'm flush with cash from the Tucson show, ready to invest it. Jessie leaves me twenty-two pounds of white walrus ivory as collateral. There is an extra thousand to buy fossil ivory with. If all goes well, I will get 100 pounds of legal fossil walrus ivory, and make $20,000 profit when I sell the ivory. If I only double my money, I think it can be sold in a week. Sweet! My plan would be to sell some fossil material wholesale and make enough quick cash to cover my investment, then raise the price to retail, and spend more time getting the higher dollars. Just like Jessie describes what Savoonga wishes to do. I could high grade some, cut some knife handle material, polish it, and get even more money, way more money, after I get my investment back. I'm not strapped for a quick turnaround on borrowed money, nor high interest rates through a bank loan. Likewise there is no 'Big Brother' silent partner collecting a 3rd of our pie.

Jessie contacts me in two weeks saying he is back! The deals did not go as expected. The material he had seen a couple of months ago sold. The people he needed to see, who had the good material, were out at camps when he arrived, so he did not get to see them. He got some material though, and would bring it by. Jessie shows up. There is some nice material, but only a few pounds, and he needs $50 a pound not $30.

"I picked up some seal teeth, a whale tooth, some other stuff for you." I am not looking for these other items. I'm not sure if seal teeth are legal to sell, though probably no one will care. I reluctantly accept this and that.

"Miles, I can finance another trip to Savoonga as soon as I sell all this stuff. I can pick up your fossil ivory then, do not worry!"

What can I do about it? I am stuck going along with the program. This is not the sort of deal I could go to the police with. Maybe Jessie will come through. I believe at least part of what he says. I believe the deal existed at one time. He went to Savoonga, and the deal he expected did not happen. His dream of how it would go did not meet reality. Can he make up for it? I tell him, "Nothing sells that you can offer me like fossil ivory. That is what the deal is for!" Naturally he does not have money or trade goods to pick up his white ivory I hold as hostage. I feel like I am in the exact situation I was afraid of getting into.

He does not have collateral that means anything to me— that I can use. I get the impression he is not interested in getting his white ivory back. He has everything out of the deal he wants. Much like the mentality of those who drop items off for cash at a pawnshop with no expectation of ever paying for and picking up the items. I suspect now he can get all the white ivory he wants, as the Eskimo has limited outlets for it, and can sell it raw only to another native. Eskimos are good traders. They have been in the business for thousands of years. They know fossil material is worth more on a world market legal to sell to anyone. With Loretta being native, they are going to pass on as much white ivory as they can.

Jessie had told me how respected he is in the village. "I have been doing business most of my life and know all the elders. I have helped them out a lot and am a respected person among the village people." I believed, at the time he told me, this is probably his inflated opinion of his self worth. I wondered what the Eskimo would say about this statement. In my business, I try hard not to judge. I buy and sell from a great cross-section of society. Many of my suppliers are uneducated by white man standards. Many cannot read or write, or make out a receipt. In some areas, a piece of paper and pencil is more rare than fossil ivory. I'm making deals on the river at fish camps.

I tell Iris, "Imagine going to the headwaters of the Amazon, or the middle of the bushman people in Australia!" I pause while she imagines that. "Now imagine asking to see ID," I pause. "Imagine asking for a receipt." Not going to happen. Like Indiana Jones, I sometimes meet with unsavory characters who do not have the same sense of ethics I have. Sometimes Indiana Jones has to hire one eyed machete wielding bandits to boat him to the dungeon of doom because no one else will go there. Few know the way, or that's just how it is. It's why no one else walks in his shoes! The very thought gives the average sheep the shivers! Like anything we do in life, if we want in the game, we have to lay our cards down and get dealt in. "Or Iris, put another way, with the fish on your side of the net. Suppose village people were in charge, making the rules we all must abide by. "Where is your compass, matches, meat jerky?!" This is what village people travel with and it's the law.

"No, Miles, not relevant in the city. That would be silly rules to abide by and accomplish nothing!"

"So you'd ignore it, right? I mean, would you carry meat jerky in your car glove box to be legal? " her sour expression and head shaking at the thought is answer enough. Point made.

There is also a percent of white people who live among the savages, not by choice as I do. They are here because they are not very bright, or got rejected by society for some reason, a quirky personality glitch. A bubble out of plumb, one French fry short of a happy meal. There are also Indians who give the whole tribe a bad reputation. *Kind of like a few lawyers give the whole business a bad reputation.*

"My point, Iris, is I cannot expect everyone I deal with, to be like me. If Jessie is a storyteller, I'm not going to run him off. My mistake was not securing collateral I can use." If I had gold, or an artifact collection I could say, "No problem, Jessie, maybe next time!" And sell off the collateral. If he could get me fossil ivory at a later date, that becomes a separate deal.

A couple of weeks later, Jessie tells me, "Miles, I have been experimenting with turning white ivory into mineralized fossil ivory. I heard talk among my friends in Savoonga that they have a mineral spring of hot water they toss white ivory into. A year later fetch it out of the pool as legal fossilized material!" I believe this is possible. New studies about fossils indicate some natural fossils are not as old as they look, and some that are truly old, do not show much mineralization. In other words, the rate of absorption of minerals can vary by a lot. Under perfect conditions, ivory can absorb minerals in as short a time as ten years that visually looks like and has passed for a thousand years old.

"So, Miles, I have some white ivory in buckets of rusty nails, copper and other natural minerals to see what happens."

From a scientific and artistic standpoint, an interesting experiment. We exchange a few ideas. I tell him about a mineral called Vivianite. The chemical that turns materials blue in nature—a highly sought after color. Jessie looks it up on the computer and finds a source to buy it to experiment with. I tell Jessie I'm experimenting as well, but with a different purpose in mind. I am treating wood. Also experimenting with junk mammoth ivory. I want to know if there is a way to take garbage mammoth ivory, and treat it in some way to make it stable, with nice colors so it has a commercial value. I do not want to throw it away. One of my growing markets is artifact seconds, good for making necklaces. Like broken ivory harpoon heads. They have little value to collectors, but they are in fact real ivory arrowheads from thousands of years ago. Good for medicine bags and art objects to wear. If I could get them to have sheens of colors that sometimes happen in nature, there could be a market for this, as the colors can match clothing, and stand out above just plain tan or yellow. Instead of being worth $25, they might be worth $65.

My chosen market is among the lower to mid-income level. I tend to avoid high end collectors with big dollars. One reason is such people are very discriminating and want the best of the best with no damage and like to haggle. Partly I do not have this knowledge to invest big dollars to mark the item up. Damaged goods are much easier to acquire! I want to sell to craft people like myself, more than collectors. I like dealing in items harder to move, that few want. 'The garbage man.' Buy it by the pound, sort it out, sell it by the piece. I somehow gravitated to this position, as a way of life I enjoy. I prefer a lot of deals, and I like moving volume. As a child, I had wanted to be a garbage man!

One friend, Dodger, finds ancient dolls now and then. This is a big market, but a market where single items go for thousands of dollars to collectors. Another doll that looks just like it could have been made by another clan, and worth a few dollars. It's not good to make a mistake! No thanks!

I'd be honest and call dyed stabilized material ' restored' or enhanced or stabilized, (mixed in with dyed some place in the fine print). In the same way turquoise is treated. I do not think Jessie is on the right track. He is not so interested in what I am doing. He is just soaking in cold solutions. I am playing with heat, vacuum, and pressure, and a variety of secret chemicals and natural concoctions. Some mixes speed up chemical reactions. I'm getting extremely good results. Vinegar, for example, softens ivory so other chemicals can penetrate. Salt makes it hard again. I am not so interested in taking illegal material and making it legal.

The issue I am having is how long it takes, and what it is costing me. It's not economical to do so far. The biggest issue for me is the stabilizing, not the dye. I am working with soft materials. I try a little white ivory along with fifteen other materials. The white ivory is more solid than my other materials, so is not working out by my methods. I'm even trying soft rock fossils like dinosaur fangs and trilobites. Because it would be cool to use these items in necklaces if I could get them strong enough! I just enjoy experimenting.

It is fun to show something to a customer "Cool ,Miles, how did you do that!"

And smile back, "Talent! Magic!" I recognize if I can pull it off, it would be a niche market no one else is offering. Out at the cutting edge few could duplicate without knowing the methods. That's how to make money. Having fun is more important than making money. From a legal standpoint, my focus is on taking legal material that has little value, and turn it into material with enhanced value. Jessie has the focus on taking totally illegal material and pass it off as legal. As I get to know Jessie, I want to disconnect from him. As soon as I get paid off.

"Miles, when I get back to the north again I am going on a polar bear hunt and kill a polar bear!" He has no need for the meat. Has no room in his house for a mount, rug, or a trophy. He just wants to kill a polar bear. I do not trophy hunt. Everything I killed, I ate, or killed in self-defense.

I get told, "Death is death Miles, the animal does not care why!"

"True for the individual animal, yes." However, if we kill to eat, the number of dead animals is limited to how many we can eat, it's a limited amount. If we kill for fun—trophies, it's easy to over-harvest.

I explain to Iris, who is still learning the business. "The animal products I carry are 99% byproducts from a subsistence lifestyle. Now and then I end up with horns or claws off an old rug or trophy that has fallen apart and is being thrown away." I cannot always control, or be sure, where a product originated, but in most cases I know my suppliers as wilderness subsistence people. It is obvious to me that when Jessie and I talk about hunting and exchange stories, he is envisioning something different. I'm appalled at Jessie's views. Likewise, he does not care where his white ivory comes from. If he can get it from poachers and disguise it to sell it, that is fine with him. He cares nothing about the walrus. He'd gladly kill the last one.

"I'm untouchable, Miles. My wife is Eskimo! No one touches us, we can do what we want." There is a sad truth in what he says. From a legal standpoint, it is hard to believe that attitude will see Jessie through the court system as a legal defense. I suspect the government will find a way to clean his clock. While the Native is untouchable, Jessie is white, and it does not look good for anyone to flagrantly advertise to the extent Jessie does. There are radical terrorist groups like Greenpeace that have a lot of money and political clout who would scream rape if they heard of Jessie and his plans.

"Miles! Hey buddy! You have a great website and know how to sell stuff. I can get a lot of white ivory. More than I can handle. I need you to sell it for me on your website. We could make a lot of money!" I think Jessie is nuttso.

"Jessie, that is big time crime! There is no way you can do that! There is no way I want any part of it! All I want is the legal fossil ivory you owe me and you take back your white ivory!" I do not want to piss off Jessie while he still owes me, but his talk is getting out of hand. I've been smiling and going along with the program until now. Jessie has misunderstood that for agreement and weakness.

"Miles, do not piss me off! I'm getting tired of your crap!"

"That is interesting, Jessie, because it is me who should be pissed at you. It is you who went back on our agreement. It is me who is out several thousand dollars."

"Plans change Miles, you have to be adaptable. Friends and smart people learn to go with the flow."

"I understand that, Jessie, but it is always your flow we adapt to. Where is the flow coming my direction, in the form of goods I can sell, or money?"

"I'm going to come through for you, Miles, but you are not making it easy! You are not letting me pay you back! Here I have this great idea, better than the original plan! You could get rich!"

"The original plan was legal, Jessie, that makes a big difference."

At this point, I realize part of the issue is my fault. For many years I had the nickname, 'Wild Miles.' I considered animals in the wild to be sane, understandable, with God. I'd say, "You know, like Tarzan." So what is wrong with Tarzan, besides not being like you, civilized? I look at what civilization is doing to the planet I love. I feel horrified, sad, angry, want no part of what civilization is doing! I did something besides talk. I changed my life so I could walk what I talk. I expected respect. Instead of respect, I got misunderstood. Civilization hears, 'Wild Miles,' and thinks party hardy, crazy, drugs, drinking, violence, and outlaw. Wild Miles conjures up the nickname of an especially nasty Hell's Angels biker. I could have done more to straighten out the misunderstanding.

Partly I did not fully understand the consequences. The misunderstanding is humorous. How little you understand me! Partly the reputation brought me attention, got me remembered. I played the part of Clint Eastwood as if life is a movie. We are all actors. Clint was harsh in a harsh land. Maybe violent, anti-social, but fair, honest. Out there at the edge, but he got things done—his way. Now and then he'd get suspended, reprimanded, but welcomed back, ending up with awards and a thanks from the mayor. In real life, Clint does things for others and his community. The public knows mostly his act. I saw nothing wrong with that. How is that a problem?

All my life I am told, "What others think does not matter, Miles, being true to yourself is where it is at, the heck with what others think!" School taught me about the right of individuals. Personal freedom is everything. In my day, smokers had the right to smoke and society put up with it. I still think it hurts you way more than the rest of us. If it means that much to you, go for it. I may suffer somewhat, but we all suffer for the rights of the individual. I breathe your car exhaust, you breathe my wood smoke. Your home blocks my view, your dog barks. Your car takes up parking space I could use. You are in line and it would be nice to shop with no line. We are social beings and put up with each other. That's how it is. That's how I was raised. A flower child,

"Peace brother, like chill out, man." There is no need for anger and violence. Along those lines there were demonstrations for women's rights, black rights. Because we all have the right to be ourselves.

"Come on, Miles, everyone knows you are an outlaw! Why are you getting squeamish on me?" While Clint Eastwood as Dirty Harry might be inclined to bend the law to help clear a decent human being, he does not help mean, corrupt, evil people. Jessie is not a man to piss off. To play the game on his terms is a road to violence. I've met the personality type before.

"Jessie, I do not bet into other people's games. You know I am a loner. I do not work with others in a partnership. That was never part of any agreement between us, you know that!"

"Well, I set this up and you are messing with it. Do not cross me! I know where you live!" I take this as a threat. If I thought the law was honest, I'd report his plans and agree to help stop him. Jessie is a menace to society. But I do not see the law as any different from Jessie. If I reported Jessie, for all I know Jessie is paying someone off. Or it would be me investigated, not Jessie. Or I would not be believed, Jessie would get wind I turned him in. I have no doubt he has the personality to kill me, or kill Iris to make a point with me. Not to cross him. Perhaps others are protected by the police. But it will not be Wild Miles. I'm among the unprotected.

I wish that arrangement I asked for from the court had worked out. At my request, the judge had ordered Fish and Wildlife to assign someone to me I could turn to with questions. It would be nice to have someone to work with and trust. *Like right now.* Someone I could ask the exact legal aspects of my situation, and what is important to keep track of and what might get overlooked. I am reluctant to ask too many questions and get under the microscope. I accepted seal claws from Jessie. I do not know anyone else who has any, or sold any. They are a byproduct of subsistence taken game. It is hard to imagine anyone killing seals to get claws to sell. They are not worth much. So morally I have no issue with this. Would the law agree? Or is it one of those unspeakable subjects for which one might go to prison for ten years? I'm not going to go ask. I plan to just keep Jessie calm, be very vague and non-confrontational. Let him fade out of my life without my getting killed.

At this point, I am pretty sure Jessie has no intention of coming through for me on our deal with the fossil walrus he owes me. So now I have a pile of tusks I have no use for. I am not quite screwed, however. I think it would not be a serious legal problem if I got these tusks back in the hands of Native Americans who can legally work and sell them. Especially if I gift them. Indirectly I should get some thanks back for gifting. Even if it is just good for my karma or paying it forward. This is not a situation I would deliberately set up and am not interested in repeating. It's more like damage control.

In every business I feel there will be situations over which the big cheese will hold his hands over his eyes and groan, mumble under his breath, and hope the problem gets resolved with the least publicity and fan fair, and goes away as a lesson learned.

I gift one tusk to a native friend. He just got out of prison and is trying to get on his feet, get back into a craft he is talented at. I donate a few tools, and a tusk to help him get started. Maybe if he does well, he will feel inspired to get other raw materials from me. I can keep much of the ivory for my own use. I make a nice set of pistol grips for my gun. Poof. The rest is off my mind. I now focus on the positive. Jessie's materials are in boxes in the shop to join hundreds of other boxes of 'stuff' I may use, and may not. Who knows how or when. I have boxes I have not looked through in twenty years. I call it ' retirement' money—increasing in value faster than interest in the bank. Who knows, in twenty years, laws might change in my favor. A museum might buy them. I'm not going to dwell on it. I do not give many details to Iris about my business, but she tells me she does not think much of Jessie, maybe is someone to avoid and disconnect from.

THIRTY BOXES that we shipped flat-rate priority arrive from Tucson. I am busy sorting and getting involved in projects, putting my new materials to use. I'm excited by some new rocks I got a deal on. Larimer is hard to get. I acquired good quality in the rough from a supplier who likes my work and wants me to have some good material. I got several pounds of number one grade rough to cut and polish. Opal is a favorite material I enjoy. I have lots of this to work with. I have been doing the show for fifteen years now. I get fossil cave bear fangs thousands of years old from Nords. I visit the old man from India I once set up next to; he gives me the best deals on moonstone and other cut gems. I see the German couple in the back of the Ramada for meteorite slices. A special dealer who has the best price on megalodon fossil shark teeth. Another vendor has the best amber with bugs in it. There are several guys in the African village I have been buying from for ten years or more. There is a guy at Electric Park who trades with me. Another guy in the same area trades me for items he wants from Alaska for dinosaur bone slices he digs up himself.

It is time to create and redistribute surplus raw materials I invested in. I tell Iris, "It used to take me all year to break even, selling off enough material to pay for the trip to buy it. This year it has only taken a month. From now on, everything I sell is profit." I've moved $25,000 worth of material in a month through my website. I have over 95% customer satisfaction rate. My goal is to have a loyal customer base of those I trust and am on the same page with. Most customers are repeat, long time buyers. I know what they want, they know what to expect. I may or may not have sold a $30,000 tusk for cash. I may or may not have acquired a tusk from a certain ivory dealer I trust, that looks just like supposed tusk A. Everything done is legal. I just do not like anyone knowing exact provable details of my business. Partly the burden of proof is now on the accused. I do not go about my life with 'being able to prove it' on my mind. I have never been audited, never met a fish and game officer in the field, never been asked to show a permit. Never been stopped in a car and asked for my license, or questioned. I'm lulled into a sense of security. *Or I forgot the bad incidents.*

I do not like the details of most of our lives being available on the Internet through Facebook, twitter, Google Earth, drones, and what not. Though Iris tells me she does not understand computers and cannot help me answer emails or help with the business in any way, I notice she knows how to use Google maps.

"Miles, look, here is my mother's house near Cleveland." She zooms in and we can see cars, people. "I see she still has that silly flag on her balcony and the old mailbox!" I do not say much, but wonder what the world has come to that anyone in the world can look in your yard and make fun of your mailbox. Or insult the flag you choose to wave in your personal private space. Bad people of the world can look around and see who to rob. See what kind of car you drive, where the back door is, when the lights are on, if you have a dog in the yard. What kind of lifestyle you live. How close the neighbors are, if the back alley is clear, and where it leads as a getaway. There are things I do not want the world to see in my yard.

CHAPTER SIX

THE SEARCH WARRANT, CONFISCATIONS

Iris Google's our home. There is my boat trailer out front with no license plate on it. Anyone in the world could turn me in. What if a picture showed wolf carcasses piled up in the yard ready to go in my cooker. There is an entire world out there of terrorists who would take that picture, make it go viral, and I'd be lynched. Or worse than death, my home burned down, wife raped, both of us tortured. In the name of PETA, or Greenpeace. In the news as another victory for those who love animals. Not just possible, but likely. People are not kind.

Iris randomly zooms around on google, looking in on the neighbors. "Oh, look what so and so has!" Other details people may consider their own business is right there. Even if supposedly for now, google earth is six months out of date. I have no proof of that, nor knowledge this will not become real time. Even six months ago is very revealing. So and so got a new roof, we wonder where they got the money. This over here looks like a few pot plants hidden in the garden. People now drive our neighborhood with a car, cruising slow, looking for gossip material.

Example Mad Jay saying, "I drove by your place, Miles, and saw a twelve foot mammoth tusk in the yard you were cleaning. I inquired in town what that would be worth and was told it is illegal! I also wonder what your tax records show." This has been repeated to everyone in the community. In the translation of being repeated, "Miles is in trouble with the IRS!"

"I wouldn't buy anything from Miles. He uses illegal materials."

"Miles killed a mammoth, they are endangered!"

These people can now buy a drone and look in your windows, snoop around your yard. A neighbor just bought a drone for their kid as a Christmas present. I assume they are affordable, not restricted, no permit needed. Hunters are now buying them to track game down in the woods. Google earth pictures can be printed, posted on public bulletin boards. Things that are personal, private, sensitive. A scary aspect is the public goes, "Huh? What do you mean? Have you got something to hide? I do not! Fine, look around all you want!" So I can use a drone and post how many sheets of toilet paper you require? What color your underwear is and where you buy it? There are now cameras up at every parking lot, in every store, and at every street light. It is not possible to go anyplace in civilization without a record of it.

I remind Iris, "Our friends in Tucson got pictures in the mail of his daughter going through a red light and being ordered to pay the fine. There is a clear picture of her driving. What if she was with someone her parents did not approve of also shown in the picture? Or she was someplace she did not tell her parents she was going?" It does not have to be something illegal. Just part of anyone's personal and private life. She could be going to a doctor for any number of reasons. Headed for a church of her choice. Looking for a present for someone in a certain neighborhood. Suddenly having to explain herself because of a secret picture taken, automatically arriving in someone else's hands. The whole concept of automatic tickets generated by computer with no human involved is not fun to be seeing. The digital world with no human intervention has investigated, collected evidence, made a determination, judged us, found us guilty and punished us.

All of my mail, no matter where I send it from, is found, deliberately slowed up, with packages deliberately smashed and destroyed. I had committed no crime, been charged with nothing, was not told there was a problem. Possible now because everything is digital, recorded in a computer, easy to target.

There is no way to say, "Stuff it dirt bag! Give it your best shot!" An irritated officer only has to push a button to make your life hell. Because you slept with his daughter, didn't give him a cut of your action, have long hair, born of a minority race, and what not. All the various reasons people love to hurt each other. Such a person can do great damage, and I do not even know who. We no longer have the right to face our accuser.

I sought advice from a political friend with connections. His advice was, "Go in and talk to these government people. Ask them what the problem is, and how it can be resolved."

I point out something else to Iris, "Remember being over at our friend Al's?" He runs the taxidermy shop in town, and was on the Fish and Game board for a while. We often talk about the animal parts laws. I try to figure out what is legal. Al agreed it is not about being legal and gave an example of what happened to him. This is said by someone who is on the game board.

He told Iris and I, "I went in to talk and get a permit. I have a customer who is

Native, the right color, who has a few seal hides he wants me to tan. This animal is on the city's protected list, so I need a special permit, and records kept to tan these hides. I know it is possible and show up to make it happen." The story, as told us, is that the agent agreed it is legal. But if Al does this, his business will get shut down.

"We will find a way. You will be inspected regularly and you will not pass." If they have to plant evidence, they will.

I tell Iris, "I believe Al. I think he had such a conversation. Fish and Wildlife would do what they said, go against the law in order to enforce what they wish. No different than any other criminal. On whose authority are they operating? What other criminal activities are they capable of?"

That is the big issue. Trust. What is the agenda, what is it the government wishes to see as an end result? What is it willing to do to get there? Not everyone agrees anything sinister is going on. There is no plan, or hidden agenda, or illegal activity by the government. Anyone who says so is a problem person who needs to be reported to the proper authorities.

"Give it a rest, Miles, geez!"

We have a guest coming, sort of a friend, all the way from Virginia! A customer wants to come here to meet me. I'm flattered. This has happened before. I had for a long time, a Japanese customer who flew to Nenana to buy from me. I have had several 'fans' come to Nenana to have my autograph and speak with me. The Virginia guy asked for a good time to visit. I suggest tripod weekend, when the community celebrates the raising of the tripod on the ice for our Ice Classic. Tickets are sold on when the tripod will go out with the spring ice.

"Worth 300 grand. Vendors set up to sell! There are all kinds of contests, a dog race, weight pulls, events for kids, and a fun time." He wants to quit his regular job and run a business something like mine. He hopes to get some advice and pick up some inventory to get started.

"I carve duck decoys. I want to start adding raw materials like you carry, when I set up at shows!" He sounds all excited to get up and going in a new business he will be happier with. I need to email him again and look up his file. I have communications going back over a year.

From: Erick Marshall
 Sent: Wednesday, October 20, 2010 1:58 PM
 To: miles@milesofalaska.net
 Subject: You out there today?
 Hey Miles.
 Was watching a show on the History Channel on gold mining and I thought of you.
 It is amazing they say the only two constants are death and taxes. I would add gold to
 that also. We as humans have been using gold as currency forever. I wish I bought in

when it was $300 an ounce. How do mining claims work in AK? Do you have to be a resident to get a claim? Can you just claim a piece of land and start mining? Anyway, if you don't have time for my silly questions, don't worry. I am just thinking out loud if you will. Thought I would say hi. Hope to hear from you soon

Erick

Hey Erick

Bottom line is, there are no free lunches. If there is enough gold to make money, someone covets that land. Staking a claim- think you do not have to be a state resident, as it is a Federal issue. Only on the right land that is Federal without any classification designated for anything else, like a park. Most who want to fool and do it as a hobby just go do it. If you have a legal claim, there are fees and assessment work. You have to find gold within a certain time limit or you lose the claim. Anyhow got to run, work to do. **Miles**

Miles I saw on the weather channel that winter arrived...Is this correct? Has winter arrived? I bet you never got my email. I was looking at getting some art from you. Let me know when is a good time to contact you to discuss a purchase. Been out of town —travel, travel, travel. But it was all good. Made some money or what I hope will make some in the future. Let me know. **Thanks Erick**

Hello Erick

Well, if you emailed in the past month, I do not see a previous email—so must have got lost in fiber-space. Yes, winter is here, has been a while now. Winter here begins in Oct, even the end of September. I have been running the snow machine a month now, mostly to go get firewood. A good time to contact me? By what method? Email works best so I can email pictures or you can cut and paste off my website items of interest so I know what you like. A good time to call me on the phone? You did not give much information. What kind of art–jewelry, custom knives, fossils, my book, watercolors? Xmas gifts? Do you own a shop, and need wholesale inventory, low end, high end?

I need a sign you know me or were on my website at all. I get 300,000 visits a year to my website. 30 emails a day to reply to. Usually legitimate interest is not so vague and unclear. Sorry for the hesitation. So just give me more information so I know you are an interested customer. Oh, I keep a file on customers after about ten repeats. Otherwise, I file by first name by the month and can find a repeat customer only if I know what month we did business, otherwise you are a new customer. 300,000 is more than I want to keep track of. **Have a good day. Miles**

Miles,

No spam here. I am the real deal. Sorry about the short message. I have read your first book and conversed with you over email about it also. Anyway I will do a better job on my emails in the future.

I want to buy an ivory box, similar to the one on your 'over $250.00' page. I like simple ivory items. That is what I generally buy, and that is what I bought on my trip to Alaska. I think I may have seen your art at the fair in Fairbanks this past summer. I was a little intimidated by all the stuff.

I have been carving duck decoys for many years and sell simple carved items as well as decoys at duck decoy/waterfowl shows on the east coast. I also started selling some of the ivory items I bought in Alaska at the decoy shows in New Jersey. I have had good success selling walrus tooth zipper pulls and other small carved items. I bought a bunch of them that were already made from a guy in Barrow. I have been able to double my money on them. People on the east coast have never seen this stuff and they like to ask questions and are willing to buy items priced right. My carvings are rough, but I work hard at it and tell people if they want to deal with the real artist they need to go to Alaska. Any way that is it for now.

I hope you realize I am serious and I am sorry for making you think you were wasting your time.

Wolf carcasses bought from local subsistence trappers all winter get cleaned in spring and sold. Not everyone would understand if they looked into my back yard and saw this.

Hello Erick

The only ivory box I have in stock right now is the picture enclosed. I have a Dall sheep horn box with ivory lid with turquoise unicorn in top—but larger, and the ivory does not dominate. Oh, I have another box of wood with a nice fossil ivory duck carving top sort of plain $150. It's with my fair stuff still. I forgot about that one. **Miles**

I need to write again [1]

This item I show from my web site is one of the ivory items approved as legal and accounted for in a previous agreement with Fish and Wildlife

Hello Erick

Nice to hear from you. Yes, I still have the box I showed you. I live a village life these days, at home working in the shop a lot. Almost a senior now. No more sled dogs. I snow machine now. Got stopped from fishing for the dogs—forced into a snow machine a while back. Forest fire wiped out my 200 miles of trapline that took twenty years to cut. Oh well.

So far this year, not much going on. We had record warm, then four days of rain, then thirty below zero with no snow. No one has gone out yet, can't get around in the wilds so far... Jan 26th we go to Tucson for the big fossil gem show—not back till mid Feb. That is not a bad time to visit, then and into March. Light is coming back again, and there should be snow to get out to do things in the woods. I'm guessing the roads will be better. I have two snow machines we could get out on.

I cannot make any special plans. I never trust what anyone says they will do and work around that. When people show up, I make plans then. I expect to be around. I should be able to take a few days off. Maybe see the northern lights, see a moose, maybe wolves, hard to know. There are things going on in Fairbanks too, worth seeing, like ice sculptures, the museum, etc. I have a good friend here in Nenana who won the Iditarod, who is great to visit, and talk to, and maybe run dogs with him. We can see how it goes. If you have dates, let me know, and I can mark it down. You'd fly into Fairbanks, I'm fifty miles away. If you come into Anchorage, that is too far to go get you. Well- tired, late, got orders to fill, and a local show to get ready for! Always fun here to do the shows. **Later. Miles**

Hello Miles,

Ok I will figure out the Paypal, $250.00 is a good deal on that art.

Well, I am going to start to work on my trip. I picked out a date. I want to arrive in Alaska on March 5, 2011. That is the day I am shooting for. I need to start my research now, so I am prepared. I don't mind driving in the snow, but we don't get much anymore, so I am out of practice. I don't want to be a pain in the ass, so you just tell me when enough is enough. I am flexible. I figure if I get to do a couple things that I want to do, then the trip is successful. I am also excited about being able to be seeing your art again first hand.

Well, as the date gets closer you will have to help me with my list of stuff to bring, and if you are going to have time in your schedule to do things. Anyway, thanks for extending the hand, I am looking forward to hanging out with a "local. " Have fun at the show, Christmas art fair? We don't have that small town stuff anymore. Nothing is handmade here.

Talk soon. I will pay for your art and pick it up when I arrive.

Erick

Hello again Miles,

Hey, I have been thinking as I continue to read books from Alaska; I am amazed how much happens in the winter up there. I am going to try to start 2011 out right and I want to make a trip to Alaska in the winter. Dog sled, ice fish, learn about trapping. I need to get away from the east coast and all the hustle and bustle of New York City. We don't have much winter anymore.

I have a bunch of air miles to use up from all my travel. What is the possibility of visiting you in Alaska and maybe learning a few things about winter life and survival also? I would guess there are plenty of chores that need to be done, always. I have outdoor experience and am pretty tough for a city guy, so I think I know I can make it. Even if you don't need help, I am planning a visit to Alaska after the new year.

Let me know.

Thank you

Erick

I am not especially thrilled to be responsible for someone's good time in Alaska, and have my brain picked, offer my assistance, take people on free trips. I used to be more open to this idea to help others. But I am not a guide, so I cannot be paid to take anyone on any trips. Such trips cost thousands of dollars if people go through legitimate normal channels. A lot of people want the experience and do not want to pay. People want me to line it all up for them, give them a place to stay, use my connections. I get a thanks, told what good buddies we are. They get a vacation worth ten grand for almost nothing. I get a handshake. It is different if I choose to make an offer to someone who has done me a kindness. This Erick is someone coming to me with a Jessie,

"Hey good, buddy, help me out." Erick is saying "I need…" No, it is not me with a need, it is him. But he may buy a lot of art and materials, a customer I should be nice to.

Hello Erick

Glad art arrived and is appreciated. If you call, I do not mind talking. I tend to not like to call as it seems to take me three to four tries to dial all the numbers right—and then get the wrong person at the other end. Up to Alaska in March? You know it is still winter? It can be thirty below. Usually getting enough light to be warmer. No leaves out yet, no summer birds here yet. No RV park open yet. No attractions open yet. Denali park closed etc. Anyhow got to run. **Miles**

Hello Miles,

Ho ho ho,

Hey pick up the mail today (no, the post office does not deliver in all types of weather) and thank you for sending me such beautiful art. I am going to buy more.

We got some really wintery Alaska weather. Twenty inches of snow, wet and heavy. Wind about twenty degrees. Everything was closed. These people freak when the weather goes to crap. They cannot survive. There is always a run on the grocery stores and the shelves are empty. You would think the end is near the way they act. They all could use some of your survival training.

Miles, not sure if you feel much for talking on the phone. I would like to talk with you about my trip in March if it still works for you and about my next purchase from you. Let me know when is a good time that you are not too busy and I will call you.

Thanks

Happy New Year

Is it still dark and cold?????

Erick

There are a couple of phone conversations that result in Erick making plans to arrive for a visit during Tripod Days as I suggest. I keep telling everyone, Iris and I do not drive in winter. We do not carry insurance during the winter. The truck is too old and unreliable in cold weather—the heater does not work, the tires are bald, the engine is gutless. It does not have all the oil pan, transmission and battery heaters required to keep a truck running in an Alaska winter. The newly acquired car is worse.

"No problem Miles, I can rent a car in Fairbanks!"

"I wish we could be more help. We got you a place to stay at the local Roughwoods motel. You can join us for meals, and we can get out on the snow machine. I lined up a dog sled ride with my Iditarod winning native friend, Josh." Erick is excited to get here. He brings us a bottle of wine as a gift. There are obvious cultural differences between us. Neither Iris or I drink. Among our friends, exchanging wine is not customary, and seems strange. We get the impression Erick drinks a lot. He hangs out at the bar. Erick comes across as a city slicker, not the outdoor type he portrayed himself as. Suit and tie, white soft skin, disoriented by an outdoor environment. My first impression is that he is going to have a hard time selling animal products. He does not walk the walk, and the talk is memorized jabberwocky. He needs more help than he let on.

"So, Miles, let's see your shop, I have heard so much about it and am looking forward to seeing it!" Flattery works. I like to please people. "Wow, look at all this stuff! I'm impressed! It sure represents a lot of knowledge and connections! I admire your lifestyle. Alas, I am stuck in the rat race, trying to find a way out, and here, you have the perfect answer!" Iris invites him for dinner of moose roast, and canned vegetables from our garden. "My God, you eat like this every day!? I sure envy you!" Erick tells me he makes pretty good money on his job, so can invest in materials. He seeks my advice.

I reply: "I suggest you begin with some of the basics that sell well, nothing complicated or legally marginal. You want to first identify your market. You are known for selling duck decoys, so what kind of crowd is this, Hunters?"

"Yes, Miles, but high-end collectors as well. If they hunt, it is for sport. They own horses, boats, but do not have time to get out much."

I think I know this group. "Wearing gold capped lion claws on a thick chain. Artificial tans, into wolves, bears, large predators."

"Yes, that's about it. But other groups. Young people who like folk art."

"So low-end, but cool items. Porcupine claw earrings, his and her matching wolf claw pendants. Cute and romantic. You can sacrifice quality for flash and dash. Keeping the price down is the priority with this group."

I show Erick how porcupine claws look a lot like hawk claws. He would have never thought of that, so we set aside a bag of those.

"Erick if you carve, I suggest moose bone, and you can carve different things from that to sell." We set aside some bones of different kinds. He likes my toe bone beads. Erick notices a dead frozen raven on the floor in the corner in an unheated part of my shop. He wants it.

"It is so big, so majestic! I am into duck decoys but also taxidermy of birds. This would be so awesome to have Miles!"

"Sorry, cannot sell ravens. It's a shame. I do not know what I will do with this. I'm not supposed to have it myself." It's on the floor discarded. I add, "It will probably end up in the compost pile."

"Wow! What a shame, how disrespectful to such a bird!"

I agree and explain what I am doing with it, how I got it. "A trusted Native friend of mine brought it to me. He runs our community cultural center where I once worked. He did not know what else to do with it or who else to bring it to. I suppose I am sort of a shaman to many people. It is part of his culture not to waste anything, to show respect, honor the dead things. It would be disrespectful for me to say, "No, take it someplace else!" It is better in their mind that a Shaman perform the ceremony or treat this situation."

"Miles, I understand! It is like in our culture when we want a priest to perform last rites for the dead! Or bury a pet for us!"

I only nod and explain, "This Native told me a DOT government driver hit the raven and stopped. The Raven was not damaged, but dead. He tosses it in the truck, not knowing what to do with it. He knows my Native friend and gives it to him frozen." He is Native, so probably no legal issue with him. I'm sure the legal aspect was not on his mind. Nor on my mind. Honoring the dead is more important. But honor the dead in what way? It is winter, no good way to bury it. I actually put it out of my mind. I have no plans. I forgot about it. Maybe another Native would want it who can legally have it. At some point I was going to ask around, maybe. "But, in truth, put it in the compost, let it become fertilizer for the garden."

Erick is astonished! "Wow, what a waste. I cannot understand our government sometimes, they sure go overboard with these restrictions!" I agree. Erick goes on, "I will keep it for myself, not offer it to anyone else, just my personal item in my private collection no one else will see. I can honor the raven!"

"Well, add it to the pile. I can give it as a gift, I suppose. Or, we make a big pile, we come up with a single dollar amount for the pile and it all comes out in the mix. Some things can be called gifts, other items paid for in a very lose and vague agreement."

Erick smiles and nods. We have a pile I think will get Erick started in his new business.

"But I need some cooler more exotic stuff, Miles, have you shown me everything?" I do not agree that Erick needs to begin his business with the rare, expensive, or exotic. But he insists. It is common for people to come to me for advice, and then not take it. We go into another room of things I do not usually show people, of my own stuff.

"Erick, I am not running a store open to the public. I have no hours. I am more in the manufacture business. I sell at shows, on the Internet, not much out of my home. Usually I bring out some items to show over to the house if anyone is interested. The public is not allowed here in my shop. So some things might be for sale, some not, some are my personal items, nothing here is priced or offered to the public for sale."

"Wow, Miles, how about this walrus tusk! This is so cool and just what I need to draw attention!" He has spotted one of Jessie's white walrus tusks. I am alarmed, and shocked Erick would want it! He needs to know his laws better, if he hopes to survive this business.

"No way, no how Erick! White ivory for you is totally off limits!"

"Well, I have sold walrus teeth before. They sell well and I had no problems."

"Erick, you see what I wrote down the length of the tusk in magic marker? It says "For Natives only." I wrote that for a reason."

"Why do the Natives have special rights? Isn't that discrimination? Is that legal?" We talk a little about how, in general, the Natives are not very grateful, nor has this 'special privileges,' classification helped them much. Many insult the white, many insult me, insult Erick. Toss their special privileges in our face. Leading to a conversation of the incompetence of the government.

"The government does not deserve our respect, Miles!"

"I agree to a point. I do not respect the morality or rightness of our government, but respect the power of the gun at our heads." Erick feels we should take the law into our own hands and do what we feel is moral and right. "If so, Erick, you have to be smart about it. There is no way you can show this white ivory tusk around and not get in trouble. It will draw attention all right! The wrong kind!"

"So what are you going to do with this white ivory, let it sit here forever?"

"I have a Native friend I think can use it. He can legally have it. He has one tusk. I thought he might end up needing more, maybe all of it. So far, he has not done anything with what he has." We walk away from the white ivory. Erick focuses on some polar bear fangs, my seal claws. Again, I am alarmed at his interest in such 'up to the line legally' stuff. He does not have the knowledge to successfully deal in these items. Nor does he have the classification as being either Alaskan or subsistence. His rights will be less than mine. Some items he could have as an end user, not to be resold.

"Sure, Miles, my private collection works for me!" But I do not believe him. When Erick first contacted me and first looked at my materials, he spoke of decoy wood, my cut stones, interesting wood, wolf claws, nothing that would raise a red flag or alarm me.

Erick is impressed by the events the community puts on for the Tripod weekend. I am proud of my community, so talk it up in a good light.

"Miles, you have items out for sale you said you would not sell me! Why!" He sounds offended.

"I am subsistence, selling some items to local Natives only, or to end users who will keep and not re-sell the item. This is Nenana, a remote subsistence village off the beaten path, off the grid. There is sort of an understood agreement with the local government. The same situation would not exist for you selling these same items in New York." I mention some items are state regulated and can remain in Alaska, but become an issue if leaving the state.

"Miles, you cannot control what happens to your products after you sell them, can you? Can anyone? I mean, once it leaves your hands, the items are not yours anymore to control, right?" In some ways, correct. I can offer advice. Once an item is sold and out of my hands, I have no control over that item, or what someone does with it. I can tell someone the law as I know it, and make suggestions. As long as I am covered, how much responsibility do I have for anyone else? One issue here is, I have a customer who has made a pile of a thousand dollars' worth of legal goods. Am I going to jeopardize the entire deal over some stuff I do not think is a good idea? *More a problem for him than me.* I'm thinking. "I believe in people's rights to make their own choices." Nor is it my job to police people. *I do not agree with the ads on TV, 'Friends do not let friends drive drunk!' If I am responsible for someone else driving drunk, what else might I be responsible for someone else doing?"*

I mean how much trouble is it going to be if the do do hits the fan and I am saying, "Yea I gave a guy a dead raven. I'm sorry. *What are you going to do, take away my birthday?* Ok, I should have tossed it in the trash and did not. So fine me." It's what level of a crime? I might at worse get a $100 fine? Is this worth getting my undies in a bunch over? *Hardly!* Dead birds of all kinds, bones, skulls are the sort of 'stuff,' found in most village yards and homes in my area. No, it is not common for civilized people, possibly beyond their comprehension, that this is how remote people live. Dogs drag animal parts and dead animals hither thither and yon, up and down the roads, dropped who knows where. I took a picture of a dead moose gut pile in front of the downtown fire station that stayed there two months, as an example. It's just a different culture than city people know.

You have aluminum cans, plastic bags, car tires in your ditches. We have dead ravens, feathers, animals in our ditches. Each feels the others garbage is appalling! Each is used to their own garbage. If I said, "Cool! A broken beer bottle! I want it, will buy it from you, I can make a cutting tool from it, arrowheads, all kinds of possibilities! Get me more!"

You'd chuckle "Have at it!"

If worse came to worse, I'd face a jury of my peers. I am confident any such jury would say, "Why are we here, why are tax dollars being wasted on this? Evidence?" There is no receipt, no money exchanged, *"What Raven?"* It is not as if I killed it or am promoting the killing of ravens. It is not like I deal in dead birds or trophies or offer them boldly on the Internet, or promote the sale of such items. It's an anomaly, one-time deal, done, gone, over, forgotten. It seems doubtful the government would expend large amounts of money to get to the bottom of what happened. After an entire weekend Erick wears me down and 'fine, whatever.' I'm not good at saying 'No', so just want him out of here. Get paid, have a good life. My good buddy, Erick.

The Tripod show goes well financially, as usual. I know everyone in the village, locals have been buying, trading, bartering, with me since forever. A local Native trapper has five wolf carcasses to trade me. One girl has a few huge pinecones from California, another has some Macaw feathers off a pet in Hawaii. I almost always say 'yes', and eventually find someone who has an interest is such items. Some items are gifts, "I do not know what to do with this stuff. I'd throw it out, if you can use it, here." It is part of local culture to thankfully accept a gift. Much like the tradition of potlatch, where food is handed out. We sit with a plate, and food is brought to us, and put on our plate.

You do not say, "No thank you, I do not eat beaver meat" or, "I do not care for fish." You are grateful and say, "Thank you." If you wish to take it home and feed it to the dog, or throw it out at home, do so quietly. I adopt this way of thinking. Again, I have nine buildings to store things in. I am not likely to run out of storage room. My peers understand this way of thinking.

SPRING IS ARRIVING! New light, time to order the garden seeds, and begin a new season! Life is good. What a wonderful time of year! Erick is gone and off my mind, but I get a communication.

Hey Miles,

Hope all is well. Have you gotten out on the snow machine to look for wood? Been busy, sold a few of the items to a good decoy customer of mine. Sold him the polar bear tooth and some lynx and wolf claws. Have you stabilized the other polar bear teeth? I am still interested in them and am in a position to make a good profit from them. Let me know. I was thinking if you had some wood you could put the teeth in with it. Talk soon

Say hi to Iris and the cat for me.

Erick

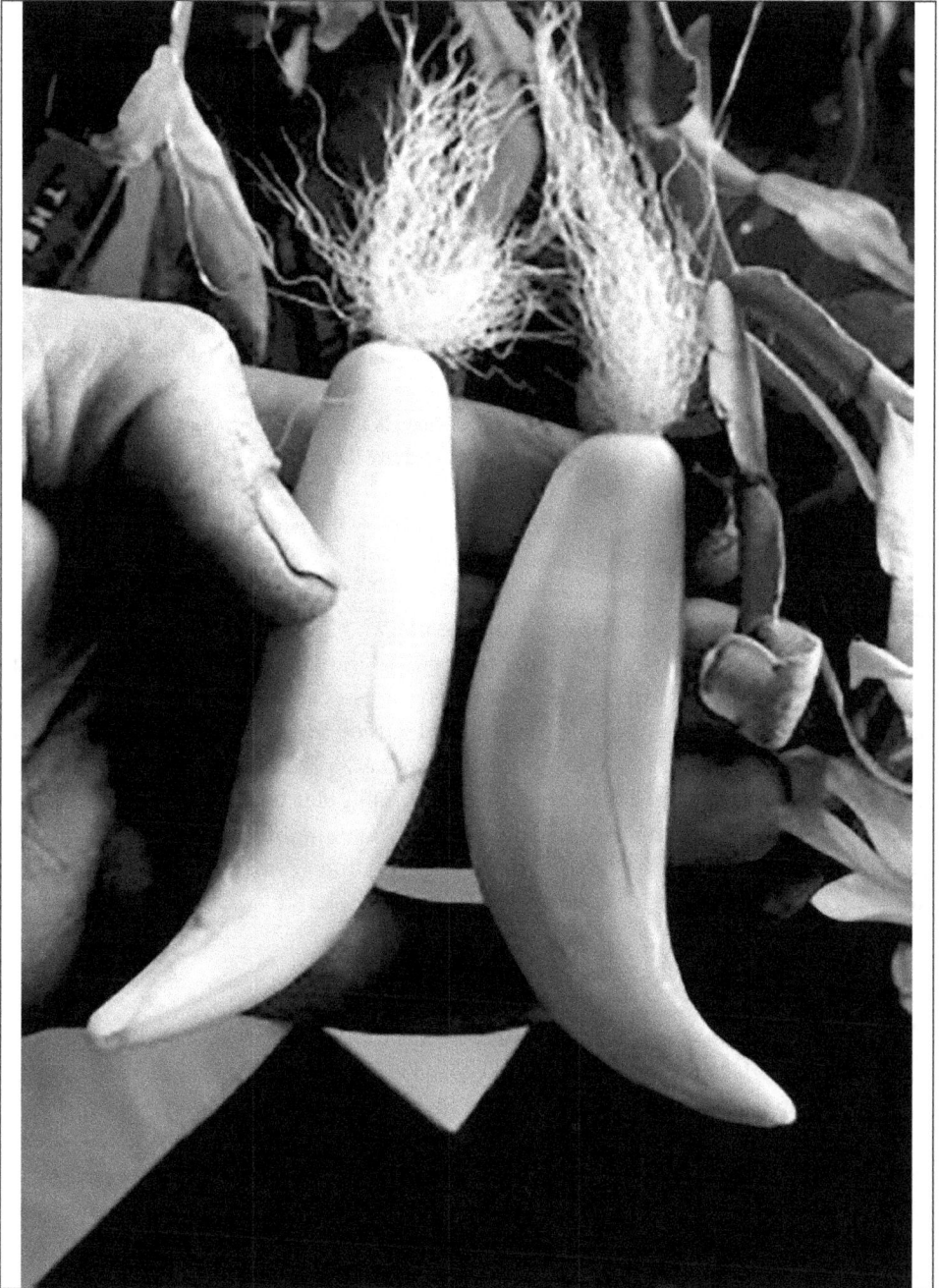

Two fossil fangs I show Erick are legal to sell as authentic native craft I have paperwork for.

Hello Erick

The polar bear fangs? I meant to get a picture today... I have been so wrapped up in the knife blades I have not even come in to dinner at meal times.

Twelve blades just came out of etching and need a polish. Then I have five more steps to go through to see how they came out. I wish I didn't have to sleep. Well, it might be easier for me to fix em and send them to you as bring to the house and take pictures and discuss them. I had kind of picked them out for a customer who collects such things who keeps asking me. Haven't had time to tell him I got two from Tucson.

Well, I got a wad of money right now and do not need money as much as time. Money I guess buys me time to 'fool' but by fooling I lead up to more money, weird, huh? So, ya, $200 each, I will send, and you can pay me when you get them or when they sell or if not wanted, return them. Oh—I came across in storage two nice spruce burls that could be cut into a square to fit in a box. Is this something that can be carved well? Nice swirly pattern. Or do you get a lot of that? I'd think a big burl of anything is worth something when you need big pieces.

Let me know I might cut and pack that and include the fangs. Have not gone to get firewood, as I say, too busy with the blades. **Later. Miles**

In most cases, polar bear fangs would be illegal. However, I have a source at the fossil show in Tucson for fossil fangs hundreds to thousands of years old. They are often costly. I try to acquire cracked or broken fangs I can restore. I am getting good at restoration. This becomes add on value. I target the craft trade, not high end collectors. There are four to five materials I make 75% of my money on. The rest almost needs subsidizing. There are not many fossil polar bear fangs available in the world. There is no way to make a living off that! I acquire huge, fossil alligator teeth, old whale teeth. One or two of something, and no more. I'm getting good enough, a museum in Italy asks me to do a fossil restoration project. Now and then I get asked to identify something.

Hello Erick

Glad items are selling. No, have not done much with the fossil polar bear fangs. I have been working on custom knives and got an idea I think will sell well so all hyped up about it, and it occupies my time right now. And fixing the website. More in the cart and adding pages, like new custom knife page, and blank blade page. There are separate pages for art I have already sold to look at, for those who want to cut and paste. Customers can show me what they like and would like me to make. Still no large birch that is spalted. Much along the trails may have been cut for firewood. **Later. Miles**

Hello Miles,

Love the knives, especially the Damascus steel! I can't wait to see the new web pages. Don't worry about the wood, I was just curious if any luck. I am sure you will find some. Don't go crazy trying to get it. No rush on the polar bear fangs either. I understand when an artist has momentum and doesn't want to change directions. If you can send me a photograph of them, I can show my customer at the next show and hold his interest until you have them ready. I don't remember if we discussed price, but throw me a number to pacify the buyer. I know it wasn't cheap. I think they were marked around 200 each. They are so polished and pretty the picture will tell the story and solidify a good sale.

I think I am going to be working this weekend. We got a small oil spill. Looks like someone dump their bilge water in the Lyden River near Newark. Same old shit, but it will pay good.

Talk Soon

Erick

Tuesday, April 05, 2011

Hello Erick

Here is a picture of the two fossil polar bear fang art pieces so you can show your customer. Getting sent tomorrow, Wed priority mail, with a box of spruce burls, expect four to five days. Two fangs at $200 is $400. $30 for wood maybe $20 to ship, wait till shipment arrives. Contact me then about what's owed. Make sure everything is ok.

Oh, best to sell the polar bear as 'Eskimo art'; leave the tuff of polar bear fur on. If you make a receipt, it needs to say 'Native art.' To keep it legal. Once owned, it can be altered to suit, but then not legally resold, maybe as a fossil, but art is easier to see and prove then fossil. Anyhow… hope all is well. **Miles**

I'm concerned with how Erick wishes to handle these fangs. How he resells them. There are delicate laws with subtleties to understand and distinctions to make. 'Native art' is the simplest, easiest way to keep it legal in the situation he is in. 'Fossil' is legal, but harder to verify, and may require money spent on an age test to prove the legality. I do not trust the legal system on this. I get the impression Erick wants to just call them, "polar bear fangs." I'm trying to help him stay legal.

Meanwhile, my focus is on getting garden seeds sprouted and under the halogen light in the back room. I have a single high-intensity light that runs on a twelve foot tracker I designed and built. It takes half an hour to make a run down and back the twelve feet. Some amount of spring light comes in the big picture window. A total of ten flats are started. Eventually the plants go into four-inch pots. Coming up with potting soil requires finding old pots under the snow full of dirt, and cooking the dirt in the oven to kill weeds, seeds, and fungus.

Iris asks, "Did you start our tomatoes yet?" We have a Siberian breed of seed that is now in its fifth generation here in Nenana that does very well for us.

"Yes, but also some yellow variety, some arctic, and cherry." Cucumber is important, as well as some of the herbs we enjoy, like basil. When the outdoor temperature gets above freezing regularly, it is time to move the bedroom Toyo oil stove into the greenhouse. I light the wood stove in the greenhouse so the oil stove should not have to kick on. Plants are in their four-inch pots and are a foot tall when they go into the greenhouse in mid-April. Ashes are put on the garden soil to help the sun melt the snow. The ground is showing.

I am in the greenhouse as usual at six in the morning, working on transplanting, mixing soil, setting up the timers and drippers. I see movement outside. *It must be a loose dog in the yard.* I keep my eye out and see a person dressed in a flak jacket, crouched down with automatic weapon at the ready, sneaking, looking around, coming around the corner of the house ready for combat. The agent has not seen me in the greenhouse. He is far enough away; he is not likely to see me. *Should I go out the door and into the backwoods, disappear?* I am not especially worried or scared. *I am not a criminal.* So I come out the door and show myself calmly saying:

"May I help you? I assume you are looking for someone, I assume me."

Another agent comes around the corner. I see they both have radios, rifles at the ready, and one says, "I found the target." There is no aggressive behavior towards me. I am simply walked to the front of the house. I notice many police cars out front, and many agents about. One seems to be in charge, informing me of the reason for the visit.

"We have a search warrant for this premises." I nod. I am still not concerned. Have at it, what do you expect to find? I do not believe I have anything seriously illegal to be found. I had, after all, received a warning months ago that I may be under investigation.

One of the first questions is "Where is the trophy room with the polar bears?" I'm puzzled and amazed. It is obvious a lot of money has been spent for these guys to be here. I'd assume they would have somewhat accurate information. I see a satellite map of my property in his hands.

"No trophy room here, look around, does it look like I live that lifestyle? But have a look if you wish." I'm served a search warrant. I do not take in what it says. As I am being addressed, there are a bunch of guys with rifles and armor on. I'm focused on not getting shot. I feel safe for now, I admit, but know if I make a sudden fast move, turn and run in a panic, or start an argument, I could easily end up dead. I'm going to go along with the program and put everyone at ease. What a piece of paper has written on it is irrelevant.

I believe this is not about being tried, judged, and punished. The job of these people is to serve a warrant and collect what is on the warrant. These guys are not lawyers, may not know the law, are not judges, or juries. I see Iris is out in the front yard in her nightgown under guard.

I get asked, "How many guns do you have?"

"I'm not sure. Do you want me to show you where they are?" No. I am not allowed in the house till the house is secure.

"We will find all the guns!"

I'm thinking, Good luck! I'd think me showing them where the guns are would save a lot of time and effort. But then again, they do not want me near my guns. *They had assumed Iris and I would be still asleep at six am. They assumed this would be a surprise on a sleepy couple caught in bed. I'm sure the impact of serving a warrant by gun toting government agents has a control advantage over half awake people.* I vaguely wonder what time they had to get up to leave Fairbanks to be here at this hour. Questions come at me.

"Do you mind answering a few questions, we need a secure place to talk away from the house."

"Depends what the questions are. I may require a lawyer on some subjects."

"Fair enough."

We go over to the shop. I want to know what is going on in the house, what is being taken, damaged, photographed. Since this is a warrant for a search, I do not know why I cannot be present to see what is taken. Or why I cannot be with Iris.

"You cannot go back in the house. No."

I'm asked about a moose. Did I poach my last moose? "No" I am shown pictures I posted on Facebook of a nice bull moose on a sandbar. There are two armed guys in the room with me as I get asked.

"We have satellite pictures of you getting this moose, would you like to change your story? It will go better on you if you tell the truth."

Before I answer, I am thinking. *I was alone. No one knew what day I left, where I was, or when I returned. The day was very cloudy. I have already seen an updated present time satellite photo of my property.* Due to the pause, interrogator number two adds, "We watched you and your friends…"

My expression never changed. I have never gotten my moose with anyone else. I do not hunt with anyone else. I am always alone. No one knows any details as a fact. That's part of survival. Have no witnesses. I never tell anyone the day I get my moose. I wait a month, and may vaguely refer to the fact that yes, I am eating well, have lots of meat.

Interrogators ask roughly, "Miles, who is the preacher? You took a preacher out moose hunting." *My phone was tapped.* I do not let on I now know that. I did in fact take a preacher friend and his father out to my homestead for a wilderness experience. I did not get paid. It was resident friends I took out so they could hunt. I did not help them hunt.

Preachers, spiritual leaders rarely get paid. It is common to thank them with favors and donations. My way of saying thanks was to give him and his visiting father a good Alaska experience I can easily offer that means a lot to them. I'm hearing how facts can get distorted, twisted, turned around, and made to be illegal. I'm trying to be nice to a spiritual person who does a lot of good things for the community. I'm vague and do not reply in a way that indicates I recall or understand what this is all about. While I come across to the community as the village idiot who has a big mouth and tells all, "What can you say as a fact, dear community, that you saw firsthand, that I did not tell you? Not one of you has ever been in my shop or worked with me." It's dust in the wind. Rumors, contradictory facts as I tell everyone a different story. I'm legal, just not very trusting.

I say to these agents, "If you have satellite pictures, then you know this is a legal moose. Show me the pictures, maybe I can explain, if there is a problem." Spy satellites in the sky, watching everywhere I go. These guys are trying to have me feel paranoid. They are lying. Are they allowed to lie? We change the subject. First topic has to do with a nonexistent trophy room full of polar bears, next topic has to do with a legal moose. Where is this going? Why? Pictures are brought out.

"Do you recognize these items?" *My buddy Erick is an undercover agent. Everything we said was recorded. Even around the dinner table. Secret pictures were taken.* That is regrettable, but not the end of the world. I still feel all I did was legal. I'd just rather not have to pay a lawyer and go to court to prove it. "What about the raven, Miles! Here is the picture. That's worth about ten years in prison." The agent is getting loud and aggressive. I am not. I remain calm.

"That is not Federal jurisdiction. If you want to tell the state all about it, feel free to do so. Ravens do not migrate or cross state lines, they are therefore state regulated."

"They are on the Federal migratory bird list."

I shrug my shoulders. "Then ravens are erroneously on the list and need to be removed." In court, I'd win, it's that simple. I'm not flustered. I know the state is not concerned unless I am killing ravens right and left, or making a regular business of selling ravens. I'm shown some pictures.

"Do you know either of these two people?"

Pictures of Jessie and his wife. I see no reason not to admit I do, there is plenty of proof I know them. I suspect where this is going. I'm shown a walrus head mount and asked if this looks familiar, as it is supposedly an item I sent overseas to Argentina. I'm puzzled at first, as I did send something to Argentina, but it was not a trophy mount, and not related to this picture. I'm thinking: *Jessie emailed me this picture! Asked me if this was of interest to me. I emailed back that no, this is not fossil, this is a trophy. I do not deal in trophies.*

As far as I understand, we are now getting into an area of grave consequences if I am wrong, where answers can be critical if used in court. Up until now, nothing has been serious. Ivory is a big subject. I reply. "This is where I need legal advice. I am not going to discuss this subject without a lawyer." One reason is, there may be no proof anything at all was sent to Argentina, and there is little reason to offer up a confession. I'm guessing, since the Feds do not know what I sent, that they know very little. I also think these questions have little do to with a search warrant, and items I have in my possession, or that the Feds have in their possession. I'm also guessing if they had anything, I'd be under arrest.

The interrogators hear over the radio the white tusks were found. "In the suspect's secret hidden room." Erick must have said I had a secret room they are to look for. It is simply a room with a piece of foam leaning up against the door to help regulate the temperature and isolate this room from the rest of the shop so it does not have to be heated. Items in this room are not obviously out in the open if I have guests, or local thieves breaking in. I can see they are going to say, 'Secret hidden room,' if we go to court. The trophy room they were looking for? *I wonder what Erick said.*

Iris later Googles the business name Erick gave us and finds him, we think. It looks like he is an alcoholic who got arrested. Our guess, it was deal time, "Help us set this guy up." If so, he may have exaggerated his story. He spent a lot of time in the bar, so being an alcoholic fits.

I answer questions I think the Feds already have an answer for, or is easy to find out elsewhere, or if the issue seems open and shut if I explain. However, these guys are trained professionals at what they do and I am an amateur. They know how to work a suspect, get information, intimidate, brainwash, confuse.

I'm diabetic. I have now not eaten two meals, almost six straight hours of interrogation. I flat out say I need to eat; we need to stop! I am groggy, weak, lightheaded, confused, unable to think. It is not a good situation when the interrogators are deliberately trying to get me to agree with their needs. This is in my mind not useable interrogation. I am told if I leave the property I cannot come back.

They are worried I may come back armed or with a gang. It is true, I would not mind returning with witnesses who could testify in court about how the search warrant is served. I wouldn't mind getting hold of a camera or tape recorder to have a copy of my own version of what happened, got said and done.

The long day is coming to an end. I'm brought to the house from the shop where the interrogation took place. On the way I see two trucks packed to the gunnels with sealed boxes of 'my stuff.' My computer and laptop are packed up. I'm bummed out they got the main thumb drive I operate off of. The one I'd grab and hide or destroy if there was an invasion. My customer list, tax records, vital statistics. In my view, nothing illegal, but private anyhow. Not something I want in the hands of people I do not trust.

"Miles, we need you to sign off on this list of confiscated items." Said as if a minor informality. I think not.

"How do I know what you took? You would not allow me to watch and see." *As far as I can see, this is a shakedown. How do I know this is not outright robbery? I'd be very surprised if we go to court, because I think I'd win. I also doubt very much I am going to get my confiscated goods back. So exactly what is missing?*

"Look around, take inventory Miles." Yeah, right. They are packed, ready to head down the road in the next five minutes.

I'd need the same seven hours to verify what is taken, that they spent to confiscate it in the first place. I answer with, "Try to be in my shoes and understand my situation. As you see, I have nine buildings full of boxes of stuff that would fill twenty dump trucks. How do I know what you took? Two truckloads does not put a dent in my inventory. I'm not signing off on anything saying I understand, know what you took, unless it is the truth, and I know what you took." With no forthcoming answer, I go on. "As far as I am concerned I should have been allowed to watch and take my own notes, even take my own pictures, make my own recordings. That is what would be honest and fair."

If the Feds can collect information for a prosecution, I should be allowed to collect information for a defense. Isn't that reasonable? I take time to scan the search warrant for the first time, now that I have specific concerns. I notice right off, that many items have been confiscated that are not in the search warrant. Also, items listed in a Federal search warrant, that are not under Federal jurisdiction. I repeat what I said earlier. "You have bear claws listed in the search warrant. Bears are state regulated, not Federally regulated."

The only situation I can think of would be a case involving the Lacey Act. Though I did hear something about bears on Federal land being under Federal jurisdiction. Any claws on my property were acquired in Alaska, have remained in Alaska, and have never been on Federal land. *By what right do you have bear claws listed in the search warrant? By what right have you confiscated them?* I ask myself. In particular are grizzly claw necklaces that are my personal necklaces not offered for sale, and in fact in a tray in my bedroom with a note 'not for sale.' Necklaces worth thousands of dollars each, for insurance purposes. I think they are confiscated so they can be sold by the Feds as a fundraiser, or kept by agents for their personal use. I do not think these will ever be seen or turn up any place as evidence.

"Where are these high end necklaces listed here?" The agents and I both look. The guys were writing it down, so should know what they called these necklaces, and being so high end, should recall what happened within the past few hours. We cannot find them. There is an entry simply 'tray of artwork.'

I do not find that acceptable. "This is a tray worth ten grand, and you do not bother to list the items, but refer to this simply as, 'miscellaneous art work?' Would you find that acceptable, if I went into your home and confiscated $10,000 worth of your personal jewelry of that value, calling it simply 'a pile of art?' Would you trust me to produce it later? Think you'd have any legal recourse for getting it back once I left with it?"

I see a necklace on the table. I ask why this necklace is an issue. It is obviously made of fossils, rocks, gemstones. I add, "I have a photo of me wearing this necklace before 1973, so it is obviously pre CITES (Convention on International Trade in Endangered Species of Wild Fauna and Flora) material. I am concerned, because this necklace is worth $5,000 and I see no reason to take it. Least the value be questioned, I sold one not as nice as this for $3,500, and another one similar to this for $5,000.

"Well, there is one bead in it, I question, Miles."

"If so, that is a five dollar bead, let me cut it out and give it to you." I'm concerned, what other items like this are disappearing into their truck of confiscations.I have trouble believing there is a problem with one bead in the necklace. I look around, and in plain site is an entire jar of handmade ivory beads, just like this one in question. Why isn't the jar confiscated? Likewise, I see a lot of items I'd question the legality of, that are not confiscated, and items that are absolutely no question legal, that are missing, worth a lot of money. What's that all about? Is the issue the legality, or the value?

I look at the table of items in zip bags to be confiscated. These are just last minute items they have not packed yet. Less than one percent of what they have already loaded up. I notice wolf claws labeled as eagle claws. I point out the error. "I'm not signing off you confiscated illegal eagle claws when they are legal wolf claws." There are other mislabeled items on the table. I spot large lynx claws labeled as lion. Having me wonder *what has already been packed that is also mislabeled. I am getting no place with my questions. I feel, if the officer was legal and honest, he'd show some concern if items are not properly labeled, as wanting to do an honest confiscation. What is being done constitutes being framed.*

This would be the same if this were a drug raid and baby powder and sugar was taken from the cupboard, put in separate bags and deliberately labeled heroin and cocaine. Or a crime scene where blood is extracted from the pet dog, and the bottle labeled human blood. I come to realize these guys have the guns and can do whatever they want to. Who am I? I have zero rights. If I do not like it, I can get shot right here and now. What would the story be? I ran. Resisted, drew a weapon. Where are my witnesses? Nothing but cops in sight. I am not allowed to take pictures, recordings, or have my own witnesses present.

I've been interrogated seven hours. I just want them gone. I just want this to end. A typical feeling, I'm told. Ready to confess to anything. Part of brainwashing and interrogation. I have no choice but to sign if I want to live and want them to leave. They have $20,000 worth of my goods I am never going to see again. That I know. I also know at least three quarters is for sure legal. They must know it too. My conclusion is this episode is about intimidation, proving who is in control, even in hopes I protest in some way so they can have the joy of cleaning my clock. I have heard the words out loud while speak of people like me. *Save society a lot of money if we just get rid of these vermin.* Heard it enough I accept it as a truth and reality with no interest in proving it to anyone else. I know what I know.

I am not expecting a follow up arrest. I do not expect to get my goods back. I assume I am the object of a shakedown. Complain to who? This is not the first time this has happened, nor even the second time. Happiness is not in the direction of anger. I tend to simply pretend it never happened and move on. Focus on the positive.

I tell Iris, "At least they did not take our money. That is weird. I wonder why? You'd think the first thing thieves would take is money!"

Evidence bags are left behind filled with items not taken—each marked with an evidence number they had logged as confiscated. I had written down evidence numbers of mislabeled evidence I saw. In this way, if I ever got to court, I might ask to see evidence number blankety blank, to be shown to the jury. If it is a jury of my peers, someone will know the difference between a wolf claw and eagle claw. Some inventoried items cannot be produced, because I have them. Possibly the entire process and all the evidence is in question indicating an unprofessional job was done. Leading to the question of stupidity or was there a reason? *Were the agents ignorant, stupid, did not know what they took as an honest mistake? Did they deliberately mislabel? Did they deliberately put mislabeled items in plain view for me to see? If so, why was 'inventoried in as evidence,' items left behind?*

As weeks go by, Iris and I notice various missing things. My passport is gone. I had seen it on the table and asked specifically if my passport is being confiscated. I got a definite "No!" Yet it is missing. My entire cabinet of records is gone. This holds the deed to the house, my homestead, and all my medical records. I need the medical records for the VA, listing my medications and blood work, blood pressure records. My main address book, and the duplicate I keep in case I lose the main one —gone. Without it I cannot get in touch with my son, mother or friends.

Iris says, "We have your mother's address on an envelope, Miles!" So we can piece some things back together, create a new address book.

I do not have my computer to run my business. I cannot afford a new one. We get a call that I can pick up my computers. These are the only item returned, the desktop and laptop back up computers. "But I bet the computers are not the same anymore, Iris. They are not returning my computer as a favor to me. It has a bug in it now. Can I trust it?"

"Stop being so paranoid, Miles, the government is not that interested in what you are doing, geez!"

I agree, but then explain the reality. "If I had told you a year ago there would be a raid, and twelve swat guys would arrive in enough cars to surround the entire block, would you have believed me? Anyone who knows me would laugh and call me paranoid, right?" Apparently I was not paranoid enough!

I had been told I am being watched by satellite. This leads me to believe the government wanted me to feel paranoid, believe I am being spied on every minute of the day. The government wants to get me to panic, do and say unbelievable things to the world, so I have no credibility. So when I talked, babbled about conspiracy, spy satellites watching our every move, everyone would laugh. Like a commercial on TV I just saw. "And did you know there are spy cameras in the cheese?" As a crazy man stabs the cheese. If I am off the deep end, I cannot defend myself. The jury will grin and make hand circles around their ear, the sign of, 'this guy belongs in a nuthouse.' I think the agents deliberately fed me crazy stories to accomplish exactly this. The Feds would say, 'Yeah, right! What a crackpot!' How wonderful it would have been to be able to make my own recordings! It is difficult to know what to believe, what is real, what is even possible or even likely when it comes to what the government is capable of.

A local fisherman told me his story. "Not me, but my brother. He went out to check his fish wheel. The wheel cannot be turned on before 6:00 am. But every hour counts because the opening is only for a day. So my brother leaves the boat landing, figuring how long it would take him to get the five miles to the fish wheel. He does not own a watch." The story is, the brother gets to the fish wheel a little early and does not know it. He turns the wheel on five minutes early. A satellite picture was taken of him doing so. The picture is so clear you can see the buttons on his shirt. The brother I am talking to says he saw the picture. His brother was arrested and lost his fishing permit.

Is this a true story? Was it exaggerated? Is there more to it that makes sense as to what happened and why? I try to imagine what it is like to be watched everywhere you go, even in the wilderness.

I was asked, "And what were you doing on a sandbar in the middle of the day for several hours?" I know our cell phones record where we are, even when they are turned off. I know our local police found a runaway teen by pinging the cell phone in her pocket, and by triangulating to a small enough area to find her at her new boyfriend's house.

I'm guessing it is possible, but very costly to track by satellite. Is it worth catching a fisherman turning a fish wheel on five minutes early? That is what I wonder. Where is the money coming from and why? What might be worth it is, having the story spreads like wildfire.

"Big brother is everywhere. Let me tell you the story I heard. We are being watched at all times, we can do nothing without being seen!" What a great message to disseminate through the population. Now I can add fuel to the same fears. What is that kind of advertising worth? Millions? "Yes indeed, let me tell you my personal story about a million dollar raid to confiscate a dead raven! Let me tell you about $20,000 worth of legal goods confiscated and nothing I can do about it, a shakedown! The government is not your friend!" Flamed on by daily news reports of cops shooting people in the back, planting evidence, officials getting caught in crimes worse than the crimes of the people they are arresting. Every day in the news! The twelve-year-old with an easy to identify toy squirt gun shot by cops, determined to be justified in court! *It was more than a dead raven, and less than $20,000! Keep the facts straight! Indeed, it is difficult to remember, and the memory itself changes quickly. So do the rumors.*

As an intelligent, sane person, what am I to make of all this? As an intelligent teen long ago, my decision was to leave civilization. I feel forced back into civilization, so now what?

"But, Miles, what is going on with you is not going on with everyone! Look around! Most of us are safe! Happy, with jobs and a good life! Left alone by the government! What is going on, is you brought it on yourself!" This is what I hear from the protected. But try being black. Try being Native American. Try being white trash, who lives with, and calls these minorities 'my peers.' Try wanting to be a mountain man. Tarzan could not swing through the vines because of the weight of all the permits he'd have to carry.

Past flash

My father. I'm with my father in his truck and I am in my thirties, visiting him in Plattsburgh, New York. I repeat this story a lot. Dad's truck is having problems and sputters. We pull over and lift the hood to see what might be the problem.

I see a cop car coming! My gut reaction and words are, "Oh, oh, here comes a cop, dad!"

My father's reaction is totally different.

The cop pulls over and walks up to us. I expect the cop to say "Let's see some ID, up against the truck now!" Followed by, "Get this heap off the road!" As would be normal in my life. Instead, the cop smiles and asks if he can be of any help.

Dad explains the symptoms and, "I think it is water in the gas."

The cop goes back to his squad car and comes back with a can of gas heat. He puts it in the gas tank for dad and says, "Maybe this will help. Have a nice day." Then leaves.

I'm left speechless. There is no way any cop is ever going to suggest I have a nice day. Yet I remember cops being like this as I was growing up. Maybe cops have not changed, but I have. Dad is in a suit and tie. He has three PhD degrees and is Dean of a college. He pays to have his hair cut, looks neat and sharp. His socks match. He is among the protected. He is not necessarily a nice person. *Or more, how would the cop know one way or the other? How would the cop figure I'm not worth protecting? By how we dress?*

Later in life, another memory. Dad tells me someone has been stalking and threatening his wife. Dad always has younger, nice looking women around. He is concerned and goes to the police station. "I'm thinking maybe I need to buy a gun for protection."

The police will not do anything. Until she is accosted, there has been no serious crime, or maybe just one person's word against another and no time to investigate. For my father, not fun to hear when he feels he deserves more protection. He expected his word to mean something. So now he wants a gun to protect his scared woman. There is some sort of sixty day delay between saying you want a gun and being able to have one in your possession. A background check has to be done and what not. The cop said, 'in his shoes he'd get hold of a gun.' Not through a gun shop or dealer. Avoid all the legal paperwork. I replied to my father this is one reason I live in the wilderness. I am allowed to protect myself. The implication from the incident is the law doesn't work. When life gets important, we are on our own. Later in life, I hear Dad got in trouble with the IRS. He lost everything, died a pauper. So even the protected can have issues.

I've been told many times throughout my life by government officials. "If we want you, we can find something to arrest you on. No one is so law-abiding we cannot find a law broken." I learn from this, the important issue is not following the law, but getting along with those who run things.

My father had told me once, "It is ok to be poor and good to be rich. Neither pays taxes. It's the middle class that needs to be avoided. The poor get everything given to them and pay no taxes, the smart rich keep their money in overseas accounts." Yet he was not protected after all. The IRS made him a pauper.

Past flash ends

Iris and I drive to Fairbanks to get our computers. She is too scared to have us stay together. "What if they grab us both? Who would know, we could never be heard of again!" We decide to stay separated so one of us can escape. We are terrified. I will not go in the building.

Iris had told me that during our interrogation, she was held outside the house in her nightgown all day in the cold, not allowed in the house. She had been offered a cop car to sit in, but she says, "I was scared to get in, they might take me away and make me disappear." They did, after all, have a gun on her.

The agent brings my computers to the door. "Where is your car?" I panic. I tell him my wife is going to meet me after he goes back inside. We are meeting 'Someplace.' The agent rolls his eyes up and goes back inside the same government building I had been in years ago asking for a permit when a feather was confiscated off my hat. I notice again, a place with a tiny plain sign you cannot see from the road. A dirt parking lot with no cars. A dull gray building, with tiny foot square dirty windows. The look of an unfriendly place that says no one comes here voluntarily.

Iris and I get away, and home, safe, with a sigh of relief. I hook up the computer and turn it on. On the screen is a message "Insert secured disk number 16432=-B to reset password." I assume the Feds did something to my computer and did not put it back to the way it was so I can use it. I'm thinking a partition with a separate password that can be accessed by them remotely whenever they wish to retrieve information. Maybe a program that records every keystroke.

I call up the agent. "I need the disk or the password to unlock my computer after you messed with it. Can I have that, please?"

Mr. Agent Man says, "I do not understand, all we did was make an exact mirror copy of everything in your computer, it is exactly the same as when you last had it." He pauses and says, "Well, I can talk to our computer expert and get back to you if we can be of any help."

I say to Iris, "Yeah, they screwed up. After they did their alterations and installed the bug, they put in their own password, forgetting to give my password back so I can have access to what is now their computer."

"Buy a new computer, Miles! This one is compromised!"

Why bother. I can never trust any computer again. None of my disks can be considered secure now. There could be a Trojan on any of them. My website may contain a worm, a large cookie. I access my website with a new computer and 'poof', the Feds are in. It can be done any time I get on the internet or through my server. Anything can be disguised as a necessary update. Part of an automatic update I am not in control of. It is better to assume there is no such thing as privacy, not anyplace.

Iris is worried that the bedroom is bugged. We were not allowed in the house who knows what was done? Friends suggest I have the computer professionally scrubbed.

I think the government can control anything and order professionals to leave their bugs alone. Or, be sophisticated enough not to be found. As a computer geek told me, "The internet was a government project to begin with for the purpose of passing on military information. They voluntarily turned some bandwidth over to the public. Have you ever heard of the government volunteering anything for free? The price has been a great way to watch and monitor us. Control, ultimately, is with the government." This may or may not be true. I am unwilling to take a chance yet saying that is is preposterous.

We know our phone has a funny hollow sound, and a funny long pause now when we receive or make calls. Different than it was before the raid. *Is this just a coincidence?* We do not think so. There are rumors it is possible to watch and hear people through their TV, even when it is off. *Is that really possible?* There are certain words we no longer use, and things we no longer talk about in our own home or in the car. Like where we keep our money, or how long we will be gone. There is no one we trust. *Perhaps these feelings will go away, eventually?* Yes, most likely.

The garden gets planted. Life goes on. I continue to make my art, run the website. The raid was like lightening, a forest fire, a flood. It is a disaster that just happens. We never know when or why. Are we 'responsible?' I say not any more than we are responsible for a flood. I do say we are responsible for what we do about it. How we handle and deal with it. Sort of like, if you live along a river in flat country, sooner or later you will be involved in a flood. In this way, we are responsible. We enjoy the benefits of the beautiful river most of the time, the price might be a flood. I refuse to let this ruin my life.

There is an ongoing story in the news. An old time river man is arrested for not having his boat registered. I have the story saved in my computer. I know Jim a little as an old time seventy-year-old river rat who spends a lot of time enjoying river activities. He is certainly very qualified to be on the river after a lifetime of doing it!

Photo Section

I make a rubber mold from an Indian artifact and cast it in copper to use as a knife guard.

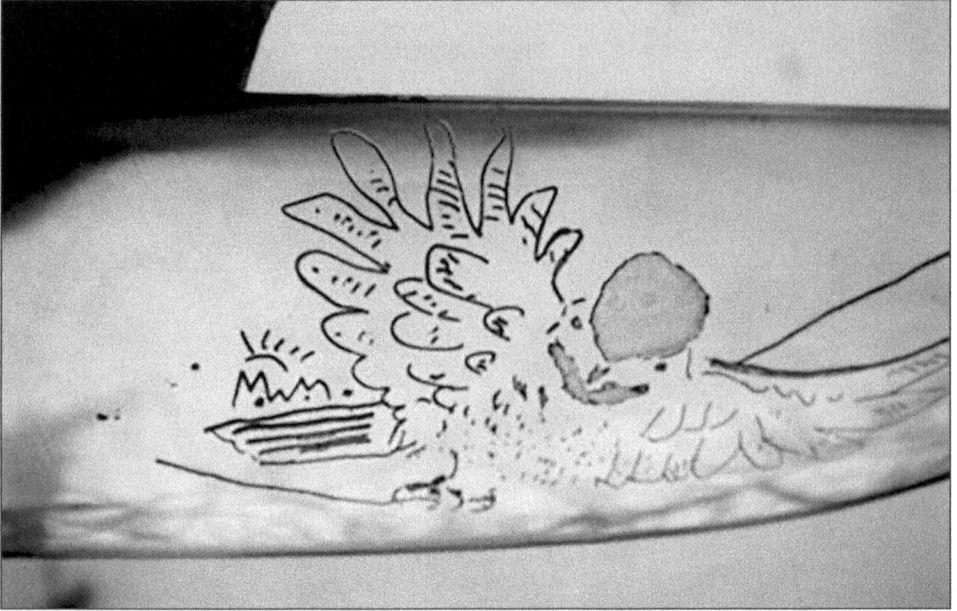

Acid etching in knife blade. Hand drawn, etched in stainless steel. Few know how this can be done, and can do it. This helps my knives be unique to me.

A custom tool I designed and made that allows me to true up and square or sand blocks at a specific angle. Constant pressure saves me holding the wood by hand.

Boating in the cold.

I'm happiest when boating on the river.

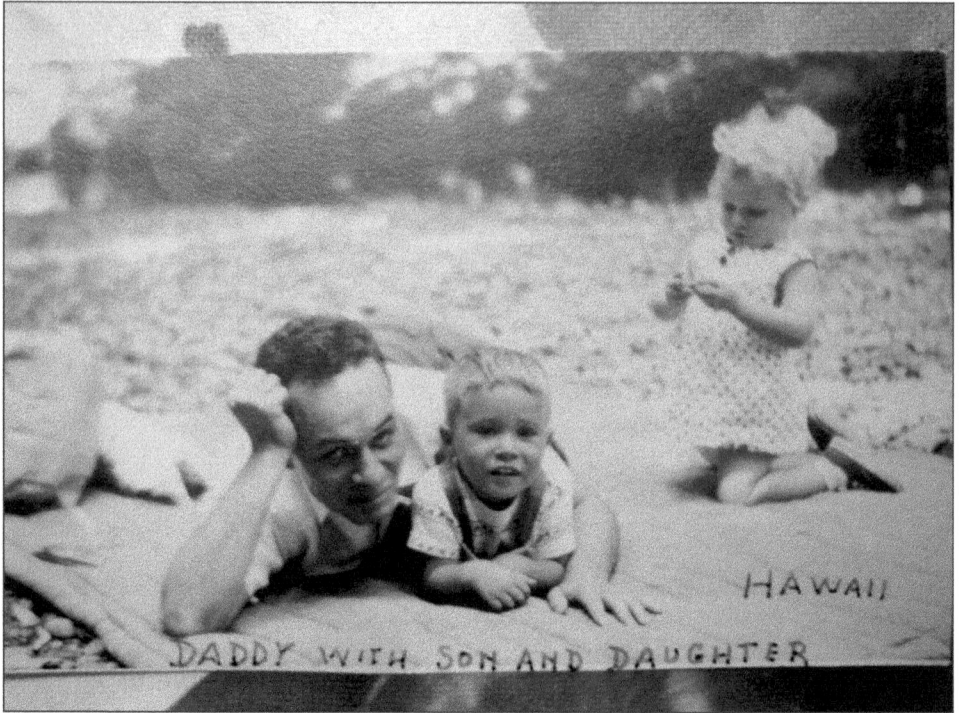

DADDY WITH SON AND DAUGHTER

HAWAII

My father, me, and sister. I'm three years old. I can see even in this early picture, my sister looks left out, entertaining herself. She had a hard time in life, affecting all of us.

I find, buy, trade, fossils. This is a 60,000 year old socket a mammoth leg bone fits into.

I make deals on cut stones by the pound. They are considered seconds—imperfect in some way—damaged, cut off size, but otherwise quality stones I can use, or sell individually. They need sorting and grading, but a stone I pay five cents for can often resell for five dollars, times 500 stones. Oh yeah. It might take a couple of decades to sell them. Minor detail. I buy a lot of things 'at the source,' 'cheap.' I see it as better than money in the bank. Normally raw material value increases faster than interest in the bank. I take advantage of nine storage buildings I own, with low taxes or overhead. 'Stuff' is my bank.

My 1916 cabin in winter. The moose rack over the door was among items confiscated by Fish and Wildlife.

I built this seven station rock shaping machine. Water cooling is five gallon bucket and gravity dripper. No running water in the shop

In one area at a Indian claim along the river where I get fossils, the cliff calves like a glacier. House size chunks of cliff randomly fall in the river. While the money is good, there is great risk.

CHAPTER SEVEN

LAWYER, PRESS RELEASE, OUT OF BUSINESS

From the news articles, I gather that Jim and his elderly wife were on the Yukon going through a park preserve. Jim saw a boat across the river that looked like it was having trouble. A jet boat, one usually considered too big for the area and not recommended in these kinds of waters. It was pulled over in a bad place to stop. Jim wondered if they were broke down and needed help. As he approaches he sees these are young men new to the state, Federal park rangers.

They reply 'no', they do not need any help saying, "And by the way, where is your boat registration?"

This subject has created a great deal of controversy over the past decade. Remote people in villages have no easy access to an agency that registers boats. Villagers feel this is not necessary, and is a way to collect more fees, with no services in return. Most villagers refuse to have their boat registered. So far, this has been overlooked and accepted when out remote, as Jim is on the Yukon, and his being an old established river man. These new young agents wish to adhere to the letter of the law as they know it from the lower states.

These youngsters rubbed Jim the wrong way, partly due to cultural differences as well. They came across like they were experts who know what they are doing, and as such have the authority and knowledge to give advice to Jim, and tell him what is safe and not safe. From his perspective, it is these young bucks who need to learn about the Yukon River. I am guessing Jim did not handle things in the best way and got abrasive. I can understand. He comes over from across the river to help someone who looks like are in trouble. Out of the goodness of his heart. In return, he gets insulted and threatened. If he had minded his own business and stayed on the other side of the river, he would never be in this situation. I understand better now why civilized people are known for minding their own business and not trying to help each other.

A friendly, "Thanks for stopping, 'yes' we are fine," was expected. Maybe a, "By the way, things are changing, and we want to see boats registered in the future, keep that in mind."

It's possible Jim gave them the finger or swore. The story is not clear. What is clear is the agents pulled guns out and ordered Jim to shut his engine off and stop in the middle of the river. This is extremely unsafe! Locals rarely do this. Jim says later, "My engine is old and hard to start, so it is not safe to shut the engine off in the strong current." Without the engine, it is difficult to steer the boat out of the river's dangers. Usually when we wish to meet on the river, we point and pull over, stop, and both tie up to visit, not drift with engines off down the river in rough water. Apparently Jim refused to endanger himself and wife. He headed for a safe place on shore and was almost shot. He ended being pushed to the ground, taken away in handcuffs. I think leaving his wife and boat behind. Even though Jim was out of line cussing and showing disrespect, it was also out of line to pull guns and toss a seventy-year-old to the ground over a boat safety issue.

I take note of the story because it has me feeling it is not just me having problems with the Feds. My issues seem similar in some respects as part of what Alaska sees as Federal overreach, and heavy-handed tactics over issues that are state issues. I know some details of the case with Jim. I know him a little and talked to him. I know his lawyer, read the news, talked to others who know him.

The argument the state uses is the river is not the park, the land is. The river is state jurisdiction, until someone gets out of the boat and gets on land, the river is state run. A registered boat would be a state issue. I quote from my saved notes in the computer.

Friday, April 15, 2011

Ongoing Wilde story about the seventy-year-old on the Yukon stopped by Federal park rangers for a boat inspection. Ended up hauled off in handcuffs. Many articles in the paper on the subject- concerning laws, rights, the authority of the state, substance rights, native rights, land use rights, etc. Very interesting as the court case develops.

"Eagle Fights Back" A letter to editor on April 15th, 2011 from Nenana Resident Brent Crowder (who I take out on the river for the university)

"I sat through the entire Jim Wilde trial last week"..."Honey Wilde, Jims wife had a gun pointed at her by rangers. Last time that happened she was eight years old and held at gunpoint by German Nazis." She refused to get out of the boat and was held at gunpoint for ten minutes. While her husband is thrown to the ground, handcuffed and carted off to jail.

Another article discusses the purpose of the rangers. Front page of the same paper

"Park Service Pledges to Change Unpopular Yukon Charley Boat Checks" A lengthily full-page story. One point made I take note of, "The Park Service has done a good job protecting bird habitat and preserving the areas' mining history...but they have not done much with subsistence." It was stated earlier what the purpose of the park preserve is! "To protect a way of life, included in that way of life, is subsistence."

Monday, April 18, 2011

Continuing on the Wilde Story… April 13th, Pete Buist, "I hate to say it but 'I told you so' about thirty years ago in a weekly column I wrote for the News Miner. As a former National service ranger myself, I predicted when the Alaska National Interest Lands Conservation Act passed that the NPS would eventually refuse to adhere to the letter, much less the spirit of the law." And goes on to say further in the article how the park service is, "making sure that Alaskans do not actually get to use the Yukon Charley and Gates to the Arctic parks, or the state owned wildlife that roam there.

We have a power hungry superintendent who seems to think it is perfectly acceptable to use Swat team tactics to threaten an Alaskan at gunpoint because his boat might not be registered or not have the proper amount of life preservers." There are some words about disobeying the law themselves, and how the rangers assume Alaskans will allow themselves to get pushed around like folks in the lower 48. NPS did not expect to get resistance, or so much publicity over this.

I get asked, "Geez, who cares, Miles! On and on about legal stuff, who has jurisdiction! What does all this have to do with a wilderness life?"

"YO! I might be correct. Who cares. Life goes on. However, anyone interested in life off the grid, homesteading, living like an Indian needs to understand they will be a minority. The consequences of a life choice needs to be considered." I press on. "The Federal government is taking over other levels of government. Game management is supposed to be state regulated, and so is the river system. Much Federal land was, by law, supposed to be turned over to the state as an agreement in our constitution as a condition of statehood. Land that was never transferred as agreed. The Feds are getting around this by creating vast public parks."

Iris and I go to a meeting, a fundraiser for Jim. I meet with a few people who have sympathy for my situation with Fish and Wildlife. I find out who Jim Wilde's lawyer is. Saddle is reputed to be the best, the one you want if you can afford him. "He's a little like the Nenana lawyer Mic, but with a tiny bit more class."

Mic is not around anymore, but had helped me out in the past. Legally gifted. The court system does not like him because he interrupts, objects, calls up obscure protocol no one else remembers, and deals in technicalities. He knows how to get things postponed, and evidence made inadmissible. This irritates the court system, so you do not want to lose with this lawyer. Mic is not 100% legal or ethical. He has his own sense of justice. He is capable of looking out for the underdog, does not like to see the accused get railroaded. He likes to make a name for himself by winning on righteous cases of his choice, or that draw publicity. Mic likes to be paid big bucks, so focuses on drug dealers, the ones with money. I do not know how many of these qualities Saddle might share, if the two are really similar. I run into a lot of people I know at the gathering. There is a lot of antigovernment sentiment.

"It's like Nazi Germany now in the US!"

"We need to fight back!" It would not surprise me to hear the government has taken pictures, and is recording who attends the meeting, and cross references the list to create a 'person of interest' profile. A lot of joking, "Miles, you are already on that list, that's for sure!"

There is a lot of talk against lawyers. I reply, "Some lawyers are no good, out to rip us off. This describes a lot of people in every field. There are good and bad in every profession. I have met lawyers, cops, politicians, and doctors, I admire, respect, and even would call a friend. Likewise, I believe in peace." Partly said because I think there are government plants at this meeting looking for radical dangerous types. Putting feelers out, trying to record people saying things they could be arrested for. It's one reason I'm already in trouble blabbing my mouth off about how we can't trust the government and need to figure out how to avoid doing as we are told.

Someone else brings up the old Joe Vogler story. "He was killed by the government you know, to shut him up!" I personally agree, but do not say so in this setting. Joe was an old time miner involved in a lot of things in the state of Alaska. Known by many people. A no nonsense sort. He was a lot like Jim Wilde. He was a little abrasive, but this was, at the time, a rough state with rough characters. He had a reputation of being honest and hard working.

One big issue he had was crossing remote park land to get to his mine with a bulldozer. I believe the trail he used existed before the park was expanded, cutting off access to his mine. Because the trail was his only access, Joe felt he should be grandfathered in. There was some issue about the park and a bulldozer. Joe was pretty mad. He was the founder of the Alaskan Independence Party and helped organize the Alaska Liberation Party. One big issue he talked about was his view that Alaska was illegally taken as a state. I am not sure if that is so, but it is a moot point; the Feds will certainly never allow us to secede from the country. Joe's argument, as I recall, is that the people of Alaska voted not to become a state a couple of times. The Feds wanted us, so gave the vote to the military, which should be illegal, as they are not residents. With the vote of the military added, the vote was in favor of becoming a state. I heard Joe was going to bring the subject up to the world court. Word is, the government did not want this to happen. So killed him.

I happen to know Joe's campaign manager as a good trusted friend, who had some inside information. Joe himself believed the government was going to kill him, or try to, and said so. He had plans in place to defend himself. Joe left instructions in case it happened. When he was killed, it was supposedly by 'some kid,' who got caught soon after, a simple robbery. Joe was taken someplace else to be killed. There are details my friend has about Joe's hat, his dog, factors that seem not to add up or make sense. I do not know the exact details, nor have any evidence, and do not want to know. I consider this information not safe to have.

Like Kennedy, will we ever get to the bottom of conspiracy talk, who killed him and why? Key witnesses and those with undesirable facts tend to disappear. I recall the news getting released about Kennedy and it appeared to me, even as a child, to be very biased and controlled. Yesterday's accurate quotes from reliable witnesses, forgotten and contradicted today.

I get caught up in the: "I have one for you," and add some new shocking first-hand tidbits about a swat team raid and how I was treated to a sympathetic group of people. It's me getting attention; easy to exaggerate to get more attention. But then it is hard to get the truth believed.

Some say, "Yeah, right, I bet it was one agent who was not armed!"

Others add, "Totally unrelated to Jim Miles, you are a poacher and have been, everyone knows that!"

While others say, "No one deserves how you were treated, Miles! I will follow how it goes and hope you are not arrested. You are not doing anything most of us who live in the village do not do. If you can be in trouble, so can most of us here!"

I'm not especially happy with the attention. It is not fulfilling, positive. I do not feel better. I am left feeling empty. I feel like how people look in a bar telling 'sorry me' and 'victim' stories to justify why they are drinking and not surviving anymore, if they ever were. Nothing positive got accomplished. Except maybe I got the name of Jim's lawyer. It seems to me that once I go down the path of conspiracy theory, the subject of Kennedy comes up.

Then Waco, and that gun dealer, what's his name who had his dog, wife, and child shot on the doorstep by the Feds. Or whatever happened. It is hard to keep the stories and facts straight. Often the conversation turns to seeing Big foot, invasion of aliens, and zombies in our midst. At some point I stop agreeing and question my own facts and sanity. The sort of stuff to forget as 'negative' and 'let's focus on the positive.' The stuff to pretend it never happened. Till it happens to you.

I contact this Saddle lawyer guy. I pay $300 to come in, say hi, and chat for an hour. I find it interesting he has no computer to keep any records on. "Not safe. I have handwritten notes I keep in a safe, and have my office swept for bugs once a week." He keeps the shades drawn for security reasons. The newspaper states Jim paid $40,000 to Saddle, and lost his case. The bottom line for the lost case being, "When an officer of the law commands you to do something, you comply. Your opinion of is it safe to, legal, or not, is not relevant. Nor is thinking you know more about the situation then the officer. Absolute, total, blind trust, is demanded, and will be had."

I say to Saddle, "Too bad Jim went over to see if he could be of help. I assume he knows better now."

"Well, the case itself was interesting and news worthy. I'm not sure his behavior helped any." I nod, and we get down to the subject at hand—my case.

"Saddle, a lot of Fish and Wildlife things were confiscated. It's been a couple of months, and I have not been charged. I have not heard anything on the subject." I explain how, as far as I know, items were legal under the situations I had them. "It looks to me like a shake down. I am not going to get charged, but I am also not going to get my goods back." Saddle nodded that this sounds familiar.

"A Mexican standoff, Miles." After a pause, "Miles, for about $40,000 I can get your goods back."

"So for that amount I can get back $20,000 worth of my stuff?" We both agree the Feds know I am not likely to do that. Saddle tells me the Feds are very powerful. A good tactic might be to not piss them off.

"Let them keep your goods and forget it, Miles. That's the option I suggest." After talking, Saddle gives an opinion. "I think if you ended up in court, you would lose. Not because you are in the wrong. Unlike Jim, your personality would be very helpful, and do you well. The subject matter would be your undoing." Saddle explains the subject is dead animal parts. The public, in his opinion, is not going to look any further to get the details. Headlines read, 'Animal parts,' and the public goes, 'Hang him!' Saddle seems to know his job.

I think about what he says and have to agree. Few will care about the details. I explain, "Years ago, the public sentiment may have been different. I once had an issue with the Feds. The New York Times got hold of the story and did a big double page story with half page pictures of me and my lifestyle. The flavor was the bad government bullying a simple subsistence person. Possibly the article slowed the Feds up, for a while anyway."

"That will not happen again, Miles." In other words, I cannot threaten the Feds with going public, because the subject this time is dead animals, and the public, as well as news media, will side with the Feds.

I'm trying to find some leverage. Or a bargaining chip. I'm looking for a situation where I approach the prosecution off the record saying, "Ok, maybe I did a few things I should not have. You made some mistakes, did a few things you should not have. I'm willing to forget your indiscretions, if you forget mine." Because this is how the world operates.

"Tell me about the eagle parts, feathers, and claws." I'm surprised this is the topic Saddle wants to hear about, not the ivory. I agree this is the most legally touchy. By law, no one can have any eagle part for any reason. Except sometimes Natives. But to be legal, the parts have to be registered with, and issued by the government. These laws are so strict, I heard of a guy who stopped his boat on a river sandbar and bent over to pick up a feather. He steps into his boat with it, and Fish and Game arrested him, confiscated his $60,000 boat. The guy did not even know what kind of feather it was. One of those rumors with a grain of truth, but no real substance? I know 'eagle' can be a scary subject. *The guy was white!* So why would I be in such a situation?? I admit to myself, at least partly because, who is going to stop me? The situation takes place in the remote wilderness with no witnesses. I have no specific intentions for the eagle. It will end up on my property in my personal shop no one visits, and or in the compost pile. There is no reason for this to ever be publicly known.

No, you cannot pick up a feather on the ground and keep it. Unless you are an Indian. Many Natives I know have eagle claws and feathers hanging from car mirrors in plain view. Many Natives in the villages I travel through have feathers hung in windows at fish camps. Enough to where it is common. None were legally issued by the government as required. That part of the law is overlooked. It's no big deal. Because I am subsistence, and feel I have similar rights as the Natives I live around, I too was not overly worried. It might be worth a warning, a reprimand. A small fine. Not worth going to court over. *Not worth it for the Feds to bring up the discrimination issue and make subsistence issues public.* I am not in the business of dealing in eagle parts. No one kills eagles to supply me. There are plenty of eagles around. They are not endangered. Heck, back in the 50's the government of Alaska had a bounty on eagles! My friend Al, the fur tannery guy told me he has an issue of Alaska Magazine, with a hunter holding a dead eagle he killed. The cover of the magazine! Now, more serious a crime then killing a person.

I tell Saddle the story. "I was out boating in a remote area near a Native village one late fall. The ice is running." I pause to recall the incident. "I come across another boat. A Native guy I sort of know, but who knows and respects me, calls me by name. This Native has a frozen eagle in his boat. He hems and haws and says he does not know what to do with it. He found a young frozen bald eagle. I have seen similar situations this time of year to believe him. There is no blood, no evidence it was shot. It is common for larger birds like eagles and swans not to mature enough during an Alaska summer to fly south or survive the winter. I have seen such birds sitting along the edge of the river shivering, covered in ice, dying. Once it was an eagle, and I debated trying to save it's life, maybe get it to the university or Fish and Game. But decided it would look bad to have an eagle in my possession. I felt torn, to see the bird suffer. I had to leave, and let nature take its course. I'm sure this Native faced the same dilemma, only being Native he does not face the level of threat a white man does.

This Native knows me as a shaman among his people, one who deals in animal medicine. One of them, depending on the land, living as Natives did years ago. He wants me to take the eagle off his hands. He is in a dilemma not knowing what to do with it, but not wanting it to go to waste as part of his beliefs and mine. He did not think it was a coincidence he ran into me exactly now, after not seeing me for years. The dead need to be properly cared for, even animals. It would be rude not to accept this gift. I accept this frozen eagle. I had no specific plans for it. I often simply collect things for no particular reason. When I got home, I tossed it in the yard, knowing there is not much I can do with it. The ground is frozen. I saved the claws and a few feathers. The rest went in the compost pile. If I had any thoughts at all, it was that maybe a situation would come along where I could gift these feathers and claws to worthy Natives who will respect them and use them in a traditional way. "I feel from a legal standpoint this is not a great offense."

Saddle twists his pencil and leans back in his chair, thinking. When he speaks he says, "I do not think you would be good on the witness stand." He does not say why. I'm puzzled, and see no problem with the truth as spoken. A jury of my peers would understand. Anyone with river knowledge knows this happens, larger immature birds die at the edge of the river when winter arrives. I could produce this Native as a witness if I had to. There is no evidence I was trying to sell the eagle or its parts. They were confiscated from my personal stash of items not for sale. But at $300 an hour talking to Saddle, we are not going to get into any deep discussions.

If I end up in court, we will discuss two major issues I think the Feds do not want made public, or want to discuss. Subsistence and discrimination. Subsistence is not about race, but about a lifestyle that I can prove I qualify for. If I were Native, none of these items would have been confiscated. Is discrimination by race legal in this situation? If so, show it to me in writing, that we believe in discrimination by race. I do not think the Feds want to go there.

I add, "If I do not qualify for subsistence, why was I issued a subsistence license? My permit does not say 'White restricted.' It is the same permit Natives carry."

"And for several hundred thousand dollars you can make your point, Miles.

Federal cases are complicated and costly. The Feds have unlimited funding to prosecute."

I do not have the kind of money Saddle talks about to defend myself. I am under the impression public defenders are good, and do a good job, because the court does not want to try the case again because of incompetence, so they make sure a good job is done the first time. Like being poor and going to a dentist who does charity work. The tooth gets pulled the same as if you spent $1,000. The dentist does not want to get sued. He's usually ethical. He's even the same dentist you pay $1,000 to. So I am not overly concerned by having a public defender if it comes to that. I would want a descent ethical, not corrupt, law-abiding human being.

"Well, Saddle, I am glad to at least have a good lawyer for some basic advice. If I am grabbed in the middle of the night and put in jail, at least you have some background information, know what is going on. You can take care of my immediate emergency needs." I agree I can pay Saddle by the hour if anything happens where I need help. "Maybe you can help me get a good public defender if the need arises." It feels better, and worth the $300 to me to have in my hand a card with a lawyer's number on it and when I say, "I want my lawyer," I know who I mean, and here is his number. I pay my lawyer to submit a request to have certain specific legal items returned.

I'm of course disappointed we cannot easily get my goods back. I need my medical records like 'now,' and am not happy to be missing deeds to my house and homesteads. I could sell my homestead to raise the legal fees fast if I needed to, but would have to have the deed. I need my passport this winter to get into Mexico to have dental and eye work done. I am not happy the government can conduct a shakedown, and nothing I can do about it. I'm not someone who gives up or accepts defeat easily. Nor am I one of the sheep who rolls over and bleats as I get sheered.

I do not think it is wise of the government to make an enemy of the people. There will one day be a price to pay. *'What ye sow, thus shall ye reap.'* I find it puzzling that the news media asks us to wonder why anyone but the guilty would run from the police or feel threatened by them, not see them as the good guys. In recent news, airport security shoots a boy with a backpack who runs when ordered to stop. The shooting was determined to be justified because innocent people do not run from the police. *Said Hitler to the Jews.* The pack was filled with the child's school books.

Some children are taught by their parents not to talk to strangers, to get away, go find your parents, run, especially if a stranger makes you feel uncomfortable, or orders you to do something, like go with them. I find it understandable a child may not understand the exceptions. Many have never met a police or security officer before. I find it understandable the parents and neighborhood might want harm to come to the police and the government for shooting their son. Why is this a great shock, and incomprehensible? I certainly understand. I just remain hopeful there is a peaceful solution. Meanwhile, back at the ranch....

All I get back is my passport, after a long argument with the Feds saying, "No, we do not have your passport!" Suddenly it turns up. With no proof or receipt, simply labeled, 'documents.' No proof they ever had it.

THE GARDEN IS PLANTED and growing well. I back off some products since the raid, but in general run my legal business as usual. I tell Iris, I am not going to try very hard to get a moose this season.

"We have so much left over from the last moose. That was a huge animal." We made 500 pounds of sausage and burger. Still have roasts and maybe another 500 pounds of general meat for a total of 1,000 pounds. Figuring this had been a 1500 pound bull. "I had a hard time skinning it, Honey. Getting old. I needed a come along to roll it over. It's work now. It used to be just all fun!"

My crab apple trees are growing and bloomed this season. "I planted these for the purpose of grafting real apple to the branches one day!" It is time. "Next spring let's do the grafting!" I have been digging up wild edible plants and transplanting them around the property. I have some currant bushes, and raspberries growing well. There are blueberry bushes, wild strawberry, as well as some foods that get planted and keep coming back, like horseradish, chives and wild mint. We have been focusing on heirloom seeds when buying seeds, so we can save seeds for next year's planting. "The cost of seeds used to be insignificant, Honey. But I notice now we can pay five dollars and get only ten seeds. Depending what the crop is. What would we do, anyone do, if the seeds suddenly cost $100 each? Or are not available at any price."

I HAVE a reference letter dated On June 14th to Saddle from Karen Loeffler —**assistant US Attorney 907-271-5071**, stating my lawyer and I seem to be offering cooperation rather than a proffer letter. The Feds expect me to admit my wrongdoing, and if so, my cooperation will be considered. But first I must offer all I know, with names and useful information. I ask my lawyer, "What wrong-doing? Is it smart to admit to anything I have not been charged with? Nor even told what the problem is?"

On June 28th, Saddle sends a reply to the June 14th letter to us from Karen. Stating we do not think it is appropriate to request and enter into wholesale admission of all matters. A proffer letter usually covers specific charges and does not involve speculation on what the charges might be. I am not willing to engage in wholesaled proffer of potentially criminal activity. We request a list of potential charges.

I had been lead to believe by officers like Jeremy Kley of Fairbanks, that there is a good possibility of 'working things out,' some kind of plea bargain or cooperation in which, if I help out, the payback might be, forgetting any issues we are looking at. I was told probably in the Jessie case, I might be asked to testify. In anticipation of this cooperation I was not going to the news media, or stirring up problems in any other way, like seeking political help etc. I'm waiting to see what the mood is of the prosecution. Or a chance to meet with someone, the prosecutor, a judge-to explain myself, to either clear this up, if there is a misunderstanding, or hear what it is I am charged with, and why. *No reason to escalate a problem that does not exist by being on the attack. My first desire is to settle this peacefully, if possible.*

I had spoken to Saddle confidentially about the possibility I might retire soon because of my age of 60. I will be eligible for Social Security in two years. By way of suggesting any continued problems may well simply go away, because I'm getting old and would consider getting out of business. It is an idea to offer as part of a deal. I am discouraged and depressed. Saddle gets a reply from the prosecution to a letter forwarded suggesting we talk.

"Miles' actions seem to indicate lack of cooperation and being insincere." The reason given is, I had applied for an export permit renewal recently. A $100 basic permit needed to do most anything overseas. As much as half my legal business is overseas. I had wanted to make sure I remain legal and have everything in order as it should be. My existing permits had been confiscated, so I did not recall the expiration date. I figured I better get a new one in case.

My permit fee was returned to me with no explanation. Refund voucher 9971011D032A dated 06/24/11. Apparently, applying was an indication I did not intend to retire as promised. But I never promised. The idea was tossed out informally, verbally, to my lawyer to convey. I expected some informal hint that if I were to actually do this and put it in writing, many of my problems would go away, as had happened with the state when we sat down and talked.

I understood my informal, "I might do this" would get an informal, "We might do that in return." By way of an introduction of good faith before we sit down to finalize a legally binding agreement in writing. I got no reply on the subject. I had no plans to quit my business 'today.'

I explain to Saddle, "I have legal art orders I was committed to sending that were already paid for by customers that I feel I should have the permit to ship." My intentions and integrity are questioned. "I have gone to both Fish and Game, and Fish and Wildlife, to try to get answers over the years as to what the laws are exactly. Even the investigators pointed out I had at one time requested an officer come to Nenana and inform us at a meeting what is legal, so we may be informed. I agreed yes, I had requested that and made it happen. I care about the laws." *Workable laws, that is, and working within an honest system.* Officers are puzzled by what looks like an anomaly. How can a hardened killer, poacher, have anything that resembles human qualities? Very strange to them! There is talk of a press release the prosecution is very upset about.

"Oh. The press release. I'd like to address that." The press came to me. I did not go to the press. I was told by the news writer, someone in Nenana called and reported I was thrown to the ground, handcuffed, and am under arrest. This was going to be the report. Have I got any comment? I decided it is better to say something, rather than have that news reported. I did not consider it an attack.

Addressing the prosecution, "I said you were polite, did your job, no problems. We'd see what came of it in a civil way." Even when I said I was a little concerned for my girlfriend… I think I added, "But she was given the option to sit in the squad car, and she chose not to." The press is begging for an oppressive Federal government story. I could have given that, but did not. I could have offered a statement and proof that some items were wrongly identified when confiscated, "Those bungling incompetent agents! Look at this!" Oh! I know how to make them look bad all right. Yet I did not.

If you think that was a bad unfriendly report? Ha! I'm a writer. I know how to draw a crowd. I know what makes news. I know how to make headlines. I'm waiting to see if I need to do that while being polite. My concern is that this is a timely subject. In a couple of weeks, no one cares anymore. If I need to defend myself and make the Feds look bad to force them to back off, now is the time! The Feds need to let me know if we are going to do this the easy way, or the hard way. Play hardball for millions of dollars, or politely come to an agreement at a low cost.

For the Feds to feel offended seems like a joke to me. It is me who has more right to be offended. The Feds released a news account in which it is stated only a few officers showed up. No mention of them being armed, a swat team, or surrounding the entire block. The release is an outright lie. It makes any complaints I express later seem laughable. This talk of an agreement and showing good faith appears to be one sided. What I understand is, I am expected to behave like one of the sheep. Anything can be done, while I just bleat and look helpless at the mercy of those wolves. Mistreating the sheep is normal. Sheep have no rights. If a sheep truly protested, or bit anyone, they'd be killed, no questions asked.

A press release is written and hidden in case I disappear. I consider that possible. "Why was up to a million dollars spent to get the goods on Miles? Why? What are you up to?" It does not make sense! Thus, what is it you want? For that kind of money, a lot of things can be made to happen. We have a new government changing very fast. What kind of government is it? If I disappear, perhaps someone will make the story public.

Saddle suggests contacting Don Young without asking for legal help, but mention protection of subsistence, and state rights. Don Young knows me by name. He is the longest seated state representative in the country.

Write about rejection of export permit, ask for document file under freedom of information as to why the permit is denied. Check on the possibility of Nenana Federal jury trial. It turns out Nenana has a Federal court. If there is ever a trial, it would be to my advantage to be in my home village. Gather people around me who are credible. Contact Fren. Fren is a respected native elder who has sat on the Federal board of fisheries and the game board. Fren knows me and has told me if anyone qualifies for subsistence, I do.

I am asked by the prosecution, "What would you like to plead guilty to?" and, "You know what you did!" That seems absurd. I asked what I am being charged with, and I will respond. I have not been told in six months. This seems to perk Saddles interest for the first time.

"What are they up to, Miles? This is out of the ordinary. It makes me wonder if they have a case. Maybe they do not have anything on you." It might be like I said all along. Lots of things confiscated, but does any of it have any substance as a charge? Much looks bad on the surface, I agree. *But investigation further should show it is all covered under various laws. But more important than loopholes' is what and who has been hurt by my deeds?*

Tuesday, July 19, 2011 jlegallaw@aol.com;

Mr. Miles—

This email follows up my telephone message left on your residence telephone this afternoon; I have been appointed by the Federal Defenders' Office to represent you as a person of interest in the ongoing case of United States v. Jesse Joseph Leboeuf, 3:11-cr-00043-TMB.

My name is Joe Legal; my office address is blank blank, Fairbanks, Alaska; my telephone number is (907) 457-blank; please make no statements to anyone except me about anything you know or think you know about the Lebeouf case. Please call so we can meet and discuss the situation. Thanks. **Joe Legal**

I paid Saddle to help get me a descent public defender. I'm told it is unusual to be assigned a public defender without ever having been charged. Right now I am part of another case and may have to testify. I argued I need legal advice, since I am involved in this case and a search warrant was served. I do not wish to get set up, incriminate myself, so worked hard to have legal representation. Not much goes on beyond working on getting my goods back. No word if I am a witness in the Jessie trial.

THE TANANA FAIR comes and goes. I make more money than last year. All legal stuff, of course! I back off some of the more controversial items, but apparently these items are not a huge impact on my business. It's not about money, as much as freedom, and the right to do, and not being wasteful. The garden is harvested. The usual 50 to 80 quarts of foods put up in the form of sauces, pickles, relish, our own ketchup. Because of my diabetes, we use no sugar or salt, and I am able to control my blood sugar with diet and a pill.

Friends and customers are asking me what is going on. They read or heard of the articles in the news concerning a raid. Some offer help. A good friend and fur dealer comes by and asks if I need more tanned fur on consignment.

I tell him, "One of the issues with the Feds is if I had a permit to sell furs at the Tucson show." My friend is puzzled. As far as he knows, no permit would be needed for me to take tanned furs to Tucson and sell them. "They asked if I had a fur dealer's permit. I told them I did not own the furs, you did. That would be under your permit." My friend is still dubious if any permit at all is needed, but tells me he will help me out in any way he can if I need him, including a witness in court.

There had been a lot of talk of polar bears from the Feds. It's a big issue, with global warming and polar bears in the limelight right now. I'd had some fossil fangs, two sold to the undercover agent man. But legal, as the bears died thousands of years ago, having zero effect on present-day populations. There had been one other issue. A two-inch square of polar bear leather and fur. This was off an old registered rug, sold for tying flies. There was a certificate number and permit number with the fur to verify its legality. The guy who sold it to me in Tucson is a friend and told me 100% legal. He as well is willing to go to court to prove it if need be. Just to be sure, the friend who sold me the fossil polar bear fangs swears they are legal, pre-1972 and he can name the Eskimo who turned it into a work of art if need be, and testify for me if it comes to that. All are indignant these items are confiscated and made to look illegal in the news. These items confiscated from me are freely and openly sold by my friends with no consequences.

Finally, word on property I request to be returned.

Reference letter dated August 9th 'Property receipt' file # 2010704152. There was not a list of what was kept, nor what was returned. Being told, "Because the list would be so long." The receipt simply says, 'documents.' My disappointment is that there is no record of a seizure or return of my passport. It was simply among the items returned with no explanation. I was told it was not confiscated, and I had it. If

I had not hired a lawyer, I am convinced I would not have my passport, or records, maybe never. The records are no longer in order, so am not sure what got returned and what kept.

Iris and Saddle have watched the comments on the internet to the articles about me. Few are complimentary. "We all know Miles is an outlaw, and he finally got what he deserves!" Is a typical comment. I note people are allowed to comment without giving their name. Saddle advises me it is not in my best interest to respond. I do not like seeing what I consider my good name trashed.

I say to Iris, "I do not understand how it is acceptable for people to bash each other, maybe ruin each other without accountability. Possibly, deliberately give false information to discredit a rival, for example." I do not cruise around the internet looking at gossip. I can understand that Saddle can keep his finger on the pulse of public sentiment this way. I wonder how often people stand up for each other here. From seeing little of what Iris brings to show me, there is a type of personality that takes delight in hurting others, sharing in a general soup of mirth, despair, doom and gloom. Those that partake become what they sip.

"I must irritate people in a way others, like my friends do not. I do not understand it. Like I was the only one in all of Nenana who had to go get a driver's license just to ride my snow machine and four wheeler in the village. When every ten your old does so without it being an issue." This depresses me. I'm not someone to play, "Woe is me." I try to focus on the good stuff. That gets hard as my world caves in around me. In the way it is not appropriate to laugh and make jokes at a funeral. The government is absolutely trying to put a monkey wrench in my gears. Without telling me why. Without accusing me of anything.

"I have not changed in my life, Iris. I am the same person I was forty years ago. I am doing the same things I have been doing for forty years. Society was entertained by my stories, envied my lifestyle, invited me to its parties as a guest speaker, flattered me, issued me it's rewards of various kinds. So what has changed, Iris?" I do not expect her to have an answer.

"No. You are not going out in public wearing that shirt! Go put another one on!" I open my mouth to assert my manhood and somehow it is gone. I get as far as, "But," and understand what is going to happen if I say just one word! By that look, now familiar on her face. I go change my shirt. *My favorite shirt I always wear everyplace I go. I think I even wore it to a wedding ten years ago.* "That's better! Don't you feel better looking, more appropriate?" No. I do not. *Of course I do not. What a dumb question.* But it's all about compromise and tradeoffs. I smile and nod that yes, everything is much better now.

I notice none of my friends in the animal parts business who are successful, are on the internet. Or even have a business card. They do not promote themselves, and are never in the news. No articles are ever written about them. None have ever written a book. I feel like Tarzan. Left alone in the wilds. Get Tarzan into civilization and he's not a cool guy anymore. Where is his safely helmet swinging from those vines? What about damage to those endangered vines? Where is the permit for the poor endangered monkey? No shoes in public. No burn permit for that fire. Peeing in public. Trespassing. No ID. Jaywalking. No insurance. No medical. No credit or bank account. The list of violations would never end. He'd never see the light of day if the truth were known. The hero everyone wants at their party is suddenly bad news.

"I do not know him." A sinking ship. It's not fun to understand. Difficult to know what to do about. At my age it is not like, "Can we try that again?" I'm going to do what? Be who? It's too late to head back to the wilds and stay there. *But I got a woman who stands by me no matter what, and will be at my side through it all. Things could always be worse!*

Well, we need a purpose. Something beyond us that gives us a reason to struggle. Art does that for us and writing. It will all make another good chapter in our book! Whatever happens, we will record it! The ending times. Or will it be? What effect can we have on the outcome? What story will get told? Do we have control over that? It can be a story of overcoming! A story of doing our best! No matter what happens! So this gives me a sense of being grounded and keeps me at peace. Part of the time. Human failings tend to get in the way of noble purpose. Is it 'failings' or is it just us, an individual keeping that individuality. Fail in whose eyes? Gods? Ours? Our parents? Society? Is the opposite of 'fail' 'success?' So what does success look like? Can't that mean different things to different people? *That would be my guess.*

Dinner is ready? Tomatoes and stuffed squash from our garden, homemade biscuits, our own pickled beets. Moose sausage in the squash. A fairly typical meal every dinner time. Nothing out of a can. No frozen dinners. No fast foods. Witty, only a couple of blocks away, runs a small farm and trades throughout the community. Iris and I trade for eggs, yogurt, pork, domestic goose, as we have been doing for a long time now. This year I trade smoked salmon. I did not get the salmon or smoke it.

I traded the use of my fish net with Crazy Lawson. In return he passed on some of the smoked fish he puts up by the hundred pounds. I could use the smoked fish, but Iris prefers the eggs and pork. So in our lifestyle things get traded and re traded till it ends up used by someone. Witty likes one particular metal design I cast of a fairy with wings, holding something in her hand. The something in her hand can be a cut gemstone, an opal, a piece of turquoise. I cast her in two metals. The wings are brass from a barge propeller; the body is copper from old water pipes. I use my own rubber mold and cast the wax, then cast the wax in metal. Since I control the entire process, the final product has a distinct look hard to copy. My methods are unique, not by the book. So is the outcome. This fairy sells well for Witty. Her hobby is making glass beads for necklaces.

Witty puts in a garden, and sometimes grows things we do not, so we trade things from the garden, and exchange seeds we produce in our gardens. This year she lost her worm farm, so I gave her worms from mine. Witty had gotten a hold of some northern grapes and is trying to grow grapes! This experiment failed.

"I think the chickens got at the plants, Miles." She is not sure. Having a few pigs and cows, Witty has a surplus of fertilizer. I come get that to mix in my compost.

"Putting it in straight last year created a lot of new weeds we never had before, Witty." Composting should break the weed seeds down. So goes the plan. Much is a constant experiment. It is so easy to give up because half of what we do fails! Witty and I both know many people do not understand growing things. "Witty, I hear so often from city people who dream of getting back to nature, how they will simply plant a garden and eat from it!" As if it were simple. I have been at it for over thirty years and still learn!

There are years it would be hard for my life to depend on what I grow. There are simply bad summers for growing. We get floods and the soil is too wet. We may not get to choose what we will be eating for the next year. One year, only the kale grew well! I had kale by the hundred pounds, and a lot of meals had to focus on the wonderful ways to eat it! I had hoped for a hundred pounds of turnips and got five. This is a lifestyle some will not enjoy or adjust to. City people are used to wanting something, then turning that want into going to the store and getting it. It is absurd to go to the store with a blank mind, see what is there, and dinner is determined by what you come home with.

Even when Iris and I shop for some foods, we tend to come home with what is on sale or in season. We do not always know when the price of something will drop. If ever.

"Remember last year, how we got all that corn on sale?" We found corn in abundance and bought almost a year's worth, paying fifty cents an ear. Another year we saw a sale on cherries and bought twenty pounds at almost two dollars a pound. Instead of wanting cherries and buying them in winter for $10 a pound. It's a lifestyle. A way of thinking.

I learned that nothing is gained by suggesting there is no savings in collecting coupons. I can see collecting coupons is something Iris enjoys doing. She is at peace snipping from the paper. It is exciting to gather them up on the day we go to town. It is rewarding to calculate the savings. I have zero connection to the process. I would not enjoy keeping track of them. I think the store is trying to get us to shop here, when we may not normally. Getting us to buy a product we may not want, but do because we have a coupon. I feel irritated. Iris and I do not go shop some place else for a forty cent savings on butter. Nor do we buy a brand we do not want in order to save thirty cents. Life is not just about money savings anyhow. I remember my earlier years when the same was said about me and my activities.

"Just get a job, earn the money, and buy it!" I'd make it all myself. I'd spend weeks making something I might buy for a few dollars. Like making my own soap by dripping lye from stove wood ashes and rendering my own bear fat. There was joy in the process. However, I never argued I was saving money. I think I wanted a connection to where all this 'stuff' we need to live, actually comes from, besides the store. There is a possibility there are things I do that are not money makers, yet I say it makes me money. When it does not, I forget, do not focus on that. Perhaps dealing with reality is a better life battle plan than thinking positive. By the time I am wise enough to understand that, my habits are already set.

Since I do not see the bad, and it does not exist, then it is hard to protect and defend myself. I am not good at covering up. I tend to be open and honest, it's all good, right? Friends nod in agreement. It is easy to view the world through friends, happy customers, and like-minded people. How big is the other world made up of those who do not agree with me? That's negative. I do not dwell on negative things. The garden does well. Iris and I talk about the potential to sell pickles and produce at the farmers' market and bazaars. Because the government is upset and the confiscation of my stuff,I wonder how selling produce would look.

I tell Iris, "The old man, Jim, who makes Jim's jam to sell during tripod days is not likely to get asked for his permit. He has no business license. His food has never been inspected or approved. There is no certification it is safe or quality controlled. We do not know if he uses dirty jars, if his temperatures sterilized the product. No one cares." I explain I think the reason is, he does not make more than $100. It seems to me we can do about anything we want to make $100. We are free. What happens if Jim begins to make $1,000? Or $10,000? As soon as anyone makes over $1,000 doing anything at all, suddenly the rules change. I'm understanding that for the first time.

If we sell a handful of jars of pickles and a box of veggies at the market, no one cares. I see the potential to sell dozens of cases and make $1,000. Suddenly our problems would never end. We'd need an inspection, a permit, insurance, a lawyer, an accountant. There goes any profits. Now you need to make $10,000 gross to make that same $1,000 profit you make when no one cared. That's what it means to say it is good to be poor or rich, but not in the middle.

I'm only slightly interested in making $100. Civilization requires more than this. $100 buys one night out on the town. Big deal. I see the ability to make a grand. I am not interested. I am not good at, nor do I enjoy paperwork, dates, times, records, doing it the right, approved way. The argument is, "Well, we are protecting the public! You need to follow certain rules with food so people do not get sick!" If so, how come no one is concerned about Jim and his jam, huh? Is anyone concerned about getting sick? Has anyone gotten sick off anyone like Jim selling food? Ever? Anywhere? In the entire history of mankind?

"All the times I recall issues with food, public notices out, it had to do with a big company. Never once a small-time operator." I think of the fishing industry. Locals who put up salmon. Suddenly the Feds tell us we have to have stainless steel sinks, running fresh water, not river water, controlled temperatures that sterilize. Permits. Rules impossible to meet in the remote areas where fish are put up. I tell Iris, "One of our politicians is in the fish processing business." I was told by a commercial fisherman who was connected to the board of game, what things look like from what he knows. This politician pushed for the upgrade and enforcement of the fish laws. Now their business is booming! They have almost a monopoly on kippered and dry salmon. The competition was put out of business. If this is the truth or not, I believe myself, things like this happen for these reasons. The public buys into it.

"Yes, the government is taking care of us! We are now safe, and will not get sick from improper fish processing!" Not one person, ever, in the history of Alaska got sick from improperly put up salmon. So explain why and where the reason for the rules came from? Where are the food poisoning stories coming from these days? I say again, high production certified big name food sources. What does that tell me? Personally, any time I ever got sick on food it was at approved inspected restaurants, or off processed city food. I never once got sick from anything directly off the land, or my own processing, or cooking, nor that of my friends who traded me their put up food.

I just cannot imagine making $1,000 selling pickles without any permits or permission from anyone, without getting arrested. My sense of freedom in my younger days was based on the freedoms of the poor. I was not aware I'd be stopped from getting ahead. Because then I'd suddenly be competition? I do not know. If I could make 100 grand I could pay someone to take care of all the details that are not fun to take care of. I could pay off everyone who needs to be paid off to get left alone. I could keep twenty-five grand for myself and be happy. A new game. Something different to try.

I HAVE a letter from someone who talked to me on the phone. She wants me to make a couple of molds. She called and wanted caps made for creating pendants and asked me to make them. I suggested if she has artistic ability, I can send her wax, she can carve that and make wax caps. "Send me the carved wax back. I make the mold, copy them for you." This will save her a lot of money. She can create her own cap design. We chat a bit about lifestyle. After calling on the phone, she emails. Discusses the details of the molds she sends and adds, 'PS I did read your book

'Going Wild' years ago. Inspired me to take the unbeaten path. I have a life that everyone wishes they had. And I dragged my husband into it too! He loves it! **Barbara in Lusk, Wyoming** '

This is a good time to get this, since I am struggling with my sense of self-worth. I tell Iris, "I wish we humans would be more accepting of each other." This is on my mind because this woman changed lifestyles after reading my book. She feels this is how she wishes to live. I do not know how many people think it is stupid, ridiculous. Some people will and have gone so far as to stop people from living this way.

The Feds imply the majority of the population they represent are appalled by my lifestyle and behavior. While representing the majority sentiment, who wish to interfere with my purpose in life. Put a stop to me, my ideas, and lifestyle. [1]My memory goes back to when I was in the Navy at 17 years old. I got to visit other countries. I got to see how the US treats other countries and I was shocked. I saw firsthand what other countries think of the US. I observed, and was part of, arrogantly deciding how others should live, and force them to do so.

"You will have democracy or else!" Our version of democracy. Which is not even democracy. At best, it is a republic. Meaning, we vote a representative into office, who promises to look out for us and represent us. Once in office, there is no legal obligation to live up to promises made. I wondered when young, why we cannot just leave people alone as long as they are not bothering us. I had been told this is what our country stands for. Was I brainwashed? Is this not true?

Even among ourselves, on a small scale, it seems normal to look at your neighbor and demand they live like you! Your house has to be up to the neighborhood's standards. You should get up, work, go to bed, at the same time, in the same way, as everyone else. Dress in a similar way. Have the same religion. That is how to get along best. This is one of the issues I have with this new google map Iris introduces me to on the computer.

Can people be trusted to be kind, understanding, accepting, or will we demand others live as we do? Will all others google for fun and merely snicker and talk? Or will there be those who do something about it? For example, I buy wolf carcasses from the local trappers who are throwing them away, dumping them in the river. I may have twenty-five carcasses collected over the winter in a pile, waiting till spring when I can cook them down to bones, and then sort the bones, dry them, sell them. Teeth, claws, skulls. I pay $25, and part them out for several hundred dollars. Civilized people may be disgusted or find it weird. *"You have that right to disagree. But if it is legal, not the right to act out that disagreement."*

"That terrorist group Greenpeace could search randomly, or work off a list using google earth. Spot my yard with a pile of wolf carcasses. I could imagine such pictures, described in the right way, going viral on the internet. Me never seeing the light of day again."

"Miles, why do you keep referring to such groups as terrorists?" Definition of terrorist activity: 'An activity engaged in, in the name of a minority group, to persuade the majority to change their views, by using intimidation, lies, threats, and destructive illegal tactics.'

"Well, just because an individual claims to be working for an organization, does not mean it has that organization's backing, Miles."

"In the news a few years ago was the sinking of a whaling ship with a bomb by Greenpeace. Described as a win for Greenpeace. The boat was engaged in a legal activity that a minority of people do not agree with."

On another subject then, thieves can google to view escape routes, where windows are, who might have money. One could look for abandoned antique cars to steal, spot items without plates like trucks, cars, trailers, to steal or report. People who need blackmail information and make a living at. All kinds of 'things out of compliance' in remote areas. That used to be no one else's business. Trouble makers just need access to a computer. Street people can go to the library and drum up extra funds blackmailing people, or collecting rewards. A female's car in a driveway when the wife is gone—stuff like that.

Iris points out a news article she thinks is of interest.

News miner Sept 21, 2011 Nation A-7 "California town bans fur clothing." West Hollywood—population 36,000 "Lawmakers see themselves as national trend setters," and "City Council unanimously approved an ordinance that would ban the sale of fur apparel-the first such ban in the nation."

Ever-growing, eye popping, often symbolic measures, in hopes of pushing animal rights and other causes onto the national stage.

I comment that I heard a community in California is going further by trying to ban all animal products.

"It is hard to imagine how this could be enforceable and what people are thinking. Things like, most perfume has an animal castor base, plastic uses fish oil. Leather is on all kinds of things. Would a distinction be made between domestic and wild? Would meat be banned, sable fur? Animal extracts are used in lots of medicines. But anyhow, whatever. The world has gone mad. We have lost touch with the land we come from and the facts of life."

My friend Tusk contacts me. He saw me at the fair and wants to know if I have any mammoth tusks for him to buy. We ramble about the topic at hand.

"Miles, I have had to have a lawyer before, and get some facts for my case. There are over 10,000 laws on the books concerning wildlife. Also, no fish and wildlife Federal case has ever gone to jury trial. Not ever. There are in fact, fewer and fewer trials of all kinds. Most, maybe all, are ending in plea bargains."

"So people agree they are guilty, in return for easy terms, when they may in fact not be guilty?"

"That's how it looks, Miles." I have some mammoth ivory, but prefer not to let Tusk know. Tusk is a good person to buy from, not to sell to. He often has deals on scraps I need for making knife scales or art objects. Tusk is so often strapped for cash that offering him cash gets very nice deals. When Tusk buys, he wants to trade for things I do not really need. I think, because he does not have any money. Or, like Crafty, wants slave labor prices. From these experiences, I learn to be careful when I suggest trading with customers. I feel them out, encourage them to trade, but am willing to drop the subject and give them cash without any fuss. I know many need that cash! I feel I am never in a cash bind, always ahead, not in a situation where I sell cheap because I have bills to pay and need that money.

"So, Miles, did Jessie ever come through for you?"

I am not sure if Tusk is working undercover. This seems like a question Tusk would not inquire about. I also consider my phone is tapped.

"I got that bit of fossil material at the fair from him when he stopped by. You were there, remember?" If the phone is tapped, I want a record of the fact Tusk witnessed a conversation and exchange of legal fossil owned material from Jessie.

"Yes, I was not paying attention, I do not know what transpired." I am not sure I believe that. Tusk is someone who tends to remember deals with competitors. He would normally be inquiring how much the fossil material is worth, and how much cheaper he could get it to me. His reply has me thinking he also suspects our discussion is being recorded, and does not want to get involved, or is already involved, and needs to look good.

"Anyhow, Tusk, no more business with Jessie. I think I will stick with mammoth ivory anyhow, no more fossil walrus. It's too controversial."

There is an example in today's emails of the chance to sell tusks retail on the internet, without going through Tusk. In fact, I am getting to be in the position of Tusk, a dealer and buyer with many contacts.

Hi Miles,

Please send the pictures of mammoth tusk to this address, and we'll start from there.

Thanks, Tom

Dear Sir,

I found your web store while searching for mammoth tusks and ivory.

Blaz

Dear Sir,

My name is Golf. And I'm interested in Mammoth tusk ivory.
price $160 a pound.
Can you supply mammoth tusks around 50-100kg / month?
pls give me a best price.
Pls contact me back as soon as possible.
Thanks Golf

Wednesday, September 28, 2011
Hello!
I'm looking to buy a wolf-tooth necklace. I'm not sure if this is too idealistic of me, but I'm hoping to get a tooth from a wolf that hasn't been hunted down through commercial means. Where do your teeth come from? What is the history behind the teeth that you sell? Please respond to me at your convenience - I hope you have a wonderful day!
Sincerely, **Lauren N.**

I record a lengthy reply I do not send. If I did, I would lose a sale and would be considered a rude seller.

I do not send my long stream of thoughts; I reply instead:

Hello Lauren!
Thanks for your inquiry!
Yes, all my wolf parts are harvested off naturally dead wolves found by local Indians in the forest of natural causes during the Natives subsistence life activities. A special prayer is said to give thanks.

If you want to know the truth about a used car, do not ask the salesman. Pay a mechanic, make time to check it out, or expect a nonsense answer to a nonsense question. Well, no. Not nonsense. Wolves who die in traps have died of natural causes. "Great! Another $400!" is a form of prayer. I offer on my website references, a facts page, my books that review my beliefs in depth for those who are truly concerned. For those who do not have the time, 'poof.' I absolve you of the guilt you are feeling. Sometimes I decide to reply to such inquires.

"I do not think you would be happy with my products, have a nice day." This customer begins saying her mind is made up. She wants to buy a wolf tooth. The question is to buy from me or someone else. No one can give a better answer than me. I'm the source. Bigger suppliers get them wholesale from me and know less than I do. Put your money down, lady, and share the guilt.

I do care. I spent my early years in the wilds struggling to understand nature and its laws. Having been raised on Walt Disney, I was shocked by the reality of the actual world. Life feeds off life. Almost by definition. 'You are alive, therefore you consume. 'You are alive, therefore living things must die. To what extent, and under what circumstances, we can be a little in control of. I am not in the business of explaining the facts of life to customers.

Hello,

I want to purchase a knife from you, I've attached a photo from your website of the style that I want. I will be replacing my old puma knife that was stolen from me two weeks ago, I really like your work with 1095 Carbon Steel… I will be using this knife for gutting and skinning caribou in the winter. I would like a 3″ blade +/- ½″ will be fine. I would also like my last name "Waterman" on the blade or the sheath if it is possible. You can call or email me, I will be waiting for your response. **Thank you.**

Hi Miles,

Just checking in....haven't heard from you in a while & wanted to make sure you got our email regarding an order for $300-$400 worth of handle material and also concerning carrying some of your work in our new store. I'm sure that you are busy but we've had lots of trouble with sudden lost email recently & not sure you ever even got our note. Some emails send multiple times & others never send. Just drop a quick line when you have a moment...we look forward to hearing from you!

Gary & Pam Smith
Smith & Sons, LLC
Leather and Fine Cutlery

Hey Miles,

I found your site today while I was scavenging online for some nice pieces of fossilized walrus tusk. I like your site and I think I would like you too! I would like to buy some good pieces which I could carve into pieces about 1 inch by 1 inch by 1/4 thick and a little larger also when finished.

I need some that is fairly light and even and also I would like some of the bluish ivory. What ya got for me?

Thanks, Christina

This is a hair piece I made from 40,000 year old mammoth ivory. Does it fall under the same laws as elephant ivory? Whose land can fossils legally come from?

CHAPTER EIGHT

NEWS ARTICLES, TUCSON TRIP

M y lawyer is clueless about animal product laws. He looks up the basic headline, sees 'illegal' and stops. Such as "illegal to sell ivory," as was stated in the charge against me years ago. I find in my notes a letter from a lawyer at that previous time, whom I hired for legal advice somewhere along the line. Peter Aschenbrenner is now a judge, but here is his letter as a lawyer.

July 10th 1986.

"A favorable exception to the above is the fact that from the spring of 1976 to June 30th 1979, jurisdiction over walrus was granted to the State Department of Fish and Game. During this time any subsistence user, native or non-native, was allowed to hunt walrus. Raw ivory taken during that period was etched with a seal or a number by the department and is exempt from the Federal possession restrictions. You could conceivably purchase an entire white tusk harvested between 1976 and 1979 and use it as you wish."

Not a lot of people know this. Few dig far enough to find this. Maybe Fish and Wildlife even forgot. Maybe it makes their job easier if everyone forgot. Some radicals say forgetting may fit in with a hidden agenda. That does not make covering this up moral or legal. I acquired such tusks with tags during that time period and still have some. I was here in Alaska; I knew natives, and I stockpiled. There is no problem when the tusk is whole with the tag on it. The issue comes up once the tusk is cut up. Proving where all the pieces came from is difficult.

I had assumed all along, there would have to be proof of a tusk 'not' being legal for there to be a problem. It kind of sucks to have legal stuff, cut it up, have it in a box during a time no one cared, and now, how am I going to prove that? I have the original tags, but there is only my word the tag connects to the box of scraps I have. My activity in the 70s was under a different set of laws the USA operated under. We were innocent unless proven guilty. How was I to know that one day the burden of proof would have to be on the accused? The past with Peter had been a 'hire a lawyer and pay for legal advice'. The present is a 'public defender' situation. My public defender is not diving as deeply into the laws. I'm even wondering, questioning if my public defender is even my lawyer. He's the public's lawyer, as the term states, 'defending the public.'

Since I do not trust my phone, my website, or even the mail, I ask my lawyer how to handle this situation with Bill, the customer who wants to talk about ivory while I am under investigation. I do not want my customer to get in trouble and get investigated like me. There is also the possibility the Feds have gone through my customer file and are contacting people, trying to set me up by blackmailing my friends and customers. My lawyer approved an answer I send to customer Bill.

> **Thank you for your email**. As you know, I have always prided myself in conducting a lawful, proper business with all my customers, including you. While acting and operating within the law, I have also prided myself in having satisfied customers, like yourself. Because I am not a lawyer, I cannot offer you legal advice, but suggest that you contact an attorney of your own choice, should you so desire to do so. **Best regards, Miles**.

I am in hopes the stiff style of my communication that is uncharacteristic of me will be a hint to be careful, if my trusted customer is unaware of what is going on. I do not know what other items he has from other dealers. I am told by my lawyer, it would not be a good idea to outright warn customers. They may be under investigation. It would be a crime apparently, to interfere with an investigation. It's nice in this case to be able to say, "My lawyer helped me compose a legal reply." It cost me $100 out of my pocket to reply. I review the actual transaction with this Bill customer, to spot any potential legal problem I might face. We had written back and forth, but this email sums it up.

> **Hey Bill**! Well, it is better in my opinion to stay away from white ivory altogether. I know you have a few customers who want it, and that is hard to turn down. All I have is this one small tusk that is legal, but could present problems if not handled right. I have papers for it, but papers may not matter if you end up in court and win, but pay thousands in legal fees. I confess, I'd as soon get rid of this tusk, as in my opinion laws are only going to get more restrictive. I could get stuck with this, and no way at all to

sell it in the future! I'm glad you can use it. I can give you a good price since it is not native connected. Do not try to sell any finished product containing this overseas. **Miles.**"

I'm not sure what a jury would have to say about this. I never expected my communications to be made public. I consider my emails as private discussions. Till now. I was not thinking,

"What would anyone else say about this if they read it?" I assume every business, every family, every relationship between friends, or anyone includes, 'some stuff,' we'd rather the world did not get wind of. Touchy stuff. Either personal, or hard for anyone else to relate to and understand. We pass insider information along, help someone we know get a job, give someone a special deal. Offer advice on a love matter we hope certain people never know about. We have a garage sale and do not report the income to the IRS. Insult our president in a private communication to a trusted loved one. Make a racial comment to a trusted friend. Read a book we should not be reading, visit a website we'd rather the world not know about. We may not wish the world to know how many sheets of toilet paper we use, or that we are afraid of spiders. Or as a Christian, having doubts about God.

I tell Iris, "The Feds spent maybe a million dollars, with hundreds of hours, analyzing all my phone calls and emails over a long period of time, and have come up with what they feel is the dirt on me. It looks bad. However, if I had the same million dollars, man hours, ability to tap the Feds phone for four years, and read all their emails, all the agents wrote and received, I bet I could make them look just as bad!"

"But Miles, you will never get that million dollars and man hours to do that. That's the problem."

"Yes, I notice the Feds had their own recording of everything! Their own pictures taken serving the search warrant. I was not allowed to take pictures, nor make recordings for my defense! Is that fair? Whatever they are allowed to do, I should be allowed to do as well, I'd think. How can something be legal for them, and not for me? Shouldn't we be held to the same standards and rules, to be fair?" But I am just spouting off. There is no answer. None is offered.

Deals like I made with customer Bill look bad under one sided scrutiny. Bill may have understood the deal to be 'slightly illegal.' Now he wants to fix it. What would he say in court, if it came to that? To save his lard, would he say, "Miles made me do it!"?

I HAVE an email from someone who has been trying to reach me.

4th try... get a mail return each time... Sorry if this has reached you before... Just was gifting one of the last pieces of jewelry you made me to a very ill friend. Any update of possible return and new creations from you? Sounds like you had a great fair... performed at the state fair in 1980 in Anchorage with the Pickle family circus... and was at the 1989 see Alaska fair... in Haines.. Hope all is well, **Marc**

I had forgot about Marc. Dang. He sent me his legal bear claws with paperwork and asked me to cap them for him. I had his box of claws with receipt and paperwork in the box. This was among items confiscated. The claws do not belong to me. I wrote, explained, apologized. Marc is not upset, said he loved my artwork. What a shame I am in trouble over this. I've been trying to get his claws back so I can return them to him. My lawyer flat out says, "Stop worrying about everyone else!"

Hello George...Yes, you got the payment right and I will send the 4 musk ox slices out tomorrow by priority mail. Expect 4-5 days. **Miles.**

Hello George... Are you in the USA? I cannot ship out of the country.

Yes, I am in the US, Pennsylvania. I bought mammoth ivory from you a couple of times. The musk ox horn scales, if they are 8 inches or more, would even be better.

My $100 export permit has been denied. I have not received a reason yet. Saddle tells me the reply from Fish and Wildlife is, "Giving an answer might interfere with an ongoing investigation."

Vendors in the past have said, "No big deal, it is just a $100 simple permit that lets you do business overseas in a variety of materials." Yes, simple, and cheap enough. Until it is denied. I've never been asked to show this permit. *It's like paying the mafia for protection.* This permit number is never asked for on any shipments. It's easy to forget. It is not the $100 that is the big deal, it is the control. In this case, effectively cutting off a multi thousand dollar part of a legal business. I have been accumulating a list of lost revenue due to not having this permit, in case I ever get to court and win, and can show damages.

Hey Miles, Stuart from Montréal here, just checking back if your international shipping woes are sorted out... I said I would check back, and I'm on the verge of decisions for my chef knife so just to be sure, are you able to ship Mammoth ivory again?

let me know

Normally mammoth ivory requires no permit of any kind to buy, sell or ship. Or, 'as far as I know.' It has been pointed out many times we are responsible for knowing the law, but government agencies are not responsible for making the laws and changes public, or easy to find. So those of us in the business speculate, exchange interpretations, legal advice we have received. We pass along what we feel is acceptable practice. Our rivals may not tell the truth.

Hi Miles,

Declan here in Ireland. I have just sent you payment via Paypal for those mammoth ivory scales. thanks again.

I will send a photo of the finished knife. loved your website by the way, especially the bit about having "two good friends in the world and you ain't one of them buddy"

I'm still chuckling away There must be a bit of anti-establishment Irish blood in you!!! You'd fit right in here.

All the best to you, and continued success.

regards

Declan Looney

I have no export permit for this deal to be legal. I return this customers' money.

Miles! I feel I know you! What a wonderful envious life you live up there in the wilds! Such stunning pictures! I have been looking for a long time for a moonstone for a project. I'd like free form, maybe loaf cut, narrower at the top than bottom, ten mm long. Can you help me? **Lori**"

Iris sees this and rolls her eyes at me. "What have I told you about helping others all the time!? Learn to say no!" Iris is referring to the conversations we have about how many times I get such requests that I will lose money on big time. Such a moonstone might be worth $10. But might take me an hour to look for. I may not have what she wants after spending that hour. I've done the math, even told Iris, even tried to explain on my website.

"I get 30 emails a day on the average. At least a third ask me to look for something. I average half an hour per search. Out of the ten who inquire, three buy something. That is five hours a day 'looking for stuff.' The average sale resulting from looking is $20. That's four dollars an hour. These are not fun numbers." The bottom line being, I can't stay in business operating like this. Iris points out what I already know. I can ignore these people and make $30, $40, up to $100 an hour.

"So why do you reply to these people and go look, Miles!"

I have no logical practical reason. Partly, "I want to help them." *But do I really?* The truth is, I find it annoying and frustrating. The truth is, I do not know how to say 'No!' Iris tells me as she observes me operate in life, this is a critical problem that even gets me in trouble!

"I guess Iris, I was not taught how to say no." When I do, I do not do so politely, I tend to blow up and be rude. I am reluctant to talk about where some of this might come from, so I make up excuses like it's ok. It all works out, so why sweat it? I'm the one who gets hurt, so who cares? Growing up, I was beaten, punished for questioning adults or authority. My parents were both no nonsense rigid types. Mother told me on my last visit to her in Tucson, "You never smiled. You were never allowed to be a child." I assume I was not a happy child. I have no memories related to this. I do not blame my parents. They were raised the same way! I was taught to mind. To be helpful.

Mom repeated many times how easy I was to raise, not a problem at all. No one suggested that some people will not have my best interest at heart. Or even that some authority figures would do very bad things to you if you do what they tell you, go with them etc. I wanted to please, be loved, so said, "Yes, yes and yes!" However, my parents did not know me, or understand me, and in my view, made a lot of wrong decisions concerning my needs. I was not asked what I wanted. I'm a child, with no vote.

"Children should be seen, and not heard" This is how both my parents were raised. You do not talk back, say no to adults! I had to learn on my own, that no one knows what I want more than I do. I cannot leave my happiness in someone else's care. It might be possible, if you are taught how to pick the right one to listen to. I did not learn that. In fact learned from a dysfunctional family how to pick the wrong ones. I became most aware when I was sent away from home at sixteen to go into the military with my parents' consent.

I tell Iris, "I probably told you this before?" Well, sometimes things need repeating. "Anyhow, my father just got remarried. I assume now, they wanted to be alone together without the stupid kids around." I explain how my sister was sent off to be with her real Mom. What a disaster that turned out to be! "She never recovered." I gave my sister and parents my opinion, that such a move would be a disaster. Mom did not take custody of us in the divorce for a reason. Usually children automatically go with the mother, certainly in the 1960's!

I was better off than my sister. I was sent into the military during the Viet Nam war. But more than that. It was a last minute decision I had no time to prepare for. Dad was in such a hurry, he could not wait a week for me to go to my high school graduation. I missed getting my diploma, and the class party, prom and all that. "I mean, all the years of schooling is supposed to be about getting your high school diploma, right?" The lifelong memories of the prom, the celebration. I had a girlfriend I was close to, friends I loved and trusted. I was the most socially adapted, and healthy as I have ever been in my life. I had somehow managed to get my life together in high school. I got good grades, had good people for friends. I was not acting out so much, or getting in trouble to get attention.

Both the girls I cared for most, ended up being very fine adults. One married, became a nurse, well respected in the hospital, a loving wife with nice children. Maggie is the other one I have referred to throughout my books.[1] Maybe the one who got me straight, introduced me to the right group of people, trusted me, had confidence in me, truly cared about me, understood me, as no one else did at the time. If I had not been sent off to the military, there is a good chance I would have married one of these two and had a much more ordinary life, probably a life with fewer issues. I'd have been much more socially adjusted. *Not that I have any regrets! What good are regrets?*

My father was very pleased sending me off, telling me how I'd love the military, how he loved it. He forgot to tell me he did not stay in and did not reenlist for a reason. Dad did not seem to understand, nor care that I was leaving my friends and loved ones behind, my girlfriend. He had a puzzled, "What does that have to do with anything?" attitude. From his perspective, women, girlfriends, love, is all unimportant background stuff that is not as important as your job and duty. Being young is about sowing your oats, checking the world out. I believed him and happily did as he told me. Dad may have just assumed I was too young and we all 'get over it.' You know, our first few loves. Maggie was stunned. It was such a surprise I am off to the war. We and our friends had talked such summer plans! Looking for work, college, or who knows? We were seventeen, with a life ahead of us, school is finally over, for the first time we have choices! All our families had money.

Maggie's father was one of the teachers at our school. One of our friends had a swimming pool and tennis court we used. All of us had homes big enough to have a band come to practice and play at our parties. Many of those high school friends took a break to travel! It was common to be rewarded by family for graduating, getting good grades, getting a diploma in good standing. Some got new cars, or have college plans. One good friend went to Italy! He ended up with a job stomping grapes. I recall picturing this guy with such a job! He loved it. He met a woman, married, came back to the US. Lives in the same area he was born and raised. Unsure what he does for a living. But emails me pictures of his boat, his property, with many acres. He has children, a good wife, and unstressful life. That might have been me. We all hung together.

In defense of my parents, I indicated I did not care for school. There would be the assumption its rewards did not interest me. No one asked children. Parents told children. What do children know? There was a time parents even decided who we would marry, what our occupation would be. I tell Iris, "It's not like I am complaining. Just stating how it was and the effect it has today." We did not talk back to our elders or those with authority. "If someone says, 'Go fetch!'" That's what we did, if we did not want to get punished!

I was gifted with art, a good photographer, smart, got good grades, actually good at anything I attempted. I was well liked by Maggie's parents, who may have assumed she and I would be a couple. Because for over a decade, I was asked when I was coming home. She and I corresponded for many, many years. It was me who disappeared into the wilds. She married while I was gone. When we were together during those high school years, I felt safe and secure, recovering from an earlier childhood. But when I got sent away 'again,' I think I lost that sense of trust and security in others. *It is best not to get close to people as it can all be taken away, and then what?*

I could somehow not get it together socially in quite the same way after what was a last final setback. A critical time in my late teens when we are most adaptable. I never again believed that I could be in control of my life, with anyone else in it. I never again trusted getting that close to anyone, or group of people. I would try to do for others, be nice, but not comfortable with kindness in return. *"It is better to give…"* I went in a direction where I could be in control of my life, and what happened in it.

"So I end up with control, authority issues. Oh, well!" I grin. Some sort of 'need to please,' without being happy about it. Getting sucked into stuff that is not in my best interest. *I must get something out of it though?* Is it healthy? More like, the issue is, 'This is how it is, deal with it!' Make the best of who we are. Hide and disguise our weakness and not let it show. Make jokes, excuses. Focus on the positive. Pretend all the bad stuff never happened. Yet my unconscious knows, and looks out for me in ways I am not in control of, ways that may not be logical. Odd habits, various key ins I am not as in control of as I wish, or think I am.

"I'm aware of some of the key ins!" Words like normal, never, always, can't. Phrases like, 'This is how it's done.' People around me say 'Can't' and I am most likely to respond. "Can't? Here watch me!" Followed by, "Don't you mean, 'should not?'" For 'should not,' implies a choice, 'cannot,' implies there is no alternative. I am big on 'there is always an alternative.' I prove it. No one puts me between a rock and a hard place.

People around me are puzzled, "Where did that come from, what's his problem?"

All this is behind a simple, "Just say 'No, Miles!'" I have been there. Wanting answers to know something, to find something, and no one interested in helping. I have empathy. I will not be like everyone else. I want to help if I can.

Iris goes, "Humph!" followed by, "And people take advantage of you!"

I prefer to see the times people appreciate what I have done. Not focus on the times I lost money or got cheated in some other way. "I'd rather be the sucker then the suckee!" is a common reply throughout my life.

Speaking of sucking, an alcoholic guy I know says, "I'd rather have a bottle in front of me, then a frontal lobotomy!" Yes. Better to have a problem we understand, that is definable, than a solution society comes up with that leaves us a vegetable. For the solution will be 'drugs!' *As it was for my sister.* So it is better to be a sucker. I can live with that. Better than to let the truth out.

Eventually 'stuff' seems to go away. Slowly I learn to say no, or I hand the phone to Iris and she screams, "What part of NO don't you understand! Go away! Leave us alone!" and slams the phone down on the telemarketer. In this case, I think I know where my moonstone is. I find something I hope this Lori stranger will be happy with. It requires taking a picture, editing it and emailing the description. There are at least three choices, so we have to discuss the merits of each. I have a good hour invested. She spends the average $20 on a $10 moonstone. Paying extra for personal service, no one else would offer her.

I tell Iris, "Who knows, maybe she will remember, and shop with me when she needs her next stone."

"Sure, even probably, and once again you will work for minimum wage. She will want another deal from her buddy, Miles!"

"Yes, well, maybe she will get a bigger order or something worth more next time."

Over time, I see Iris is correct on some important points. People hardly ever change. What they do once, they are likely to repeat the same way. The poor hardly ever come back to me as the rich. The needy hardly ever come back as the giver. Those who need special services for minimum wage will most likely always be that way. Those who waste my time probably waste everyone else's time and are probably just like that! They are ones who are not even likely to be sincerely grateful. Often as not, I am just an enabler, a sucker. I am not necessarily doing them a favor by helping them. But as I intellectualize that, and see it, understand it, my unconscious gets the message.

In time, my unconscious is capable of adjusting accordingly. Good people tend to not waste my or anyone else's time. Those I make a lot of money from are glad I make money, ask the least questions, are the easiest to please and deal with. These are the ones I wish to reward. I learn to do that. I learn to say stuff like, "I might go look when I am not busy. I have a lot going on right now." Life is not easy to figure out.

"And further more, Miles, I told you I did not like that Jessie when I met him. He seemed to me like someone who spent time in prison! You always try to think the best of people and believe people, Miles. You just cannot do that!" Luckily I have not heard from him in a while and now expect I will not. I think he is locked up now. Iris had shown me the news article. The Feds went to his place with a search warrant. He greeted them with a loaded gun. Tried to run them off. The news reported he was trading drugs and illegal guns for truckloads of white walrus ivory. He had a partner in the lower states who put them on the internet for sale. One of the guns he had, was used in a killing in a state where Jessie used to live. The murder went unsolved, though Jessie was a suspect. Now they have the murder weapon. "Why would he hang on to a murder weapon all these years?" Anyway, looks like his goose is cooked. Not getting my $2,000 worth of fossil ivory from him, seems like a minor detail.

"Who knows if the newspaper report is correct. But usually there is at least a half truth in a news article. I do not think the news media totally makes up news from scratch. It may have been one truckload of ivory, one gun and some minor drugs traded. Drugs may have been pot. It's hard to know. Except a search warrant ended up with Jessie in jail. "Honey, it says in the article Jessie and his lady were not married." He said he was, and I assumed so. As such, his legal connection to her native rights is gone.

Hi Miles,

It's Kathy, your Dad's 3rd wife, I'm sure you remember.

I'm writing because to celebrate my 70th birthday, can you believe?, I'm taking Avon, Dana and little Max on a cruise to Hawaii. We'll spend one day in Honolulu and hope to drive to the North shore of the island. Your father often told me about living there and driving up over the mountain to get to the Naval base on the South side. I'd like to see the area where he and Dolores lived and you were born and point it out to Avon. So only your Mom can tell us where it is.

Could you help me get the information from her or give me her phone # so I can ask her?

On the map I see a couple of town names on the route North from Pearl Harbor:

Waipahu, Wahiawa, Waialua, Haleiwa

Whew, I'd never remember, but maybe she does.

If you think it will upset her, don't tell her I want to know, just ask about your birth and where their house was.

You told me she still wants to know why Miles left her. I could tell her, and it might make her feel better. He always loved her and spoke of her in only the fondest terms.

How are you? Still with your lady-friend? do you ever get down to San Diego to see Mitch? You know I'm only an hour North of there and it would be easy to see you if you get here. **Fondly, Kathy**

I show the letter to Iris. I rarely hear from family, so this is a big event, sort of.

"She is the one Dad wanted to spend time with and sent us kids away over. She's ok. Good looking and sexy. I can see why Dad was wrapped around her finger. But Kathy and I were never close. I was away from home after that. I think I was glad to be away. Missed my friends, but involved in a new adventure." The letter brings up memories. I'm not sure how she got my address. Must have been Avon, my step-brother, Kathy's child. Max, I think is the Russian kid Dad adopted and promised to take care of, someone in KGB asked Dad to look after him, take him to the US. Still puzzled over how that came about. (?)

"Miles. Are you going to the WIN meeting? It's after 12."

"This is Tuesday?"

"Did you forget? I reminded you this morning." I could remember if I wanted to, needed to. *It's mostly that Iris takes on the role and enjoys reminding me of things and organizing me. It pleases her to be useful. It is easy for me to simply forget, think of other things, let her remind me. It pleases her that she is smart and remembers, while I am stupid and forget.* "What is on the agenda today, Miles, do you know?"

Sort of an important day. I'm to give a report from the committee for the borough fact finding board that I am on. Appointed by the city council. I was on the same committee five to six years ago when the issue came up back then. I had to review what took place last time and go into the computer for my notes. I scan through it to pick out the points of interest. The Question of Nenana being in a borough or not has come up off and on over the years, and once again it is a topic of discussion. The Mayor agrees this is a subject that needs discussing, and a while back a city council meeting made up a task force to investigate the issue in an effort to gather facts. Alan Baker is head of this task force.

At the same time, the WIN coalition also brought up the subject as an issue effecting the health of the community. *At the last city council meeting, the efforts of WIN and the city council were combined when Miles was asked to be on the task force. Dale–a strong participant at WIN has put a lot of energy into a plan.* The potential nearby gas fields and possible revenues that might be generated is one of the most pressing matters.

"Let's wait and see if there is even any gas!" I have heard from many citizens. This sounds reasonable.

"Fighting over money that does not even exist yet, and may never exist, seems nuts!" This as well is a good point. Others say there is an unconfirmed rumor Fairbanks borough is looking to absorb us. Likewise, the Denali borough. Politically, word is, there is an effort to push for all communities in the state being in an organized borough. Nenana being absorbed would fit in with this agenda.. Delta has been facing similar issues with Pogo mine nearby and has gathered a lot of useful information and done a lot of groundwork. They have a very informative website with seventy pages of information

"We do not need another layer of government, more taxes, more officials telling us what to do!" is a very strong sentiment. Many do not need or want facts, and have already made up their mind, while others wish to hear both sides of the story.

The plan for now is to have the borough commissioner Mr. Brochorst speak to us one day and on another day have John Coghill speak to us (known to be against forming a borough). Mr. Brochorst has been here before to give us basic information and came across as ready to answer questions without bias. So if you have strong opinions, you can bring them to Alan Baker or Miles Martin, and your concerns can be brought to the city council or incorporated in the questions to be asked at the public meeting. It is the task forces hope to have Minto, maybe Tanana, Minchumina, and surrounding communities involved and informed. Maybe not at the first meeting, but this would affect them if it turns that the goal is to have all communities in a borough if we like to or not. Again, this is one of the issues to get to the bottom of.

"Well, you know me Miles, want to stay out of politics!" Yes, I know. We have discussed this many times. Iris knows my view. I have explained it many times. I like to be in control of my life, value my privacy, and wish to stand up for individual rights. When I was in the wilds, my life was affected by nature—the weather, movement of wildlife. I learned to work with and understand these things. I move to civilization! So what controls my life now? The city council, locally, has a big effect on all our lives. So I wish to understand how it works, stay informed, be 'cause' over events, instead of just affected by what goes on. I see many people complain, but unwilling to do anything. So I get involved. It's volunteer work. This whole borough issue is an example.

"Iris, there are some people so riled up they are arriving at meetings armed, and threatening people on the committee."

"Geez, Miles!" Yes, mostly people who rarely, if ever, show up at city meetings or stay informed except at the bar. Some are from out of the city limits, worried we in the city have a plan to tax them. Right now they pay no taxes. I explain that many of the families have children who ride the school bus to go to our school who pay nothing for this. They receive emergency care, get fire protection, and pay nothing. Such people are going ballistic they might have to pay something. I asked one such irritated person who is a provider for her family, and a friend of mine. She tells me her family has it covered. They shop in Nenana. Thus contribute to the community to the extent they receive from the community. By paying tax on goods they buy at the local store. They in fact shop in Fairbanks like most of us do. She has told me this many times in the past.

"Anyhow, I doubt very much the city is up to anything. I attend most meetings and stay informed, so think I understand what is going on and why. It's just a fact finding group, so we can stay informed." I'm on this committee, and could be on the city council if I wanted. Some asked me to run for mayor. It's a thankless job I would not want. But nice to know many want me. I understand our community. I live like the subsistence natives, but run a white man's business. I was head of the Chamber. I have attended churches, yet have friends who drink a lot. I know just about all groups. However, I am not good on the phone, or good at dealing with paperwork or working with others. Neither do I like to be in charge. I like to be in charge of myself, but not anyone else. I do not like to tell others what to do. I had quite a learning experience getting the Art Train to stop. I was in charge of that. What a lot of work! Ha! So yes, off to the Wellness meeting! Iris thinks the group does not get anything done, accomplishes nothing but entertain ourselves. Possibly so. That's not what I dwell on.

A BOAT TRIP is coming up.

I want to go down to the Yukon River, to hunt moose late in the season when it is getting cold. The moose might be in rut. I also just want to get out and have a nice boat trip! I had not been out in the boat much all summer. I start with eighty gallons of fuel on board. Burning two point five gallons an hour, doing about twenty-five miles an hour. Considered slow, but easy to read the water, and safe, more enjoyable than going faster. I get to Fish Creek by dark, a usual stop spot for the night. I catch a pike, very big! I turn it loose. The pike is lightly hooked, so will survive. I did not want to eat pike unless I have to. *There was a day I could give the fish away to someone who valued it.* But I do not know anyone anymore who would consider being given a pike a blessing.

Weather is cloudy. Rain off and on, just above freezing. I am able to keep warm by the use of my new electric 'heated seat.' I bought a twenty watt warmer that goes under my vinyl boat seat. Sold for snow machines, but works for boat use too. Next day I am in my moose hunting area, open till the 25th of Sept. I know this area a little from all my boat travels over the years. There is an area I like, with a nice scenic view, a creek to explore, and an island with a small lake, good for moose hunting. Good, because a smart moose will choose an island as a defendable area to keep his cow harem.

I see moose tracks, so am encouraged. Too late in the day now to do any tracking. I need to dry out. The sunset is a nice purple, blending to red, that matches the hot coals in my camp fire. In the morning, the only moose I see is too far from the river for me to haul if I shoot it. I decide not to shoot this one, who knows to stay in the middle of the island. I see where another big bull crossed a creek, but he is long gone and not coming back. While hunting, I take time to look for rocks I can cut and sell. I have gathered good rocks in the past in this area. There is a special jasper quartz mix rock I look for, bright red. Another is a green, like jade, with inclusions, sometimes black, sometimes different colors of green. I found what I thought would amount to $300 worth of rocks, enough to pay for the gas used on this trip.

In my lifestyle there is no such thing as a true vacation. I can do fun things, but need to find a way to pay for it, to find a money angle in about everything I do. I am happy to find these rocks. I can hear my friends now,

"But Miles, doesn't it take the fun out of it to be thinking about 'money'!" Talking to me, as if everything with me is about money, "The root of all evil, Miles!" The basics of life are important to us all. Food, and shelter, for example. If my life is not about being at a regular home, or going to the store for food, then I have to think. *Where will I spend the night? What will I be eating when I am hungry?* This is constantly on the mind, but just in the background, not dominating my every thought.

If I see a batch of ripe berries, I know to gather some up, without giving this a lot of thought. If I do not have a regular paycheck, then, "Where is money going to come from?" has to be on my mind in the background. Gathering dollars, becomes like foraging for berries. Is berry picking, work, or play? I'm sorry so many people I know hate money. Do they as well, hate berries? I assume they hate their job, that they associate it with the need for making a living and necessity of having money. Is this the same personality that a million years ago, hated hunting, gathering, building fires, picking berries instead of dollars, and hauling water? I'm daydreaming such thoughts when…

I run into some Natives from Tanana hunting moose, using a cabin I had never seen occupied before. One guy says he is from Rampart.

"I know you!" he tells me. His wife knows me as well, but I do not remember who they are. I stop and have coffee with them. We talk about old times. I showed them the rocks I am getting. Natives in general have a different view than civilized people. There is rarely room in their life to haul a pile of rocks around in the boat, and call them pretty, worth hauling anyplace. It is beyond comprehension for these two, to imagine white men saving rocks, selling them, wearing them for jewelry. They are just rocks!

Similar to a person in the wilds collecting broken bottles as valuable to make arrowheads. These two are being polite to save my feelings, but I see them look at each other, *This guy, Miles, is nuts!* I can run into these two at the fair and show them finished jewelry. They want it! I think it is just hard to imagine all the steps from this raw muddy rock, to finished art. It is like magic. Indeed, it is in fact, magic. *Watch! Behold! And be amazed!*

I do not mention moose hunting; I know they are hunting moose. They may not like me around Indian country hunting. It is good they believe some crazy white man is gathering rocks. Rainy, cloudy cold weather persists.

At my camp, a boat comes by at close to dark in the rain. I step out to see, and the boat turns to come back. It is Paul with two guys I do not know, but Paul had introduced me to this one guy at the Tanana fair. Both are now totally plastered. Neither of them can even stand up and walk, or talk, and be understood. Open beer cans shine like diamonds all over the inside of the boat. Paul who introduced me, seems to be a leader; and does all the attempts at talking.

"Hey! Shwhat are you doon here! You can't be hur white man! You need pay me to be here!" Both guys are armed with rifles. This wise guy is wanting to make trouble. "What ha you got in you boat?" He jumps in my boat. "What's in dis can!" I tell him:

"My clothes."

"You hur getting mammoth Ibee, and you need pay me cut! Dis ma land!" It is not his land, and is not even Native land, it is a Federal preserve. Or at least the part he is all worried about me going on. They are out hunting moose too, but had not got one. I saw groups of boats go by, some with big moose racks on the front. Fancy boats owned by rich people outside our area. None of us subsistence people here got a moose.

I'm trying to be polite, not wanting problems with local Indians. It is extremely rude to get into another man's boat like this uninvited, and demand to know what is in the boat, or what you are doing. This is the equivalent in the civilized world, of having a drunk get in your car at a stoplight, and make demands. These Natives could shoot me, dump me in the river, and no one would ever know. Here is Mr. Hot Shot threatening me, trying to extort money out of me, trying to make me afraid. I show them the rocks I can sell. Hot Shot is not impressed. He wants money.

Paul says to his buddy, "Come on, its late; we need to goo! Leave dis crazy white rock man alone!"

Hot Shot asks, "So dis you last trip right?" With the tone, *It better be, or you're in trouble!* A tone of, *If we see you around here again, you will be shot.* So much for a pleasant getaway vacation. I in fact, have a mammoth tusk in the boat. I have it hidden under a mosquito mesh. The two drunks are not seeing the tusk and are even stepping on it in their quest to find out what I have. They are drunk, armed, and in my space. If they see the tusk, I feel certain they will steal it.

I am always armed; my 357 pistol is stuck down my pants, under my shirt. Usually ready for bears, but ready for anything that comes up in the wilds. I move my hand and keep it on the handle of the pistol, ready to draw and shoot if this situation gets nasty. I'm even thinking of options and how this scene can play out. I decide if I do have to shoot them, I will dump them in the river, turn their boat loose, leave, and say nothing, see nothing, have no idea what might have happened. White man kills two Indians? It would not matter the reason, or circumstances, my life would be over.

"Let them rob you; let them kill you." That is how it is because my race stole their land, so I deserve whatever happens to me. They are armed. I study them and decide their reaction time is much slower than mine. Even at my age, I think I can draw and shoot faster than they can raise a rifle and pull the trigger. I'll shoot the drunkest one on the right first, jump to my left to make it harder for the drunk guy on the left to know where I am. *He will be confused, his reaction time will be slowed, seeing his friend shot.* I'm ready, studying the two. It is not a racial issue for me. Only for them.

"Deem what mun!" Spits on me and steps out of my boat back into his. His friend joins him. I am not going to escalate this situation by reacting to being spit on. It's not worth a life. I appropriately apologize for being white.

Future Flash

A year from this incident. One of these drunks is in the Kangas family. He and his father kill a police officer in the village of Tanana. The police officer has responded to a domestic violence call. A young, well respected cop, is dead.

News article says there is a group of Indians at war with the whites, wanting to kill all of us. I know I have stopped visiting this village to buy gas, spend my money, or visit my friends. These feelings have been building for years. More than once, I had been stopped in this village by Indians who were hostile to the extent I felt threatened. None of my white friends stop here either. The school, post office, white owners of the store, are all feeling the hate.

The village is going broke, and I wish them luck taking their land back. They can go back to the stone age and maybe be happy. I feel they have that right, as long as their hand is not out for free handouts and support. If there are Indians who do not want this, they need to keep the radicals in line and their village safe for other races. I sigh. If I had killed this man who stepped in my boat, insulted and treated me as an armed intruder, probably this cop's life would have been saved. However, we never know the future.

Even knowing it, what would the legal and ethical aspect of my act look like, and how would it have been treated? I do not understand civilization enough to make that call. I do not have the social standing with my status being among the unprotected. I may well have deliberately not pulled my gun, and let the two drunks shoot me, as being better than the alternatives.

Future flash ends

I pack to go home, puzzled about gas consumption. I seem to be burning more than the gauge tells me. It is hard to get an exact independent estimate, as none of my containers are full, because I can't lift full containers. The engine is acting up. Not serious, but seems to not want to idle, and stalls when running slow. Mostly annoying. Wondering if this could be related to fuel consumption. How can the engine burn what is not being recorded though? Is it dripping, leaking? I look all around and see no indications of a leak.

On the way home, I see a big boat stuck on a sandbar. I slow down, but my engine wants to quit. Another boat trying to help, so figure I cannot be of much use with an engine that will not idle. I'm having problems restarting it when it does quit. The stuck boat has two guys around it unloading fifty-five gallon barrels of fuel onto the sandbar to lighten the boat so they can try to push it off the sandbar. A lot of work ahead. They may have to dig a trench in the sand to get the boat to water. I believe it was their own fault. I know to get that high on a sandbar they were traveling way too fast. Like fifty miles an hour or better. I have never in my life been that high and dry on a sandbar. I feel a little guilty for not stopping, but again, not much I can do.

Soon after this, my engine quits. It takes me a few minutes to check out why. I am out of gas in my big tank. Something is wrong all right, as this tank should have gotten me almost home, and here I am 100 miles from home. I am tied up. Now I have to find the problem, or will not make it home. I have fuel in other tanks. I look for fuel in the bilges of the boat indicating a leaking hose or tank. No gas. I have been looking under the cowling of the engine for leaks, and see nothing. I no longer think the engine can be burning this much extra fuel, or it would not be running as smooth at high speed, but would foul out the plugs. I'm puzzled where the fuel is going.

I decide to rev up the engine in neutral position and go back and watch the engine hoses; the issue might be a high-speed carburetor jet, intake, or fuel pump issue. The high-speed fuel pump hose is spraying fuel when the engine hits high speed. I had at one time pulled this hose off to pour gas heet in the line to get rid of water. The filter had filled with water that went through into the engine. That had been a mess of a job. I do not have a hose clamp. I am able to use baling wire around the hose, and twist it for a clamp. I had not seen any fuel because under the hot cowling the liquid gas was vaporizing. This fixes the problem—but now, will I have fuel to get home? Manley Hot Springs is coming up where I can buy fuel. I calculate my fuel consumption.

I am within a gallon or two of making it home. Why take a chance? I cannot get up the Manley slough, so have to run six miles further around the river bend to the boat landing that is also six miles from the village. I meet Josh's brother at the landing, fishing with a crew of people. He will give me a ride in his truck to the store. Fifteen gallons of gas cost $89. I buy my Native friend food for dinner as payment for the truck trip, so almost $100 for fifteen gallons of gas. I will make it home and have extra. I want to go up the Kantishna River, maybe as far as my homestead to check on it. There may be moose there and also places to look for mammoth tusks. A night is spent at the old Burke cabin at the mouth of the Kantishna. I leave a note to add to the other notes of people who stop to use the cabin.

The weather is not great, so I go slow and reach the ivory cliff. Mud is still sliding into the river. This is a good sign. I see where someone else stopped, so am disappointed. I see the blue outline of what might have been a matched pair of mammoth tusks someone else found and retrieved, probably just a day ago. *Geez. If they had not stopped I would have seen the tusks.* Average find of this kind, $10,000. *Oh well.* I poke around and find some bones. I see the tip of some small bone and go to pull. It is a big bone, so I pull more! Out of the mud comes a big bison skull!

"All right!" This will pay for my trip. There is a broken shoulder blade, some leg bones, all from the same animal, I think. I am about to go, but some new mud has been sliding at a spot I looked at just over an hour ago. A tusk has been exposed! It is in two parts, and one part comes to me easily. The rest has to be dug out of the ice. I can hardly reach it, so the work of digging is hard.

There are mastodon flowers around me to cut out of the way. The flower biologists tell me does not exist. This fact empathizes how far out in the wilds I am. The sky is gray, cliff is gray and my boat is gray in this light. I'm in a black and white movie. There is a damp chill in the air that makes me shiver. I expose almost two feet of the tusk and tie a rope to it, come down the cliff, and tie that to my boat. I use the boat power to jerk and pull on the tusk.

This is dangerous in the strong river current. Each time I come to the end of the rope, the boat jerks in unpredictable directions. Sometimes sucking the edge of the boat gunnels to the waterline. The tusk finally comes loose! Not a full tusk, but part of a big diameter tusk. It later weighs out to sixty-five pounds. It felt heavier getting it in the boat covered in mud. Later I discover the other section was not off the same tusk, not even off the same animal! If I had known that, I would have looked closer in the mud at the bottom to see if two other tusks, or parts of these two were below in the mud, or still frozen in the cliff.

Uprooted trees float in the river current. The loose bow rope used to pull the tusk is still in the water and gets tangled in a tree root wad. Before it gets tangled and inseparable from the tree, I run to the bow and work the rope loose. The tree roles over and wants to wind the rope. I get it free before the tree can claim it. I have learned not to lament what I could have, would have, should have done to get a tusk, or anything else. Be happy with what is. I'm lucky I even decided to check the same spot twice. A place that an hour ago had nothing. Why look again? Here is proof that even an hour can make a difference. An hour before I showed up, an entire head could have slid in the river, or an hour after I pass. There is only a tiny, tiny fraction of what is here ever found by anyone.

The engine runs great, idles, and running good on gas-so well I stop to explore some creeks I have not been up in a long time. One creek is a disappointment. The entrance has split with an island, and neither entrance is deep enough to let me in. Maybe never. Logs are beginning to block this creek off. Eventually there could be a new mouth to the creek half a mile away. Another unnamed creek has not changed. There is a narrow entrance, hard to find, that opens up into a large body of water a few hundred feet up. I recalled this so take the time to work my way into the narrows. Geese, swans, fish, beaver, every kind of creature known in the interior lives untouched back in here. I do not need meat, so just enjoy the view and get some pictures. Good video cameras are not around yet, but I keep my eye on the prices and quality. It looks like no one traps or hunts up in here. *I could build a small cabin back in here if I want.*

I have been trying to work out a design for a portable shed I can build at home and bring out in a boat as a pop up easy to assemble in a short time. I have seen designs for some that can easily be setup for ice fishing, taken down and hauled home after the weekend of fishing. Why not such a shed as a portable camp? Something very small, maybe 4 x 8 with headroom, like a smallish tent. But bear proof, with windows, maybe bug proof, slightly insulated for a small stove. I could build it from two x two wood, keep the total cost under $300. I have to dream to set these up, all over-some in summer to visit in winter. I grin. I could get out of the weather; store stuff. I could take it down and leave if I am trespassing and it's a problem. I'm finding out this project is not so easy! If it folds, one side has to accommodate the thickness of the plywood, yet be able to be hinged. Locking the sides has not been figured out. Keeping the roof solid against snow is an issue. There are some pop up ideas.

I see a perfect place for camp at a fork in the creek-nice flat ground with dry grass. I decide to stay, look around, check the area out. There is a nice view of the sunset. I see fresh moose tracks, with a pond out of sight I could easily walk to and investigate quietly. I am not unhappy with just living on the boat. I tried and still use a dome tent on the deck, but also have a pull up called a Bimini-canvas on an aluminum framework that hinges in one place, so folds down and out of sight in the back. It pulls it up in a few seconds and I strap it in place with hooks. All my supplies are on the boat and I have walking room. Totes work as a bed. I have both a wood stove I built for heat, or small buddy-heater propane stove. There is a zipper front. It's not perfect-wind can come under and it is not totally bug proof. I have a mosquito net that drops down from the Bimini over the bed area so I can sleep in a bug free zone. I do not like mosquitoes and can burn pic when I am awake. There are flexible plastic windows. The beauty is it is always with me no matter where I stop.

I have been in a rain squall and stopped, pulled up this waterproof Bimini, got the heat going and read a book for an hour until the weather cleared. I'm warm, dry and rested. In my youth, I did not care. I just got wet and smiled. As I get older, life is not just about being tough. The boat gently rocks in the evening breeze coming up. Rice and duck is cooking on the can size woodstove. I have a book to read by kerosene lantern. I sit in my heated boat seat, but decide to move to sit on a mammoth leg bone closer to the lantern. The breeze keeps the mosquitoes knocked down. I am not in a rush, not on a time frame, not expected anyplace, no job to get back to, boss to explain an absence to. I eat when hungry, go to bed when tired, get up when I feel like it. I do not even have a time-piece with me. A mammoth tusk sticks outside the boat under the Bimini to make room for the tote needed for the bed. In the dark, I turn the kerosene lantern way down to go to sleep. The small flame offers some heat, and if I wake up in the dark, this is a night light.

Twice in the past I have heard bears pacing the water's edge, unwilling to step on the boat. I think the small lantern flame is strange enough to give them pause. The smell is offensive and fire is never a good thing to wild creatures. I have had bears step on the boat, but never when I was aboard. This is grizzly country, so it is good to be aware of my surroundings.

I awake in the morning to a beautiful sunrise through the willow trees. It takes a moment to recall where I am. I can lie in bed and lean over and get a new fire going on my woodstove. Water is heated and tea made before I ever get up. I have seventy-five miles to get to the nearest road, at the village of Nenana where I am headed.

I get home to the usual business emails to tend to. Iris has stalled some people and asks how to reply to some others. She makes out some receipts for me as I get orders ready.

"Miles, what about this customer, Ra, who wants a wolf claw, but then says he decided it should be plastic! Which one did he settle on real, or plastic!" I cannot recall. I look over the emails.

"Plastic!" I pause and want to make it simple for Iris to fill out. "Just leave the receipt as wolf claw! The guy will know what he got, it's just a receipt!" *I hate paperwork.* Someone else wants an eagle feather, but sounds like it is for a child or young city person. Rather than discuss the law with a child, I decide to send a large legal turkey feather.

"Miles, is that ethical!" Iris asks what others have asked me in astonishment. I feel annoyed and defensive. I'm in business. I have to make a judgment call. It's not always fun or easy.

"Look at the price. Any reasonable person would be expected to know a real eagle feather is going to cost a lot more." I get tired of playing lawyer for all these idiot customers. I put it another way, as I have many times before. "If you get a ring out of a bubble gum machine for a quarter and the paper tag on it says, 'Diamond ring', would you expect it to be a real diamond, and if you did, do you think you'd get far in court suing the gum company for false advertising?" I go on, "Decisions get more complicated than that, I can assure you! I often substitute large coyote claws for wolf claws when shipping overseas. I'm not certain of the legality of shipping wolf. I read I need a $25 permit for each shipment, even one claw! Who would want that added on to their five-dollar order?" I explain to Iris I have gone more than once to Fish and Game, and Fish and Wildlife, and asked about such a permit. No one has ever been issued such a permit in the history of the state.

"I have never even seen such a permit." I was told once, "One claw? Just send it and do not worry about it." Some agency at the other end might care. The worse thing is, the claw gets confiscated. I do not trust what I am told. So if I can get away with it, I ship large coyote claws to those who would not know the difference, or maybe not even care. To legally protect us both. "Only a lab could tell the difference! It keeps me legal, Iris. I put 'wolf claw' on the receipt. Who cares what I call it, so long as it tests as non-wolf in the lab!"

Iris is dubious about these methods, but she has not had to run a business and make money for over thirty years. I wish people knew the difference and cared! To a majority of people, any large dark feather is eagle. Any claw is a wolf.

Anyhow, I do not want to talk about it! Humph! "Tell em to go shop someplace else if they do not like it! I have not received even one complaint on the subject in 10,000 transactions!" *So there!* She implies I have learned too much from my friend Crafty. No, I would not send a turkey feather to a native American who needed something special for a ceremony. He needs the real thing, understood. But an eight-year-old who only has two dollars to spend gets a genuine turkey feather.

"There is no way to get a real eagle feather to anyone, Miles, I know that much!"

"Maybe, but there are a lot of Indians out there with eagle feathers. It's possible without a lot of publicity, to quietly gift something special."

"And you are the man who can make it happen?"

I shrug my shoulders. "Some see me as a Shaman, and I act as a middleman in gift exchanges. It's part of a spiritual belief we share. Nothing I want to talk about." Iris has never had a vision quest. Would not understand a Sun Dance. Few do, so it's better not to talk about 'everything.' Isn't religion one of those subjects that is personal?? *Maybe in time. In time, two people who want to get along can blend ideas together, and eventually share a common hybrid view We do not have to argue, or draw a line in the sand, do we?*

We had just been to Denali park and walked through the gift shops. 'Alaska Rocks,' is a shop with about zero rocks from Alaska. I know the dealers they buy from in Tucson. I recognize the material from Brazil. We eat in a pizza place with full moose antler chandeliers. How did they get those antlers that are not legal to sell intact? Who is asking? It's the famous Princess tour line.

Iris wonders about the legality of someone like myself, choosing some moral stand that suits me to live by. I repeat what I often say. "I ask myself what my peers would have to say if I had to explain myself in court." Not the average civilized citizen. They are not my peers. Peers are your equals, from your own station in life, who have similar occupations, social standing, spiritual beliefs. Savages like me-the bottom line being, 'one of us.' From my planet. I envision having to explain myself to my community, for example. I care. I talk and ask, "What would you do? What do you do?" (In these situations). Asked of people who face these situations. Iris is more street wise than I am and is dubious. Most people are letter of the law types. I am more 'situation ethics' oriented.

I remind Iris, "One of those reality TV shows did a background check on me when considering hiring me. They told me I have the cleanest record of anyone they have ever investigated. Doesn't that speak for itself?"

"You have a habit of remembering what you want to remember, Miles. I hear things maybe you do not. Some people do not think much of you, Miles!" There are people I do not think much of, so what?

THE PERMANENT OIL dividend checks come in, and as expected, Alaska Airlines offers flying specials to encourage us to spend our money with them. The checks buy our tickets to Tucson every year, with some left over. Even though the trip is months away, buying now costs about a third of what it would cost trying to get tickets a week away. It is already time to think of what might sell at the show and getting materials ready. I have opals in the rough I can cut, shape, and run through the tumbler, along with some other favorite stones that sell well.

Larimar, picture jasper, jade, and local Nowitna River Agate. *Slices of mammoth teeth are selling well lately.* My books need to get sent ahead. Now that I have my passport, a Mexico trip for teeth work, and have my eyes looked at. The VA does not cover this. Iris needs serious eye work done. She has cataracts and is losing her sight. She has no insurance. We can afford to pay without financial help in Mexico. Iris will have Medicare when she is 65 in a couple of years. *A lot about getting older has to do with health care! Geez! "You know you are getting old when..."* We both laugh. We are both concerned with the new 'Obama Care' that Iris was told will cost her $700 a month. Automatically taken from her retirement.

***'

Fossils need slow drying and care. Throughout the late fall, early winter, I wrap and unwrap, then turn the fossils so they begin to dry. The first stages are most critical. I have a prehistoric bison skull four feet across. Several mammoth teeth I wish I could slice, but need to slow dry correctly, so better wait. I make plans to keep certain valuables off the property so they do not get 'stolen' by Fish and Wildlife.

"Confiscated, Miles, don't you mean confiscated?" 'Confiscated' means you might get it back, something is going to happen, like a trial, or a fine, or an arrest. There is a record of what is missing. 'Stolen' is when it is gone, and will never be seen again. With no charges or explanation, and no record. My lawyer suggested I forget it, "Let it be, this is how life is, accept it. Bend over. Take it like a man. That is the lot of the poor."

It appears I am doing that well. My attitude is, "Hey! Where is my stuff! Tell me why you have it or give it back!" Forcing Fish and Wildlife's hand. *They are not likely to admit they were wrong.* It's not wise to punch a big, powerful bully in the nose.

I'm all geared up for the annual Tucson trip to see my mother and do the big show. Tickets have been acquired, show fees paid, goods to sell boxed and shipped to both my mother and one of our friends we are getting to know and trust better, who has been helping out. Foil lives near enough to Tucson to commute and does much of his shopping here. I like Andrea who has helped longer than Foil, and sleeps in the tent, but he lives in another state so cannot help us during the rest of the year.

"Miles, I have a spare trailer and can easily pick up supplies you send and can store them there!" Foil has been picking us up at the airport and checking up on Mom, offering her a chance to get out and grocery shop and other such kind favors.

"Sure Iris, I give him really good deals, even give him materials he wants, but it's still nice he does this for us! There are $500 worth of boxes sent, what is that, thirty-five flat rate boxes? More than Mom can deal with at eighty-five years old!"

I catch the headlines in the news.

News Miner. Hundreds of plants, animals up for protection. The Obama administration is taking steps to extend new Federal protections to a list of imperiled animals and plants that reads like a manifest for Noah's Ark." "Decisions about 60 more species covered under the settlements are expected today, the Fish and Wildlife Service says." Seeking $25 million for the listing program." "Cost to the economy $125 million for the Whooping Crane and $58,000 for the false Astor, a flower."

In the news on the radio not long after, is the state's suggestion, "The Feds want to encourage all marine mammals in Alaska being on the endangered species list so that the Feds gain control over the oil rich arctic. This is a hidden agenda not made public." This thought fits in with my issues maybe, as the Feds' search warrant was for marine mammal parts.

I was told, "Possessing parts of marine mammals for art is hurting the species." Such a blanket statement sounds reasonable. I and people like me are selfish and deluded, thinking what we do is not harmful. I'd argue, all the animal parts I have acquired were from subsistence taken game, not trophy, not poached, not killed to supply the ivory market, or killed just to supply the craft industry. I'm dealing with the surplus waste of game taken for food, self-defense, or natural caused deaths. My business got started as part of a strong subsistence belief of not being wasteful.

Sure, I look for a money angle in everything I do because the bills have to get paid and there are few ways to make a living in the wilds. This is my niche place in the scheme of things. The animal parts garbage man. Mostly dealing with materials from the dump. The only exception I know of is Jessie, and I disconnected on my own. Getting the public in an uproar over the craft industry could be a move to change the focus of blame. If this is being done covertly, unethically, even illegally, to get the desired results of a hidden agenda, as the state implies. This is worth remembering.

Hi there Miles,

I shot (legally) a mountain lion last year and would like to have one of the claws turned into a necklace for my brother (he was there) as it was his first lion experience. The local jewelers only do something fairly extravagant, which is $300 + for a silver bit/design that they say is way better than the cap (which I read about on your website, and they said pretty much the same thing). Is there an 'in-between' or how much do you charge to make it into a necklace/pendent?

Thanks in advance, **Louise Batt**

Hello Louise

I can cast a cap in bronze or copper. The cast cap will fit just that claw and be plain, maybe can write brother's name on it when in wax, a date, something simple, maybe stamp the wax with a basic design before casting it. Will have a loop on top for the chain and be sturdy. Looking at **$30 plus** whatever shipping is for the claw to me and back to you guessing $4 times 2 ways so total **$8 shipping.**

THIS IS a similar deal with bear claws that got confiscated by the Feds. *Didn't I learn anything!* What is there to learn? I have not been told what crime I may have committed. I have what I feel is a legal answer for everything. *Almost everything.* Yes, well, ' everything' in the same terms as the average person might feel about an IRS audit. There could be a few minor disagreements we can come to an understanding about. Minor compared to the Feds confiscating $20,000 worth of my goods in what I now consider a shake down at gunpoint. I learned I can't trust my government. Or I am confused. How far and under what conditions does this mistrust go? I trust my local government.

I'm friends with the mayor, know everyone on the city council. They are not monsters. They got elected as 'one of us.' So where does the 'one of us' concept disappear? I sort of trust my state level government. We began a relation of distrust. I talked to them and they visually appear to be human. It turns out they understand reason. Like a human might. They eat food like I do, and do not plug themselves in at night to an energy source for recharging, taking off their human zoot suit. They appear to have been born of a woman who is their mother, and they appear to have children like real humans do. It turns out we are closely enough related we can understand each other. It's the Federal level my trust disappears. At what point did humans get replaced with monsters?

I see no harm in helping this guy and his brother, turning these claws into memorable necklaces. The cat is already dead and was not killed to get the claws. If it was right to have killed the cat in the first place, is a different issue. There are people who do not believe in killing such majestic life. I would suggest such people not kill one! I would not kill one unless it attacked me. I do not trophy hunt. I am not in the area this guy lives. I am not in a position to judge if there is a surplus of game to be harvested. I assume the checks and balances of the laws are at play. If that is not working, that's not what I am going to focus on. Partly, this is part of the world I live in, understand. Hunters, trappers, those close to the land, often middle class to poor. I have more issues with people who seem to have no idea where food comes from, what animals are, how nature 'is.'

My son came to visit and would not eat anything out of the garden. "It might have a bug in it, Dad!" Explaining, "It has no seal of approval from anyone. It is not out of a can, a box, or plastic wrapped, therefore it is suspect. I might get sick." So who will my family be? My tribe? It is my customers.

Those who come to me at my website say, "I like what I see, I agree with how you live." I never give thought to how many might see my website and be horrified, angry, or simply disagree and go someplace else. I focus on the several hundred thousand who visited my site, looked around, and contacted me according to my web visit stats. I focus on the million people who make it to the biggest fossil show on earth, in Tucson. I focus on any show I do anyplace, and the fact you give me a crowd of ordinary citizens, and I sell. It would not occur to me to focus on a billion people who hate my guts. Let them hang with their own people at Greenpeace, PETA rallies, Friends of the Animals and what not.

I remind Iris: "I met a gal once in the Audubon Society and assumed we would get along great! I love Audubon!" I repeat this story often. That's what the elderly do. "What an artist! What a lifestyle he lived!" He ate game he killed around camp-fires with trappers. He did more killing than I care for. Propped up dead things, drew them, and walked away. You know he said once, he did not consider it a good day unless he killed at least a hundred birds! I explain that is a lot of dead birds!

Wow! "So anyone who joins a group in his honor I should get along with, right?" Even more! The lady is a top artist in the nation. She did a Federal duck stamp! That's what stamp hunters get when they pay the fee for the right to kill ducks! "But I find out she is not a hunter at all! The Audubon Society is an animal rights group! Talk about being out of touch with reality!"

Iris has no comment. Do I have a meaningful point? What may matter is, it is me who is out of sync with the rest of the world. I get out of all this, it is possible my son represents mainstream America. If food stops arriving in cans and wrapped up with a sticker on it, would mainstream America starve to death? *No! People are adaptable! Still, it's a steep learning curve, with this issue being only the tip of an iceberg.*

So even though I am not a trophy hunter, I understand the concept enough to feel closer than I would to a bunny kisser. These guys at least wear boots that touches dirt. These guys duck under branches of real trees. These guys hear robins, see blue skies, breathe real air God created. I tell Iris that I asked a bunny snuggler once, "If you were driving along and there was a person and a dog in the road, and you had to make a quick decision and hit one of them, which would it be?"

The woman says without hesitation she'd run over the man. Her reasoning being, "The man knows better. The dog is innocent."

Reminds me of an incident I tell Iris about. "I was with a woman once, headed for the Palmer Fair to check it out." I go on about how this lady slams her breaks on! The car behind almost rear ends us. This is the middle of a highway on a straight stretch, where this behavior is unexpected from other drivers. The car behind us runs off the road to miss us. I ask her what that was all about. "There was a bird in the road." She did not want to hit it. If the car behind us hit a tree and everyone in it died, I am not sure she'd be sorry, or do anything different next time. These are my limited experiences with bunny cuddlers.

"I do somewhat agree with these people. There are too many people in the world, and something ought to be done about it." I am even secretly pleased when others raise their hand to be counted among the ones to step aside and make room for the rest of us. Very noble of them. Those who commit suicide decide to take the road of the drug addict and remove themselves from the competition of the workforce.

But to me it should be a person's choice, not me deciding who to eliminate in order to save the bunnies, the birds, the bees, or all of nature and the planet, including mankind. I agree it all needs saving, all right. I agree if man was not around, the planet would be safer, happier, more healthy, and better off. I even agree that one day our time in the sun will be over, and some other species will have its time in the sun. As was so in the past. History will repeat itself. With any luck, the earth can heal. But meanwhile, back at the ranch. There is a certain reality to deal with. I am here, and plan to make the best of it. Meanwhile, $30 and eight dollars shipping. Will that be paper or plastic?

I chuckle to Iris, "Some of my customers want the real thing and not a plastic replica, yet want to pay me with plastic! Go figure." What's good for the goose should be good for the gander. You want the real thing? Pay me with the real thing, gold! Ha!

Iris agrees, "It's a plastic world."

"Yea and the plastic industry is one of the most polluting nasty poisonous industries in the world!"

Iris agrees adding, "Conservationists heat their homes with oil, saying wood is wrong because it pollutes our precious air."

"I can see how such a thought would be to the advantage of, and be promoted by, the oil industry. What bothers me is that the public buys into it." I pause because that is not the real issue. Let the public be duped; no skin off my nose. But it does become skin off my nose. I burn wood. I eat living things off the land. I sell the leftover for craft material, as our ancestors did and Native Americans say they do, and the white man tells the savage how noble this is.

The public wants to lynch me. I wonder if these people represent the majority or not. I know I am not hearing very many people saying what was done is wrong! Josh says, "Yes, well, you have to realize, Miles, most people are afraid of their government and will not speak up." Is this true?

"Miles, how come you hate permits so much. You should be paying along with everyone else. That's what I hear people saying. What gives you the right to have it all for free and not contribute your fair share?" Josh is just being an instigator. He hates the government with a passion. Anyone who can slow the government up and make problems for the government more power to them, as far as he is concerned.

But I answer his question. "I believe in paying my share, Josh. Proof of that is, I donate more to my community than I pay in taxes. I donated art to the school kids for fund raising, the library got a prize I donated, the Ice classic, and it amounts to hundreds of dollars they raised from art I donated."

In the lifestyle Josh and I live, we believe in trading, bartering, and this is the lifestyle of our entire community. There used to be people who mowed the city grass instead of paying taxes. Those who contribute fish, services, goods of different kinds. The fuel company paid the city by donating fuel for city equipment. Permits are not often about covering costs. It's about extortion, control, power.

"Josh, we rebelled against England because of taxation without representation, permits, fees for everything. We threw tea in the harbor in rebellion, went to war, formed our own country to get away from 'all that.' Now, are we right back where we started?" Josh does not answer because he has said the same thing to me many times. But no use getting wound up! The road to happiness is not going to be a road of protest and anger.

"How are the dogs, Josh?" He brightens up at the mention of his sled dogs.

"Miles, I have two really good leaders coming up! All I need is a few more team dogs! Puppies look like maybe next year they will be ready!" It's nice to see Josh smile. It is not long before he brings up a bunny petting story. I interrupt before he gets all wound up, or gets me upset.

"I have been going to WIN meetings for a while now, Josh, and there are a couple of bunny sniffers in the group. They seem almost human. Like it would be possible to work with them." *Only maybe.* Josh does not believe it.

"Hey, Miles, you and Iris going to make it over for Thanksgiving?" I have been going over to Josh's for Thanksgiving for thirty-five or more years now.

"Sure, thanks for inviting us. Should we bring anything?"

"Maybe that good bread Iris makes!"

"We'll be there!"

TRAPPING season begins and I do not go out, and am not even interested. Those days are truly over for me now. I am anxious to get out and cut firewood across the river, though. It's the same routine that has gone on a lot of years. I enjoy this as a ritual. Gets me out, seeing the sunrise, the animal tracks, birds, breathing fresh air and doing something to stay fit. There is that reward of doing something that is important, providing my house heat. I still like to get ahead in wood by a month and no more. I like to get out at least once a week and cut just a sled load at a time. The winter routine involves getting into the shop early each day at 5:00 am and creating art, knives, preparing raw materials so they can be sold. Before long, it is time to get to the Tucson show! I feel lucky I was able to get my passport back! *Too bad it cost hundreds of dollars and a lawyer. In my old remote life, that would have been a year's wages!*

I get a message from my friend, the fossil dealer, Tusk, asking me to stop in; he has fossils to show me. I'm curious what he has. The Native fossil hunters often bring in their summer finds late in the season, sometimes after the freeze when they can snow machine or dog sled into their village. These fossils can be from a world with no roads, off the grid. Many of us in the business, buy, sell, trade items of interest. I stop in to see Tusk when I get to Fairbanks for groceries.

The subject of my search warrant and confiscation comes up. Tusk is surprised I have heard nothing, not been arrested or received my things back.

"Miles, be careful, those guys are not nice people." I know Tusk has had his dealing with the same department. We both know what happened to Sidmore. "But at least you seem to be recovering and getting your motivation back." I wonder what he means; Tusk goes on, "They want to break you down, make you feel like dirt, get you to give up on everything, even living." I kind of know what he means. I fight that feeling and did not know it was universal. "Miles, these guys are professionals. Professionals at interrogation, even a form of torture." I know what he means. They can threaten us with all kinds of things. It is hard to separate rumor from fact. What is possible from what is impossible. What is likely, from what is actually happening. Tusk feels ordinary people break.

I think I know what he means and reply: "I had to drop off something to a friend. I could not reach him on the phone. He will not answer his phone until you get on the answer machine and he recognizes your voice. Even then, he is not sure, and might ask a security question." His door is barricaded, his windows are taped with blankets so no one can look in. I dropped a Christmas present at his house, and I consider he may not know who it is from, and decide it is poison left by who knows who, or a bomb. Or has a hidden microphone. Was he always a nut case? How did he get this way? Why do I meet so many with these symptoms?

I explain that some of what my friend says has a grain of truth. Yet at some point he gets unbelievable. Like people who say they met an alien, or were abducted, or had a run in with Big Foot, or according to the Mayan calendar the world ends today, stuff like that. Warning us to be prepared. Stuff you better not go around repeating to people if you do not want to be locked up. But here is Tusk bringing this kind of stuff up!

"Miles, they had me convinced my car is bugged, I am being followed by satellite, and there is no place I am not alone."

"Yeah, Tusk, they did the same to me. Swore they had evidence from a satellite of me out in the wilderness. Photos they would use in court if I did not confess. Very compelling and convincing. Yes, quite good at the job, call it brain washing of sorts." Tusk only nods he understands.

I add, "They had me wanting to confess to all kinds of things, just to get rid of them. Hours of interrogation. I understood they could, with a flick of a finger, cut off my bank account, my credit card, intercept all my mail, my computer, and take away my life. Without an effort."

"Yes, it is easy to talk about not cooperating, telling them your rights, but you are right, there is nowhere to run, no way to get away. If they shut off your bank account, how long will you survive? Where? How?" I want to change the subject! *Maybe we are being recorded. I'm not going to say the words, 'stashed cash.'* The Feds would be running all over my yard with metal detectors looking for buried coffee cans.

"This is a nice pile of fossils, Tusk! What's the deal on it?" He knows I am getting ready to go to Tucson to the fossil show and wants me to sell some things for him. No, wants me to buy stuff he feels I can sell. I trade him my four-foot bison skull plate, with the horns on it. "Tusk, this is something worth money all right, but hard to ship to Tucson. Not the sort of thing you put in an ordinary box! Ha!" Tusk has some items worth as much, but much more compact. A black fossil whale's tooth is of particular interest. Neither of us understands how this whale looking tooth got into the interior of Alaska.

He says, "Well, there was a time all of Alaska was under the ocean!" We both agree that was a time before the ice age, when the mammoths were here, so we are seeing different layers of time, maybe a million years apart.

"Where did it come from, Tusk?"

He will not give exact specifics since we are in competition, but says, "The interior–up by Kobuk." I do not know that area well, but within 200 miles, dinosaur parts are being found. There is no paperwork exchanged between us. Tusk agrees we meet people in situations where no one has a pencil or paper, much less a receipt book, or a permit of any kind. Tusk was on a job working with National Geographic. This was a little side trip.

"Sweet, Tusk!" He laughs.

Tusk is nervous doing any business with me, as I am nervous working with him. Either one of us could be working undercover for the Feds, recording, taking secret pictures. Trying to trip the other up on a technical detail. Even though we have known each other over twenty years, no one can be totally trusted. We both know there is no one the Feds cannot break. I was told if I cooperated, they'd go easy on me. If I named my sources and gave details, I might have things easy.

"Think about it," they had said. What they meant was, consider giving up your friends like Tusk.

Before I go, I say to Tusk, "Tusk if I ever communicate with you, cough, and tell you the dust has been bothering me, that means I'm wired and ordered to set you up. I'd appreciate you doing the same for me." Naturally, if what I just said was recorded, it would not look good.

1958. My family went camping a lot in summer. This may have begun my interest in the great outdoors. It was one of the few times I saw my parents happy.

CHAPTER NINE

FEDERAL TAKEOVER, JOHN LENNON, OTHER CASES

New Miner Jan 18th 2012 'Man Accused of Meat for Heat Hires Lawyer'. Troopers issue a news release. "Buying, selling, or bartering game meat except snow shoe hares is illegal"

Update Jan 19th: Fish and Wildlife changed its mind and dropped charges. Apparently about 150,000 commented to the news article from across the country in support of this guy.

What also came out, is the board of Game just proposed the removal of 'barter' from subsistence uses of game. Interesting in that this was done without the public's knowledge, input, or comments. If this had passed, we would be responsible for knowing the change we were never told about or asked about. Due to this case, the board changed its mind. Otherwise there would have been a change no one would have ever heard about till someone was arrested. Since I have the paper in my hand I scan through it.

"Game Board delays considering more bear snaring," The board has decided there are too many bears. The solution proposed is to snare them as a way to cut the bear population down. This is supposed to help the moose population. However, the argument goes, that snares kill all bears, protected grizzly, mothers, cubs. An argument I am not hearing is how come they do not let hunters harvest more bears. Within a few hours of death in a snare, bear meat spoils if not gutted when out in the sun. Nothing is salvageable, neither hide nor meat. This is especially true if the animal dies while overheated and does not bleed right after death. So how is it Fish and Game can engage in wanton waste while the public cannot? *More to the point, why is anyone considering such waste?*

I come back to the first article about trading meat for firewood. Josh is Native, and has a lot to say on this when we meet, and the subject comes up. "Miles, subsistence is important to all of us in the village. It is common for people living alone to be unable to eat a 1,500 pound moose within a reasonable time. It is common for such a person to be poor! It is common for such a person to trade some of it to someone else who has no meat, but maybe a surplus of firewood to trade! What is wrong with that?" Subsistence is about feast and famine. Part of the lifestyle is, we often have an abundance of something, followed by none at all! Part of our survival is to trade with others who were lucky in other areas of necessity. If you live in a nice forest and there was a fire, there can be a surplus of standing dead firewood for a few years.

Others got lucky and caught thousands of salmon on a good fish run. Someone else got a big moose, but does not have access to a river and salmon. Survival is partnering up and redistributing the surplus of wealth the land offers, so we can all survive. In a subsistence lifestyle, we look out for our parents, grandparents, and all elders in our tribe, and community. It is common for me to visit senior housing and bring wild game to the elders who were raised on it and miss it. Many on fixed social security cannot afford good food. Many are diabetic, and processed foods are not good for them. The old folks' home is not going to provide salmon meals!

"Josh, Edmond loved rabbit! I bring him a lot of my snared rabbit when rabbit is on a high cycle and abundant." I have no answer for Josh concerning the government's attitude. It might simply be lack of understanding of a lifestyle. Not caring, or might be part of a deliberate plan of some kind. My opinion is that subsistence people are such a minority, we are not worth considering. We have no lobbyist to speak up for us. I head home and check my emails.

Dear Miles, My husband finished reading your first book this week and enjoyed it very much. I gave it to him as an early Christmas present. He works in an automotive stamping plant, but I think he would have been a mountain man if he had been born 150 years earlier. While he was reading it, I would ask him about your adventures and what your belief in God is. He handed me your book and told me to read page 200, so I did. Since we don't have books two or three yet, I don't know if you write any more about your faith, but it struck me that maybe you hadn't heard much about Jesus, so just in case, I would like to tell you about him...

THE LETTER GOES on a while about Jesus. I reply kindly, thanking them for getting my book, and glad they enjoy it. Discussing religion with strangers is not a great idea, so I simply smile and appreciate the concern for my salvation. While saving the email, I look around at stored communications. I had a recent conversation with the owner of the café where I hang out.

Rain, the owner, tells me about her past fish case in court. She and her husband went to court over fishing on the Kantishna River. They homesteaded at the same time I did, neighbors only 50 miles further upriver. They argued for subsistence fishing and went all the way to the supreme court and won. However, it took four years. In the meantime, they were forced out of a lifestyle, and came to town, got the restaurant. Won too late to be of any help to them or me. Years later, the biologist who spoke against them at the trial came to the restaurant and apologized. Said he needed his job, had two kids in school and could not afford to lose his job, so had to support the state against her. Even though he knew she was right. She seems bitter about it.

"No one joined us in our fight, Miles!" *At the time I never heard about their case. No one asked me if I'd support such a case.It is too bad they handled it alone. Together it might have been easier.*

In the news, Jim Wilde lost his case. Spent $40,000 and lost.

Related headlines on such issues are more common than the past, such as today, "Resist the Federal Takeover" by Mike Kramer. Summed up, the article is about how Alaska, when we became a state wanted to preserve state rights, the rights of the individual, and the fact we are a last frontier, and wanted local control not far off. Control from Washington was designed to be limited, with state protection included in our constitution. "Then we found oil. In 1980, Congress approved Alaska National Interest Lands Conservation Act" that put millions of acres under Federal control.

Tony Knowles promised to appeal a Federal court decision to grant Federal government the right to manage rivers as a way to discriminate among Alaskans for fishing rights. This was not done. "It will take state intervention in these challenges to make a difference, yet the state has so far resisted supporting either lawsuit. Our economic dependence on Federal funds has fostered a culture of conciliation and deference to Federal claims of authority. Those of us who value individual and state rights need to demand that our state government get off its hands and vigorously defend what few rights we still cling to."

I GET AN EMAIL.

You don't know sh+*&t about me. I have no need to justify or defend any of my viewpoints, but your pompous "I-live-in-Alaska-so-I'm-superior-to-you" bullshit is obnoxious and unwarranted. I know more about the real nature of wolves than you will ever hope to know. Murder does not bring you closer to nature, just separates you further from it.

"Come up to Alaska and kill it yourself or I'll kill it for you?"

I smile at that part. This is a quote off my website I'm guessing. I forget.

Yeah...you REALLY must respect animals. Salvaging their claws for profit. Bullshit. I've heard it all before. I pray you are able to purify your murderous karmic stains before you find yourself in a future life being hunted for your claws and pelt. Ignorant actions will produce ignorant results. And NO, I don't hate anybody. But I despise your actions and the way you make your living, with your bullshit online enterprise of selling bodies for money. Our strength is defined by how we treat those weaker than us. An innocent animal is the perfect example of that. You are clearly a very cowardly person. Have a good life, a+_s hole. F*&CK YOU.

KILLING WOLVES, BY FAR THE MOST MAJESTIC CREATURES ON THE FACE OF THE EARTH, TO STEAL THEIR CLAWS AND TEETH FOR PROFIT. YOU DISGUST ME. TO DO THAT TO ANY ANIMAL IS BAD ENOUGH, BUT WOLVES?! DO YOU HAVE NO MORAL COMPASS WHATSOEVER? BURN IN HELL, YOU PIECE OF SH*&T.

I'm curious why this person was even on my website reading about things that are obviously so upsetting for him. He sounds violent and dangerous. I hope I never meet him. I have just added a new concept to the raw materials part of my website. I have a lot of customers not understanding the difference between 'finished' and 'raw' materials, nor understanding prices. So I ask what level you would like to come in on?

I begin with big headlines *"Free raw materials!"* Mentioning the wolf claws as an example. Free! All you need is a ticket to Alaska, a $10,000 snow machine, a $400 rifle, warm cloths, knowing where to go, (etc.) and you can have free claws off a wolf! Or… you can have me take care of all that. For $10, I can offer a bloody frozen foot. If you can accept a smelly package in the mail and know how to boil and clean it. Or, I can cut the claws off and boil clean for you for $10 a claw. I can drill a hole, put in a screw eye, grade, sort, dry, put a chain on it, put it in a box, label it, for $25.

"So what level would you like to come in on?" Spelled out from zero to $25. Written for those who want cheaper and even less. There is no way around the fact, the shiny pretty finished claw started out on a live wolf, and someone saw the claw through the process described, either me or you. A raw bloody foot offered, or a finished claw necklace, represents the same wolf, in the same way. If you are squeamish or lack the skill, let me put the worm on the hook for you, so you may go fishing.

Same with wood. I'll sell you the whole 2,000 pound tree for $20, the same price as a few ounces of stabilized dyed knife scale sets. All you need to do is meet me at my homestead when I am home. How you arrive is up to you. I will point out a nice tree. "Have at it!" "If you would you like me to haul the tree to town, cut it up, dry it, there will be fees." So again, "What level would you like to come in on?" I see no reason to yell and scream about the subject. You do not and will not heat with wood and are not interested in claws off wolves? Great, Next!

Dear Miles, it was an absolute pleasure speaking with you yesterday afternoon. You are obviously a man with immeasurable knowledge, talent and individualism with a real down-to-earth attitude. I truly admire these traits in a person. I appreciate your time, patience, and sincerity more than you know, after wasting my time calling and talking with people in the business who couldn't find their a=-s with two hands!

I think you could be a f-cking genius. I have heard of people like you. They do not want the world to know how talented they are. They keep a very low key, low profile image. Just enough exposure to **make a living...**

JOHN LENNON HAS BEEN a hero most of my life, someone I admire, and look up to, and am inspired by. There was a special about his life on TV last night, so I learned things about him I never knew. I only knew him during the Beatles days. In the early 70s when other things were going on with John, I was in the wilds, out of communication.

I was struck by an interview in which he says everyone thought he was paranoid. His phone was tapped, the phones of his friends were tapped, he and his friends were followed. He was secretly photographed, the subject of investigations, and threatened. There was a major government effort to have him deported from the US. The reason? He was protesting against war. People listened to him. He had the ability to affect millions of people. Also of note, John always 'detuned' his D string, on purpose, saying, "So you know it's me playing,"

So very much like me, leaving an imperfection in my art on purpose, so you know it is me. I did not know till now, John and I had this in common. I do not care for perfection. The world is not perfect. It is the flaws that give character, meaning and personality. That is the difference between art and science. Art has no instructions. With an out of tune D, John was among the best in the world at what he did. Imagine. I have a better understanding after reading this, what the New York Times photographer meant after staying with me a week taking pictures: "You guys," clarifying, "People like you and John Lennon." Adding, "One of the best in the world at what you do."

But what is it we do? I record a phone conversation in my records.

"Miles, I got the second shipment ok. It was labeled fossils. I also got a notice on what happened with the first package. It was confiscated at the border as illegal. I was told the wolf claws were not legal to send."

I asked, "What about the other items?"

"The whole shipment is held up. I was told I can fight it, but there is no phone number, only an address, and I have fifteen days—or after that, the whole shipment gets destroyed. It took them over a month to send out the notice. Yes. Well, I guess we have to write the shipment off then. I had been told in the past it takes about $30,000 to fight a government agency. This would be international, so even more money. Glad at least to know I was not being ripped off by you, that you did send the shipment out."

"Miles, what was that moose meat all about, geez, we had to toss it out! There was a hair in it!" Oh yes. I forgot. The school teacher. I had given him 25 pounds because he said he wanted it. "I assumed you'd at least clean it, Miles! Dang, what if I got sick?"

I do not reply. Am vague about what might have happened that went so wrong. Many people who are used to food from the store judge it by how it looks. What they cannot see does not concern them. There is a minimum quality standard met with store products. If there ever was a hair, it gets absorbed in the process, bleached, ground, disintegrated with chemicals etc. It's cut well, wrapped and packaged 'pretty.' There will be no loose ends, no strands of fat clinging to it, no blood left. At one time in the process when it was fresh, it looked much like my gift. Few among the civilized know or see that, or would accept that. So while they tell me, "Oh, I want fresh wild game!" They may visualize all the good things about store meat, but with all the good wild game add ons. Just like packaged in the store, only no steroids, red dye, or enhancers! Wow.

I handle my meat closer to civilized, compared to many Natives I know, have dined with or received gifts from. I have been served meat with the hide and hair still on it. The custom is to eat the meat off the hide and leave it and the hair on your plate. I have been served small game with the guts still in it, cooked. You set that aside on your plate. I visited a Native guy who was having a garage sale, who shows me moose in his freezer. The quarters stuck in the freezer, uncut, unwrapped, with hair frozen all over it. But dang, it's 900 pounds. A lot to deal with. I miss a hair here and there. *Beggars can't be choosers.*

I HAVE ALL my Christmas cards done up before Christmas. Mostly for friends, people I have kept in touch with, gosh, some for thirty years or more. People who want to wish me well and want to know what I have been up to. I am still used to sending out sixty to eighty hand painted cards every year. Been doing that since I was ten years old. I get them done and realized I have no one's address. Both my address book and my back up address book were confiscated in the Federal Wildlife raid. I'm discouraged. I assume I'll get over it. Because I am stronger than the average bear. I thought that, as friends write me, I'd copy their address in a new book, and update them. Life would go on. As time goes by, I do not get to it. Mostly I do not know what to say.

"Sorry I have not written; my address book was confiscated." I agree with myself, that sounds lame, or the beginning of a long discussion I do not what to have at Christmas time. *What are we going to do with all these cards?* They get bundled up in batches of half a dozen and priced to sell as handmade cards.

Christmas to me is not so much the religious time it was meant to be. I see it as a time to specifically remember friends and loved ones, and get in touch. It is easy to forget during the year and be busy. I use this time to interrupt my busy life to remember all the people who have influenced me positively. I smile and nod when Christianity is brought up.

"Yes, yes, I have been saved!" I have an issue with Christianity. I do not want to identify with the crusades. Or locally, taking Native children from homes to teach them a new, better way in a dorm setting to be turned into Christians. My mother was put in a convent where she was abused, beaten, not fed well, and relates unpleasant conditions she does not have fond memories of. I do not find Christianity to be a very kind religion. Though I enjoy many of the bible stories and find them inspiring. In Christianity, animals were put on the earth for man to have domain over. I do not agree this is our relationship with nature.

I recall a conversation I had a long time ago with God. (Or it could have been my unconscious posing as God during one of my time alone periods). At any rate, I heard a voice I believe to be God. I asked about the bible, wondering why I am being visited, considering I am not a bible thumper. A voice says, "The bible is provided for those who like contracts, want to see it in writing. For believers in handshake agreements, just come to me directly." Made sense to me. So that sums up Christmas. Iris is not big on celebration of holidays either. We do not get involved in the mad rush, nor put out decorations. *It's better to just try to be kind to people, value what we have and such.*

One of my buddies tries to cheer me up with a joke, after hearing about the raid and a discussion on 'security.' Yes, when we live remote, we get innovative. Security does not have to cost a lot, or require expert installation.

HOW TO INSTALL A SOUTHERN HOME SECURITY SYSTEM
1. Go to Goodwill and buy a pair of size 14 -16 men's work boots
2. Place them on your front porch, along with a copy of Guns & Ammo Magazine.
3. Put four giant dog dishes next to the boots and magazines.
4. Leave a note on your door that reads ...Bubba, Bertha, Duke, Slim, & I went for more ammo and beer. Be back in an hour. Don't mess with the pit bulls. They got the mailman this morning and messed him up bad. I don't think Killer took part, but it was hard to tell from all the blood. Anyway, I locked all four of 'em in the house. Better wait outside. Be right back.
Cooter

I reply: I have an innovative security system. I discovered locks fail in the super cold here. It is easy to lose or not have the key with me. There are two dozen 'things to lock up'—nine sheds, a boat, toolbox, and other things. Two dozen locks cost a lot, with a lot of keys to keep track of. I tried locks with a common key, but a dozen is the usual count. So which key opens this lock? I solved my dilemma. I drill a quarter inch diameter hole in the door and the doorjamb that line up. I make a pin with a fake piece of dirt on the end. The pin goes through the door or lid, and into the frame, so it will not open. The dirt or fake screw-head sticks out a bit to grab and pull out. But who would look around and think that piece of dirt is holding the door shut? It's foolproof, in that it does not need a key to remember, does not stick, and is not complicated or costly. I make a hole nearby to store the pin in when not in use. I can handle it in the dark, or with cold fingers.

We agree security is to keep honest people out, maybe low level drunk, stupid, or lazy criminals. The serious will figure out how to get in about anything. Same as our computer. Yes, same as our computers. I was shocked at how fast the Feds got in my computer and retrieved everything they wanted. About ten seconds. So much for 'password protected.' Security is an illusion. I assume there is a back door people with authority can get through in case of emergency. Same as our bank account. I am not worried about some kid hacking in. The biggest thief is the bank itself, the government, or a big company. A threat of a bunch of pit bulls and Bubba with a baseball bat is not going to help much. Those were the good old days when we could defend ourselves with the easy means at our disposal. So goes the conversation. What good comes of it? I'd as soon not get all wound up about things I have no control over, and can do nothing about.

"Oh yes, we have control! We can vote!" My buddy says sarcastically. Followed by, "If you think your vote counts!"

I chuckle that, "The newly elected President is being welcomed into office, while we in Alaska are still voting." My buddy mentions Acorn, and more votes than there are people in some states. It's the Obama years. I answer, "I wanted to live a simple life in the wilds with nature, away from the maddening crowd. Now that I am getting plugged in, I have no answer."

"Besides bend over you mean?"

I acknowledge to myself that sometimes voting makes a difference. Now and then I hear how a million protests get the government to back down on an issue. I watch in my own community how voting makes a difference on a small scale, where we all know each other.

That's the problem when I get on these subjects with people. It never ends. We get all worked up and upset. Someone inevitably brings up the word 'revolution,' or 'conspiracy.' If said on the phone, or in an email, I think this triggers off computer generated automatic recordings. It is not hard to program a system to key in on, and target specific words or phrases. Heck, my book writing program does that! I ask, "Find" and type in a word or phrase, and any place in the computer this phrase exists, I get told.

"That would not be legal for the government to do, therefore it is not done!" This does not hold up to existing evidence.

I knew or suspected this in the 1960s when I decided I wished to be alone in the wilds. I used the word 'safe' a lot throughout my life in the wilderness. I tried to explain the concern for bears, the cold, getting lost, as not big deals, compared to issues in civilization. I said back in book one that civilization will be my undoing, not the wilds. "I have more reason to fear you, than you do to fear me."

Josh asks me, "I notice you did not go out trapping this winter, Miles; are you ok? Not sick are you?" Josh is a strong connection to the old ways, subsistence, the Native ways. We have discussed many times the advantages of living a simple life with the land. Trapping has been a huge part of that in our conversations. Josh cannot imagine life without trapping, though he himself does not trap, because racing dogs consumes all his time. Trapping is a symbol of a lifestyle we both highly value.

"I might get back to it, Josh. I do not have a good dog team anymore. The snow machine is not reliable, kids are trying to move into the trapping area. There is little fur, so I am regrouping, figuring out what to do." This is only partly true, but satisfies my savage friend.

I am not sure what the truth is, or how to put into words how I feel. It was never the trapping and the furs that drove me, or excited me. Nor was it just the beauty of the land. If I had to put it into words, the term 'safe' comes up again. Followed by 'free.' Combined with good thoughts of feeling like 'first man,' alone in the wilds. If there is a big thrill, it is seeing the trail as the first one, with no other human sign. Just

God and me. I have never been happy seeing other trails and footprints. I do not enjoy traveling with others in the wilds as a group. The vastness attracts me. The overwhelming emptiness, void of human intervention. I feel like Tarzan, a character in Clan of the Cave Bear, someone who crash landed the starship Enterprise, and will not see anyone till there is a rescue in thirty years. What wonderful thoughts.

My old trail is used by many now. There are sounds of homesteaders, planes, saws in the distance, others moving in and having to defend a dead lifestyle. Officers showing up with helicopters wanting to see permits, asking questions, takes the joy away. Having to know the time, the day, the month, takes the joy away. I am not alone, so I am not safe. Who understands that? I think it is not a political issue, but a spiritual one. I am not interested in a radical, angry conversation. It's a private matter. Nothing I care to discuss with anyone. I have said many times, I can kill bears if they become a problem! Now that I understand them better, I usually do not need to, and do not want to. Civilization wants to hear about that rare encounter, though! Oh yes! I think to assure themselves they made the right choice to be sheep; the fear of being eaten by a slathering bear is greater than the fear of life as a serf. I even think 'powers that be,' encourage such fears.

The reply can be: "Let us help!" I realized long ago, when everything is fine and society is without fear, we have no need for big government! It is not to big governments' advantage to solve society's problems. Help just enough to stop us from revolting. Or offer the illusion of help. Control disguised as help.

It is true, there are still a few who live the old way not bothered. Or at least still there, unsure about the 'not bothered' part. People ask and I reply, "Yes, I know a few still out in the wilds." This keeps the dream going.

Civilization owns and controls the entire world, with nothing out of its jurisdiction. This gives civilization the right to regulate all that is on the map within the lines referred to as 'our country.' This thought gives its citizens the right to demand a fair share of what is owned. I see it as a British thought of conquering by arriving and placing a flag. Some higher up person says, "I bestow upon you this land and title of lordship!" To someone who is owed a political favor. William Penn gets all of Pennsylvania, for example. Arriving at the crucial question, "What is ownership?" Who told the inhabitants of Pennsylvania they now have a master and by what right? They are now servants, renters, and not owners. Mr. Penn owns all the water, trees, and deer in the forest. "You, and who else will make me pay rent, follow your rules!?" For a long time a joke, there are not the resources, maybe not even the interest, to make it clear who is lord of the wilds.

Until there are desired resources, the answer civilization laughingly gives is, "Leave it to the bears and the savages!" Yet one day, there is in fact, enough power to say to me, "Me and the helicopters and armed men are here to tell you what to do."

If I harvest a moose, snaffle some game trapping, fry a fish, flock bust some geese, away off in the pucker brush you have never seen, never will, what's it to you? Why is that your business? I, we, have to eat something to stay alive. If I am not eating wild game, I am supporting some other death, some other evil. I am supporting some potential dust bowl due to over planting to support the masses. I'm supporting genetic alterations, pesticides, fertilizers, pollutions of all sorts. I choose to have a choice to pick which may live, and which may die, so I may eat. What is wrong with that?

I believe the public is better off having me in the wilds as a caretaker than the big business moving into the wilds after forcing subsistence people off the land. I think more damage has been done by the gas exploration and timber interests in the past year, then I have done in the past twenty! But how would Joe public know? Besides what Joe reads. Joe has not observed firsthand. Anyhow, I'm sure I have said enough. Like everyone else I know, I gather facts, supporters, statistics, opinions, that back up my personal view.

I most often hear, "Sure, Miles, and where would we be if we let everyone who wanted to, harvest all the wild game, by whatever methods, whenever they wish with no rules!" It is easy to envision disaster! Because we envision civilized people suddenly turned loose to help themselves to the cookie jar. My view is, very few civilized people have the knowledge, ability, money, resources, to get to where they will compete with the game I harvest. I confess more people end up in the wilds than deserve to be there due to modern inventions like GPD and reliable boats, planes, snow machines. Most people with enough money to buy all this 'stuff' do not need to eat wild game. Trophy hunters lose interest after the big ones are gone. There is some damage, I admit. But it is not the devastation envisioned. Most people cannot handle the bugs, the cold, the alone. They simply do not have what it takes. They tend to get lost, scared, are not at home, are not smarter than the game. I watch weekend warriors run the river full speed one after the other in their quest to find the big bull moose. I rescue such people all the time. They shoot the stupid moose that stares at them as they approach. Smart moose learn fast to step back and be still till the boats are gone. Or stay away from the river for two weeks. There is a vast swamp country hunters cannot get to, that moose love. Yes, given time, thousands of idiots could kill off the moose.

There should be some rules. Just nothing I should follow (smile). In my opinion, those few of us white people living as savages, should be grandfathered in to the old ways we believe in. This might be fifty people in the state. Not enough to bother the balance of nature. Someone who has done something legally for forty years should not be told, "You have to change now; we came up with some new ideas we are going to try out." The laws I live by worked for the past 40,000 years. Civilization is going to make improvements? What has civilization shown me about its ability to manage its environment? In the past 200 years of civilization we have been a cancer on the land, a foreign invader, a virus.

"True Miles, but look at our growing population! We can't go back to living like savages off the land! We have to accommodate all the people now." Again, grandfather in those fifty people who have proven to be at one with the wild. Give them the rights of animals. We can be a source of education and knowledge we can all benefit from. I had said once before that I think of a place I visited, if it still exists, in Valley Forge. There was a replica of a small village of yesteryear. Those who were employed and lived there, baked bread in stone ovens, worked iron in a forge, used horses, dressed and lived in a past way. Civilization paid to watch, take pictures, ask questions, and learn. There are classes on how to make bow and arrow, start fires with flint, survival skills of all kinds. "What is wrong with considering those like me in the wilds as savages, part of the original landscape along with the other wild living things that are in balance with nature?"

"As in, Look mommy, there's a bear, oh look, there's a savage!" Click, click goes the camera. I pause, "Just think of the rewards to society of having a few people who have knowledge few others have." I go on. "There is always a price for life, for choices made. Maybe I ambush a moose you might have been able to take a picture of next year. Who can say? Instead of the picture of the moose I denied you, you get a story, a custom knife made by Wild Miles, with appropriate provenance." I've been watching the antique road show! Such conversations can go on and on and never end. 'What if?'

I'm in the routine of spending time in the shop creating art from the materials I got in Tucson. I have a knock out hunk of amber with a bug in it. I know I can make a gorgeous necklace out of this amber. I have a plan for it, using a nicely cut amethyst, set in a casting on the side of the amber. I just got done cutting and shaping a raw piece of turquoise the size of an egg. I have a faceted piece of Smokey quartz the size of a dime I plan to make a custom setting for, and hang by itself. Each morning I greet the sun. This time of year we gain a half an hour a week of light. I greet the sun on the way to the shop, filled with project ideas, then turning ideas into some really awesome product. I feel lucky, and blessed, to have been given such a talent. My shop is my man cave. A world I created, that I am in control of. Where I am not drug down by the doom and gloom of the world, according to the news and the gossip.

The WIN group helps me see the good in the world. The group donates time, tries to do something about issues we see in our community. We work together to have a health fair once a year. We arrange guest speakers for the community on topics of interest-gardening, bees, tax preparation, whatever subject that might help people out. Again, all volunteer work. Helping out the poor and what to do about the drinking, and drug problems is a common topic.

One night Iris wakes me up. "Miles, there is someone in the house!"

I sit up a moment and snort, "Yeah, right! You are having a dream, go back to sleep!" For years and years I never locked my door, no one did. Not even when I am gone. There were no problems. I began locking the door when gone, mostly to please Iris who is from the city. But lock myself in, when I am home? That is nuttso. What kind of world would that be!

"Miles!" Once again. "I hear someone in the house!" The urgency in her voice has me sit up and listen more carefully. Sure enough, a voice.

"Miles, Miles, are you awake? I need help." The voice is at the bedroom entrance. This does not sound like someone in an emergency, so I am doubtful there has been something like a car accident in the street. I keep my Ruger Blackhawk 357 pistol over the bed, and can find it just by reaching up in the dark.

With gun in my hand, I say sternly, "If there is a problem, go outside and I will meet you at the front door! You are in my home. I do not know who you are, or if you are armed, and what the situation is, you need to leave, now!" I feel reluctant to simply blast whoever was in my doorway. I cannot see in the dark anyhow. What if there is an emergency; someone is deathly sick. It is possible they knocked, and we did not hear them. It could be my neighbor, a friend. You'd think though, whoever it was, would identify themselves and state the emergency, understand how this looks!

Once again, "I need help, someone is chasing me." A man's voice, a young person. The voice even sounds familiar, but not frightened, in a panic. The tone does not match that of emergency mode.

Iris is scared out of her gourd. She urges me to shoot whoever this is.

I say sternly, "You need to leave, now. Neither of us is dressed. Go wait by the front door and whatever is going on we can deal with it!" The person is not leaving, and in fact comes closer. I say louder, "I do not know your intentions, or if you are armed. You are about to get shot!" I pull the hammer back on the gun in preparation to shoot. No person with honorable intentions would come closer when ordered to leave at gunpoint. But also no sane person, not even a burglar.

The situation is simply 'odd.' My gut feeling is, someone is very whacked out on drugs. So whacked out they do not understand the gravity of the situation. I hate to shoot a whacked out teen who simply does not know where they are, or what they are doing. Still, whacked out teens in this situation are capable of very evil deeds. Just ask Squeaky, of the Charles Manson tribe. My gut feeling is, if this person had such evil intentions, they would not have been calling out my name. If this person were armed, I'd know it by now. This person sounds distressed, not angry, demanding, or violent. For these reasons, I do not pull the trigger. Whoever it is, retreats a bit and I get up, put my pants on, and go to greet them with the light on.

It is one of my neighbor kids, Phil, of the Evans family. "Phil, what in the *&!^^ are you doing here in my house sneaking around? I almost shot you!"

"Miles, someone is following me with a shotgun! I ran through the swamps and came in for protection! Help me!" This is hard to believe, as Phil is not sweating, or breathing hard, like someone on the run. If he ran through the woods and swamp, why are his shoes dry, and his white socks still white? My guess is, he is so whacked out on drugs he is hallucinating. I simply tell him I cannot help him and send him out the door.

"Go home, Phil!" I could call the police, but then he would go to jail. I'm not convinced jail is what this kid needs. Likewise, it would be me interrogated and under suspicion. *Why do you keep a gun by your bed? Is it registered? Why is it loaded with unapproved hand loaded ammunition? Huh? The law clearly says guns need a safety lock, with the key in another room, and ammunition in a 3rd locked location outside the building.* We have the right to bear arms, but they can't be made functional without half an hour's preparation. I'd go to jail, buddy Phil would be laughing at the way the system works.

Iris gets up and points out Phil's footprints on the floor from the mud on his feet. Phil went over to my computer, into the bathroom, must have opened some drawers. So now I am not sure how whacked out he was, if he was alert enough to have been trying to rob us. Was calling out my name, a coverup, in case I heard him and woke up? Oddly, he had locked the door behind him when he came in. Why would someone break in and lock themselves in your house with you in the house? If I had shot him, there certainly would have been a reason to. He is lucky to be alive. He is one of the kids I have been trying to help. Phil has been in and out of jail, involved in all sorts of hanky panky, mostly whacked out on drugs. Yes, Dorothy, there really are Zombies! I spread the word among his relatives and friends that he broke in and I almost shot him. Maybe someone will keep an eye on him and get him help or something. What should society do about people like this? It costs us a lot of money in resources and loss to deal with such people!

The WIN group brings the subject up. "It's a disease! We have to treat it as a disease!" I keep hearing. But maybe every aberration among us is a disease.

"The devil made me do it!" As one criminal said.

There was the hostess cupcake case, where some fat kid tried to sue the Twinkie company, "You made me do it!" While high on sugar he killed his parents, or some such deed.

The WIN group discusses the subject regularly. The bottom line I see is drugs is big business. It is not going to be stopped by some church goodie two shoes. About the time lives get threatened, people back peddle fast. We had one of our members stand up to be counted! The local drug lord threatened his wife and dog. That was the end of that stand-up comedy! Law-abiding citizens cringe and call 911. The police appear to be few in number, underpaid, and unwilling to risk their lives for whatever rewards there might.

I was told many times by cops I know, "We let these people deal with themselves. There are too many of them. We only respond when there is blood. We would spend our time nonstop taking these people to town every time they beat each other up or overdosed. They tend not to live long." There are entire neighborhoods in cities, left alone, where cops do not even go. So I'm told, or maybe read in a news article. Zombie land. Like in Brave New World. Outside the protected area, where no civilized person goes. Where people live in the stone age. Civilized people put up barriers to keep them out. Hired police are instructed to keep them out of our neighborhood.

It is because, whoever you are, you are a Zombie. The walking dead. The unprotected include every race. Certain low life occupations. The poor. The uneducated. Subsistence people. Written off as the train of progress leaps forward on its tracks headed for the future. There is not room on that train for everyone. Some will necessarily be left in the dust. I am not sure that will, can, or should, be changed. Change would require the train to slow down, even stop to wait. We'd have to give up on the idea of free enterprise, democracy, survival of the fittest.

We'd have to believe in, 'No child left behind,' and all go at the pace of the slowest person. I'm spoiled. I like to live by the idea if I work hard, I get to keep the money and buy cool stuff with it. I do not like the idea that half my money should go to support some low life degenerate who deserves as good a lifestyle as I have. If you can't cut it, step aside and make room for those who can. That's how I was raised. I learned even before I could walk, if we fall down, no one will pick you up.

How much time can I spend on the train, looking behind me at those screaming, running, trying to catch up and get on this train we call life? I can reach out and grab the hand of a few, risk getting pulled off the train. Or I can turn and look inside the train, set myself down and relax. Share lunch with those looking out the other window at the beautiful scenery, a plate of overpriced sprouts; a cup of tea in front of me. My little pinky finger sticking off appropriately to the side saying, "Why I never," like the rest of the sheep. That's the real world. Survival is in facing reality. Survival is being one of the Romans, not Jesus. Playing Jesus is a good way to get nailed to a cross. I have what I feel is a personal answer that works for me. I do not call 911.

Civilized issues leave my mind when I am out with Nature. I love winter. The forever darkness, but the hints of colors of a sunrise below the horizon at noon. The northern lights. I am out gathering firewood in the dark. The temperature is twenty-nine below. Not cold, just normal. I stop to breathe in the air and stare up at the northern lights. I sit down on the wood-pile in my sled.

My wood cutting area has been the same for almost a decade now. This is an old forest fire burn of standing dead trees with no bark and no limbs. I section the trees into ten-foot lengths to fit in the sled and stacked four feet high. This should last about two weeks, maybe. I hear a hawk-owl not far away; I suspect, made nervous by my presence. I picture his extra long tail going up and down. It is too dark to see him. I hear snow fall off the tree branch as he flies, close enough for snow to land on me. We have a normal amount of snow-fall for this time of year, about a foot over the past month. I'm reluctant to head back home, but give a sigh and haul the wood into Nenana.

On December 17th, 2012 I am served with an indictment. To me 'out of the blue.' I'm stunned. I tell Iris, "It has been a year and a half since the search warrant was served. Without knowing, or being told what I did wrong, I assumed it was a shake-down. Now what?" Or if not a shakedown, a 'mistake!' Fish and Wildlife does not want to admit to that, so just letting it go is not an option. There was no trophy room full of mounted polar bears as they thought. Is that too embarrassing to admit? How could they have spent a million dollars and not know me better than that? Weird! What is their source of information? Who would say something so outrageous? A rival? Fish and Feathers just made it up out of the blue to prove to me they can say anything, and prove anything they want? There is nothing I can do about it? This is unexpected, to be charged.

I read over the issues I face.

There are twenty-eight separate felony charges listed. The biggest, perhaps, is selling an illegal white walrus tusk to an undercover agent. Then sending a fresh walrus tusk overseas. There is the sale of an eagle feather. The sale of about six wolf claws from sales of one per individual, all separate charges. The sale of a dead frozen raven. The sale of a single polar bear fang. The sale of an ounce of polar bear fur. The sale of some lynx claws. Each charge comes with a grand prize of three to ten years in prison, and up to $200,000 in fines.

I review not just what I think, but what I have saved as notes, copies of laws, 'proof' on what I might use in a defense. This becomes mind-boggling. My brain locks up at the sheer mass of material and things to organize, remember, sort, cate-gorize, rate in importance. This can-will take a very long time. Time I do not have living a basic life. A life where, if I am not productive, I do not eat. I have no work-man's comp, sick leave, etc.

At the top of the charges is the notation. "Not a Native American." The assump-tion being, if I was, there would be no charges, and this is how I understand my situation. I have been acting like an Indian, while I am not. Now I will be punished for that.

My main defense, in my mind, revolves around the word 'Subsistence.' The biggest issue is, if I qualify or not. There is a belief subsistence is an 'Indian only' issue, as stated on the charges. I read laws, saying discrimination by race is illegal.

Fish and Wildlife is among those saying, 'No,' I have no subsistence rights. I find a legal quote I need to file, here it is. The subject is fishing, but this is all I can find for now in my pile.

Page 5 Under AS 16.05.251 (b), subsistence uses have priority over sport and commercial uses if the board finds it necessary to restrict the taking of fish to assure the maintenance of fish stocks or to assure the continuation of subsistence uses. In a footnote at the bottom are definitions. 'Subsistence uses' means the customary and traditional uses in Alaska of wild, renewable resources for direct personal or family consumption of food, shelter, fuel, clothing, tools, or transportation, for the making and selling of handicraft articles out of non-edible by-products of fish and wildlife resources, and customary barter and trade or sharing for personal consumption. Family means all persons living within the household on a permanent basis.

This seems clear to me. Nothing here says you have to be in Indian. *But maybe it is stated someplace else, I better keep looking.*

Here is a relevant newsletter concerning parks, I saved from 1979. I saved this because at the time I was homesteading and trapping near a park boundary, Denali park was being expanded under the Carter administration. I was concerned with what to do if my stomping grounds are within the boundary of the park expansion! I did dip in and out of the park at the back boundary. Can I harvest a moose, or trap in a park? What about other subsistence activities? Need I be careful what I say about where product #1 was harvested?

Headline concerning park activities allowed.

Federal Register/ Vol. 44. No 126 Heading is Subsistence. "Direct the secretary to promulgate such regulations as are appropriate, including regulations of the opportunity to engage in subsistence lifestyle by local residents."

This is a lengthy writing, a dozen pages of small print, that spell out issues of cabin use and building, trapping, access, trails, and other concerns one might have. I see nothing to contradict the basic premise that subsistence is encouraged, even one of the reasons to create a park, to set aside land that is sustainable for local subsistence activates. It is clear that there are in fact much more restrictions for the general public, then for subsistence people. Ah, here is something else from this same writing:

13.43 Subsistence permits for persons who permanently reside outside the resident zone. "May apply for a subsistence permit to engage in subsistence uses within the park."

Yes, I have such a permit, and again I see nothing about having to be an Indian.

Why wasn't I told I could not have such a permit because I am the wrong color? Why is it so darn important to settle this 'Indian only' issue I hear about? I explain my thoughts to Iris. "One good example is the Jessie case I am part of!" I explain that I read Jessie was trading drugs and illegal guns, including machine guns, to Natives for fresh, white, illegally killed, untagged walrus ivory. This is none of the ivory I received from Jessie; mine was government tagged and in the system as legally harvested, with assigned numbers I recorded. "No Natives have been charged. Why? They traded poached white ivory for drugs and guns."

"Miles, that is not a great example, something else is going on. This is not about subsistence rights! No one can do this, not even Natives!" I mention it because it is on my mind. I'm arrested, but not the Natives he was dealing with? What's that all about! I could use a better argument, I just come up with a blank. It's not a good defense to say "But what about them!" Pointing fingers. I understand that is not relevant to my case, which is all about me taking responsibility.

Sometimes I make a connection, a leap into my brain filled with snippets of data. I grab at the first sticky note my unconscious finds and spout it out. I wish I could pull out the correct, appropriate relevant piece of knowledge, at the time it would be most useful. I could use this snippet on another subject, but by then I will have forgotten it! Where the prosecution has a whole team of highly paid experts who had years to put their evidence together. Charges state I have been investigated for four years. I have a few weeks for a rebuttal defense.

I'm not even sure I understand how our government works! What are laws anyway? Where do they come from? Who makes them up? The writings I read appear to come from the legislature. So do such people have to follow the directive? Who stops this person or group from ignoring the directive and doing what they wish? That would be the head of the Fish and Game department. Who does he report to and who is above him? How free can this person be with what they decide? What is the check and balance here? There is supposed to be an advisory board. I showed up once and saw it was all Natives. I was told, "Go back where you came from white man!" So where do I turn?

It is my understanding that if the directive is not followed, and someone gets arrested, like myself, a case comes to court. The prosecution points out past cases. The defense finds other cases, with a different outcome. A judge or jury hears both sides and makes a decision. Can anyone quote the directive handed down? I'd think so, since all of this is about intent. In other words, what was meant, what were the lawmakers trying to accomplish when they made a law?

I review what I have been told over the years in conversations with politicians. Charley Parr, one of the Coghills, Don Young, our local magistrate. Unless I understood wrong, all say, "There is no such thing as a law set in stone that is a universal truth that cannot be changed, or for which there is not an exception." I pause to let that sink in. "It's all in flux, constantly changing." *So how do laws change?* "Cases go to court and set a precedence." The problem I am having is that court cases are not in alphabetical order, nor is there a book of them, with a table of contents by subject. It takes a lawyer. Someone must know a case number, a name that reads,

"So and so, Vs so and so," at the right level in the court system. There are a good four to five levels I cannot even name. Some cases become famous and easier to find, others would be more obscure because they did not make headlines. The subject of the sale of animal parts is not the same as murder, rape, and robbery. I have no way to find relevant court cases. As such, I am helpless in the legal system. I need a lawyer. Saddle spelled it out. "$40 grand, cash today, to talk. Looking at a total over 100 grand, are you in or out?"

"Can I hire you by the hour, to take care of specific tasks I do not understand, to take care of immediate needs?" Saddle looks at me impatiently, like he does not know how he can be of service. I give an example. "I have no choice but to approach the court and request a public defender. I'm guessing there are a variety of levels of these defenders. Some might have Fish and Wildlife knowledge, or have a personal interest. Some might be more ethical. I want someone willing to go to court and fight this if that is what is best, and not be afraid to."

Saddle nods his head that he understands, agrees this might be wise. I press on, "Maybe you have some influence, might recommend someone to the court." I'm thinking this request looks better coming from a recognized top notch lawyer. Explaining, "I wish to switch lawyers." Meaning I now have Saddle who is a recognized top lawyer. No one needs to know, 'for a very short time to complete a specific task.' It's a form of name dropping. It's a way to not look like a total destitute who has no clue of the proceedings. I can make the situation appear, 'one lawyer who knows the system, requesting a change of lawyers, with a recommendation.' Saddle is an outdoor person, hunter, and been around many years. I assume he knows everyone, as well as knowing who might have outdoor knowledge as he does.

"Yes Miles, I know a decent public defender I could recommend." Possibly Saddle can have zero effect on who is chosen. I have peace of mind believing I have an edge. A tiny 'in.' While we go through the process of getting me a lawyer, I look for relevant information I think applies to my case. I do not know how to do the lawyer's job. I do not know what is relevant in court. I know what is important to me, that I base my behavior on. *Ah, here is another piece of paper referring to my subsistence permit.* This has to do with fishing, but I understand sets a precedence for other game and resources.

From the Department of Fish and Game. I know enough now to see this refers to state level. May 21, 1991: addressed to me from the area biologist Keith Shultz. So I understand now this is a biologist, not a legal document as I thought, but I read this anyway. "You were issued a 1991 Subsistence salmon permit # SA-31-91. For fishing is sub district 6-A which includes the Kantishna River. I have enclosed a 1991 regulations book for you to review. It is up to the individual to abide by the regulations that apply to the specific location being fished." I pause to think about just this part. One big issue over the years is the 'specific location' referred to. Often when out remote, my specific location is not named on any map. There is less clarity on just what the rules in the wilds might be. Most people are on the map someplace. My stomping grounds is an area the size of Rhode Island with no roads in it. 'Off the grid' does not even apply. More like off the edge of the earth. I catch one part of interest.

"The issuing officer was in error when she specified on your permit that only Coho salmon may be taken after August 16th." This cost me an arrest, a trip to town, a court appearance, hiring a lawyer, and loss of fishing time, which affected the ability to feed my dogs all winter and trap. I notice there is no, "You will be compensated for the damages the error caused." Just a, "Whoops! We screwed it up!" The laws are so complicated, even those who write and enforce it cannot keep it straight. Yet, if it is me who does not understand it, I get arrested. But anyhow, no time to get worked up. Most people who are not investigated tell me they avoid these controversies by avoiding the subject entirely, simply stop engaging in the activity in question! Well, isn't that wonderful! That these sheep can afford to do that. Do what they are told, without question! One issue is, there are so few people in my position, who are white, yet living like an Indian. I wonder if a white person were living with headhunters in the upper Amazon River country, wouldn't the same laws apply as the rest of the tribe lived by? Would he be arrested for fishing without a permit?

Where would our country be today if the old trappers, mountain men, prospectors, those who founded our country, decided, "This is mighty controversial from a legal standpoint. I best avoid any problems and just not do this! I better not live with the Indians, learn to trap and live off the land. I need to stay home and do what I'm told!"

"Wow! I better not step on this Mayflower boat! Looks like a liability to me!"

"Go to the moon? Discover light bulb? Explore the unknown? Isn't that illegal?"

Another issue I notice is, What is a regulation? Compared to a law? Or a directive? Which is more important or stronger? I had been told, "Just because we see something in writing, does not mean it must be followed! A booklet a department writes up is not the law. Oh, you can be told to abide by it, but told by who, on whose authority? There is usually a higher authority that can be quoted." *I think I get it! It's like our constitution, right?* "Or the ten commandments."

When it comes to our constitution it is somewhat basic, outlying the intent. All 'the stuff' underneath that, the reams of volumes of legal words. All they do is give examples and specifics, but none can disobey the original intent, as laid out in the highest document. Sort of like you can quote the bible to your heart's content, but if you disobey one of the ten commandments, all that reading, of all the various scriptures is worth diddly squat in terms of being holier than thou, and getting into heaven. If, for example, you covet thy neighbor's wife, what use is reviewing the finer points in small print? Or showing up in church every Sunday.

Many belief systems can be summed up on one page. Companies and organizations often have mission statements. What is an organization about if it ignores its mission statement? Communism has Communist Manifesto. Democracy has the constitution. The constitution is not complicated or long. One beauty is, it does not change! Once you understand it, you understand it forever. I found myself in a quandary. I want to 'do the right thing' but for most of my life lived out in the remote wilderness without electricity or communication. I could not keep up with the changes in fine print. The solution I chose was to understand the purpose laws are made. I reason, if I understand the purpose, and uphold that, how far astray can I go?

All my proofs and pieces of paper will mean what? I sigh.[1] I am overwhelmed with fear. My brain locks up. I'm in deep trouble. Not because I feel I am a criminal, but because the Feds want me for some reason.

I see a modern video, with home surveillance footage of an armed swat team in a residence with guns drawn, 'invading.' The reason and charge was a small farm family selling their own milk. It's illegal under federal law to sell raw milk. The husband is carted off in handcuffs and died in jail. Did this not happen, was the footage faked? The wife said she believed they were legal based on state laws they were complying with, that disagreed with Federal ruling. She assumed the state would work it out with the Feds.

There was Rodney King, and similar footage shot of people beat up, killed.

Are any crimes I have committed really worth a million dollars of tax dollars spent? Does that make sense? It does not to me. This is all this scary to me. It has always been 'someone else.' I assumed, 'I must not have all the facts,' and *"My government would not do that! Somehow all these people deserved it!"* Almost the exact words the farm woman spoke as her husband was carted off. Without 'proving' anything; what matters is what I believe and how it affects my behavior. I chose to live alone in the wilds, away from civilization.

There is an article about a guide who had a customer on a float trip on a remote river and finds a mammoth tusk in a creek hundreds of miles from no place. She let him keep it; they sold it to someone and got caught. A $4,000 tusk, a smallish one. The tusk was on Federal park land in the Brooks Mountain Range. Hundreds of miles in a remote wilderness area, no one can be expected to go for years. No digging, just picking up a tusk from the water. Damaging nothing, hurting no one. First time offense. Lost her guide license, and can't work for five years. Something like $200,000 fine. Her life is over. They might as well take her out, make her dig her own grave, shoot her and dump her in it. What will her life be, can't work for five years, at the same time paying a $200,000 fine?

A judge friend told me, "Arresting offenders randomly reaches more people, faster, cheaper, more effectively, then taking ads out, and putting up fliers."

I go back to the exact charges again. My eyes will not even focus. I read but cannot understand. The link between my eyes and my brain is interrupted with survival drugs and shut down time. Pulling my blood to my inner core in preparation for being shot. I hear radicals speak sometimes. "I refuse to pay taxes. The government has been illegally demanding we pay and does not have that right!" I actually agree that this was long ago, an illegal move. However, I know how such people will end up. Paying taxes, in jail, or dead.

Joe Vogler was going to world court to prove Alaska was illegally taken as a state. I believe him, I know his evidence. I would not support him, saying, "So what!" The USA government is not going to allow Alaska to secede! Joe was killed. Many, including me, feel the government killed him. I'm not interested in proving it or protesting. It's called "This is how it is." Is my situation similar? Who cares if discrimination by race is illegal. I'm going down. I hear, as I would say to Joe. "What did you expect, Miles!"

I had a dream of being a mountain man. The state offers homestead land saying, "We expect you to live subsistence off the land."

I reply, "I can do that!" I get a special subsistence permit that looks exactly like an Indian's permit. Subsistence is defined as a lifestyle, not a race. Most people shake their head and walk away. Obviously I do not get it.

There are twenty-eight total charges to review. Some seem obviously frivolous and easy to win on. Others seem out of the Feds jurisdiction. Other charges I feel the Feds have their facts wrong. There are a couple of items that in my mind, I might have trouble explaining and getting away with. Just two out of 28. The eagle parts and the raven. The charges the Feds want me on, and what 'this' is all about, the ivory, I think I can win on.

"But win what?" I tell Iris, "If the Feds 'want me' and the purpose is to shut me up, get rid of me, send a message out to my 100,000 fans, then that is going to happen."

We agree, the details of how it happens are irrelevant. If I pay a hundred grand to a lawyer, I will never be out of debt. With no money, there is no progress on anything. *A canoe without a paddle, that is what life is without money.* Spinning around going no place, not a threat to anyone. Allowed to live in a soup line. Effectively shut up and shut down. Without money, I can never get what I write in print. Oh well, I have to do something!

Here is another snippet of information in the hodgepodge file of stuff I need to know. I printed it off the computer, more updated information concerning subsistence. Again, I am so terrified I cannot think, cannot get together a defense. What did the Jews do? What could they do? Offer what as a defense? Point out whose laws? How far does, *"But you can't do that! I have rights!"* go?

Federal Subsistence Management program- Questions and Answers: 'At its May 18-20 2004 meeting the subsistence board adopted new regulations allowing the sale of handcrafts made from brown bear fur' and further on the page, 'subsistence users may sell handcraft articles made from black bear fur which can include the claws, which has been allowed since July of 2002.'

This is of interest, as one of the issues of confiscation and on the search warrant was bear claws. But not among the charges. I suspect the judge who approved the search warrant was unaware of the law. The prosecution pulled the wool over his eyes by quoting either some outdated law or the big general picture. It all hinges on, if I am subsistence or not. I read further: "Federally qualified subsistence users may continue to barter fish or wildlife or their parts taken under Federal subsistence regulations. The sale of these items is a customary practice consistent with the intent of title V11 of ANILCA"

And further along, "It is the opinion of the Federal Subsistence board that Federal regulations governing the sale of handcrafts made from subsistence harvested wildlife extend to any legally taken subsistence wildlife, regardless of where the actual cash transaction takes place."

This clears up a couple of issues on my mind. For example, it makes clear some amount of cash is traditional and accepted concerning game animals and their parts, if you qualify for subsistence lifestyle. It sounds to me like internet, even overseas sales would not be excluded from the intent. The intent is to meet subsistence basic needs and not get rich. The intent is to not overly tax our natural resources. I have had subsistence experts point out that all ancient tribes were traders and dealt with people from all over the world. In fact, innovation is a huge part of subsistence survival. *We need to argue that in court!*

Another snippet, Senate Bill 231 from 1985 "An Act relating to the taking of fish and game for subsistence use." Hmm, this pretty much backs up everything else I am reading. I recall this might be the time period when the state and federal government were at odds. The Feds saying the state is out of compliance with subsistence laws, that laws must be bought in compliance with Federal 'or else.' State called on the carpet. It stated, "Be it enacted by the legislature of the state of Alaska." This states a recognition that taking of game is related to the health, safety and general welfare of rural Alaskans.

'Subsistence uses' means the customary and traditional uses by rural Alaska residents of wild resources... food, shelter, fuel... clothing, tools... for the making and selling of handicraft articles... for trade, barter in accordance with AS 01.10.70 (C)

Here is a news clipping in a folder not dated: More than 150 accused in online wildlife sales. "Authorities disrupted on line wildlife trafficking operations involving tiger, leopard, and jaguar pelts, elephant ivory and live birds... announced the arrest... undercover from 16 states... three Asian countries... Operation Wild Web." Summed up, "Our message is clear and simple: The internet is not an open marketplace for protected species." Hm. Well, I assume I am part of this big bust operation. Some of my confiscated items include deliberately mislabeled tiger, lion, leopard, parts (claws) that are clearly legal lynx claws. I say 'deliberate,' because I pointed the indiscretion out when there was time to have the mistake corrected at the time of labeling. I took pictures of such items with the confiscation number. *Let's bring that up in court.* A lot of people would be able to see the difference from the photos between the porcupine labeled as eagle and real eagle.

I read, 'protected species,' and in that scope are 'wolves.' The subject of wolf hunting and protection has been in the news a lot. The Feds call wolves 'endangered and protected', the state of Alaska does not. I saved numerous articles on the subject, if I could find them. Showing tax dollars spent on planes used by biologists to aerial hunt wolves as a method of moose control, and often leave the wolf behind unsalvaged. Likewise, it is legal and encouraged by state biologists, in some places in Alaska to go into wolf dens and kill puppies. Wolf trapping is still legal and encouraged in Alaska, with a season and no bag limit.

I remind Iris of what I have repeated often, "When biologists were hunting wolves and shooting them from a plane they lost a plane, paid for and replaced by tax payers!" Humph! "Not me, though!"

"I pay diddly squat in taxes. If I were someone like Seymour..." I trail off. "While trappers appear to be the scapegoats and cause of all the problems, like lack of wolves and imbalance of nature, as well as the ones getting arrested! Do you see the state biologists getting arrested?!"

"Ok, well, calm down, Miles. You already have high blood pressure."

I have chosen to side with the state on this issue, and sell wolf claws the state considers legal activity. So who exactly are the Feds referring to, when discussing the sale of protected species? The entire State of Alaska?

"Iris, my friend the fur dealer Don, has told me for many years, that Alaska trappers and the state are following sound scientific data based on studies over many years. Don says the Feds base what they say on emotion, not facts. I've been told by many people the animal rights, preservation radical groups, have never been involved in a public debate at a meeting. The reason, I'm told by hunters, is they'd lose on the basis of laws, sound judgment, and biologically sound studies. All the preservationists have to back up their side is emotions." Iris gives me a look, causing me to reply. "Ok, I agree, I also wonder who is doing the studies. Are the studies rigged to produce desired results? Would I trust a government to do any unbiased study of any kind?" Or anyone? Iris still gives me her look. "Ok! I agree Iris, I also think many laws are bonkers! I pick and choose the ones I agree with, and ignore the ones I think we all need to forget about!"

My point is still valid. If I am at fault on the wolf issue, so is the entire state of Alaska.

There is certainly another side to the story. I am sure evil things are being done by some poachers. I would like to see that stopped for sure! There are laws in place, legal ways to catch and punish those who hurt the environment. But wait! I am one of the bad guys? How did that happen? The article is continued on another page, let's see, Oh yes, "As a major platform for the illicit trade in wildlife, the internet has become a dangerous place for animals." Said Jeff Flocken, director for the International Fund for Animal Welfare and advocate group that worked with the Federal task force. "Wildlife crimes pose a threat to national and global security" Flocken said. "Illegal wildlife trade generates an estimated 19 billion dollars a year worldwide and ranks fourth on a list of most lucrative global illegal activities."

An animal rights group from California is working closely with the Federal government. The state that has communities advertising they want to ban all animal products from its borders. In the news, described as the cutting edge of the future, and direction the entire country is going. I confess this is too deep for me to grasp. I want to be a subsistence person in a remote area. I'd prefer to not even have electricity, no news, off the grid, I leave you alone; you leave me alone. Understanding politics is a full-time job. Doing something about it is even a more full-time job. What I want may not be possible. Or legal.

I recall my friend, Will, telling me he heard the NRA does not back trappers, will not join our organization or defend it. That is hard to believe! It must be a rumor! Will dropped his membership with the NRA over the issue. He said to me, "I think the NRA made a deal. That went something like 'ok, you back us up over here and we drop our affiliation with trappers, mountain men, subsistence people.' Some behind-the-scenes agreement that sold us out, Miles!"

I think possible, but not likely. However, I heard the NRA is getting big, powerful, political, and in the end as much part of a problem as a solution for some of us. Maybe they would follow the money and power. Thus view the number of trappers, Indians, subsistence, in the world as insignificant in number from a political standpoint to win votes. It is true, many of us do not have much money. Almost by definition,' subsistence equals poor', so are not big spenders on guns and gear, and tend not to vote, get involved in politics, so who is going to stand up for us? Maybe no one, as Will points out. "Miles, we are a minority so small we do not even qualify as a minority group!"

"We'd be better off being black, Will!"

"Or Indian! I'd give my left nut to be an Indian this day and age!"

"Try and discriminate against a black, a woman or an Indian and see how far you get! Suddenly you would face an indignant advocate group, a top lawyer and millions of dollars in compensation. Front page news! Not to be tolerated!"

This reminds me of another legal angle! I forgot! There is a possibility to toss out there that I am in fact an Indian! A trump card to lay on the table, get out of jail free, do not pass go, collect $200. Yeah, right! But am reminded I am for sure part Indian on my mother's side. Algonquin, mixed with the French Canadian. Mom even remembers a relative who looked pure Indian she used to visit as a child. Maybe her grandfather. On my father's side, he told me once he recalls visiting a reservation in upstate New York to visit a relative. But has no idea who that person was. He was never told. Back in those days, many people did not want to admit they had any Indian blood in them. They hid it. Even went so far as to have records altered.

My grandmother, my mother's mother, told me she did a background check on my father when he said he was Irish. She told me, "No way in hell that man is Irish!" I agree. He, we, do not look Irish, have no Irish traditions, have no pictures, no relatives, no stories, that resemble the Irish. We practiced no Irish traditions. Zip. Nada. I know for sure we have a lot of black in us. My grandfather knocked up the bar piano player and had to marry her. So goes the story through the grapevine. Unrecorded history no one will ever find evidence of. She was from Jamaica. Her father was one of the first black dentists or doctors in all of New York. Word is he paid all the bills, got my grandpa a home, and maybe lived in what must have been hush hush disgrace. I never even met the woman, but she sent expensive presents every year all through my childhood. To where I do not care for presents much. I felt guilty for these nice gifts from someone I never met, who I was told loved me very much. I have no clue about what she ever looked like. Mom only met her once.

Word has it as well, grandpa had organized crime connections (cool!) and he paid to have his son's records changed to say he is pure Irish, so he could go to college. In that part of New York, you had to be Irish to be anyone. You want to go to college? You better be Irish! Indian and black? Dream on, not going to happen! I believe the unrecorded verbal history whispered and hinted at. It matches certain family pictures and behavior. Makes sense. Grandpa was a boxing fighter manager operating out of a bar. It makes sense, fights were rigged in order to survive, organized crime connections were a must. Piano player girlfriends make sense. Fast women, fast money. I see it in the blood. I feel it. I nod. I get it.

So now the real question is, "What part Indian am I on my father's side?!" I only have to be 1/16th to have my get out of jail free card. I agree, that sucks big time! It's prejudice against whites! I believe strongly in being who we are, regardless of our race, religion, etc. I stand up for a lifestyle, not a race! I have said many times, "All

300

races of people, all over the world, had and have a deep connection to the land! Not just Indians! To raise my hand and say I am deserving because of my race is wrong!" So I have avoided 'proving' I am Indian so I may have more rights! But to save my bacon? I might be facing a lifetime in prison. Depending why the Feds want me. I have said some antigovernment things now and again. I have the skills to teach people how to go underground. Not get found. Live without an ID, totally untraceable. I can teach anyone how to disappear.

Are there people afraid of that kind of knowledge getting taught? Do not want it taught? Do not want anyone inspired to tune in, drop out, and ask questions? In short, teach sheep to stop bleating and jump the fence? Offer them another choice! Is that worth putting someone out of business and shutting them up? Only because I do not get it. I am doing and living about like all Natives do in every village in the state. What is the big deal? So anyhow, prove I am an Indian. Worth investigating. All forgiven. By saying, "I am Native!" How cool would that be!

I could be adopted by a tribe. I should have done it years ago. The offer was there actually. I was asked. I said at the time, "No thanks, I know I live like a Native, and may even be one by blood, but the truth is, I was raised white, and have white ways, a white background, and that is what I am in everyone's eyes, 'White.' I look white. I am not going to be adopted in order to gain certain rights." At this point, I hear it is possible to have a DNA test done. I hear it is very costly and am unsure if a court would accept the findings.

Though one thought is, the court might feel embarrassed, unsure how to handle me, if we go to court and argue white subsistence! It's a hot topic I think the court system does not want to touch, because the court has been ordered to define and deal with this, and it has not been done. Someone wants subsistence to go away! No group wants to set a precedence with a court case, is what it looks like to me. If this is so, it might be an easy out in a plea bargain.

"Hey, I'm Indian, just let it go. Explain to the world it's ok, I'm an Indian." I can make certain promises saying I'll be good. You can do some finger shaking, and everyone can go away happy. "I got it. I shut up, you shut up, it all goes away. "

My public defender is silent. I can tell he thinks I'm nuts. The legal world does not operate like that. Of course it does. It is this lawyer who is not that bright. Saddle could make it happen, set up the appointment to talk. Know how to offer the details in legal terms. For 100 grand. "Of course, this is how the world operates! More decisions are made on the golf course then in the courtroom. As it should be! Let's have dinner and figure out how to resolve this." Like that. It's how couples resolve issues, small governments, big governments. Court is for last resort, cannot figure out how to get along problems. When Saddle and I talked, we were on the same page. His own words, "A Mexican standoff."

I'm a businessman. I know how to negotiate. I just lack the grease that makes the gears turn. I'm good at stand offs. I'm not scared. The worse that can happen is you die. Dying is easy, it's living that is hard. Dying does not scare me. I have lived a long, full life. When it is time to go, "Oh, well." I'm right there saying, "Go for it! Make your move!" Been there, done that. Being wounded, a cripple, out of business, a nobody on the street corner is worse than death. Getting wounded as a martyr in a Mexican standoff with the Feds is acceptable. Because if I was only wounded, it would mean I got them. Made the Feds back down. It'd be like Clint Eastwood in Hang em high. Yeah, with the Jews harp playing! Time for the one liner! Like, "Make my day!" or, 'You call that a knife!' "For my next performance I'm going to light myself on fire!" or, but I interrupt myself.

"Miles, you are a second offender." I scowl in puzzlement. The public defender is looking at some files. I recall what this might be about.

"I had an issue a decade ago. It was a violation, misdemeanor, taken care of in traffic court." I recall more details. "Something I could easily have won if I went to court, but was told I would not have free legal council if I chose to fight. I was advised to simply pay the small fine and plead guilty." I did not have the thousands of dollars to defend myself. I had no choice. I paid and forgot about it.

Mr. Public pauses a moment and replies. "You were told what the problem is, 'stay away from ivory!' But you did not listen, and so here you are—back again."

This part is true. "The ivory the undercover agent purchased was among the item inventoried in as legal for me to sell." Now it is my turn to pause. "The white ivory was never mine. I was holding it as collateral. I made sure it was legal government tagged, turned over by a Native with signed paperwork and the numbers."

"The prosecution can probably prove you bought the ivory, and Jessie used the money to buy tickets to Savoonga."

"Maybe. However, I have signed paperwork from an Eskimo saying different, and if I invested and meant to sell, why would I still have ten of the twelve tusks over a year later? Why would the ivory be labeled 'not for sale Natives only' and in my private room, not open to the public?" I realize some of the recorded conversation with Mr. Undercover would not look good. "However, I never sold any of Jessie's white ivory, so what would the charge be?"

"You made an agreement to stay out of the ivory business."

"It's not business if you do not sell, and that was white ivory."

While he is frowning and looking, I remember Penny, the woman who was arrested for selling the mammoth tusk that was in the news. I emailed her and gave my sympathy. She emailed back!

"Miles, you do not know the half of it. The news misrepresented the facts. I was in the park service a long time ago. I quit because of illegal activity I saw and did not want to be part of. It was the people in the park service that turned me in, even set me up, and lined up the buyer who was a previous customer I had who wanted a memento of the raft trip. I was not aware it was illegal to sell fossil mammoth ivory under these conditions.

In fact, as far as I know, it is not. No law was quoted and we never went to court." Like most of us, she did not have the hundred grand it took to have a lawyer and fight the case. She had to take the plea bargain. Concerning my case she says: "Well, of course Miles, you will get told the same thing, that you have a choice. It's supposed to be a plea bargain, but you will see, it is an ultimatum. There are no two sides, just one side. Take the deal or leave it!"

"So this dead raven, explain yourself." Mr. Public peeks up above his glasses. He is old, past retirement age, gray, tired looking. He look content in his suit and tie.

I reply, "The simplest, to the point and shortest way to deal with the raven part of the charges is, this is not federal jurisdiction, next!" I really need say no more, but explain anyway, "Not Federal jurisdiction because the raven does not migrate, or cross state lines. Therefore, it is a state concern. If the state wishes to press charges, that is a different, separate case."

"Miles, I looked it up, and the raven is on the Federal list of migratory birds!"

"Then it is erroneously on that list. Most Alaskans know ravens are a winter bird that does not migrate."

The lawyer snorts, "We'd have to go all the way to the supreme court to change that!" Said indignantly, with a 'dream on' attitude as in 'me and who else is doing that, on whose dime ha, ha' attitude.

"I agree! It is a bummer for whoever made the mistake. It needs to be corrected. I'm sorry correcting the mistake will cost so much! That is not my fault. It's not my mistake. I do not understand the process by which it gets changed. That is what lawyers are for. I'd be just as happy to have that charge dropped to save all that whoop la. I could promise to keep my mouth shut about the error. For certain considerations, I might not go to the public with the incompetence and ignorance of the Federal Fish and Wildlife."

I do not think the raven being on the migratory bird list was an error and an accident. I think this is exactly what the state has been talking about—illegal, deliberate, Federal overreach of power. Big smile on my face. The lawyer is still not saying anything, so I add, "Hey, it is not me on the attack here! I am only defending myself. Keep that in mind."

Twenty years and a $200,000 fine for having a dead raven, are you nuttso? Someone needs to fix that! Clean the Feds clock! Saddle was right, though. This guy is at least honest and up front, not lying to me. He's telling it as he sees it. He is not bullshitting me. I appreciate that. Through this lawyer, I see my problem better. This is the guy defending me, and this is how he feels. Imagine how the prosecution feels! I am not angry. I can honestly see this through his eyes, from his perspective.

He is elderly. Old school. He loves the courtroom. The legal system is his friend in the same way the laws of nature are my friend. Suggesting to him, the legal system is in error, is the same as suggesting to me Mother Nature has it wrong. Everyone in the legal system is his buddy—the judge, the secretary, the prosecution, probation officers, bail bondsman. They all go have dinner together after a hundred trials together. They exchange favors, are kind, honest, treat each other with respect. This world defines the human race. Everyone else is not quite up to standard. He is not interested in upsetting the apple cart. Examining the system for serious errors, how it works, trying to fix it, is not his goal in life. He looks for the good in a system he believes in. His whole life, who has he admired and looked up to? Judges. Lawyers. These are his heroes, the ones who keep it all in balance. He plays golf. That is as much as he knows about the outdoors. Subsistence is like some freaky cult thing. Me and all the alien illegal's! I want protection? Act like a citizen, speak English not 'poor people talk!' Mr. Public wants the world to be a safe place from the likes of me and my kind, who ruin America.

He loves his suit and tie. He loves the feel of the rug on the way down the hall. He loves the guys at security who all know him. I see him straighten up at the respect they show him. He inhales and smiles. At peace, at ease, safe. It is beyond his comprehension this might be perceived by any honest, sane person as a hostile environment, or scary, biased, cruel. I understand better what my father's concern was when I announced the path I would take in life. My father would be among the protected, fit right in with this group of good old boys.

Mr. Public knows no other world. He is not rich. He has not traveled. Nose to the grindstone, a perfect sheep. He does what he is told, without question. If he were in Germany, he would absolutely say there are no concentration camps. The SS treated blue eyed Germans with the utmost respect they deserve. Life is good for those who obey. He has no adventurous thoughts. It would never occur to him he is boring. He takes no chances. I'm sure he runs right to the bank with all his money, as a safe place to keep it. He is happy with the interest rates. He would never go sky diving, bungee jumping, mountain climbing, or go where there are bears on the loose. He would never think of flying to two poles on the earth in a single-engine plane. Old John Wayne movies are a little to risqué for him. Adventure is trying the new soup of the day at the place he has eaten lunch for 35 years.

How can I fault that? Life is good. He is happy. I understand the pull, the happiness in all that. It is a great life for him; there are no other lives out in the world waiting to be explored. He believes in the letter of the law. He may not even be especially bright! He just studied hard, memorized for the test, and knows how to repeat by rote. Open a book and read it. There are no interpretations. There is no intent.

There is no wondering where laws come from, or who has the authority to make them or break them. He opens the book and there it is, right in front of him. He's a good lawyer if you got a speeding ticket. None of this is 'his fault.' I even like the guy. Saddle is right. He is not mean. He has no ax to grind. He is not out to get anyone. He is honest. He is in fact what I asked for.

I am on a fast learning curve here.

"Miles, do you want to separate out any of the charges?" Huh? Do what? *Apparently charges can be separated out and become part of what? A separate case? Two trials?* No. Surely, he does not mean a separate trial after you deal with one trial; face another all over again? Mr. Public slowly explains it, and I still do not get it. Somehow there is a method by which certain evidence is heard and only applies to some charges and not the other charges. The jurors are asked to remember this and ignore what you were just told. *Yeah, right! Like jurors are going to forget?* What planet are these lawyers from? Mr. Public thinks we should focus on that. I do not know enough to understand the advantages and disadvantages. There is no time to explain. I'm guessing he was given an operating budget for this case. My guess is it is a few hundred dollars.

It turns out if we go to trial, I may not have the right to trial by jury, or even the right to get on the stand and speak in my defense. That somehow this is not often wise. Mr. Public thinks I would be bad on the stand, and should not do so. I talk too much. If I am not on the stand on trial, who is? I do not get it. If not me, will there be witnesses we have for the defense? Experts we will call in? I already understand our budget. Next to nothing. Mr. Public has to ask for enough money for pencils.

I see his office. It's a single tiny room with leaking ceiling, unwashed windows, piles of papers on the floor, used outdated computer he does not understand, used furniture. It would never occur to Mr. Public to protect his computer like Saddle does. No one is interested in what is in his boring computer files. He has one over-worked minimum wage secretary typing away. My guess is, we have $1,000 max to spend on our defense. I ask how much the prosecution has!

"Try a trillion dollars." Said without any sarcasm, just the truth. That is what we are up against. I guaran—F*&^%—tee, if I had the prosecutions money they spent getting the goods on me, I would come out smelling like roses and the entire Fish and Wildlife zoo would be in prison! If I had four years' time I could tap into every-one's computer including employees' homes, record all phone conversations, see all emails, look into all bank accounts, watch the money move. If I had a fleet of trained personal lawyers, investigators, computer experts to analyze it all? If I had labs to analyze finger prints, voice recognitions, video footages from secret cameras, if I could plant an insider undercover. Oh my, how different all this would look. This is all amazingly one sided. Railroad job, to say the least. *If it were an equal playing field— but dream on!*

Mr. Public knows as little of my world as I know of his. He has probably never even heard this word 'subsistence.' I insist the entire case revolves around this word. He had to look it up in the dictionary. Not a relevant word in his world. And it is not going to be, not on his salary. I get it. I understand. *But now what?* Because this is not how I envisioned our system being!

What I understood was, we got good public defenders because the court system does not want to retry cases so they want to do it right the first time. It's the same lawyers that one might hire. Kind of pro bono. All the lawyers have to serve their time in donation cases thing. They want to do a good job and look good, so they get better jobs and publicity. Right? Kind of like public dentists and doctors. I assume they get tax breaks for helping the poor, do a good job because they do not want to get sued. Like that. I never noticed a difference between a free tooth pulled on public assistance and a tooth pulled for $1,000.

I understand the court system because I watch Perry Mason. He understands wilderness life because he golfs and watched Lassie as a child.

My buddy, Tusk, happens to be friends with lawyer Saddle. I get a little inside information. Tusk tells me Saddle said of my case, "Kiss your friend Miles good bye. We just sold him down the river." Turned me over to a public defender. It's all over but the fiddle music. I figured that out on my own. I tell Tusk, "I had hoped Saddle would take the case out of personal interest, maybe the publicity. If we fight for white subsistence, it would be front page news around the country." Tusk agrees. I tell Tusk what Saddle told me though, "The animal parts is not going to win!" I pause to see if Tusk gets it. "In other words, the reason we lose would have nothing to do with the law." Tusk agrees. Saddle does not want to be associated with defending the harvest of animals.[2]

"In the past you had fishing for the sled dogs issues, trail use issues. You made the New York times as a poor subsistence person being picked on by bully big government. It made good news at that time. It will not make good news now. Animal rights people will jump all over you and hang you." I agree. I did not agree before I understood how the system works.

"The world is not open-minded, Tusk." He adds, "As a society, we do not respect how others want to live. We get into everyone else's business and tell them, order them, force them, to be like us, the majority."I tell Tusk about my time in the Navy as a teen. "I saw how we treated other countries. 'Be like us or else,' I was embarrassed, ashamed. I thought we should let other countries run their government and people run their lives as they see fit. Why do we have to be bullies? I assumed I joined to help fight for people's rights and freedom."

"I am not sure, Miles, that life would be any better in any other country!"

"So I am told Tusk, how would you or I know?" I do not get into it with Tusk. There is a possibility he is wired and working for the Feds. He is a competitor. We have had some issues off and on. He wants me to sell my mammoth ivory and fossil finds to him. He may be upset I cut him out as the middle man. That was his own doing. He did not treat me fair, so I left. Other middle people I deal with now are happy to just double their money. Fair enough. I would not want my comments recorded. *Trust no one.*

I have heard the US has a higher percent of its citizens behind bars than any other country in the world. Thus, we are more likely to end up in jail than in any other country. More people, and a higher percent than Stalin had in his reign. Is that just a rumor? Why is it said so many in other countries die trying to get here for a better life? Possibly the sheep have it better in the US in terms of the world's average standard of living. Which might be much better, because we are the greatest exploiter in the world. I'm not sure, I have no answer. I hear how so many countries have people dying, while trying to get to the US, what a privilege it is to arrive, how lucky they feel. The land of opportunity. But is it the best place to be a free person? Living as you wish, not bothering anyone? Are there countries where such a person might expect to get left alone? Is there a place a person could own a cabin in the woods, a canoe, live off the land, coming into a village a few times a year for rice and beans and not get hauled off in handcuffs?

Tusk thinks I would have been left alone, except I got on the internet! He is upset about that, "It hurts us all in the business, Miles. The rest of us are trying to keep a low profile!"

"So subsistence is ok when we are poor, keep our eyes down, go to the back of the bus, say yes, Sir? Low profile, out of everyone else's way, not competition." "As soon as we say 'Hey, I love it! Life is good,' society frowns? As soon as we get good at a lifestyle, suddenly it is wrong?" "Is that how it works, Tusk, and is that ok?" It's like saying black is beautiful up till you want a white man's job. Or that being a dumpster diver is ok till you enjoy it. Until you enjoy it, people feel sorry for you and put pennies in the can you hold out. There are food stamps, the Salvation Army, help programs. As long as you get involved and, "Yup, doing good, got me a hot meal, cot for the night, and a blanket, life is good." But if you found stuff at the dump and sold it on Craig's list, then what? I know what. People frown. Suddenly you are competition. It is not cool to be a successful dumpster diver, anymore than successful living off the land as a subsistence person. Transfer stations are to help the poor, not run a business.

Running a business is not about 'low profile.' How can you tell someone in business to keep a low profile? Just don't advertise! I was trying to make some OK money my last few years of working before becoming a retired senior, later in life, doing all this as a hobby, with less stress about bills.

"Well, Miles, if you do well, then supposedly you no longer need special privileges to snaffle the endangered game." Tusk would not have this outlook, but many do. He's playing devil's advocate. I understand this concept. However, the law and intent only view the money as one of many factors. I tell Tusk what I have read about the law. "Lifestyle, tradition, where you live, all are major criteria in defining who is subsistence. There are in fact eight major criteria looked at."

"Still, Miles, you are looking for legal loopholes it sounds like to me."

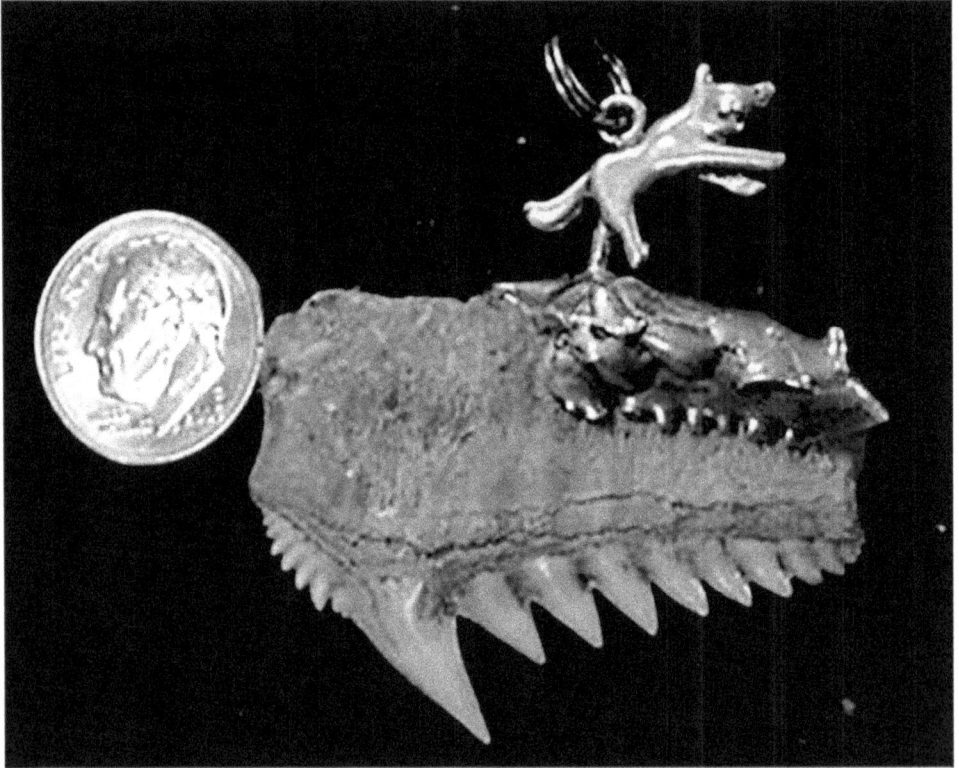

I take shards of bones, teeth, fossils, and try to use them in my art.

CHAPTER TEN

SUBSISTENCE PRIORITY LAWS, FEDERAL LAWS

I review the news article that came out in connection with my arrest.

News Miner Jan 5th 2013.

'Man accused of sales crimes' in smaller headlines, 'Charges stem from online business' ...have charged Nenana artist woodsman Miles Martin with 28 felony and misdemeanor counts for illegally selling and exporting parts of Alaska animals including polar bear teeth, seal claws, walrus ivory, and wolf bones.... Slew of charges dating back from May 2009 to April 2011... on line business selling animal parts.... Conspiracy to buy illegally obtained walrus tusks... nearly two years after Martin's home was searched...

The headlines on the follow up page read—

"Charges: Man charged with violating wildlife laws". Shipments include wolf teeth, lynx claws, destined for the United Kingdom, Czech Republic, Australia... each charge has a maximum sentence of 10 years... conspiracy to violate the Lacey Act... timeline coincides with arrest and conviction of Jessie, Loretta, Richard Blake the trio pleaded guilty... Marine mammal Protection Act forbids the transportation, sale of any marine mammal part or product... it allows some Alaska native groups to take and possess... for subsistence or creating handicrafts. Martin's arraignment is set for Jan 18th.

"Miles, a new set of laws came out in an agreement with the Natives called ANILCA. You need to look that up!" I do look this up. I never heard of this agreement. I get new information, but still, nothing that discriminates in favor of Natives.

I reply to my friend, "This issue is important for anyone interested in living off the grid. Off grid, implies living outside of civilization, certainly outside the larger areas. I refer to the word 'subsistence,' which simply, means, 'taking care of yourself,' involving depending more on nature, than the government. So the topic would be if you chose such a lifestyle. Is this is even legal! Would you be arrested?"

"Well, your issue, Miles, involves animal parts of threatened animals."

"True. However, I argue this involves wilderness waste items, recycled-repurposed items headed for the garbage. A byproduct of eating or self defense. This issue concerns a way of life, with the belief we should not be wasteful. A way of life that does not have regular jobs with bosses, degrees, or always involve money. In this way, a variety of issues in conflict with how it is done in civilization become apparent. These issues can get interesting and should be considered if such a life is of interest, even if just a passing 'what if' contemplation."

I find on the internet in a google search, Congress made good on that promise in 1980, when it passed the landmark **Alaska National Interest Lands Conservation Act [ANILCA]**. Besides creating new national wildlife refuges and public recreation lands, ANILCA mandated that the state maintain a subsistence hunting and fishing preference for *rural* residents on Federal public lands, or forfeit its management of subsistence uses there.

I'm even more confused. There is a lot to wade through, with vague references, nothing absolutely clear. It looks to me like it is the Federal government that favors equality and the state that favors discrimination in favor of natives.

WHAT IS THE SUBSISTENCE PRIORITY

From a government informational website: 'Subsistence management Information' - Subsistence has been elemental to Alaska Natives and their cultures for thousands of years. It also has become a way of life for many non-Natives in Alaska. Subsistence is recognized by the United States and by the State of Alaska as the highest-priority consumptive use of resources in the state.

Subsistence is a controversial political topic because managing subsistence involves making decisions about who has access to Alaska's valuable fish and wildlife resources. Disagreements about subsistence arise between and within different groups, including urban and rural Alaska residents, Natives and non-Natives, subsistence users and non-subsistence users, state lawmakers and other groups. Disagreements include who should get rights to subsistence, how resources are allocated under subsistence provisions, and how such decisions are made.

Subsistence wasn't a controversial legal issue until the late 1970s, when demands of a growing state population started putting the squeeze on Alaska's available fish and game, and resource managers increasingly were forced to choose between users.

I pause here, as I think about how it was when I arrived in Alaska in 1972. I did not notice the big controversy as this article points out. Pipeline times, with a lot of new arrivals. I saw that. I read on.

But the underpinnings of the management controversy can be traced to Alaska statehood in 1959. On becoming a state, Alaska took over responsibility for managing subsistence from the Federal Government when it gained authority for managing fish and wildlife. State control of fish and wildlife was a leading argument for statehood, as Alaskans criticized Federal fishery management as favoring outside interests and unresponsive to resident needs.

The new Alaska Constitution established that fish and wildlife "are reserved to the people for common use" and that "no exclusive right or special privilege of fishery shall be created or authorized." [Alaska Constitution, Article VIII] For the United States federal government, the question of subsistence surfaced in 1971 when Congress was drafting the **Alaska Native Claims Settlement Act (ANCSA)**. The act addressed Native land claims that clouded construction of the Trans-Alaska Oil Pipeline. It extinguished aboriginal hunting and fishing rights in Alaska in exchange for almost $1 billion in cash and 44 million acres of land.

Hmmm, this is interesting. Did you catch that? "Yes, I caught that. Thanks for pointing it out." Alaska natives should now be considered 'citizens.' With the same rights, no more, and no less, then anyone else. There is still ongoing talk about how the white man cheated the Indian, and how we whites owe them. I understand. They were here first. It was their land and people of my race came and claimed it; took it by force and trickery. With the ANCSA agreement, the Natives were financially well compensated, as well as receiving generous portions of land. I recall some words from the past, I did not understand, that the amount given was a million dollars plus 160 acres of land for every single Alaska native. This is how my friend Josh got his land. What Josh did with his million, I do not know.

I think he told me, "Miles, this money was not given to each native but to our corporations. The issues are the same as with the white people. Our own leaders are skimming the money and not giving it to the people it was designed to compensate." Josh feels this land and money will never go to the people. The red man is no more honest, and has no more integrity than any other race. The leaders have run off with the money. Maybe not. I'm told the money is invested in oil and is paying dividends out to shareholders. Even so, the issue of us owing the Indian was settled.

"There, we are all equals now." Because of this agreement and acceptance, there should be no more talk about owing the Indian. Take your 44 million acres and billion dollars and be happy! Geez! I read on...

ANCSA didn't explicitly protect subsistence, but a Congressional conference report issued with the new law stated that Native subsistence practices and subsistence lands would be protected by the State of Alaska and U.S. Department of Interior. Congress made good on that promise in 1980, when it passed the landmark Alaska National Interest Lands Conservation Act [ANILCA]. Besides creating new national wildlife refuges and public recreation lands, ANILCA mandated that the state maintain a subsistence hunting and fishing preference for rural residents on federal public lands or forfeit its management of subsistence uses there.

The State of Alaska, which had established its own subsistence law in 1978, took note of the discrepancy between the laws and amended state law in 1986 to match ANILCA by limiting subsistence uses to rural residents. The fix, however, didn't last long. In 1989, the state Supreme Court ruled that the rural preference violated Alaska Constitution, including its "common use" provisions regarding use of fish and wildlife.

As the state no longer guaranteed a rural preference for subsistence as required by ANILCA, the Federal government moved to take over management of subsistence on federal public lands. Several attempts by the state to reconcile the two laws by amending the Alaska Constitution failed when supporters couldn't muster enough votes in the Alaska Legislature to send a constitutional amendment to the state's voters. Federal managers took over authority for subsistence on federal lands on July 1, 1990.

In 1995, the U.S. Ninth Circuit Court of Appeals, in adjudicating Katie John vs. United States, ruled that ANILCA's subsistence priority extends to freshwater bodies within and alongside federal public lands. The decision pushed the Federal Government into management of subsistence fisheries.

Realizing that federal subsistence fisheries management would impact fishing statewide, the State of Alaska again attempted to regain management. Between 1997 and 1999, a subsistence task force was convened, two special sessions of the Legislature were held, and U.S. Senator Ted Stevens of Alaska twice delayed a federal takeover of subsistence on Federal Waters through a moratorium. But in the end, the Alaska Senate failed to pass onto voters a constitutional amendment that would bring state law into compliance with ANILCA. On October 1, 1999, the rural subsistence priority was extended to inland waters within 34 federal parks, forests, wildlife refuges, preserves and recreation lands. Federal subsistence fishery management had arrived.

Congress also saw a need to protect subsistence uses by non-Native rural residents, many of whom had adopted a subsistence way of living. In making a customary and traditional use *determination*, the Federal Subsistence Board identifies communities that have practiced a particular use. Only those communities are eligible for subsistence use under such "customary and traditional use" determinations.

Yes, I remember seeing a list of eligible communities. Nenana, where I live, is on that list. I wonder how it would go for those people living subsistence out in the wilds as I had been doing. I would not be eligible because I was not part of a community? In my mind true subsistence is not sustainable by a large village, but ideally involves small isolated groups capable of following the resources in a nomadic existence.

I explain to my friend. "As our history shows, subsistence has always been about very small groups from a dozen to maybe thirty people. The environment can handle this amount of sustainable harvesting. Much as a pack of wolves is about this size and covers many hundreds of square miles."

"So mankind got crowded and subsistence is not going to work anymore."

"Perhaps. Early man lived off the land hunting with rocks and spears. It is not comparable to modern subsistence with rifles and motorboats." When I began, I tried and wanted to live as primitive as possible. I would have loved going back to pole boats and fish nets, hunting with bow and arrow or black powder. My problem became competition with sport hunters with all the modern equipment. Rival trappers taking over my trapline with snow machines as I ran sled dogs. Subsistence laws against fish nets, ordering me to use a modern fish wheel. I have another perspective to share.

"If subsistence is about sustainable resources used wisely, I will consume only what I need." With this in mind, will it matter, biologically to the environment if I harvest one moose with a rifle or a rock? Will it matter if I catch the fish I need for sled dogs with my hands, a fish pole, a net, or a wheel, if it is the same number of fish extracted from the environment? It should help the game population if I can travel further into more remote inhospitable country with the use of a motorboat or snow machine.

The issue in my mind is not to over-harvest. I argue it is politics, that favors sport hunting and commercial harvest of limited resources. As stated in the agreements, I quote, this is illegal. What is the public getting told? Try to imagine the life of a remote person who is not interested in politics, not getting any news, just trying to live off the grid. Live a simple uncomplicated life with nature, who gets told, 'Yes, go ahead, you are protected by subsistence laws!' You are doing so, when a helicopter shows up and carts you off to civilization to face charges of breaking the law.

"A nice sob story, Miles, but you are selling on the internet making good money."

"Yes. How did I get here to this position? I got carted off, faced charges, had to pay lawyers, come up with a level of income not consistent with my lifestyle. I wished to survive, I had to make hard choices, partly forced to." Yes, I am walking the line between depending on the land and forced to depend on civilization, or partly choosing to. Wondering where the line of acceptance might be. Needing about two years of ok income to be able to retire. In retirement, unable to get out to live subsistence, spending retirement working on my books, fooling with my casting and cutting my own rocks for art as a hobby, no longer being a subsistence issue. I understand the world is getting crowded and the land may not be able to continue to support subsistence in the future. This is my life, my training, my knowledge. "You cannot imagine being in my shoes, and what would you do?"

I read on:

In judging a customary and traditional use determination, the federal board considers eight factors including: a long-term and consistent pattern of use, uses recurring in specific seasons, uses involving methods of harvest that are efficient and economic, harvests and uses that are related to past ones and are reasonably accessible to a community, methods of handling and preserving resources that are traditional, allowing for *some alteration for technological advances*, uses involving the handing down of knowledge of harvest skills, values and lore from one generation to the next, *uses in which harvests are shared within a defined community*, and uses that involve reliance on a wide variety of resources in an area and *provide an area with cultural, economic, social and nutritional elements*.

These eight factors are viewed as guidelines, not criteria. A use does not have to meet all factors to be determined "customary and traditional" by the Federal Subsistence Board. The board also considers Advisory Council recommendations and public input when making determinations.

So this sums up many of the issues in general. When looking at state law, I find this:

State: In state law, "customary and traditional," means "the non-commercial, long-term and consistent taking of, use of, and reliance upon fish or game in a specific area and the use patterns of that fish or game that have been established over a reasonable period of time, taking into consideration the availability of the fish or game. "

Under state law, the boards of Fish and Game are required to identify fish stocks with customary and traditional uses, using eight criteria similar to those under federal regulation. Unlike federal regulation, all eight criteria must be met to establish a customary and traditional use.

State and federal management aren't entirely separate efforts. Federal and state fisheries and wildlife managers work together under a draft Memorandum of Understanding (MOA) that was initialed in 2000. Areas identified for coordinated actions include, but aren't limited to, development of regulations, in-season management, research, special action requests, customary *trade and barter*, customary and traditional use determinations and Advisory Committee and Regional Council actions.

http://subsistmgtinfo.org/ct.htm

I still have to find specifics on marine mammal protection. I review what I believe and see if I have misunderstood. I come across another snippet of stashed information, another news article. I realize there is an issue if I have moved into the commercial world and this disqualifies me for subsistence. However, I still qualify for a subsistence permit which I have. I find an article in the local paper.

> **"Individuals can't keep them, while commercial fishing,"** Chinook salmon are one of most precious resources. "For many of us, the opportunity to catch one of these is one of the primary reasons we live here."
>
> "Though our constitution guarantees us equal access to all our commonly owned resources, and expressly prohibits exclusive rights to fish, the only user group harvesting king salmon this summer are commercial fisherman, most of whom live outside during the winter. As total closures or catch and release regulations have been imposed throughout Alaska on personal use and sport fisheries, the commercial fisheries have continued harvesting hundreds of thousands of kings."

I pause in my reading. This is the exact issue Alaska faced when we voted to become a state and not a territory. One big issue was federal control and outside interests interfering with the rights of Alaskans. This was an important part of our constitution at statehood not so long ago. If there was ever a time for Alaskans to revolt over how our king salmon are being mismanaged, it is now.

The commercial fisherman donate heavily and lobby extensively to maintain control over our fish, while we continue to sit quietly on the shore watching the last few kings swim up the river. The drift gill nets, the purse seines, the beach seines, and fish vacuums known as factory trawlers have historically accounted for the major percent of all salmon harvested. The leftover one percent placates the rest of us in times of plenty, but in times of shortage, it is politically expedient to cut our minimal harvest completely, rather than reduce the profits of Seattle based seafood companies.

Even subsistence fisheries have been denied their fish, while offshore trawlers kill kings by the tens of thousands. These great fish are inconvenient "bycatch" to Seattle based Pollock fleet that provide cheap fish sticks to the world at our considerable expense. The commercial fish managers at ADFG have taken full advantage of the upriver closures by allocating every king salmon to the Cordova commercial fleet. You can buy a Gulkana King at Fred Meyers, but you can't catch one yourself.

I note this was on the opinion page, and not a news article, so the facts may be off. What I read does match what I have observed. By law, subsistence needs have priority in a time of shortage. The law is clearly not being followed. So define 'criminal.' This whole fishing issue is important to me because I got caught up in the politics and stopped from depending on fish. I was forced out of a lifestyle by not being allowed to fish for my sled dogs. Unable to legally feed my sled dogs resulted in having to move to town. When at the time, there were plenty of fish in the river.

I cannot dwell on that! It's a lot to understand, know about, follow. I was living in the wilds with no electricity, no news. I assumed living the subsistence life was proof enough. I'm still looking for the Marine Mammal information. I began looking for information affecting my federal crimes. Are subsistence people who choose not to have electricity supposed to have computers and be internet savvy enough to find the applicable laws? It's frustrating.

When the Alaska Statehood Act (Public Law 85-508) passed in 1958, the state of Alaska was permitted to select for withdrawal, 104 million acres of land for public domain. Alaska proclaimed that "all right and title to any lands or other property not granted or confirmed to the State... may be held by any... Natives, or held by the U.S. in trust for said Natives" (Public Law 85-508).

Contention arose when the state began to make selections that intruded on Native settlements and hunting grounds. This encroachment, in turn, spawned several lawsuits by Natives. As a result, Congress sought to resolve the issue through the Alaska Native Claims Settlement Act (ANCSA) of 1971 (Public Law 92-203)

This is the first time I see something specific to 'Native only' rights to land. This is clearly discrimination. We say we do not believe in discrimination. So I don't get it. If we think discrimination is the answer, and necessary to show favoritism to a particular race because they are that race, then this might be a good thing! But why not say so! "We believe in discrimination because..." and call a spade a spade. Instead of denying it is so!

Hey, I thought of other clear discrimination you never thought of! Yes, and what might that be dear conscience? *Well, we have ladies restrooms and men's restrooms and that's discrimination!* I agree! Discrimination by sex is illegal! I should post haste enter the ladies' restroom and announce I do not believe in discrimination!

Our entire country is off its rocker saying there is no discrimination allowed. So anyhow, it sounds like the intention in the beginning was to protect the Natives aboriginal rights, since they were here on the land first. Sounds good. And if I had been told when I arrived in Alaska, "I'm sorry you are white and you cannot go live in the wilds off the land, only Indians can." I would have understood; it is a bummer, and done something else, or moved to where I could live the life I chose. Maybe another country. Or been more secretive, understanding I am an outlaw. I may have stayed out of magazines, declined interviews and such. Or sought permission some place somehow. Maybe been adopted by a Native family, had DNA testing to prove I am a Native.

However, when homesteading was going on, the staking packet stated clearly, "Those who receive these parcels are expected to live a subsistence lifestyle." Not only permission to live subsistence, but if you do not, you will not make it. I still have a copy of this brochure given out by the state. I comply with this. I'm one of the few, one of the ten percent who saw the land acquisition to the end and got title. I find it unreasonable to be told I'm expected to live subsistence to acquire this state land, then get told, "No, that was spoken in error, get off the land."

An article I wrote for Alaska magazine discussing a subsistence lifestyle was reprinted and distributed to potential land stakers as a 'read this if you expect to end up with title to your land.' This was handed out by the state. I was told by the state, "This is the best introduction to what potential homesteaders can expect if they want to make it, that we have ever seen!" There was no mistake or misunderstanding, subsistence was expected. Likewise, how is it I have been issued a subsistence license all these years? Am I being told, 'No, it was not valid?' I think it is recognized that 'some' white people live in the old subsistence ways. If so, with the same rights the Natives have. Ah! Here is something addressing this.

Subsistence and ANILCA

One clear purpose of ANILCA is to "preserve Wilderness resource values." (§101[a] Public Law 96-487). Another is "to provide the opportunity for rural residents engaged in subsistence way of life, and to continue to do so" (§101[c[Public Law 96-487). Subsistence is defined in ANILCA as the customary and traditional uses by rural Alaska residents of wild renewable resources for direct personal or family consumption as food, shelter, fuel, clothing, tools, or transportation; for the making and selling of handicraft articles out of non-edible byproducts of fish and wildlife resources taken for personal or family consumption; and for customary trade. (§ 803 Public Law 96-487) Considering the above purposes, conflicting views about the relationship between wilderness preservation and subsistence are inevitable.

For example,

Unlike designated wilderness in the Lower 48, snowmobile use, motorboats, and airplanes are allowed in Alaskan wilderness for subsistence, traditional activities, and travel to and from villages and home sites (§811[a] and §1110 Public Law 96-487). The phrase "traditional uses," found within ANILCA's definition of subsistence, has incited a conflict reflected in a U.S. Senate report addressing ANILCA. The report states that restriction of subsistence to customary and traditional uses shall "in no way impede the use of new technology for subsistence purposes" (Senate Report 96-413). This controversy has heightened with rapid changes in technology.

I note the 'new technology' part. One strong argument has been that it is a crime for me to be on the internet with animal parts. That by doing so, I gave up my subsistence rights.

"The internet can't be used to sell subsistence crafts and materials, Miles!" Why? Because it works? More important, is if this is at a commercial level or not. Even subsistence people need a way to pay the bills, for there are things even subsistence people need that cost money. Important to note, no animals were ever killed specifically to supply me with material. All materials were a by-product of a something already dead for other reasons.

Title VIII of ANILCA contains the rural preference provision

PUBLIC LAW 96-487-DEC. 2, 1980 94 STAT. 2371

PREFERENCE FOR SUBSISTENCE USE ANILCA §804. Except as otherwise provided in this Act and other Federal laws, the taking on public lands of fish and wildlife for non-wasteful subsistence uses shall be accorded priority over the taking on such lands of fish and wildlife for other purposes.

So far, everywhere I look, I see the intention of preserving a subsistence way of life as a priority. The question is still, if my activities fall under traditional use, and subsistence protection. Even I am not sure if I have moved into the realm of 'commercial' over the last few years. If so, I had simply hoped to secure a minimal retirement of over $400 a month by working hard my last few years, after a lifetime of being financially poor. I make ok money, relative to the past, but still in the poverty level in terms of profit. I still legally qualify for a subsistence permit

In a discussion with Seymour, he says, "You got caught, Miles! Bummer! But you can't say you were not warned! You cannot say you do not understand, or that you are innocent. You cannot rightfully blame your problems on the government. You are an outlaw and always were." What Seymour says holds a lot of weight. We have worked together twenty-five years. He knows me better than anyone else. "You will not get many to listen, Miles. You are trying to make it complicated by quoting all these sources and looking for conflict, discrepancies. I can see how it is of interest to you, but what you speak of does not affect many others."

I do notice, no one I begin talking to shows a lot of interest saying, "Tell me more." "That's interesting, wow!" "Can I have a copy of that to show others?"

Even Iris has zero interest. "You got yourself into this mess." She sits over there doing crossword puzzles, while I try to look things up, organize notes, work on a defense. The message I get is, there is no defense.

Still, I do not know where all this big money goes. Nothing really stands out as a huge money drain. A combination of given away, sold cheap, stolen, bad deals, damaged, not caring overly much, investment in surplus stored inventory, lost in the creative process with a third loss through experimentations that do not turn out. If I'm 'commercial' it certainly is not big time. My standard of living is on par with most subsistence people in the village *who get Indian money compensation from their Native Corporation.*

I cannot find any definition of 'CITES' in connection with endangered species, the Marine Mammal Protection Act. I understand the history and definition. There was concern as civilization grew, for species that were going extinct like whooping crane, buffalo, passenger pigeon. Around the world there was concern with import, export of animals and parts on the verge of extinction. Several countries got together to set up some international guidelines to follow. There was a developing problem with poachers moving between countries out of each other's jurisdiction. It was hard to prosecute international crimes when there was no agreement between countries. In 1972 this meeting took place and rules set down to protect these endangered species.

This is an important meeting, and set of rules, set forth that control the animal parts business concerning endangered species. Those who had items before the treaty, became exempt, and any such items could be sold, as long as the item was in private hands before 1972, or the animal died before 1972. A list was created of animals in danger of extinction. Various levels of seriousness were created. Endangered or just protected. Violation of these rules is a serious Federal offense. The list began with marine mammals, and expanded to include any threatened species. This is a list concerning Alaskans.

Common Alaskan CITES listed species used in Alaskan Native Arts include: Bears (Polar, Brown, and Black), Lynx, Wolf, River Otter, Sea Otter, Whale and Walrus.

I find it interesting that Alaska has lynx, otter, and wolf as legal to harvest by trappers without any special fee or restrictions. This gets confusing as the Federal Government and state argue. Whose laws do we obey? Trappers are obeying state laws. I decide to do the same. In the news, the Feds reprimand the state and threaten to withhold federal funding over wolf control methods. There are efforts to boycott tourism to Alaska, but Alaska holds firm.

This becomes an issue, however, when crossing state lines with such items into states and countries who do not agree with Alaska. A subsistence trapper who decides to send his furs to the Canadian fur auction, or Seattle Fur Exchange, or to a tanner to have furs tanned and sold retail, may become a felon for doing so without the proper permits. Not all trappers are up on the latest laws and what state or country has passed what laws. Often 'since last year,' when the trapper last sent furs out. The Feds themselves implied I needed a permit to sell tanned furs in Tucson. Either they knew I did not need a permit, and lied to me, or they do not know their own laws. Or maybe none of us in the business know the latest law.[1]

Officials may not know the right answer. Opinions vary, clarification hard to come by. Serious criminals get what they deserve, those clearly wiping out a species for profit. Others trying to understand the law and being good citizens become puzzled. Many responsible citizens just avoid the entire issue. Most shops refuse to carry any animal products to avoid trouble. It is difficult to go along with that in my position, having spent a lifetime gaining knowledge and building up a business, a reputation, that has taken several decades. How do I walk away from that? What am I going to do instead? It's my love, passion and area of expertise. 'The tooth and claw man.'

While many people hear the basic simple law, "Do not do it!" That suits them, doesn't directly affect them, makes their life simpler. Most feel such laws need to be universal, as all laws should be, with no discrimination, or special privileges to anyone. Most people do not understand there are exceptions written into the law. Here is an example: Marine mammals that died before 1972 do not fall into the same protected status, and Non-Alaska Natives may use, sell and possess marine mammal parts that meet the standard of Pre-1972.

There is so much to read, to determine what is relevant. I'm focusing on a big picture for now. I have trouble getting into the details of my exact situation. My mind reels from all the laws, court cases, news stories, public opinions, state laws, Federal Laws. I realize I have to deal with the specifics. A court case that was fair would take a lot of time and involve understanding a lot of laws and issues. In the end, who would be right? Fish and Wildlife, or me?

The January 18th court date is a problem. I am set up to go to Tucson. All my goods are sent ahead. Tickets are bought, show fees paid. I'm scheduled to leave the 29th, a week after my court appearance. I inform Mr. Public I'd like to make it to the show, and put in a request to go ahead of time. Since I have not been convicted, I figure it should not be a big deal.

"Postpone the hearing," it should be understood I need to make a legal living. I mean geez, if one of the lawyers says, 'I'm scheduled to be on vacation during that date,' the case would get postponed. A lawyers, 'I'm scheduled to play golf that day,' is a conflict, the hearing date gets changed.

There will be no postponement. I do not know what to do, or know if I will even be allowed to attend the show! The tentative plan is to go ahead and send Iris ahead, so she is there to sort the goods, take care of the preliminaries. If I show up to join her, great. If I cannot, we can deal with that, but someone has to be with the goods and take care of the show.

"Iris, maybe you could hire one of the kids we work with, or our friend Foil, who has been helping us. Even Wren. Or, that young kid, what's his name."

"Andrea. Miles!"

"Yeah, good kid, he's good at setting up, taking down, lifting stuff and what not." It would be hard to financially survive without the show. There is a plan B with a mammoth tusk for sale. I had planned to wait to stabilize it and get the increased value, but selling now would make up for lost show income and various fees, potential fines, etc.

I take time to look over the contract handed me by Mr. Public. There is a description of what his role is. I pause and frown. *There is no place that uses the word lawyer!* "Yes, I noticed, most curious." I study harder to look for the description of who he is, and what his job is. *He is representing the people. His job is to make sure the noose is put around my neck legally and humanely. The noose needs to be clean and strong enough, with a working trapdoor under me. Not to defend me, or try to stop the noose from getting put on in the first place. 'What's best for society is the priority.' This is basically the same job of the prosecution.*

I understand now; you hire a lawyer who is not part of the court system to actually fight and look out for the defendant who is paying. The court is paying a public defender. Mr. Public's responsibility is to Mr. Public's boss who is paying his salary. The court pays. The same source of funding as the prosecution. That is not explained up front. I, we, the public, are getting misled. I have no representation. At best, there is a defensive response to attacks. There is no planned offense. We respond to what is being done. We do not plan an attack, an aggressive defense. The way this is set up makes it almost impossible for me to win in court. I tell Iris, "I'm not talking now if I am innocent or guilty, or even my specific case. I'm talking about the system and how it works. For any of us."

I can see where Saddle is looking out for me as my lawyer if I pay. He does not depend on the court for his salary. He does not go to lunch with, nor is friends with, anyone in the court system. These people are not his friends. Saddle would like to clean their clock. Not Mr. Public.

I do not drive, so take the senior bus to Fairbanks. I got dropped off at Mr. Public's office. There is not a lot to say. Though I'd think we'd have a lot to discuss! "Miles, you have to decide if this goes to trial, or work on a plea. A lot of money was spent! I have never in my career seen such an effort, so am puzzled why you are wanted so badly, but they have a pretty tight case against you." I do not agree, but this guy knows the legal system and how it works. "28 counts against you, any one of which carries ten years in prison. It's not good odds, Miles, to win on all counts."

We had discussed 'entrapment' as a defense. "Public, I see all the problems stemming from one bad customer and backed away when I realized what he was up to. And an undercover agent who set me up." I explain how the undercover agent posed as a friend and wanted only legal stuff at first. He comes to my home and spends an entire weekend trying to get me to toss illegal items in his order. I did not want to do that. It took him three days to talk me into something I do not normally do and did not want.

"Miles, entrapment is hard to win. Laws have changed. It only needs to be shown that you are predisposed and had the inclination to commit a crime. You are a second offender. This has happened before. You have said some anti-law, anti-government things that have been recorded. You speak of morality and integrity being more important than laws. You cannot just have your own set of rules to live by and expect everyone else to understand and respect those rules. I think we'd lose on the entrapment argument."

It's true I have the nickname, 'Wild Miles' and a reputation of not being exactly a legal beagle, one of the sheep. I'm known for being out there at the edge, a maverick. It's hard to sniffle, "He tricked me!" I'm just, well, trying to save my bacon by whatever method works. I need a battle plan, a strategy. Mr. Public is not the creative type. This is not Perry Mason or CSI. I need a rabbit pulled out of a hat here. *Maybe I can prove I'm not a Jew?*

"The main thing here, Miles, is to keep quiet, and do not say anything! You tend to talk too much!" Oh. "Let me do all the talking. Once we enter the building, keep your mouth shut. There are cameras and recorders throughout the entire building."

"Even the restroom?"

"At least you have not lost your sense of humor, but get rid of that cocky attitude in front of the judge." Yes, I understand. Bow my head, stutter, look confused, ready to do as I'm told, ready to ride in the back of the bus. Got it. My life is in your hands Masta, please do not beat me. It's like acting. I can do this, it's like being in a movie. I'm the type that would be doing a jig, making jokes, as I was marched down the plank at the end of a sword. Not giving anyone the pleasure of thinking they were doing me great harm. Take that joy away from them. I will entertain the crowd to the last.

This court appearance is to find out if this is really me as described and if I understand the charges. Maybe I am offered choices. I am not asked how I plead, I do not think. It is all a nightmare. I hear nothing. I process nothing. I said nothing beyond, "Yes, your honor." 'Poof' it didn't happen. My blood comes back out of my core. I was not shot. There is a probation officer if this is the title. I am released on my own recognizance. Another date is set far off down the road. I ask this probation officer. "My annual Tucson trip is set up, paid for, and I need to conduct my legal business to pay my bills. I'll be gone…"

I am interrupted, "No way, no how!" Rude and cheeky of me to even ask. Like a drug dealer asking to go to Mexico for one more important shipment. This is a loss of about thirty grand! *A fine how do you do.* "I'm not proven guilty of anything. I have not been to trial. I am supposed to be innocent till then." It's like getting fined $30,000, charged, found guilty, and punished in one swoop of the guillotine. I'm asked to voluntarily surrender my passport in case I try to bolt across the border.

I have already been across the border since the warrant was served. If I was going to run, it would be then! I did not say much as my public defender frowned at me. *"Say nothing, ask for nothing, shut up, do what I'm told, and let's get out of here in one piece."* Ok! I got it! This is exactly what not to be saying. *Yes, Masta! Thank you for letting me live, bow, and bow again. It is not a big deal not going to the show, it's only a year's income. I'm grateful to not be in jail, thank you!*

Iris flies down to my mother's and the show without me. My ticket goes unused. I get a refund on only half my show fee. I have agreed not to sell any animal products, or do any shows, or have anyone work for me as a condition of my release. Iris cannot set up for me or sell anything I sent down, except some rocks. She goes over everything sent down, repackages it, and sends it back. $500 to send it down, $500 to send it home again. All my regular customers are wondering where I am, why I am not set up. As the Feds want, a thousand people get the message not to mess with them when the word is spread, "Miles got busted."

Tusk says, "Been through this as well. I was investigated. This is all about getting the word out to dealers and customers not to mess with the Feds. Do what you are told. The law does not have a lot to do with it. The agenda does." There may be truth in that, as I and friends have been told, the objective is to stop all sales of all animal products. Told that there is no such thing as legal ivory of any kind, not fossil, not mammoth, not tagged, not Indian, or Eskimo. All of it is illegal.

"To follow the lead of California."

As a government representative told me, "All ivory to us, is like heroin is to the drug agency."

Tusk has heard this as well. Dealers know each other, discuss various issues we all face. This is some of the talk we pass around and wonder what it means. Tusk asks, "Do we listen, to what amounts to illegal restrictions? Or do we listen because there is a gun at our head?"

I have been one of the few bold, saying, "I side with the state, and on the side of right, moral, and legal!"

"Well, Miles, we all see where that is getting you, and that is the message the Feds are getting out, worth the million they spent. Maybe they know you are a writer. They surely know you reach a lot of people. 300,000 go to your website? I looked at the count, pretty impressive. You are practically a symbol for independence and survival, self-reliance, with all the skills and followers. A revolution could form around you, Miles."

"Is that what you think the Feds are concerned about? I doubt that." But it did occur to me that there is gas and oil under my four homesteads and entire trapline. I noticed all the subsistence people in that whole area the size of Rhode Island have been systematically made to leave. The land is now empty of permanent residents, as the oil exploration begins. "Is that a coincidence?" I have trouble believing the oil company would work hand in hand with Fish and Wildlife to get rid of people in some kind of conspiracy. "A little farfetched Tusk!"

I tell Tusk, "I was out on my snow machine this winter checking new roads the oil seismic people put in. I was thinking of trapping those trails, since it is my trapping area. I was trying to mark where the trails are on my map using GPS. Some of the exploration is as much as twenty miles outside the boundaries of their lease. There is a lot of environmental damage going on beyond what is reported to the public at meetings." I know because I attended the meetings where the rules were read, and public input requested. I saw the maps and heard the protections put in place.

"Miles, I can see how these people do not want any outsiders around taking pictures and making reports! Maybe having you arrested is a good way to get you out of the picture!"

I chuckle, "For sure the public is being told it is me ruining the land for all of us, killing all the animals, not caring, needing to be stopped! This oil exploration group has done more damage in a few months than I have done in twenty-five years!"

"How would you know for sure, Miles?"

"Fly over the area! You cannot see my trails and hardly see any of my log cabins. I have repeated many times, there are as many animals there now, as thirty years ago when I arrived. Fly over where the exploration people have been! There is a twenty-five foot wide road fifty miles long. More trees were pushed down than I have cut in my lifetime of wood heating." It is hard to explain. This is the next step in civilizing the wild.

I'm a land surveyor. The advance guard of civilization. The saw man. The first one to step foot in the area to be tamed. I know at least a little about the process. I'm sad, but not totally against it; or an enemy of advancement. We the people desire to live good, so we shall put our money down and pay the price. The issue I have is, there is not as much live and let live going on as I'd like to see.

Bridges are going in, swamps filled. Trophy moose hunters have crossed the river and run the new roads, killing moose. The area is in the news as a fresh area to explore. There is talk of other commercial ventures. Farming, timber harvest. All planned once the oil company puts the road and bridges in.

"I guarantee one thing Tusk, the animal population will never go up again. It is only downhill from here. I acknowledge we need the resources. All this is necessary if civilization wishes to live at its present level of lifestyle. I do not see civilization backing off and living simpler any time soon. Yes, I suppose I am sad to see this. I think it will never be the same for me across the river again. I may not even go back. Too much change too fast for me." I do not want to believe there was an organized effort to get me and the other homesteaders out by devious underhanded means.

"One sad aspect I think of Tusk is this. If treated right, those of us living there could make good guardians for the gas and oil people. We know everyone passing through, and could keep an eye on things. It would be possible to co-exist. Pay us a salary as 'guards' (buy us off rather than run us off). Having a reason to keep rival trappers out would have an advantage possibly outweighing the disadvantage." Writing down license plate numbers, keeping records, I'd think would be useful.

"Miles, I heard about Miss Zoro!" *Ah yes. I wondered if that would be brought up.* Miss Zoro lives across the river and has been making trouble for the exploration people. Reporting them, turning in complaints.

"Yeah, Tusk, she filed a complaint the exploration is interfering with the endangered otter in the area." Legal trapping hurt the otter more. But she knows otter are cute and fuzzy and will get the public riled up. I'm guessing this is exactly why the exploration people would like to have the area to themselves. No one knows, so no one complains.

Tusk is going to the show in Tucson. "Got some fossils and ivory to sell, Miles, already have appointments!"

This reminds me, I owe my Russian friend money. I am not going to say anything to Tusk, or anyone else, as to what I got from the Russians, where it sells, what I owe him. I contact Iris and have her stop by and finish our deal. She may pick up a tusk for me, or maybe not. Maybe one sells that I have, who knows? I play a shell game. Because I do not trust my government. It's good to be vague, have receipts for this, that, the other. I found this; I bought that. I traded, maybe, who knows. I forget.

"Miles, I'd take some of your fossils and stuff on consignment, deliver for you even, but you know how it is. You are watched, not a good person to be affiliated with right now." Tusk is scared. For good reason. Who wants to become a person of interest. It's possible I made a deal and am a snitch working undercover to set my friends up. No one can be trusted. I understand.

"Good luck at the show, Tusk!" We are rivals. I do not like his prices. Even so, there are not many of us fossil dealers!

Before we part, I look around. Tusk lives a lot like I do, in terms of how his shop and yard look. He has his back alley blocked with piles of rocks and antlers. His shop is full of dust and half-finished art. There is a mammoth tusk hanging from the ceiling out of the way, drying with clamps on it. A box of musk ox horns he got from up north is in the corner covered in mammoth ivory dust from the grinder. There are band saws, grinders, a drill press, and the usual things one needs to be in our business.

Tusk is built like me. Short, stocky, with a 1800s mountain man hat on. Ivory dust all over his clothes, face, hair. He coughs all the time from breathing it in. I do not have that cough yet, because I have more going on than just the tusks and grinding business. I have to think what to do now that I am not headed for the show! *I suppose I can focus on making a lot of knife blades! That is something fun and pays the bills.* I feel lucky to have a variety of ways to make a living, and am adaptable, not in debt with bills to keep up with. I can afford a financially slack time. Not everyone could! *Am I ever lucky!* I answer myself, "Because we have a high Jesus factor!" *Yup.*

Mr. Public does not have much time for me. He is kept busy with a heavy case-load. That's ok. I understand. He has his two secretaries write out answers he dictates. Sometimes they add information of their own when they know the answer. I move in the direction of getting information from them, who have more time. One knows a friend of mine, Witty, in Nenana. They both lived in Delta at the same time.

"Hey, I lived in Delta long ago. It is where my houseboat was built!" She knows Steamer, who was the boat builder I worked under. The other woman knows me because her father is from Tanana, and he is a river rat, who has dealt with me on the river, and bought my first book. She has heard of me.

We refer to Mr. Public as the energizer bunny! Always on the go. Whenever I see him, he is just coming in, or just headed out. *How can he keep all his cases straight? I'm always amazed how much secretaries know about what is really going on!* 😊 :)

I address Mr. Public, "Now that I am arrested, I should have the right to see the exact charges, and view the evidence against me, to determine if I wish to fight this. Maybe, as you asked, separate the charges out and divide them."

"Usually you do not get to see the evidence until you make the decision to go to court, Miles."

"How do I plea bargain without knowing the cards being held? Is that fair?" I believe some of these charges are frivolous and based on nothing. I think some evidence might be wrongly interpreted. I might decide looking it over, that I can explain myself. I go on, "I think I'm innocent of everything, or could explain myself adequately to my peers in court. I want to know what the prosecution is basing the charges on, besides legal, physical evidence confiscated. I think I have the right to know that. Otherwise, I'll tell them to stuff it!" I pause. "Well, not in those exact words. I'm sure there is a polite legal way that means the same thing, in Latin. 'Habus corpses' or something?" *You're the lawyer, you figure it out.*

Eventually we get the evidence. A week before I have to plead guilty or innocent.

The evidence arrives in the form of a black computer box, an external hard drive of about a gigabyte of information. No password to access the device was given to me. *They did their legal duty, provided us with the evidence.* Gaining access to it is our problem. Mr. Public is not interested. He knows we are never going to trial, so why play games? I want to at least look for flagrant irregularities that may exist. Highly illegal activities that I think exist in the case. Possibly so flagrant, the Feds will be forced to back way off in an agreement. The entire search warrant might be inadmissible and anything gathered from it.

The younger secretary has time to talk to me when the lawyer is gone. "Miles, I have another job. I am the computer security person for the University. I'm a code breaker and hacker. I am sure I can access this black box." I leave the black box with her to break the code.

I get word back that she has gained access. "However, some of the files were written in crime lab program code, that no one else has access to, and no one else can read, unless you have the program and are a scientist. Only crime labs have the program."

I look at what is on this hard drive. There are 250,000 files. I have access to about half of them. Most have code names for the documents that have no meaning to me, like "01-53 Mibb." This makes it hard to look up anything. It's not a date, or an abbreviation for a word or name easy to guess. *I had been accused of deliberately being evasive because I use a code for my record keeping. This is considered a crime. Like P/A/35 to me, means the item referred to is a pendant, with animal subject, selling for $35.* I explained my code, or face the felony charge of 'tampering with evidence' or 'obstruction' or whatever they'd come up with. So what is good for the goose should be good for the gander. What is this code crap? How can I honestly be told I have access to evidence my accusers have against me?

I figure out one file is transcribed phone calls from four years of tapping my phone. I read various transcriptions of the conversations. How do I know these are honest transcriptions and not biased or flat out made up? There is some assumption here. *I can't provide my version of an alleged phone conversation and call it admissible evidence.* But ok, let's say there is no misunderstanding or deceit and this is what took place.

I read in a document a recording transcription of what Tusk said. Apparently either he or someone in our presence was wired. Tusk is talking to me. "Is this the ivory Jessie owes you, that you told me about?"

My recollection is, Tusk came to the Tanana Fair to see me. Jessie arrived close to the same time and brought me some legal fossil material as part of what he owes me. But who was recording this, and why? In the 250,000 documents, how would I find further conversations Tusk may have had with the Feds. There is no time to find this. I do not know if he would be a witness in my defense, if I choose to go to court. Or he is a hostile witness, bought by the Feds. This recording is of interest because it helps prove my relationship, and the deal I had with Jessie.

I am recorded saying, "Jessie, how come there is so little? You owe me $3,000 worth!"

His answer saying. "I know, but I can't get it yet. This is all I have for now!" This in my mind proves the deal Jessie and I had was that the money I fronted was a loan, the tagged white tusks was collateral, and he acknowledges owning me legal material.

Josh is recorded over the phone talking. The Feds are asking Josh what he knows about anything illegal I have done. Specifically, ivory I gave his son who is a Native craftsman. The Feds are trying to force Josh into saying 'yes, there was an ivory deal, and the ivory was sold.'

Josh says, "I'm old! I just had an injury. My mind is not what it was. I do not recall. I just do not remember!"

"Are you sure! You do not want your son to go back to prison, do you?! This is a serious offense!" Josh holds firm. He cannot recall.

The son replies, "Oh, yes, Miles sold me some ivory and charged me way too much and ripped me off! What can I do to help!"

"You know you cannot buy ivory off a white man, right? Even if you are Native! We can send you back to prison!"

He had just gotten out of prison after a lifetime of being in for murder. He spent thirty years behind bars.

I had felt for him and wanted him to get back on his feet. Jobs are hard to get for felons. I asked Josh at the time, "Geez, Josh, you are Native, surely you have connections up in Nome with the Native carvers so you could help your son get some ivory?" The Iditarod dog sled race Josh runs ends in Nome! It is a Native village and the villagers should relate to Josh and admire him, want to help him out! I'd think.

"Miles, they all charge too much! I'm not paying those prices!"

Being his buddy and wanting to help, I tell Josh, "I am not sure how this works legally. But for sure your son can legally have white walrus ivory as a known Native carver." The ivory I got from Jessie is tagged, legally gifted to me, and I see no reason I cannot gift it back to a Native who can use it to get back on his feet. This should fall within the intent of the law.

Josh and the son were crying the blues to me about not wanting to end up on the street, no work, the desire to sell some carvings, no money, needing a break, no one helping him, and all this. So I had parted with one tusk from Jessie, gifted it to another Native, and now he is willing to say I sold it, and ripped him off? Looking to me like, "Because this is what Fish and Wildlife would like him to say." Offering him consideration, overlooking some other issue maybe. At first I am shocked and angry! But calm down and forgive him. I am guessing that thirty years of hard core prison, much of it spent in solitary confinement, will have an effect on a person. He does not want to go back, and 'survival,' for him, is doing what is expected, what he is told.

The son has thirty-year-old prices in his head. Ivory was $20 a pound. Now $200 and $300 a pound. He thinks $50 is a rip off? I'm sorry he feels that way. He never said that to me. I had sold him some basic tools cheap, but not ivory. We did talk about future possibilities. General material he could carve, sell, and get himself started. He wanted more. Now where did it get me?

I had said, "If you need more, you have to buy it!" I thought, "Make art from the free goods. Sell it, take some of the profit to buy more materials."

His words to me were, "No, first I need a full studio with new equipment and a nice apartment!" Normally we save and work for that, get this in increments.

What was said just makes me look bad. But is nice to know ahead of time who I can count on as a witness on my side if I choose to go to court. It would have been nice if Josh had tipped me off. I do not know if there were other conversations I am not finding in another folder. Josh felt threatened, not sure whose phone is tapped, or what the consequences might be if it were found out he tipped me off. I can see Josh between a rock and a hard place between me and his son. He remained neutral.

I realize I am seeing evidence I was not expected to ever see. The Feds had no idea I could break the code and hack into the evidence and actually see it. I am seeing stuff I think they did not even intend to show me. There is a video of Jessie shooting an owl from a camera in an undercover agent's ball cap. I hear Jessie in the background telling his good buddy all about his life, filled with trust while he is being filmed.

There is a snippet of a note. "Need to contact Miles' live in woman, Iris." With a comment further along. "We usually try to find someone close to the suspect to give us an in and get close for information gathering." Iris never told me anyone has tried to approach her. Did she, like Josh, not want to get involved, and so not warn me? Did the Feds actually get to her? Would she be a witness against me with recorded and filmed, 'who knows what,' from our private personal life? Inside information the Feds refer to? Iris and I are not married, so she could testify against me. Again, in all these documents and coded files, where would I find any follow up on this note? Can I trust my girlfriend? Imagine being in court and your loved one testifies against you! To save her own bacon? To get even for some slight she has not been open about?

Every business card I ever collected was confiscated. I see it all recorded, one card at a time as 'evidence,' of having done business with all these people. Hundreds of cards. The truth is, I go to a lot of places, get handed a ton of cards. I most often say thanks, take the card, and toss it in a box in the house. I most often never look in that box, ever, for anything. There, the cards stay. Just in case I might be interested someday. I could in theory look through all my cards to find some contact I forgot, or need now. By no stretch of the imagination are these customers, vendors, or anyone I even know. All meticulously laid out with all the information about what they sell, what they are looking for. Now and then I make a note on the back. "Supplies jade," or "source for lion claws." *If I ever wanted any.*

This reminds me. There are fossil lion fangs I get from this African guy. I suspect are not lion. I also suspect they are not fossil, but some fangs boiled in tea. I do not know either for a fact. I come across a comment concerning the denial of the export permit I thought I was getting, since I had paid for it.

"I say let's hold on to the permit and let the son of a bitch hang himself!" I'm sure I was not supposed to see this! I am not sure how to bookmark, or 'copy paste' and refer to this as evidence.

It is the weekend. Mr. Public is off. This is a 'read only' external hard drive I cannot edit, bookmark or transfer. Mr. Legal says he will 'look it over.' So how can he? He has a copy, but does not have the access code. It seems to me, if we are serious about any defense, we need to review stuff together so I can explain how it was. We would know where the weakness is in the attack. My hope would be, Mr. Public might say. "Wow, this blows holes in their case, I think we have something!"

Maybe Saddle would be more like this, not a public defender. I'm not sure. I get the impression Mr. Public has told the prosecution he is sure we will plea bargain. Funds are cut off for a defense. It's all settled. I simply have not been told what was decided. Over lunch, or out on the golf course. No court dates set. The word is, we are going for a deal.

I point out to Mr. Public that my emails are all read by the prosecution, since the internet is a public form of communication. It might be good to talk or have private communications. Mr. Public believes me, but does not care. "So what if the prosecution knows what we are talking about?" As if it is all a lost cause, as if he has already made the deal on my behalf. I think Mr. Public is working for the court, trying to save time and money, looking out for the taxpayers and the public. That's his job. It seems odd to not be interested in a private conversation. "To talk about what?" He asks.

I'm certain Saddle would tell me we have a case for another $150,000. Considering the case with Jim cost half a million.

Some evidence is from various crime labs. I assume results as to what animal parts really are. I cannot access any lab results file. I am pretty sure 90% results show items not as marked on the evidence tag. Including what I feel were deliberate mislabeling, like eagle claws that are really porcupine claws, lion claws that are legal lynx. Things I saw labeled wrong. It would be interesting to read some lab results. To say to the court, "On charge #26, the lab results show? Oh, yes, here we are," followed by, "And could you tell the court why this porcupine claw is illegal, and charges were filed?" Followed by "Next!"

My lawyer said, "This is not a movie or Perry Mason," for the hundredth time. "There are twenty-eight counts. Are you sure you can win on all 28? You only have to lose on one to go to jail for ten years and pay $200,000 in fines, Miles!" It is not realistic to think I can win on twenty-eight charges, especially with the defense I have.

I can lose, not on truth and evidence, but my inability to prove something. What would it cost to contact 200 business people, and ask if they ever heard of me, or if they did business with me? To prove I do not know even one of these people whose business cards I saved? Who will make the calls? How will the calls be certified, verified? On whose dime? Who will bring in witnesses from overseas to confirm a pay pal notice claiming 'wolf claw,' was really a plastic one, or legal coyote, or returned? As far as I can see in the evidence, not one of these items is in the prosecution's possession, except what the undercover agent acquired.

I recall the news article, bad Miles with all this 'stuff,' that was deliberately miss-named?

Where is the money and time to get my 200,000 that the prosecution has? Who will fork over the one or two million all this cost to put together, that I need to spend for a matching defense? For a total of four million dollars? To get to the bottom of what?

I see some honest questions totaling about a $500 value if I was 'mistaken' and willing to accept the consequences for. This one to four million could buy a new water treatment plant for my community! *This is your tax dollars at work! Are you pleased with how it is spent?* This is what I am thinking as I go through this search trying to defend myself. What has society accomplished if I am locked up, shut down, put out of business? *What is your goal here? At $80,000 a year, you will pay for me to be in prison. I will be sacrificed and my life over, and society is getting what in return besides a $80,000 a year bill?* I cannot stop these thoughts from racing through my head. It is difficult to organize what I am finding, into anything meaningful as a defense. I am simply observing this stuff going, "Huh, interesting." *I'm not able to come up with a system for how to find this spot again in a file of quotes I might create. I have no lawyer to work with.*

I'm alone looking at all this. No team of worker bees getting right on it. Iris is not interested, it's none of her business. She has not been charged. Though this was considered. The prosecution says, "We think she knows more then she admits, and helped you ship these illegal goods, knew what she was packing, saw all this coming in and out of the shop, and must have known!"

Iris tells me she was interrogated as I was, when the raid took place. She tells me she was asked, "Can you tell me what marine mammals are?" She did not know, wondered why a bear was called a marine mammal. Asked about ivory. "It's all mammoth isn't it?" Iris tells me how angry the interrogator was.

"Mammoth, mammoth that's the word of the day here isn't it!"

"Yes it is." It's true, Iris has not been a part of my business, and would not know a tooth from a claw, like most civilized people. Does not know ivory from bone, or walrus from mammoth ivory. Iris rarely steps foot in the shop. " It's too dirty, noisy, smelly, unsafe."

She used to cut rocks, and it looked at first like she enjoyed this new hobby. But think she was doing it to please me, and does not enjoy hanging about the shop. I told her she does not have to go in the shop to do anything if she does not like to. Her outlook seems to be "Good, what a relief. There is nothing I want to do." She's retired. That is how it has been. We rarely discuss business, as she is simply not interested. Good news for both of us, as after four years of tapping the phone and reading emails and such, the Feds conclude the same thing. It is me they want, and not her.

There are local rumors and talk going around as to what has been going on, what is going on, what will be done about it. *It's a good time to see who your friends are.*[2] One couple in particular leaps forward into my life in a big way that was in times past sort of friends, and sort of part of my life long ago. Barefoot was once a neighbor, and we had built dog sleds in Josh's shop together. He was around when I was accused of killing Gene. Barefoot was himself a possible suspect as we were all neighbors at one time. Gene had tried to kill me.

However, it had been Barefoot who came to me privately after the events and says, "Gene told me he was going to kill you." I believed him. " He showed me his rifle with a camera taped to it and he said he was going to film shooting you."

I smile and nod like this is normal. I ask, "So why didn't you tell me, or the police, and try to save my or his life?"

"I didn't want to get involved, Miles, you understand, he's a dangerous guy!" My relationship with Barefoot simply changed after that, to cool politeness. There are a lot of nicknames that come and go. There is a Bearfoot, a Barefoot, and a Bear. It does not matter who the guy is. In time, he meets a gal, gets married, and the couple live their own life. We wave and say hi.

The wife is much younger and very outspoken. She and I used to be friends. She had heard of me back where she came from when she read about Alaska. Maybe one of my Alaska Magazine stories, the New York Times, who knows? When she was having a hard time fitting in, and was getting harassed by locals, I defended her. Time passes, twenty years passes.

Dalia, this gal, catches me on the street. "Miles, I think you got what you deserve, and think Iris should go to prison along with you! We all know she goes to the post office with you and delivers the illegal goods!" I smile and nod and tell her,

"I appreciate your honesty, Dalia. It's nice to be told to my face instead of hearing just rumors."

"I am not the only one who thinks this, everyone says so. I'm just the only one honest enough to tell you to your face." I nod in appreciation. "Well, that's what friends are all about, Dalia, honesty!"

Much like her husband, this is not someone who is my friend. A line has been crossed that can never be forgiven. It's like a friend telling you as a Jew you really deserve to be in a concentration camp with the ones you love. The reply is "Interesting," big smile, walk away. Never to speak to that person again. Huge incalculable damage is done with this outlook of hers. I cannot discuss my case. No one will ever know all the exact facts and details. Some post public comments on Facebook, other social media. There are replies to news articles. Comments in places you do not have to give your real name.

"I know Miles, he puts all his garbage in the gas station dumpster! What a loser! Everyone in Nenana knows he is a lowlife!" Well. Someone for sure hates my guts. There had been a series of 'incidents' almost thirty years ago when I arrived from the wild. I was at 10th Street living on the boat where there is no garbage pickup. I do not drive. I did get caught putting garbage in the gas station dumpster. A public dumpster where those who drive by drop off their garbage. You are expected to buy gas. Probably it is not cool to use it and not contribute. I was told to stop, and I did. It was about a bag a month. Others I know toss their bags of trash in the river. The difference is, no one knows.

A year after the issues over using a dumpster, a survey was done inquiring whether Nenana needs a dump or not. Funding might be available to open a dump we used to have, We have no dump. Everyone is supposed to have garbage pickup they pay for. The results of a local survey implied, 'No, we are fine, no garbage issues here!' Denial.

My reply was essentially, "Are you off your rocker! A community of over 300 needs a dump, of course we do! We have people dumping trash in the river, along the roads, dumping diapers in our drain lines. We need a dump!" And added after the question, "What do you do now about garbage?" I wrote, "Dump my garbage in the gas station dumpster!" Mostly to help us get funding, to clean up our town, and get a dump! That admission had to be put into the context of the situation, and reason I said that. Here, thirty years later, someone has not forgotten. That person wants to see me fry. Whoever it is. The world gets to read about it. My lawyer tells me to let stuff go, not reply and let that stand. While people whisper, "Is that true, gosh golly, yeah, what a bad guy," whisper, whisper around the community.

The truth is, not a lot of people know much about me. Even though I am doing a lot, am on committees, volunteering, donating. I have few 'friends.' I do not show up at ball games, go out drinking with the guys, and do the usual social things civilized people do to be part of the tribe. It is true I have some weird habits, do not dress well. When seen, I do not appear to have a job. I work for myself and get up at 4:00 am, and working by 5:00 am, and by 9:00 am need a break.

"So what is Miles doing while we begin our day huh? My tax dollars support this arrogant guy?"

They do not know I have been working, and on my break about the time they wake up and begin their day. I am heading over for morning coffee and crumpets about 9:00 am, and think everyone assumes I just got up starting my day, as they are doing. I may look like I am on welfare, drugs, and food stamps.

I have a sign on the door, "Work is for people who do not know how to fish." I may speak that attitude. I do not especially care what everyone thinks, and do not take care to straighten people out. I'm not looking for friends. On one level do not want any. Life is safer that way. I assume those who 'care,' who are smart, who do not listen to rumors, have seen my art, know I have written many books, have dozens of custom knives out for sale. They have seen what I donate, what I do for the community, and speak up for me, or simply know, and do not buy into the negative stuff. It's a false assumption maybe.

Many do not like my life outlook, my saying "I get paid to have fun! You should too! Do you like your job? Enjoy life? I do not need a vacation, I love what I do! " That drives some people nuts with hate. I assume, those who hate their job, who work hard, cannot seem to get ahead, worried about the future, and see no way out, stuck. The perfect sheep, the serfs, serving their Lord Big Brother. I must be on drugs to be so happy. There are many who earn just enough to make interest payments on their loans. Maybe working two jobs, maybe a married couple, both work, no one to raise the unruly kids.

They look forward, and live for, the weekend, get a week a year off for vacation. On the weekend they catch up on sleep and mow the lawn. Get home, plop themselves down with a beer, and turn the TV on. Wore out used up, not worth much by retirement age. Dying soon after. The prefect citizen. This describes the majority. Mad at whoever they blame. Saying, "The poor are eating up my taxes, the blacks, the Natives, women." Anyone who takes their job away. Misdirected hate. Divide and conquer.

I am included in the general, "That Miles who lives off my tax dollars and is so smug about it!" Those who do not get it are being played for a fool. Angry at me who found a way out! Not caught in the net! A free man! With choices! Who eats when hungry, sleeps when tired, works when I feel like it, doing what I feel like, loving every minute of it. That image makes some people want to clean my clock. My whole life is what they see only on weekends. Of course there may even be some legitimate reason people have a real gripe that I deserve! *Ignorance is bliss.* I have no clue what my faults might be. I do not focus on them. I might tend to rub in the fact life is good. I have a happy grin as others come unglued, with little sympathy for those who volunteer to be serfs, because it is easy. Likewise, I have no use for complainers.

So here I am in this mess. This time of, 'serious stuff going on,' and people walking on the other side of the street when they see me coming. Friends like Dalia and Barefoot are happily fueling the flames. I recognize the personality type that enjoys kicking and attacking those who are down and weak. I try to find it just 'interesting.' *Wolves and their pack are like this as well.* I meet those who tell me how much better animals are then us. In a wolf pack only the Alpha male gets to breed. At a kill, there is a pecking order. The weak might get left to starve. No other will likely bring them a meal, or share what they have. If the Alpha slips, number two watches and waits for the opportunity to pick a fight and win.

"Nature is simply like this," I keep saying, " Even harmless plants kill each other over light."

I learned from a book Crafty had me read, 'Science of survival' that I thought was right up my alley, that turns out to be the major Scientology spiritual book, not what I expected. One truth I read that I had not thought of before, has to do with watching what kind of information those around us pass along. Sometimes all we hear is negative truths. Disasters, failures, sick people are the selected topics. "It's true! I'm an honest person!" I am told. But honestly doing what? Those who succeed, and seem happiest, tend to at least mix bad news with something funny, good, or rarely pass on any bad news at all! "What is your purpose, why are you telling me this," is what I ask myself when people tell me the truth. This was the bottom line in 'Science of Survival' or what I got out of it anyway.

I find it easier to understand what is going on around me. This is very important. There is an effort to get me to accept responsibility of wrongdoing. Understand what a bad person I am. Comprehend how wrong it is to step out of my class. Pay restitution to society for my wrongdoing. Become one of the sheep. Bow to the plow and be a good citizen, good serf, and serve my master. Punish me for thinking there is a way out. When there is not. Take away my rights, my income, my ability to earn a living. Let me accept this, and understand why it is what I deserve. Preparing me to be made a sacrifice.

"Be a man, admit your wrongdoing and pay restitution!" This is repeated throughout society, even by friends, as 'what is expected of me.'

"Fine Miles, but just admit your wrongdoing, take your punishment like a man, get past it, begin a new life after restitution is made. Learn your lesson, straighten out." Is the common line I get.

Certainly Mr. Public is preparing me. He wants to know why I even asked for the evidence, what I hope to gain by looking at it. "Yup, I'm guilty." I can stare at that black box all I want, and the same truth remains. There is no loophole that will save me. I'm going to fry. I'm walking the plank. We all know the outcome. Keel hauled. It is time to pray for the forgiveness of my sins. It takes superhuman strength to think, "Maybe we can look at this another way?" The power of all civilization weighs upon me. A peasant in the days of the Romans. I understand the desire to play Rob Roy, or Brave Heart. It's hard to play Jesus and go up there smiling, thanking everyone for making my day.

I recall a study being done. An experiment. Black students were in two groups taking standard tests. One group had to fill out at the top of the page, what race they are. The other group was not asked. The group that was asked to name what race they were, at the top of the page did 20% worse overall on any test given. The power of suggestion. Living up to what is expected of us. I feel lucky for all those years alone in the wilds. There was no power of suggestion. No social class to fit into. I discovered I am in the top 10% in both intelligence and physical ability. I discovered I am honestly not afraid of bears, the cold, pain, or dying. I learned that God knows who I am and likes me. More, God enjoys spending time with me. I understood how lucky I am.

This helps me forgive those who are more angry and not as happy. I have issues. I'm tweaked, damaged. That is ok. I can focus on what is good and accomplish something positive. This whole situation I am in now sure puts a spin on all that. Right back where I started so many years ago, thinking I could rise above being convinced by society I am nothing and no one, useless, stupid, will never amount to anything. Like not worth having joint custody or helping to raise a child.

"A criminal! See what we mean, Miles! Stay away from your son! Stay away from me!" I can hear what is said. What can I reply? It is difficult not to become what is expected of me.

I run into Moonshine in town, my longtime river friend. He lives subsistence on the river and does well. He has said many times, "Miles, there is no way in hell to live our lifestyle and be legal." He simply does his thing and keeps a much lower profile than I do. He is not interested in telling the world what is going on, "The world already knows, Miles."

"Moonshine, I hear you are working for Fish and Game, counting fish with the test wheel?"

"Yup." He pauses with a grin. "Putting the fox in the chicken coop, wouldn't you say, Miles?"

"Got that right!" He has all the fish he needs for his sled dogs. The fish count is whatever he wants it to be. And he gets paid for it.

"Talk about a scam, Moonshine!"

"You got that right, Miles." This is something I consider unethical; I would not do. Moonshine will never be in trouble. Here I am, the criminal. Geez. It's hard to play the 'ignorance is bliss' card when there is such overwhelming reality all around me. The unconscious can only hide so much before it all comes unraveled.

There are a lot of pauses as I see various bits and pieces of collected evidence proving I am a horrible human being. The wrong color. The wrong occupation. The wrong goals. A wrong sense of ethics. In the wilderness, none of this was wrong. Out of thousands of pictures on the computer there are a dozen that help the prosecution, that I see in the evidence back box. There is one picture of my buddy, Will, holding a gun, looking mean, as we played at looking like mobsters on a rainy day ages ago when we were eighteen. There are also pictures a jury would see of 'dead things' that are not pretty. Piles of wolf carcasses—legally trapped and tossed out. I did not kill them. I know what a jury or judge would think. People for the most part are not kind or forgiving.

I am looking at twenty-eight charges, ten years each. 280 years of prison. Maybe a plea bargain is fifty years. I do not know where we are at. Mr. Public informs me what is most likely, also the maximum. "You might get ten to twelve years at the most, Miles." Twelve years at my age is life. What would I have when I got out?

There has to be a plea bargain. In my mind this is defined as both sides sitting at a table and making offers and counteroffers, then coming to something the two parties can agree to. Because I see plea bargaining this way, I want to know what cards I can put on the table to negotiate with. I want to be able to say, "True, but you have at least a dozen items that are mislabeled. That is going to weaken your credibility." Or, "This is discrimination, that is illegal," Or, "This is not your jurisdiction because…" Cards I can put on the table that weaken the prosecution's case that make negotiation chips to put down. Balanced with concessions.

This seems better than, "You are right, I am had, there is nothing I can say, I am at your mercy." There are too many people who enjoy pulling the legs off spiders. I believe too many of them seek positions of authority and power. A high percentage end up as policemen, lawyers, in the court system. Not all, no, there are some good cops and lawyers. I even know some and trust some. It's just a higher percent of power hungry types who seek out these roles than we see in the general population. I'm not putting myself at the mercy of a bunch of unknown people who, so far, are not showing me they believe in the law, or doing what is right. Which would be to allow me time to explain myself. Which would allow me the same rules they live by. These are the same personality types who preach, "And when a bear attacks, play dead." Hope the bear gets tired, leaves, and you only lose a leg and arm and hopefully survive. My style is more to put a 357 between his eyes with the hammer back and a grin, "Would you like to reconsider your options, Mr. Bear?" In civilization it's your lawyer, not a 357 pistol, or bits of useful information. Right? No? *Money you mean?*

I was not born into the class I have chosen. I have memories of being in another class. I know what it is like to be 'one of us.' I was born a W.A.S.P. I seem to have forgotten. So tell me, dear Civilized, what is your 357? Or, do you bow down, let bear eat the parts he wants and hope you live.

There is no getting together to discuss a plea agreement like I expected, like I see in the movies. I'm waiting. Instead, Mr. Public contacts me and tells me what was decided. "This is the offer," with a take it or leave it option. There is no discussion. Time is running out, or they will change their mind. This is an ultimatum, not a plea bargain. As a reminder of my position, Mr. Public says, "Of course, if you chose to fight this in court, let me know. I'll see you half an hour before the trial."

This lets me know the quality of representation I can expect. More than this is the entire package of what is going on that seems orchestrated to a tune called brainwashing. I have read a lot of books on psychology. Mental torture, abuse, manipulation, control through social pressure. I know about the 'good guy, bad guy' technique. I know about holding out a reward and withdrawing it, making promises and breaking them, until a person is a malleable bowl of jello. I know about manipulating time, changing dates, keeping time an unknown. All you want is out. For it to end. By any method, just make it stop. Ready to confess to anything you want me to say, just make it all stop. Seeing how it is done, watching it happen, does not change it. It's on subconscious levels. *If you want to have me say I am single-handedly responsible for global warming, where do I sign!*

"Ok! Now you are ready for the plea agreement, Miles! Have we got a deal for you!" There is no discussion concerning the evidence. I would not know how to put what I have discovered into legal terms. I would not know how to enter anything into evidence, or when to bring it up.

"What is this great deal I cannot refuse?"

Mr. Public reviews it with me. "You plead guilty to three of the charges, the rest are set aside. You will be a felon. You will pay a $5,000 to $10,000 fine, serve no more than a year in prison. With three years supervised probation." There are some add on conditions. "You cannot ever sell animal products again. You will remove all references and pictures of animal products from your website. You will not help others, or give advice concerning animal products, or give legal advice to others."

My opinion is, if I could afford Saddle, I could win on the major charges. I would not be a felon. The Feds are wrong on the biggest issue they want so badly—the white ivory charges. In court they would lose the one and only charge that really matters to them. But I might get ten years in prison for the couple of things hard to get out of. Unless I win arguing subsistence, going to the Supreme Court. Like sending a wolf claw through the mail and having eagle feathers.

I think with Saddle, I would pay 100 grand, spend ten years in prison, but not be a felon. I could be wrong. Pay the money and lose. It is also possible for 200 grand ten years in court, I could win on all accounts. Or, I can take the deal, be a felon, be out one tenth the money, and one tenth the prison time. I'm not young, so what does it matter if my ending years are as a felon? Who cares? I am not looking for work. In a couple of years I will be a senior on Social Security. It will not be many years, and I will be unable to run shows and do my artwork, run a business as I do now.

There is no discussion or counteroffer. "Miles, you do not want to piss these people off!" That's Mr. Public's advice.

Saddle's outlook is, "Bring it on! Be pissed! Make my day!" *That's the difference between free and 100 grand!*

I have neglected my emails and business for a while. Too much of a knot in my stomach over what is going on. Iris has been in Tucson visiting my mother. Mom is getting elderly. I do not know how many more visits I have with her before she passes away. Her health has not been great. She had a mini stroke when she was out on one of her walks. Nothing has been the same since. She is slow, weak, slightly slurred voice. Where she used to work for others for extra money cleaning, and walking five miles a day, she now does no work and is barely able to walk down the street to visit her boyfriend, Les. Les is older than she is and is getting Alzheimer's. Mom is struggling to take care of him as he gives her a hard time. I had hoped to be there to help out during these hard times. She had looked forward to seeing me. Now does not understand why I have been arrested. Why my girlfriend is in my place.

I get a hand-written letter from Karen, the woman I lived with so long ago with her children.

To Sonshine Miles (She addresses me 'Sonshine' instead of Sunshine… No one really calls me 'Wild Miles' anymore, but many call me 'Sunshine.' They say because I brighten their day… anyhow on with her letter)

I am so very sorry to read in the news about your issues over our lifestyle. It was one reason I could not be happy anymore living with you. Remember when the officers came with a warrant to the homestead by helicopter looking for our illegal winter moose harvest? It reminded me of stories my grandparents told me of the holocaust. They described exactly what we experienced. Books tossed on the floor, interrogations, threats, house torn apart. My personal diary found and read out loud…

Yes, I recall that. Karen on the floor screaming in terror and in tears. Nothing I can do about it. *Why had I forgotten?* I have to put the letter down, lost in thought.

Sometimes wildlife is just good to look at, like this group of Trumpeter swans with eight ft. wing spans.

CHAPTER ELEVEN

ARREST, EVIDENCE, COURT, FELON

Past Flash

Late 1980s. The homestead life. Raising children, home schooling. Little Joy had not even met anyone besides her parents till she was three. I'm stepping in to fill the role as a substitute father. We live off the land on a $5,000 a year income. Half of that goes to gas to get supplies twice a year. It's a wonderful world with no other human beings in it. Just us and nature. Moose hunting laws are written for trophy hunters. The season is written so we are to harvest moose during the rut when it is easiest to find the bulls. However, this time is in September, when the weather is still hot, and assumes all hunters have electricity and freezers to keep the meat from spoiling. We discover from experience; it is almost impossible to keep a moose killed in September from spoiling without refrigeration.

We must eat green meat, meat with maggots in it. There is a lot of waste. Both Karen and I are very against waste of any kind. Our resources are precious! We feel civilization is very wasteful! One main reason we live here is to live more in harmony with nature, be more respectful, considering waste a major crime. We ate a lot of meat that made us sick, so it was not wasted.[1] Karen reminds me it is possible to make jerky from moose under good conditions. Weather does not always permit it, and hard dry meat is edible, but not like eating steak! We can moose in jars! If we can afford jars and lids. Jars are usually filled in August with garden produce.

So we begin like most who live as we do, harvesting moose in winter! We are verbally told by wildlife officers, this is fine, as long as there is no waste. There is however nothing in writing. Subsistence is a new enough term no one has legally defined it yet, nor determined just who subsistence people are! The State and Federal

MILES MARTIN

Government are battling over the definition. This has been going on for years unresolved. Meanwhile, back on the homestead, we have to stay alive. We cannot wait twenty years to get an answer.

New laws do come out concerning us.

"We will allow you to live subsistence, please come in and get your license. There will be designated areas you may gather your subsistence needs. Your fish may be harvested on the Tanana river, the nearest area, and your moose may be harvested in the separate Minto management area." Karen and I stare at each other in disbelief. The Tanana river is forty-five miles away. There is no way we can afford to move down there to get fish for our sled dogs. We'd have to move the dogs down there, be away from home, transport the dogs and fish back to the homestead. We cannot afford the gas. We'd be living in a tent we'd have to buy. Right now we fish right out our front door on the Kantishna River. The same fish as are on the Tanana headed this direction. I know the reasoning. I tell Karen,

"So they can keep better tabs on subsistence people, they want us all in the same area where we can be watched and regulated." For the same reason we are told we must by law use fish wheels and can no longer use nets. Wheels are somewhat complicated, expensive, and need repairs. They require big boats to move and set them. We use a canoe to set and check nets. Impossible with a wheel.

The issue with the winter moose harvest is that the Minto area referred to is also a long way away with no trail. I'd have to stop trapping, snowshoe in front of sled dogs, and hope the dogs can pull the heavy load home. I'd be camping out for many days in the snow. The Minto Indians have a reputation for being hostile to whites. I doubt they would allow me to take a moose out of the area suggested by law. A person could get killed and meat stolen or simply run off. For sure it would not be a friendly encounter.

We simply do what we have to do to survive. I get my moose way out on the trapline which to us makes biological sense. In an area there is no hunting pressure, where the removal of a moose has no impact on the environment. We are told, in general, the law will look the other way, and it is understood, as long as we are not wasteful and keep it quiet, our activities will be tolerated. I do not appreciate 'semi–legal-overlooked, if you keep quiet.' Like it is something shameful we can't talk about. Something we can't share with our friends. Something I can't write about.

The government showed up in a helicopter with a copy of the exact law. "Forget anything verbal you may have been told." I have to go to court at a time of year travel is normally impossible—at 'break up.' If I do not show, I will be arrested. Someone will come out in a helicopter with handcuffs. I will be carted off. If I get in for court, I may have no way back home. The woman and children will be without me, the one who knows how to run the boat when the ice goes out, is me only. This is a serious life-threatening issue. Those I explain this to are not concerned in the least, even 'pleased.'

I make it to court, and the date gets changed. It sounds like the judge forgot he has a golf game scheduled this day.

Past Flash ends

I return to Karen's long letter:

Remember how May snuck out the door and moved the ladder to the cache and hid it? The Gestapo could not get up in the cache and we told them it is unused and we have no ladder! I did not like lying, Miles, but we did what we had to do to survive. Remember, a moose roast was in the oven! I do not know how they could not smell the meat cooking. They never did look in the oven. We had roast moose that night!

Her words bring tears to my eyes. That we had to give up a lifestyle, one we both loved a lot. We did not get arrested, carted off from the homestead to jail. *But that could happen any time, and that was held over our heads.* I ended up going to court over having written, 'Got a moose' on my calendar. The case was dismissed because the state has not adequately defined what subsistence is, or who qualifies. Fish and Game was furious!

I have never after that kept a diary, Miles. I learned there is no privacy in our country. I saw no future in how we lived. I learned there is nowhere we can go to get away. The government will find us and terrorize us. So I have sympathy for what you are going through. I'm glad I am no longer with you though, or I'd be going to jail for life too.

Her letter trails off into other subjects and

Good luck, Miles

Karen and I parted.[2] She lives a more low-profile life than I do, not as remote, back in one of the villages. Not as subsistence as we lived, but off the grid at least. The girls are grown now, with families of their own. Joy contacted me at the fair. She hardly remembers when she was three.

"You do not remember the cardboard airplane I made for you from a box and a board? You'd climb in it and fly down the hill to the creek!"

"No, not really. It was a longtime ago, Miles."

I shake my head, clear the memories Karen's letter brings. I cared a lot for her. She is still my friend. *So as she says, one reason I lost a woman and family was because of these same issues I face today.* That's a heavy price to pay. I tend not to dwell on it. *That is not the road to happiness and survival.*

Another old memory leaps out unbidden, the can of worms is open.

Past Flash

I am not sure what year. I am on the trapline with sled dogs. I own the world. I am king of as far as I can see in every direction. Me and my trusty sled dogs. I was as a God among mortals. Yesterday had been fifty-five below zero and I laughed. The dogs and I love it. We covered sixty miles today, setting and checking traps. I have not seen another human being or sign in many months. If I never saw another human for the rest of my life, I would be in heaven. I sleep on the trail in the dog sled by a campfire, dogs all around me keeping warm. I just read a book, 'White Dawn,' and I felt like Sartak, or someone out of 'Clan of the Cave Bear.' Crossing the world alone.

I hear a helicopter and frown. *Is my planet being invaded? Yes, it is.* The helicopter lands in front of the sled dogs in the open flats. Out comes a young kid in his twenties, a Fish and Wildlife officer. "Can I see your trappers license please!" He has a warm Big Mac burger in his hand, just half an hour away from a place that would take me a long week to get to. I'm floored.

"I have one, but I do not carry a wallet with me on the trapline. It is not part of this lifestyle. I'd lose it. I have it at the cabin and carry it when I go to civilization."

"By law, it has to be on you at all times when you are trapping! You know that!" There is talk of the possibility of facing arrest. Especially if I give him a hard time. I have to assume the position. Bow the head. Beg for forgiveness. Acknowledge my master. The kid is ready to haul me off to civilization in handcuffs otherwise. He did not care what might happen to my sled dogs if I am carted off. They can all die for all he cares. He does not give a hoot how I will get back here again without the dogs. I have no business being out here living like a savage. I'm nothing, and no one, not even human. I contribute nothing. The unspoken message is, 'I have a gun, I represent the law. If you look at me crossways, I can make you disappear out here in the wilds, and what can you do about it, you lowlife!'

I understand his view. He is used to civilization where he is king. Where people bow before him, where he is a God because he is armed, and they are not. He is used to sheep who have been properly subdued. He believes he deserves respect and thinks he has that respect. *But respect is earned, not demanded. I am not afraid of him and his gun.* I meet this personality all the time out here in the wilds, where guns rule supreme. I was 'there' when Silka killed one tenth of the population of Manley Hot Springs. I have had guns in my face with the hammer back a dozen times. I have learned my reflexes are five times faster than most. I can bench press over 500 pounds. *Make your move if you feel so lucky today!* I'll show you the other end of that gun and stick it...." No, a human with a gun does not scare me. I'm amused.

What scares me is civilization. I make this guy disappear and I may as well kill myself. Someone else will show up and someone after that and a hundred after that, and it would never end till I was ended. *How could I get rid of the helicopter?* I feel towards this kid about like he feels towards me. He is not human. He's a monster. That he would cart me off in this flying contraption and leave dogs I love and who depend on me, behind here to die. I could never return here. It would be years trying to get back to this spot. I have no money with me. I'd have to get a job to pay a pilot to fly me out at the cost of a month's wages. Where would I stay for a month? By the time I raised the money to return, it would be spring, and not possible to cover this ground. I could not even get here to recover my sled and bury my dead dogs.

All this goes through my head while I stand here listening to this kid tell me about the law. Why I need my wallet with me at all times. These thoughts are real to me because I already went through this once. In Canada. I was hauled out of my home in handcuffs, never to return. I was not even allowed to fetch my shoes, jacket, or wallet. I had made $200 without a permit, trying to keep a village library open. Lied to by a city council that set me up. I was willing to give the $200 back. I was deported, lost my home and everything I owned. The neighbor shot my cat I read in a letter.

So here we go again. All over. It can indeed happen. I can indeed get shot here, and the fish cop can tell any story he wants. I resisted arrest. It looked like I had a weapon on me, the weapon he can plant on me afterwards. This could be a kid who enjoys pulling the legs off spiders. He might be one who lives to watch living things squirm and suffer. I meet this type among those who seek positions of authority all the time. Many get transferred to Alaska as not a prime location for civilized people. In the same way, for the same reason, child molesting priests get sent here. We are only fifty miles from Siberia, where Russians also send those they wish to punish.

It turns out this kid is just a young kid who has no clue about Alaska; fresh from outside. He loves his job and the beauty of the land. He senses he has never seen the likes of my kind and does not know what to make of me. It seems clear to him a wallet does not fit very well in the picture before him. The permit he refers to is $5, that covers hunting, fishing and trapping.

"Ok, well, I'll let you go this time! But carry your wallet from now on!" *Yeah, right! Like this punk kid is going to tell me how to live my life?* But I smile and assume the position. *Yes, Master! Thank you for not killing me this time, Master!* I long for the end of the world when civilization wipes itself out. When I can be safe among animals. I love about seventy below zero, floods, big storms. Civilization does not move then. Planes fall out of the sky, steel turns to ice and breaks. I smile and keep moving forward with dogs, wood, and leather, as a free man.

Past flash ends

I HAD FORGOTTEN ABOUT THAT! I dislike to be reminded! My unconscious remembers stuff like this and does not tell me because what is the use of being depressed? We need to move forward with positive things in life! So no. All this going on now is not something out of the blue.

I stay fixed on that incident with the young fish officer so long ago, landing in his helicopter in front of my dog team to ask for my trapper's license. He was just a young punk kid, as I was. I am guessing he meant well. Considered by all who know him as smart, hardworking, kind, nice, descent. He was as nervous of me as I was of him. I can picture his brainwashing. No, maybe 'indoctrination' is the correct word. "Rah, rah, lets go get it!" speeches. Lectures on serving his country, doing good in the world. Stopping poaching, catching thieves, upholding the good of the country, protecting wildlife. Like a football coach getting his team motivated. Like me giving the sled dogs a pep talk.

The kid being told honest citizens will be your friend! Why not?! Good people will be glad to see you, glad you are there to protect them and the environment. I'm sure in my heart, citizens offer him free coffee, thank him for protecting us, like people in the military are treated. Protectors of democracy. I'm sure he gets told, "On the other hand, there is that element you that you need to be careful of, who do not care for you, and what you stand for, the criminal element!" We all frown and look around. Wanted posters shown around the room of scary looking guys who would kill you for your shoes. Like stereotype movie villains, wearing a black hat, so we know the good guy from the bad guy. 'Them,' who we all want to see behind bars!

White man telling the savage about taking care of the environment, then wiping out the buffalo. When the savage had been in balance with the buffalo for 30,000 years, we know of. White man in charge for under 200 years. Who wiped out the buffalo? Not the savage! Or more, who is really the savage in this story? Who of the two cultures knew about stewardship and taking care of the land and resources? I need permission, need to follow the civilized rules out here in the wilds? Not out of respect. But what does this punk kid know of such things.

I am interrupted writing these words with a phone call. It is Karen! Geez. Out of the blue she calls, just as I am writing and thinking of her!

"True, Miles, I run the lodge out here at Lake Minchumina by myself these days." I ask how the lodge is doing! I had heard not so well.

"We would like to sell it, but need to keep it up so it has worth, and sell to someone who at least knows how to even live out here! The house is 200 feet up a hill. Some of the prospective buyers cannot even walk up the hill to see it!" We reminisce about such people we both have met, who could not walk the twenty feet to our cabin up the hill, much less 200 feet. Dreamers who do not have a clue who tell us how healthy they are! I ask about May and Joy.

"You were such a perfect father for them, Miles! I can say that for you. You used to read to them. Mix up the stories, tell them backwards, remember? Joy tries to do that with her kids and says she has not gotten the gift you do, Miles." I think this is kind of her to say. We seemed at such odds at the time, trying to be a family, both of us with such baggage! What family stories there would be to tell if we spoke of it. I dare not. The fight over the trash can! Oh, she'd remember all right! I screwed it down so she could not move it, and she chopped a hole in the floor with an ax to move it.

May is still working with sled dogs. Sometimes doing her own dog trips with people. There is dog cart pulling in summer for tourists. Now working with a well-known musher. Better money, but not really getting ahead financially, but probably happy. As long as there are dogs in her life, she will be happy. Heck, her first word was 'dog,' not Mom or Dad! She used to get up at 4:00 am to get her home schooling done and ask to go dog mushing after breakfast. We let her. At twelve years old, she went out on her first overnight dog trip by herself! Built a log cabin at ten years old! I am still so proud of her! So much better than how kids are raised today! Or so Karen and I agree. Joy, the younger child, keeps in touch with Karen more than me. She is settled, married, has children. The sanest and least disturbed out of the bunch of us.

"I hope they will come and live here, and take over the lodge, but the husband is not the outdoor type like May!" This could be true. "Miles, the reason I am calling is I have a prospective buyer for the lodge who wants to come here to look at it! They are your neighbors!" I am not sure who she means at first, as I do not know the husband or boyfriend. It takes me a few more hints to place who they are!

"Oh, yeah, she cooked at the school and helped you guys out at the lake cooking one summer?"

"Yes, Miles, her!"

"You will be lucky to get paid. They have no money and are behind on taxes, and water and sewer bill. How can they afford a lodge?"

"They want to be in partnership with me, Miles!"

"No way, no how. They will suck you dry," I explain. She used to take school food and use the school kitchen to prepare food to sell on her own at events. Outfitted her entire family with school food she stole. I know it for a fact, I have watched her unload it. Her daughter about burned the house down a couple of years ago. Put a log in the stove too long, and the door would not shut, so she let it burn, and passed out with all her druggie friends. The house caught on fire! The family sued the stove company! I think the company must have decided to settle out of court rather than have a long drawn out negative battle. The neighbors got a rebuild and profit out of it.

"Thanks for telling me. I suspected as much, but needed to hear it from someone who might know more. She is flying out today and I was going to show her around. Should I cancel that trip?"

"No. I'd let her see for herself she cannot handle the life. I doubt she can make it across the lake eight miles on your snow machine. I think she is incapable of even hanging on the back without falling off. No way can she make it up the hill to the lodge, but let her find that out for herself. That way it is her decision and no hard feelings." We ramble about old times.

"Miles, people ask me if I know you, and are excited, telling me I should write my own book! I tell them no, you are writing about me! You are right, Miles, my life is not interesting enough." I'm not sure I put it exactly like that. I feel bad if she feels this way. I'm sorry if I said anything in the past that stops her from telling her story.

"Karen, you know, having an adventure means you made a mistake. People who do not make mistakes do not have adventures!"

"Not true, Miles! There is river ice overflow, and stuff like that, that is normal." She reminds of when the welfare-child custody people showed up trying to take her children away from us. I forgot about that. Yes, the father of the children was upset his children were out in the wilderness, with no access to a church, or other kids and what not. So he called social services and got them involved. We had to pay for an investigation and an inspector lady shows up.

"Miles, remember her and the overflow?" Oh yes. I had to go out to the lake out back to pick her up when she flew in on a ski plane. The creek was full of water on the snow. Normal for us, horrible for her. She was terrified!

"Yes, Karen, she kept working her way forward in the sled, forcing the brush bow into the water. I told her to lean back and let the front of the sled steer and be out of the water! Geez!" People not listening had been part of our earlier conversation. I recalled, 'some musher lady,' had been in the news for having clients get lost, and having a bad experience, and needing to be rescued. Karen and I agreed the customers did not listen! They paid for not listening!

"I heard the client's side, Miles. It was my daughter, May, who rescued them and gave them a better experience for free so they could leave Alaska feeling better about our state." There was another side to the story. The lady running the tour had little money, was not set up well, had no insurance, little gear, and was operating this tour in a restricted area, on trails that only experienced people should be on. It is interesting that in Alaska we all know each other. I mention something, and she knows someone who knows someone else, and it is part of the same story!

"The guy who is running Josh's dogs says he knows May, and they went on a trip together!" "Oh yes, but May kind of looked out for him and enabled him."

"Yeah, he said May was amazingly competent." Later, this guy, Jessie, is the main person in the reality show, 'Life Below Zero.'

Karen and I are babbling away, remembering this and that, getting caught up.

"Karen, you really should write your own story if you like to write." Karen used to be an English teacher. I add, "It needs to be your version of life in the wilds. Women would love it, since you have been living so many women's dreams, living off the grid alone." I can tell by her attitude she lacks the confidence. I wonder how life would be if we had stayed together! Us running a remote lodge would be a good life? I love to fix things, build things, tell stories to the clients. Sell them my art and books. If I knew then what I know now, maybe I could have helped her with her confidence. *But we clashed so much at the time.* Years and years ago when I began writing, I wrote my first article for Alaska magazine. It took me an hour, while I was waiting for Karen to fix dinner that would be late. I sent it off, written in pencil on dirty yellow notepad paper. She came unglued, telling me,

"No way it will be accepted, Miles!" In pencil with all my normal misspellings and weird ways of writing! She is an English teacher after all, who knows her grammar!

My article got accepted, and hers got rejected, the one she slaved over for a month. I did not say so, but probably had a smug attitude of, "So there!" In response to her, "You need an education and degree, Miles!" A button for me. "You need to be neat and clean, Miles!" Insulting how I learned things in life. A chip on my shoulder she was not kind about. Reacting to a lifetime of dealing with a family who agrees with Karen! *Now I'm living in this same nightmare!* Why was I attracted to her in the first place!? I may prefer educated women? I cannot have my cake and eat it too! Many of our issues were on me! *In hindsight, of course.* We could have toughed it out and worked through our issues. Maybe. At the time, I believed I deserved so much better! It would have been cool if I wrote and she edited. She would have seen that as the flunky job, though. Working in the background, not getting credit for the story.

At seventy years old, she still carries two buckets of water from the lake to the cabin each day. Still gets firewood, crosses an eight-mile lake on a snow machine. "This is the first year I do not have dogs, Miles! It cost five times as much to keep dogs here as in town!" Yes, I know. I lived at Minchumina, and know the costs, and is one reason I had to move some place else.

The connection seems bad. Karen is on a phone at Lake Minchumina, maybe the only phone on the whole lake. One phone for all twenty-one residents. No roads, everything has to be flown in. No form of government. No taxes. I can picture the eight mile long lake, at the base of Mt. Denali. So close you have to bend back to look up and see the top. Swans, salmon, bears, moose, outnumber the residents. We have to say goodbye after an hour of talking.

I GET BACK to studying what is in this black box of evidence. But why bother? We are not going to court. We are not negotiating a plea bargain. We take the ultimatum, or fight blow-by-blow twenty-eight charges, and get ten times the punishment for arguing. *How much do I want all the details of what was found that make me look bad? Life goes on. Let it go. When floods hit me, do I study all the damage it did? I assess the basics, rebuild, and press on! Same with a forest fire, bear damage, any catastrophe. Someday it ends.*

I accept the ultimatum June 7th 2013. The judge gives me a $7,000 fine, six months in Federal prison, and three years' probation. I am given the written information before I appear in court. The judge gives me the minimum jail time allowed, and it's an amazingly low fine.

I glance over the plea agreement #4:12-cr-00015-RRB-SA0 Unites States District Court for the District of Alaska.

> Miles Martin is before this court on plea of guilty to 4 counts of 28 count indictment concerning various violations of federal law prohibiting the trafficking in wildlife and their parts. It should be clear to the court that Martin is a wildlife trafficker with an extensive history in the illicit trade of wildlife which goes back many years and which was, as indicated by the items seized, relatively extensive.
>
> In this case the defendant did not contest any of the investigative activity and agreed to enter into plea negotiations.

This is an extensive document, so I scan ahead.

History Characteristics of the Defendant-Unlawful Conduct

> The defendant is a long-time resident of Alaska and has been involved in wildlife trafficking trade, worldwide, for years. As indicated by the attached inventory of forfeiture, no item of wildlife was outside the scope of possible sale, lion, walrus, birds, elephant ivory, and the list is long. And it appears the defendant made a fair part of his income from the illegal trade in wildlife parts... Virtually any wild animal part was made available for sale-wolverine, grizzly, elephant, wolf, beaver, which establishes the defendants specialized knowledge with respect to the law and export regulations. The counts of conviction reflect the sale in migratory birds, polar bear, seal, walrus, illegal exportation of wolf teeth, and other high-value predator parts i.e., the claws of lion and wolf... With respect to market, the defendant's customers spanned the globe from Germany to Argentina and the lower 48 states.

Yes, there was in fact a lot of product. 99.9 % legal material. 'Wolverine, wolf, beaver,' is all perfectly legal. There was zero elephant ivory. *And this is what the issue was all about and the funding was for. Stopping the illegal trade of elephant ivory in 'Operation Whitewash.' Whatever, it does not matter. It's over.* I scan ahead further.

> Need for the sentence to Reflect the Seriousness of the Offense, Afford Deterrence, Protect the Public, and Rehabilitate the Defendant

So here are the stated goals of what the prosecution hopes to accomplish. *Protect the public from what?* The judge himself said he saw no victim. The charges did not stem from a complaint. *Rehabilitate?* I am puzzled. I see the government, Fish and Wildlife, and the court system as being in the wrong as I am accused of being. But ok. I may be mistaken. Here is the chance to show me the way. Enlighten me. Teach me how to be more legal, less selfish. Show me how to make a living in some legal manner of your choice. I will remain open-minded. I am ready! An empty vessel, ready to be... *Hey! I think that's laying it on a bit thick, huh?* Yeah, yeah, sure whatever you say. How would you like me to say it, Sir!? My conscious has taken on the role of the judge with wig and hammer sitting up high on his throne.

☠

I read on further to see what it is I have done and how I will be punished.

A sentence of 6 months' imprisonment, 3 years supervised release, and a fine of $6,750 along with conditions set forth in the plea agreement and forfeiture are appropriate.

With regard to deterrence, the agencies entrusted to protect and defend the resources of Alaska face daunting obstacles with limited resources to cover a state of such magnitude. Indeed, Martin was able to continue this illegal conduct for years.

It was only through the work of an undercover agent and the arrest of Jesse Lebouef, which brought the defendant to justice. Here, under the aspect of Section 3553, the requested sentence of 6 months in conjunction with the closure of the defendant's business, the cessation of that livelihood due to this investigation, and the forfeiture of a significant quantity of wildlife parts sends a strong and significant message to others inclined towards this illegal activity of the consequences of their actions and promote respect for the laws in place to protect wildlife.

Wildlife will forever feel the pinch of encroachment even in a state as vast as Alaska. The internet has now permitted anyone with a laptop and access to wildlife in the wild places the ability to sell coveted wildlife parts anywhere in the world with a few token clicks of a mouse. It permits the anonymous meeting between seller and buyer with little risk of apprehension or discovery.

Well, this sounds like Fish and Wildlife laying it on a bit thick, to a court system that has no clue. I am not horribly upset, Hey, I do the same thing! Make the sale! Turn blue into red, convince Eskimos they need to buy snow! An issue I have is, how come they can do it, and I cannot?

Past Flash

I am in the Navy, on the Aircraft carrier, 'Wasp' out at sea. 1970. For some reason a Russian boat comes alongside us. Situations are on a 'need to know' basis. It was not for seamen to understand what we are doing or why. Just follow orders. All I recall is a Russian boat next to us.

The sailors on both boats are hollering, screaming, throwing items back and forth like hats, cigarettes, in hopes those on the other boat will throw items of interest back in trade. Wow! They look human! I see heads! Arms! No horns! Nothing evil looking. Wow! They are smiling and laughing just like humans! How cool is that! What a concept!

It appeared to me that if the two ships pulled into port like this, we'd meet at the bar and have a grand time! I am not envisioning fighting. These guys want to meet us and we want to meet them! How can they be our enemy? They are not! Interesting! I look around some more, and see our captain up on the bridge, arms folded across his chest, glaring at the other boat, its crew, and its captain.

The Russian captain is doing the same thing. I am nineteen years old. I am thinking that it is the leaders who create war and strife, for reasons of their own. Left to their own devices, the human beings on both sides would try to trade, meet, mingle, and be friends. The captains did not like to see us realize this. It upset their plans for each country and its war. Maybe war is money. I do not know. I am nineteen, what do I know.

Past flash ends

My situation as described seems similar in my mind. The Internet has gotten people around the world chatting, trading, learning, and becoming friends. This scares the heck out of all governments. What if we do not want to kill these people we are meeting? What if we all like each other? Bad for governments! When the Internet came along, I had a vision, saw the potential. The ability to equalize the world. There would be much less ignorance. Many middle people would get cut out. Both from a business standpoint, but also socially. Governments could not hoodwink their people about what life is like elsewhere. We the people can look around with open eyes and see the rest of the world as it really is. At least come to our own conclusions. We can see prices, markets available, with little to stop us from working out our own deals between ourselves. Governments find that scary?

"What? Put people's lives into their own incompetent hands! Where would that lead! Where would the people be without us, the government!" As in my case, the government believes, "Wipe out all the wildlife! That's what people will do if allowed!"

What is this talk in my charges and punishment involving the Internet?

"Little risk of discovery or apprehension?" The Internet was designed by the government. It was used to move secret data in large amounts, fast, around the world. There was a lot of room, so the government gave some of it to the public. But was it given for free, really? It has been a great way to keep track of absolutely everyone. All on the net is public. Our emails, our pictures, anything we do. It is easy to find. I have a website easy to find, I want you to find me.

Google my name. Google 'teeth and claws,' and I am in the top five sites in the world. That's all Fish and Wildlife has to do to find me, or my products. I am not hiding anything. I considered what was on the Internet all legal, above board. Anything on the website or emails is all 'evidence,' easy to gather by anyone. I am pretty sure my activity is known, has been known, and was not a problem until there was a reason to make it a problem, to fulfill an agenda. I can only speculate 'why now?'

So the Feds description is a bit off. But would the average citizen know? Or the judge? How much time does a judge have to surf the net and look up who is selling what and play with Ebay? How much would even a jury know? I believe the government has a file on every single one of us. Or can very quickly create one when needed. Or not. We keep the file on ourselves! I believe as well, the government can profile us, create predictions, and charts based on averages and physiology studies that help identify a variety of issues the government might have. I believe the government can scan emails and websites for keywords and phrases, to have them pulled, gathered, analyzed, all by computer programs. Write the word 'bomb' in an email and see what happens. The 'little risk of discovery' written in my punishment is a joke. An Afghanistan war veteran who was a world class sniper interrogator, told me, "If you have a presence on a computer, we own you."

I have a gift for selling. I am not just 'anyone clicking a mouse.' I have spent ten hard years learning how to use the computer. *Let it go. Who cares. It's already yesterday's news.* Yeah, but it is my life. Even if my life only matters to me.

I see the judge. For sentencing.

"Do you have a preference which prison, Mr. Martin?" The judge wants to know.

I reply, "Well, my lawyer said maybe Arizona, since my mother lives there, that is the most likely place I would go. I suppose then, my mother might visit."

There is a long pause. "Mr. Martin, obviously you are not familiar with the prison system. No one requests Arizona. You will go to Washington to a minimum security prison there. Have you got anything to say about your crime?"

I want to say, "That should have been your first question, not your last." This is the first time anyone asked me a question through the whole process. It's been all about the lawyers and judge talking as if I am not there. No, I have nothing to say. It's a bit late, don't you think, Your Highness! I say nothing.

The judge adds, "I hear you are a writer and have written a couple of books!"

Said in surprise, like it seems impossible a stupid, low life felonious criminal, killer of cute fuzzy innocent dwellers of the forest, knows how to read and write. Have real hands like a human, capable of holding a pencil, not claws. He's impressed and intrigued a little. He wants to verify there were no drugs involved.

"No sir, I do not believe in drugs."

"Good, do not let me hear of any drug problem!" He studies his notes and grunts, adding, "It appears to me there has been no victim in this crime."

I wonder. *If there is no victim, how can there be a crime, your honor?* I have learned my lesson from Mr. Public. Say nothing. Neither Fish and Game nor the news media said 'no victim.' I am let go and am asked to return to report for my incarceration. The tickets have to get lined up and paperwork done. I got the minimum prison time allowable by the judge who could have given me a year and still be within the guidelines of the recommendation. There has been no confiscation of my bank accounts, home, boat, etc. All in all, it is as good a deal as possible. Even Saddle could probably have not done better. I explain how important in my lifestyle it is to have the garden planted for Iris. We need the food. I'm given until July 30th to report to prison so I can plant the garden.

I find out later, Arizona prisons have been in the news. 'Tent camp city.' The governor of Arizona has got prisoners living in tents. Saying, "If it is good enough for our troops, it is good enough for our prisoners!" No air-conditioning, poor food, it's got the reputation among prisoners as the worse place to be in the country. How could Mr. Public not know? Why would he suggest I request it? I agree prison is for punishment. Spending these huge amounts of money to give prisoners a good place to stay, and give them a positive experience, is hard on taxpayers, and may not accomplish the stated purpose. I think prisoners should be working, and not only earning their keep, but paying back society for the loss they caused. I feel if shop owners said, "Thank you, thief, for robbing my store! I need a new picture window, cabinets, let's see…" there would be a lot less thievery, as many criminals I have met along life's path, like to hurt people, 'get even' put a monkey wrench in society's gears.

I call billing the citizens eighty grand a year for incarceration is as much damage as some of these criminals can cause. It's like winning the war. At some point the enemy government will be overwhelmed with costs. This is the argument spoken. Street people nod approval.

Instead of 'costing,' criminalization should be making a profit. Slave labor. The old chain gangs. Put criminals to use. Send them out to pick cotton. Harvest watermelons. Whatever. No. I would not mind working. I'd in fact like to. Come home strong, with a tan, and knowledge of something I can do. Like the military was. Time I put in for my government. I disliked some aspects of my military time, but did like the work.

I have some freedom for a while to be home, wrap up stuff. Enough wood is cut for Iris to make it through the winter. The garden is started and well along. My website is prepared as well as I can, for me to be gone, but there can be no animal parts. Iris is shown how to reply to customers, and hopefully can figure out pay pal. She does not know how to work the website program. When things sell, she has no way to remove the item from the site, or replace anything. It has not been 'our' business, but 'my' business.

I'm a lot more calm and relaxed now, knowing my fate, believing this is do-able. One big concern is, "Is this it? Or, is more to come?" There was nothing said about any fossils, including mammoth ivory. Yet the Feds told me it is all illegal, and for sure the Feds want to put a stop to all ivory trade. So are they trying to build another bigger case separately? It is in fact difficult to prove where I got any of my fossil ivory from, besides a few receipts from the Russians. There are concerns for my outlook on the government, and this would be called a security issue. Others have gone to prison just for speaking not doing anything.

Iris and I look up this prison we never heard of. The prison runs a farm. There are pictures, with descriptions of how prisoners learn to farm, and leave with trade skills. The prisoners eat from the farm, so eat well from a fresh garden. Club Fed in Washington. Even so, I am concerned about my situation. After all, I have knowledge I can teach others on how to live without the government, off the grid, out in the wilds, as a total unknown. If there is a hidden agenda, against having such knowledge, I could be made to disappear. I have reason and seen evidence to think this is a possibility. Go to prison and never get out, disappear in the system.

There is the possibility Iris is a plant. There is not much we have in common. There was a brief blurb in the evidence about contacting her. I might not know how to find the follow up on that note to know the details of how much she cooperated. Or still is.

When people wonder what the big deal is about Miles?! Why so much money spent! I ask what it is about me, that is not like very many people. By way of trying to identify the why. I know enough to educate even the military on wilderness survival. Who else on the whole planet has voluntarily been in the wilds a year at a time with so little human contact? Who also has civilized knowledge, been in the military, communicates well enough to write books, has followers? If I were running a corrupt government, I'd be worried about people like me. In the political classic book 'Utopia,' the savage was a big problem. The whole book revolved around the savage. The 'problem' is well described by 'Mustava Mund.'

While I'm gone, there could be a complete systematic search for who knows what evidence the Feds missed in a single day search. Maybe coffee cans of cash. Past indiscretions of the 3rd kind. A single phone number on a piece of scrap paper connecting me to...? Whoever. Things only I know. Or forgot about. The old murder accusation. I once had some dynamite. *I might need to blow up a beaver damn, do some emergency fishing, move a large object, make a root cellar in a hurry, stuff like that. It's fun to watch things go boom.* Other potential wildlife products, possibly never discovered. Stuff I'd as soon leave dead and buried. Unmentionables.

Will the other shoe fall? But other than that, I can prepare for the known. It is nice to have the time to get my life in order. I appreciate that consideration. The situation could have been much worse!

I tell Will, "There are countries where, if you piss off the government, they make you dig a hole and jump in it where they shoot you, and your wife shovels the dirt in after they rape her." It's not smart to badmouth someone with a big stick. Or at least chose your battles.

"Yeh, Miles, except you figured you were talking to like-minded people and friends. You got set up!"

"True, but Will, there is no such thing as total trust, privacy, or secrets."

I'm paying the price. I understand. It's ok. I made a mistake. I should have been more careful, more low profile, not got the Feds so openly upset. In truth, the ones with the biggest stick are the law! I underestimated the enemy. It does not matter what the people say, believe, read, interpret. This is the sort of knowledge not taught in school. This is what is meant by 'street smarts.' There is an expected article in the newspaper. At least not on the front page. The front page news was someone getting mauled by a bear. I'm in the B section.

"Animal Trafficker gets 6 Months" followed by… results of a State and Federal investigation… Allegations… a requirement that he surrender more than 900 pounds of wildlife parts that include lion, bear, walrus ivory, parts of seal, polar bear, elephant ivory.

There were no lion parts. Bear is state regulated, not a Federal issue. Polar bear was half an ounce of legal documented fur for fly tying. There was no elephant ivory. The only relevant correct part was seal claws. But there was 900 pounds total. They got that right. Mostly moose antler pieces.

I had been told by my lawyer that eventually Fish and Wildlife would come and confiscate all animal products, both legal and illegal. Because part of my plea is to voluntarily give up all animal parts. Mr. Pubic repeated, "Confiscate what is on your property; when they arrive, that is in your possession at that time." In other words, I can have these items removed by someone else, have it off my property, not in my possession, owned by someone else. I have a month to accomplish this. The products are not Fish and Wildlife's till they confiscate it. Yet it is not mine either. Animal parts could be mine up until the plea bargain agreement takes effect. It's basically up for grabs after that. I could have, over the past two years, made it disappear.

Even legally sold it. After the plea bargain agreement, others may legally claim it before the Feds do. I now do not have the authority to protect it, salvage it, inventory it.

As was promised, the Feds came. They got even the cat's toy made of fur. The antique moose rack over the door that came with the house.

Yes, it was two truckloads. At least 500 pounds was two freezers I unplugged, full of rotting maggot filled bones from my dinner. Moose leg bones I gathered up from the ditch along the road. I was not responsible for paying the electric bill on keeping items that are not mine frozen. Another 200 pounds was legal weathered moose antlers many years old. Zero value. I had cut the tines off and sold them already. Everything confiscated I wanted them to have, as not worth removing from the property and hauling to the dump. Anything worth anything was 'gone' and not in my possession. Except the cats toy and the moose rack over my door. There was nothing else taken that mattered.

The article previously made it sound like 900 pounds of things like lion claws, and illegal ivory. It sells papers, but it's not reality. People read it and believe it.

In the same issue of the paper is this: "Obama administration propose lifting wolf protection ban in lower 48."

There was some reference in the charges having to do with the fact I sell so many animal parts, therefore it is a logical conclusion I know the laws. When in fact no one knows the laws. The laws are vague, changing by the day, conflicting, and untested in court. Those who make the laws do not understand them. Those who enforce the laws do not understand them. The state does not understand them. The state says, "I don't think so!" and ignores many they do understand. No one out there at the cutting edge knows what to do. Here is an example. The president of the United States decides to end a ban protecting wolves. We are never told what laws got changed as a result, or when they take effect.

People like myself help define that cutting edge. Hey! Did you know our hero Audubon ,the artist spent time in prison for not paying his debts!? Yup. I think died a pauper. The most influential wildlife artist in our country. "Hey! You want my autograph? I'm a felon now!"

Dalia, who used to be my friend, who married 'What's his name,' who used to also be my friend, is the village gossip now. She is the one who called the paper and told a reporter I had been handcuffed, tossed to the ground, and am being carted off to prison. That is what was going to get printed at the time of the search warrant.. Good grief! It's all hard enough to deal with when it is the truth. Life is made ten times more difficult when lies are told. Even more difficult when told by friends who have insider knowledge.

Not long after Dalia stopped me on the street to tell me how she felt about me, her son dies of a drug overdose in another state. Many people, including me, have heard her on her cell phone over the past year yelling and cussing out her son. Telling him to leave her alone, go away, she is not going to help! He apparently had nowhere to turn. A street person. Dies at a party. The body moved by the party goers. No one knows for sure what happened. Dalia is stunned, shocked, indignant, yelling at the police to do something, investigate! "That's my son!"

She was told by the police it is just another dead druggie not worth anyone's time, so shut up. A cold thing to be saying. But she was insulting the police, ready to sue them, irritating them, screaming like a shrew. The time to care, and get excited of course, was when he was alive. *What goes around comes around. It is Karma and we get what we deserve.* I never pointed that out. I was deeply hurt by her attack on Iris and I during a time we could use support from friends and community. She kicked me when I was down and vulnerable. This is the sort of thing I do not forget. I never cared for cruelty and meanness. I often wonder if she understands what she gave, and what she got back.

I forgot and now recall. Her guy had illegally killed a cow moose with another unnamed friend of ours. It had been he who shot it. He hears a plane overhead, panics, thinking it is the Fish and Game. So these two guys grab what they can on the run, leaving the dead cow moose behind, dragging a few pieces of meat through the mud and grass. I saw the meat and got told the story by 'the other guy.' There were about two meals of edible meat, and 1,000 pounds left to rot. Dalia ate off it and shared in the crime. Let's put down the, 'get what we deserve' card. So why is her nose in the air? I have no idea. But by the grace of God, it could be her and her old man facing what I'm facing.

The mayor is willing to go to court and speak up for me and even wrote a letter. Likewise, the local magistrate and policeman. Even so, Dalia's words hurt deeply. She wonders why Iris and I do not speak to her on the street anymore, "Oh, get over it! Stop holding a grudge, geez, Iris!" Her friends agree. There is no use starting a war, exchanging who said and did what. I suck in the pain and walk by.

I tell Iris, "It is good to see who your real friends are, huh. Otherwise we might never know."

My friend and survey boss Seymour stops by. It is good to see him! He is upset over my arrest. Wishes me well. I am reminded of the strawberries story by our conversation. He is very much a numbers man. His stories are written in times, dates and numbers. That is his job!

"Yeah, Seymour, there are people who define the world in dates, times, numbers. There is another sort of person who remembers feelings, sensations, trust instincts, the inner mind. Whose property is not so many feet, by so many feet, at certain angles on a plat. Their property is described by their garden, the toolshed, the swamp edge. Described by the flowers, and how they smell. The sound of the frogs from the swamp."

"Whatever, Miles, but the real world measures things with numbers, as accurate! How can there be a legal description of sensations! How can that be trusted! People can just make stuff up! You cannot prove a feeling in court!"

I sort of agree but am not sure. "You walk until you can't smell the flowers anymore and that's the edge of my property!" We both laugh.

Seymour adds, "When you begin to smell the dog crap? That's the neighbor's property line!"

"Like that, you got it! Seymour!"

"In court such a personality is screwed, Seymour." He must know how it is with us on the job. I barely remember how old I am, or my birthday. I cannot dial a phone number right the first time. It takes at least three tries. I'm one of the worse numbers, time, dates, names, person you could ever come across! It does not make me a lair. Likewise, I seem not to spot social dangers till it is too late, and when I do, I seem not to be able to remove myself easily. I can make inappropriate jokes at funerals and have funeral depression at weddings. I divulge secrets I do not understand are secret, and I keep quiet about things that it is socially acceptable to talk about.

"Seymour, it is like being wired different from others." I consciously sought out a lifestyle that would put my good points to best use, and minimize the price I pay, or damage I might do.

Seymour is amazed, I can take him on the river and not hit anything; run the river in the pitch dark when we cannot see the front of the boat! He is clueless how it is possible! Yet, has seen it with his own eyes, so is a believer. I cannot explain it.

"The world of sensations, instincts, sounds, smells." My father had once said about a subject when it comes to learning, "If you cannot explain it, it doesn't exist." I had for a while been very interested in the world of mathematics. Out there at the cutting edge of quasars, string theory, black holes, gravitons, quarks, and such things. The main reason the interest faded as a career interest is the realization this occupation requires being a team player. Funding depends on grants under other people's control.

I had some rewards early in life with my art. I gravitated in the direction of least resistance and getting attention. There is the world of being able to pick up a musical instrument and simply play it. I never did that, but think I could have gone this direction. I believe you could hand me a guitar and in a day, I could play it. In a month, be known. I did not know my locker combination in school, but was able to open my school locker. Try explaining that when you are ten years old! Or, as Seymour sees, running a boat in the pitch dark. "I'm counting rpms and running an internal clock."

"That's impossible!"

"I know." But doing it anyway.

I believe everything we ever saw, heard, felt, is recorded someplace in our brain. Much like every keystroke on the computer is there someplace in residual memory that cannot be erased, and may be retrieved by those who know how. My theory is, I have run the river a hundred times. I know how long it takes at certain speeds to get from bend to bend. I know the sound of the hull on the water as depth changes. I know the feel of the air currents, as they change when we round a hill, or pass an island. I know the echo of the engine sounds as a blind man does. I know changes in smells. If I get asked, I also say this, "The brain has a certain capacity and ability like any vessel or computer. We choose what goes in. If we load a computer memory up with video games, the computer is slower for other tasks. So is our brain. I therefore want to remember that which I want to know, that is important in my life. But also, 'something different' as I do not wish to know what everyone else knows."

I quote Einstein. He was once asked the easy question, what the speed of light is. "When I want to know that, I'll ask someone, or look it up in a book." Many people who are my heroes, who are the best there is in the world at what they do, have one thing in common. They would not do well in court.

"Do you know so and so, and did you meet this person on this date, and have this conversation, Sir!?"

"Huh?" There are other people in the world? Most would look up with annoyance from their microscope, race car engine, electric guitar, and say, "I do not know, and I do not care, and why would I want to remember?" Followed by, "Now, if you ask me what the difference between string frequencies per ten degree temperature change, I can tell you that."

Seymour once had my GPS tracking route on and was watching it. I was not. "Miles, I have been watching this instrument for a mile and you have not deviated by a foot from the track you ran a year ago. How do you know where you went before, to the nearest foot! On a river half a mile across and so twisted?"

"Because I'm the man!" Because there is no answer. Because I have a GPS in my head. Because I know every bend of every river on every trip I ever ran. Since that is not possible, it is easier to say something stupid, and be the village idiot who can't recall his age or phone number, because that is not important. My brain needs room for important stuff. More and more, I turn to Iris. "What year is this again?" "How old am I again?" "Who was that?" I still cannot make a pitcher of lemonade by adding exactly four cans of water. Or make jello by measuring out the water. How stupid is that! Yet, the university wants me to have a grant and explain to the world how I made a garden watering automatic switch based on humidity for under ten dollars. I was asked in years past to teach art at the University.

"No thanks, I'm busy." Someone else can make the jello and lemonade. Or more, I will botch it, drink it anyway and enjoy it.

I do understand there is no way I can go to court and survive. That makes me very vulnerable, when there is no possibility of winning, when I cannot even give my date of birth correctly. I do not know if Seymour notices these things or not. We have never talked about it. He simply dials all the phone numbers, does all the driving, remembers all the numbers and angles. While I do what I get paid to do and do it well.

I do not view the world in the same dimensions most people do. Again, it does not make me a liar because I have to wing it and make up numbers to fill in the gaps, to survive in a numbers world. In the same way, people make up how they feel because they feel nothing. They do not think about how they feel. That is a subject that never comes up in their world, except awkwardly from women who ask if you love them.

"I bought you a new car, didn't I! Geez!" *How do I feel indeed!* What holds up in divorce court is the new car. No one cares how you feel about it! What did it cost, that's what matters! What gets divided up in court? 'Stuff you can see and measure, that cost money!' Not hearts, passion, love, courage, integrity.

We are punished in dollars. That's what fines are. We are punished in days incarcerated, in units of time. No one cares how you feel about it. To some people, jail is home, where they want to be, where their friends are, with meals and a place to sleep, all on a nice schedule they like to live by. It's true, few really like jail! But jail time is a relative experience and relative depth of punishment. What we owe people is measured in money. Such a financial punishment is rarely a percent of what you have. My $7,000 fine is an amount I will not miss. It used to represent two years of my wages. I have made more money than this in a single day of work. Even a single hour.

I do not like to be around people. Being crammed in a single room with eighty guys may be a nightmare. I am a sensation person. The smells and noise and such are more punishment to me than some. I do not live a regimented life. There is a difference between putting a sheep in a cage and putting a wolf in a cage. The sheep can smile, lay down, go to sleep. This is normal. An inner city kid is used to chaos, being crowded, guns going off, stress, noise, yelling incidents, people breaking down, interruptions, orders, no physical space, is all 'just like home.' I feel crowded if a neighbor is five miles away. I'm going to be more effected in jail. It might even constitute cruel and unusual punishment. Where leaving someone on a deserted island with no one on it for a year, might be cruel to others, and unusual punishment, that I do voluntarily, and love it.

When I first arrived in Alaska, many Natives did not trust me, and asked what I had done that my people had banished me? It is customary in their culture to punish someone by banishing them from the village, put them out on their own to live off the land by themselves. It's considered the worst thing that can be done to a person, and what most fear. Why would anyone voluntarily banish themselves?

It's the same as someone in my culture voluntarily going to jail, because they like it.

The court system and methods of punishment are geared towards the sheep. Seymour and I do not talk about such things. I say, "Hey, I am lucky. I lived as a free man, how I wanted all my life. I only now get in trouble as a senior! It's not the end of the world."

"Life is going to get pretty changed from now on for sure, Miles! Don't drop the bar of soap!" Yeah, showering with thousands of guys in a stall like cattle does not sound pleasant. Again. I am not used to anything public. Most people have showered in stalls before getting in a swimming pool, or school gym class, etc. I'm not used to these experiences. I would not be used to being some big guy's girlfriend!

Iris shows me the prison on the internet, with its description. How everyone gets their own room! Maybe a few have to double up sometimes, but in general, lots of space! Wow!

"I might be allowed to have a computer if I do not go on line, and then can work on my books for six months! Perfect!" I'm going to a minimum security prison. I could get into typing for six straight months, getting fed, no responsibilities, all my needs taken care of. It could be heaven in disguise.

"Look, Miles, here are pictures! A garden, a farm, classes to take." Wow!

I had corresponded a little with Josh's boy in prison. We do not talk about that anymore. He got life, thirty years. Actually just got out a few months ago, after doing over his thirty years in prison. He had it rough, I assume. He got a lot of solitary confinement. He refused to take mandatory anger management classes. But he got to play basketball, took college courses that were offered. Sort of, or so we all got told. It is odd he gets out and has no education that could get him a job. So what sort of classes did he get, I wonder? But he had woodworking, was able to produce some art his mother sold for him. It is hard to get a handle on the truth. People from prison seem not to talk about it, or write much about it. Where is there accurate literature on prison life? That's not sensationalism, I mean. With such a high percent of the population having been in prison, and no one writes about it? How weird is that! No. I suppose no one wants to know the details! Too creepy!

THE END OF BOOK 6

A productive garden. You can hardly see me over the greenery.

A personal note—

Reviews help authors more than you might think. If you enjoyed Surviving Wild, please consider leaving a review where you purchased it—it would be greatly appreciated. (Really!)

Sign up for my newsletter, "Keeping Up With Miles," @ www.milesofalaska.com and I'll send you a free book of short stories. You'll also receive discounts for original Alaskan Artwork I make and raw materials for your own creations.

The Alaska Off Grid Survival Series Summary

Book 1 - Going Wild

In 1973, I am 22 years old, and a city kid. I enlisted in the Navy and got out after the Vietnam War.

I travel to interior Alaska, a 'Cheechako' (Greenhorn) by Alaskan standards. But I have been raised on Walt Disney and feel qualified to be a mountain man!

I arranged with a pilot to drop me off in the wilds of Alaska. I do not have everything I need and have things I do not need. I learn about guns, trapping, and the loneliness of living in the vast wilderness with no other humans around.

I do not see anyone for many months, then walk out of the wilds to civilization in the spring. After working odd jobs to make supply money, I return to the wilds in the fall and have a hard time my second winter. I almost die, and need to be rescued.

I decide to build a houseboat so I can travel around without having to build another cabin. I have to accept summer work in Fairbanks to pay for the boat materials and work under a builder. The boat takes much longer to build than expected.

I live as a street person much of the time to keep expenses down.

Book 2 - Gone Wild

I have many adventures on the houseboat and acquire a dog team. There are issues with the police, a bear on my boat, and a trip to see my family who live a civilized life.

My houseboat sinks. I get lost and learn other hard lessons. I start doing artwork and end up on TV. I win a land lottery and start my first homestead.

There are mail order women, and I live with a woman and her kids. Ten people are murdered in a village we visit, and myself and the family are almost among them. Family life is more difficult than I imagined.

Fish and Game becomes a concern.

I head back into the wilderness, which leads into book 3.

Book 3 - Still Wild

I acquire a couple more homesteads and cut more trapline.

I give up sled dogs and enter the world of snow machine adventures.

I winter in Galena and visit many native villages. There are bear encounters, and many survival situations to learn about.

I become a serious mammoth hunter and find fossils as part of my living. I work with a land surveyor specializing in homesteads and wilderness surveys, getting paid to use my boat.

My art sells well, so I do some big shows. I become more social and understand civilization better. I see the wisdom of being accepted by others. I learn. I grow. I try to change, as the world does.

The economy changes. It is less acceptable to be a trapper. I never become totally civilized as a city person defines it, but maybe I do, relative to the life I had in book one.

Book 4 - Beyond Wild

I am getting past just survival and doing well, even prospering. I own more than the houseboat can easily haul. Gas gets expensive. I need a new houseboat engine.

There is a homestead and trapline that keeps me in one place now. There are more bear stories and adventures into the wilds, including a 300-mile boat trip looking for mammoth tusks, which has disastrous consequences.

I find where I want to live on the Kantishna River. A river 300 miles long with about five people on it. I hang out in the native village of Nenana, spending a lot of time here.

I get my first computer and learn to build a website. People are looking at the pictures and buying my raw materials and art. This is a chance to make a difference.

Life is beautiful. Life is precious. I Dare to live it.

Book 5 - Back To Wild

I acquire a home in Nenana and start a web store. I am forced out of my subsistence lifestyle, partly because of changes in the laws. I do some serious mammoth hunting.

Unstable power causes a lot of computer data loss. I learn by punching keys to see what happens. It takes a long time to get good enough to create a book.

I continue the Mammoth hunts. The Tucson fossil gem show and State fair do well for me.

This period of 'being civilized' that I am trying out, has advantages, but also a price to pay—a big change from the wilderness life and being alone!

I am a suspect in a murder investigation. Another trapper tries to move in on my territory. There are neighbors and infringements on my property.

I fear I cannot change who I am. There is difficulty blending the two lives and ways of thinking. There are mail-order women coming and going, as well as the usual adventures and situations I manage to get myself into.

Book 6 - Surviving Wild (This Book)

Iris is my partner. Business grows, with money coming in, but causes 'complications.' I understand why I left for the wilds in the first place.

I get better at fossil hunting and have some exciting trips getting mammoth tusks and other ancient treasures. I am viewed as an expert on a few subjects and Discovery TV and reality shows contact me several times.

The new life in town causes legal issues that have been nipping at my heels off and on throughout my time in Alaska. Fish and Wildlife ask, "Why are you alone out here where we cannot keep an eye on you? We know you are up to something. What is it you have to hide? We will find out!" This mentality is that different is bad and of concern. I end up being investigated. A SWAT team shows up at my property with a dozen cars and 20 cops.

My arrest makes headlines. I'm sentenced to Federal Prison for six months as a felon. This is a stark contrast to 'Book 1-Going Wild,' where I have as much freedom as it is possible to have.

How did I get from there to here?

Book 7 - Secretly Wild

I am a convicted felon, describing life in prison from the viewpoint of someone used to freedom and the wilderness life. The same feather in the hat I wore on the cover of Ruralite magazine in 1979, is now worth five years in prison.

What do I need to do to survive here? There are classes to take, books to read, farm work to do, and people to help. There are interesting felon stories.

I observe more crime within the prison system by the system than I am accused of committing. "The prison could not survive if we operated legally," I am told by officials. I do my time. Now what? Am I a better person? I see the error of my ways. I am saved. Society is safer now.

Book 8 - Retiring Wild

I talk about news relevant to living off the grid as an individual in the wilderness that few citizens are aware of. I adapt my business, and still have adventures, depending as much as I can on the subsistence life I love and understand that is now becoming illegal as a white man.

I ponder whether the end of my life is in agreement with the views I held dear from the beginning. I have hope that even in times of control and suppression, I can still focus on the plus side, and continue to find ways to enjoy personal freedoms and individuality.

I continue to explore choices, how to have better control of my destiny, happiness, and success. I refer to this as 'Survival.' I have few regrets, and hope my life's path as written can provide entertainment and insight.

As someone who is interested in being different, not one of the sheep, I look realistically at the rewards that choice offers, but also the price that has to be paid.

Please visit www.alaskadp.com for links to the books.

Visit www.milesofalaska.com to find a bio of Miles, additional photos, stories, how-to videos, handmade artwork, and raw materials for sale.

Magazine and News Stories

Alaska Magazine

Alaska Magazine July 77—Survive by Miles Martin two pages, Photos. By Miles about my rescue, walk out on the Yukon River, five days at 50 below zero.

Nomadic House Boater Have Cabin Will Travel January 81—by Miles. Three pages, four color photos, a map. About life living on a houseboat, trapping and selling art (photo of my art), and all the adventures I have had on the river.

Would You Make A Good Bush Homesteader? June 86—by Miles four pages, six color pictures (One shows my custom knives.) A story I wrote about what it takes to be a homesteader.

Surviving The Big Lonesome— March 98—by Jim Rearden five pages, two color photos, one double page photo of Miles. Photos by world-famous photographer Jean Erick Pasquier. Describes life in the wilderness.

GEO Magazine

GEO in Germany is like "National Geographic" in the US.

Life in The Wilderness Alaska Special—87 by Miles Martin ten pages, sixteen color photos, a map

Photos by Jean Erick, one of the best photographers in the world, I Wrote it myself, winter life in the wilderness.

Alaska Special - 95 Einer gegen den Rest der Welt

Eight pages, seven color photos, three are double page. A follow up story to the first, written by New York Times reporter Ted Morgan, with Brigitte Helbing, photos by New York Times photographer Rex Rystedt. My fight for a lifestyle.

The New York Times

New York Times Magazine an insert to the paper, April 17, 1994, section six, The Vexing Adventures of the Last Alaskan Bushrat.

Six pages, four color photos, one is a double page Written by New York Times writer and bestselling author Ted Morgan. Photos by Rex Rystedt (World-renowned photographer). Facing twenty years in jail and a $10,000 fine for putting artwork on a bear claw and selling it.

Book-- A Shovel Full of Stars 95—Published by Simon and Schuster — New York

By Ted Morgan about ten pages with Miles. About one of the last homesteaders, and the lifestyle I live, of a Subsistence person.

Ruralite Magazine

Put out by Golden Valley 180,000 circulation
Wild Miles August 79, two pages, four black and white photos, Full cover page photo of Miles doing artwork. Story and photos by Margaret Van Cleve — Mostly about my artwork, some about my lifestyle on a houseboat

Newspaper, Daily Newsminer, Fairbanks Alaska

Associated Press, date unreadable, think a Thursday, and think spring of circa 74 **'Trapper rescued by Chopper;** Vows to Return to the Bush' headline, one column, National news, about my rescue after five days walking at 50 below.

Alaska Trapper Magazine

Put out by Alaska Trappers Association, a cover photo of me with Wolf. Five-page story by Miles comparing snowmachine and snowshoe trapping Nov. 99—four pages. Over the years, another six-seven articles on various trapping and related issues. Contact organization for exact issues.

Me in 1975.

OTHER TITLES AVAILABLE FROM ALASKA DREAMS PUBLISHING

Visit www.alaskadp.com to see these titles.

Books by Miles Martin:

- Going Wild
- Gone Wild
- Still Wild
- Beyond Wild
- Back To Wild
- Surviving Wild
- Secretly Wild
- Retiring Wild

Titles by other ADP authors:

- Rookie
- Alaska Freedom Brigade
- Apache Snow
- In Search of Honor
- A Coming Storm
- Arizona Rangers Series – Blake's War
- Legend of Silene
- Inspiring Special Needs Stories
- My Life In The Wilderness
- All Over The Road
- Ghost Cave Mountain
- Inside the Circle
- The Silver Horn of Robin Hood
- Alaskan Troll Eggs
- Through My Eyes
- The Professional Ghost Investigator
- The Adventures of Jason and Bo
- Seeds Of The Pirate Rebels

FOOT NOTES

CHAPTER 1

1. Web business and computer technology has changed since I got started. Many changes were not fast, but gradual. Digital cameras got more user friendly and less expensive, while quality improved. Programs to edit pictures got cheaper, easier to use and understand. Higher capacity computers could process pictures faster and offered more room. I began with floppy drive storage of 1 meg. I graduated to zip drive, then CD, then thumb drives, then mass storage devices, external hard drives etc. I may have to move to something I hear called 'the cloud.' Customers over time came to the internet to shop more. At first there were not so many shoppers! Those few were skeptical, unwilling to make large purchases.

CHAPTER 2

1. Over a decade has gone by since this conversation. I feel my retirement is going better than Seymour's. He still cannot retire yet. I've been retired several years.

CHAPTER 3

1. News miner Friday Aug 28th 2015. Judge blocks Obama administration regulations on waterways. Summed up, the present Federal administration wishes to make all waterways federal jurisdiction. This involves the EPA and army corp. The agriculture industry is concerned. Federal laws would carry over state law. 13 states are fighting this in court.
2. Throughout my life I have promoted 'good eating habits' drug free, and clean living . Off and on I have taught others, giving presentations, done what I can to encourage these beliefs. While at the same time trying to be accepting of others who have come to different concussions. Many feel it is my life that is unsafe!
3. Half a decade after this conversation vendor turn out and attendance is down by half. The craft tent that once had twenty vendors has four.

CHAPTER 4

1. **Past Flash** = a term used in all my books to represent a special past memory. A concept from the music industry 'knock out nifty of the past, golden oldie.' A song from the past that spins us back to the time the song came out, causing us to relive those times for a short period while that song is playing. Likewise **'future flash'** is a glimpse into a time when I am editing with an update, relevant to understanding how it was at the time the event happened, and was first written. In truth, my life moves up and down the timeline with ease. Confusing to others, not to me.
2. Keep in mind, this is the days before cop body cameras, camera phones, George Floyd cases and such, with 'proof.'

CHAPTER 6

1. Ivory art on my site that I am referring to is among the pieces recorded and approved in the deal with Fish and Wildlife.

CHAPTER 7

1. This is one reason I review in detail, what I think, my views, why I have them, and how these views are applied to my life. What is it society hates so much about it, and why? Is my opinion correct, or are there views a civilized person understands better than I do that involves reasons I am not aware of!

CHAPTER 8

1. I could talk more about 'the other' early girlfriend, but do not want my story to get too complicated with too many people in it. There was a group of us who hung together through high school. This was a good group, who all did well in life. Leaving when and how I did was a major event, that closed doors behind me, while opening other doors.

CHAPTER 9

1. I can pause here to comment on all my news clippings, references quotes, pieces of paper. I am overwhelmed with a good fifty pounds I collect over the years. Should I show my readers? I wish to show it is not just me making something up! My ideas did not pop up in my head without assistance. My conclusions are based on directives, quoted judges, lawyers, politicians information disseminated to the public.
2. I follow Saddle cases in the news over the years and note he defends accused rapists, child porn cases, abuse issues of all kinds, drug dealers, and human killers. Killing animals is worse. I noticed on my own, we see horror movies where we cut each other up with chain saws, but not one movie I ever saw showed anyone so much as speak badly of an animal, much less kick one, yell at one, hurt an animal in any way. Except some very old classic westerns where I once saw someone looking like Jane Fonda shooting a pheasant for dinner. Someone says "Good shot!" and "Good dinner." But that was in the 50's.

CHAPTER 10

1. Alaska and other states legalize pot, though it is federally outlawed. While the state makes it illegal for a federal agent to arrest anyone on state lands, money made selling pot cannot be legally put in a bank. This is another example of conflicts with laws that do not match. Many people choose to obey the state law, like grow, smoke pot, or trap wolves and lynx. Agriculture laws are also in conflict, as well as building codes.
2. Some people, mostly locals, went ballistic when they figured out who they were in my previous books. I have kept some people out of the events of my life on purpose, they are not needed! But at some point a story of one's life needs other people in it.

CHAPTER 11

1. Best told in my previous books covering these years and lifestyle.

2. I tell a different version at the time all this happens back in book two I think. Our memories fade, a new reality sets in. There is new insight into what was going on long ago. Truth and reality can be what we want it to be. Necessary for survival.